D1544926

RISE AND PROGRESS
OF UNIVERSITIES

AND

BENEDICTINE ESSAYS

THE WORKS OF
CARDINAL JOHN HENRY NEWMAN
BIRMINGHAM ORATORY
MILLENNIUM EDITION
VOLUME III

SERIES EDITOR

JAMES TOLHURST DD

RISE AND PROGRESS
OF UNIVERSITIES

AND

BENEDICTINE ESSAYS

BY

JOHN HENRY CARDINAL NEWMAN

with an Introduction and Notes by

MARY KATHERINE TILLMAN

Gracewing.

NOTRE DAME

First published in 1872–3 by
Basil Montague Pickering
Published in the Birmingham Millennium Oratory Edition in 2001
jointly by

Gracewing
2 Southern Avenue
Leominster
Herefordshire HR6 0QF

University of Notre Dame Press
310 Flanner Hall
Notre Dame
IN 46556 USA

The right of Mary Katherine Tillman to be identified as the author of the Introduction and Editor's Notes to this work has been asserted in accordance with the Copyright, Designs and Patents Act 1988.

Library of Congress Cataloging-in-Publication Data
Newman, John Henry, 1801-1890.
    Rise and progress of universities; and, Benedictine essays / by John Henry Cardinal Newman; with an introduction and notes by Katherine Tillman.
    p. cm. – (The works of Cardinal John Henry Newman; v. 3)
    Includes bibliographical references.
    ISBN 0-85244-449-4 – ISBN 0-268-04005-2 (U.S. : cloth : alk. paper)
    1. Education, Higher – History. 2. Universities and colleges – History. 3. Benedictines. 4. Catholic schools. I. Title: Rise and progress of universities; and, Benedictine essays. II. Tillman, Katherine. III. Newman, John Henry, 1801–1890. Benedictine essays. IV. Title: Benedictine essays. V. Title.

LA174.N49 2001
378'.009–dc21   00-066961

UK ISBN 0 85244 449 4
US ISBN 0-268-04005-2

Additional typesetting by Action Publishing Technology Ltd, Gloucester, GL1 1SP
Printed in England by MPG Books Ltd, Bodmin, PL31 1EG

CONTENTS

NOTE ON THE TEXT
Rise and Progress of Universities
In this Millennium Edition, the text on pp. 1–251
follows the uniform Longmans Edition of HISTORI-
CAL SKETCHES, VOL. III, published by Longmans,
Green & Co., London, 1888–.

Benedictine Essays ('The Mission of St. Benedict' and
'The Benedictine Schools')
In this Millennium Edition, the text on pp. 363–487
follows the uniform Longmans Edition of HISTORI-
CAL SKETCHES, VOL. II, published by Longmans,
Green & Co., London, 1888–.

Taking the text from two separate volumes of
HISTORICAL SKETCHES has created the variance
in pagination from pp. 262–363.

ACKNOWLEDGEMENTS

I acknowledge, with appreciation, the Fathers of the Birmingham Oratory in England for the use of the Newman Archives. Recognition is also due to The Venerable John Henry Newman Association in the United States, especially to the late Revd Vincent J. Giese and the Board of Advisors; to the Provost's Office and to the Institute for Scholarship in the Liberal Arts at the University of Notre Dame. I owe a debt as well to the Oratories, Colleges, Universities, and Academic Conferences, in the United States and abroad, which have invited me to speak at their institutions. For their continuing kind interest in my work, I am beholden to the Revd Theodore M. Hesburgh, C.S.C., the Revd C. J. G. Winterton, the Revd Vincent F. Blehl, S.J., and the Revd Ian T. Ker. And I am especially grateful to my colleagues and students in Notre Dame's Program of Liberal Studies. My first and best thanks, though, are due to the Revd Marvin R. O'Connell of the University of Notre Dame – historian, author, palmary colleague in Newman Studies, and esteemed friend.

Mary Katherine Tillman

A University embodies the principal [sic] *of progress, and a College that of stability; the one is the sail, and the other the ballast; each is insufficient in itself for the pursuit, extension, and inculcation of knowledge; each is useful to the other. A University is the scene of enthusiasm, of pleasurable exertion, of brilliant display, of winning influence, of diffusive and potent sympathy; and a College is the scene of order, of obedience, of modest and persevering diligence, of conscientious fulfilment of duty, of mutual private services, and deep and lasting attachments. The University is for the world, and the College is for the nation. The University is for the Professor, and the College for the Tutor; the University is for the philosophical discourse, the eloquent sermon, or the well contested disputation; and the College for the catechetical lecture. The University is for theology, law, and medicine, for natural history, for physical science, and for the sciences generally and their promulgation; the College is for the formation of character, intellectual and moral, for the cultivation of the mind, for the improvement of the individual, for the study of literature, for the classics, and those rudimental sciences which strengthen and sharpen the intellect. The University being the element of advance, will fail in making good its ground as it goes; the College, from its Conservative tendencies, will be sure to go back, because it does not go forward. It would seem as if an University seated and living in Colleges, would be a perfect institution, as possessing excellences of opposite kinds.*

But such a union, such salutary balance and mutual complement of opposite advantages, is of difficult and rare attainment.

John Henry Newman
Rise and Progress of Universities

INTRODUCTION

I. THE *CATHOLIC UNIVERSITY GAZETTE* AND THE *ATLANTIS*

This volume contains a selection of periodic publications from the middle (1854–56) and late (1858–59) periods of John Henry Newman's association with the Catholic University of Ireland. About the *Rise and Progress of Universities*, Fergal McGrath makes, without further comment, an astute and remarkable observation: 'Though far less known than *The Idea of a University*, this collection of essays is of equal, if not greater, value for the full understanding of Newman's educational views.'[1]

[1] Fergal McGrath, S.J., *Newman's University: Idea and Reality* (London, Longmans, Green, & Co., 1951) p. 319. According to the late Charles Stephen Dessain, longtime archivist at the Birmingham Oratory: 'To this book [by Father McGrath] the reader may be referred for the fullest discussion of the Catholic University.' Introduction to Newman's 'Memorandum About My Connection with the Catholic University' in *John Henry Newman Autobiographical Writings*, ed. Henry Tristram (New York, Sheed and Ward, 1957), p. 279. See also the judgement of Michael Tierney, a distinguished former president of University College Dublin: 'The *Sketches* form a very important part of a coherent body of thought.' Preface to John Henry Newman, D.D., *University Sketches*, Text of 1856, ed. Michael Tierney (Dublin, Browne and Nolan Limited, The Richview Press, 1911), p. vii.

The *Rise and Progress of Universities* consists of twenty articles from the *Catholic University Gazette*, which was a small periodical of about eight pages published weekly from 1st June 1854 to 28th December 1854, then monthly from 8th March 1855, until it terminated at the end of 1856.[2] The last two essays of this volume, called here the *Benedictine Essays*, originally appeared in *The Atlantis: A Register of Literature and Science*, which Newman instituted specifically for the publication of research by his faculty.[3] Appearing twice yearly in 1858 and 1859, and in 1862 and 1863, with a final single issue in February 1870, each impressive number was about two hundred pages in length and was divided into groups of scholarly articles labelled 'Literature,' 'Scientific Researches,' and 'Scientific Notices'. Newman considered the *Atlantis* to be the "repository and record" of the University's intellectual excellence:

> Such an undertaking naturally follows on the entrance of the Professors upon their respective

[2] Originally published as one volume in 1856 with the title *Office and Work of Universities*, these selected essays from the *Catholic University Gazette* were renamed by Newman *Rise and Progress of Universities* with the 1872 edition, as 'more appropriate to its contents' ('Advertisement'). Newman later placed the volume among his collected works as the first and major part of *Historical Sketches*, Vol. III: pp. 1–251, to which correspond the page numbers of the footnotes in this section of the Introduction, and in the correlating Notes that follow the text. For a complete listing of the multiple editions of Newman's numerous publications, in particular on the knotty problem of the various editions of *Historical Sketches*, consult the invaluable work of Vincent Ferrer Blehl, S.J., *John Henry Newman, Bibliographical Catalogue of His Writings* (University Press of Virginia, Charlottesville, 1978).

[3] See 'The *Atlantis I*' and 'The *Atlantis II*' in Cardinal Newman, *My Campaign in Ireland, Part I*, ed. W. P. Neville (privately printed, 1896), pp. 429–434.

provinces of labour. Nor will it only serve to tell the public what they are doing and what they can do; it will be their contribution to the science and literature of the day; it will be their advertisement, recommendation, and bond of connection, with the learned bodies of Great Britain and the Continent; and it will gain for them in exchange for what they send, the various journals of a similar kind, many of them important and valuable, which issue periodically from those great centres of thought.[4]

Although Newman had been involved since 1851 in the planning and the continually delayed establishment of the Catholic University, and had published in 1852 his 'Dublin Discourses' on the idea of a university, it was these middle years, 1854–56, the years of Newman's most intense and direct involvement with the university, that saw the publication of the *Catholic University Gazette*, and thus of the present volume's main contents, *Rise and Progress of Universities*. When the first issues of the *Catholic University Gazette* appeared in June 1854, the university had not yet opened its doors to the twenty or so young men who would begin November lectures in classics and mathematics. When the *Atlantis* came into existence barely more than three years later, Newman boasted that the university had 'students as many as are found in German Universities of first rank and name', that is, from a hundred and ten to a hundred

---

[4] 'The *Atlantis I*,' 'From the Calendar of the Irish Cath. Univ. of the Session of 1856–57', *Campaign*, p. 430. For more on the *Atlantis* and on the important place for Newman of professorial research and publication – contrary to so many misinterpretations of Newman in this regard – see section 2 of this Introduction, The *Benedictine Essays*.

and twenty students, 'a Medical School in full operation', library books 'accumulating faster than it can
house them', and a new University Church 'large
enough for all ecclesiastical and academical ceremonies'.[5] Newman's final year as Rector, 1858, began
and ended with the January issues of the *Atlantis*,
containing the two Benedictine essays with which the
present volume concludes.

  What follows in this Introduction emphasises the
integral relation between the *Gazette* essays on the
historical development of universities, namely, *Rise
and Progress of Universities*, on the one hand, and
Newman's 'bare and necessary *idea*' of a university as
set forth abstractly in the 'Dublin Discourses', that is, in
The Idea of a University, for neither work alone, it is here
maintained, represents adequately or without distor-
tion Newman's capacious mind on Catholic higher
education. Accordingly, and in analogous fashion, the
significance of republishing here Newman's *Benedictine
Essays* together with *Rise and Progress of Universities* is
shown to penetrate more deeply than their common
historical approach and occasionally intersecting
subject matter might at first sight seem to indicate.

II. THE INAUGURATION OF THE CATHOLIC
UNIVERSITY OF IRELAND, JUNE, 1854

On the Feast of Pentecost, 4th June 1854, exactly five
months prior to its opening, the Catholic University
of Ireland was finally inaugurated and its Rector, the

<hr />

[5] *My Campaign in Ireland* (*Campaign*), p. 429.

Very Reverend Dr John Henry Newman, priest of the Oratory of St. Philip Neri in Birmingham, England, having made the required profession of fidelity and obedience, was at last installed officially. Three long years it had been since Newman accepted the office of Rector offered him by the Most Reverend Dr Paul Cullen, then Apostolic Delegate and Primate of Ireland, with the approval of Pope Pius IX. And two full years it had been since Newman delivered his famous Discourses on university education in the packed Rotunda on O'Connell Street.[6]

In the days before the formal liturgical celebration in Dublin's cathedral, the bishops of Ireland had met to confirm Newman's appointment and to conduct other business relating to the Catholic University. Now assured at last that he could engage professors and tutors, accept students, and open the University, Newman lost no time in initiating publication of the *Catholic University Gazette*. The periodical was composed of a section of 'Notices' with university announcements and proceedings, and a second section containing the present historical essays on universities, which Newman had begun to write the previous spring and summer with a view to the periodical's initiation.[7] Each essay was always

[6] Newman's own detailed account of the multiple conflicts and endless delays in starting up the university, particularly with regard to his position as Rector, and in relation to the Irish bishops and to Rome, may be found in 'Memorandum', *Autobiographical Writings*, pp. 280–333.

[7] See 'What I Aimed At,' *Campaign*, pp. 294–95. Between 1854 and 1856, Newman also published in the *Gazette* most of the occasional lectures, in revised and sometimes combined form, which he delivered to members of the university. In 1858 he published the latter as a separate volume under the title *Lectures and Essays on University Subjects*, and in 1873, he situated them permanently as the second half of *The Idea of a University*.

preceded by the invocation, '*Sedes Sapientiae, Ora pro Nobis*'.[8]

For example, Issue No. I, which cost one penny, was dated 'Thursday, June 1, 1854', and in its Notices are set forth the informational particulars of the new university: there will be three terms; the normal age of admission will be sixteen; the entrance examination will consist of construing, parsing, and translating Latin and Greek, of Greek and Roman history, the elements of geography, the first book of Euclid's elements, arithmetic, the Gospel of St. Matthew, and any approved Catechism.[9]

Passing this entrance examination would admit the candidate as a 'Student of the University' for two years, during which time he would study classics, modern languages, geometry, algebra, logic, geography, chronology, and ancient Irish and English history. After passing a second examination on these subjects, the student, then eighteen, would receive the title 'Scholar of the University'. The young scholar might then retire from the university, or pass into the schools of medicine, civil engineering, and of other material and physical sciences, or he might continue his studies in arts and undergo a third examination issuing in the Bachelor of Arts degree. In the latter case, the arts scholar would study, during his second two years, the subjects of modern history, political economy, ethics, metaphysics, analytical mathematics, the principles of law, and the elements of astronomy

[8] 'Seat of Wisdom, pray for us' – referring to the Blessed Virgin Mary, under whose patronage Newman dedicated the Catholic University.

[9] *The Catholic University Gazette*, 1854–1855, Vol. I (Dublin, James Duffy, n.d.) No. 1.

and chemistry, exceptions being made for those young men going forward in classical studies.

In the Notices of the third number of the *Gazette*, that dated 'Thursday, June 15, 1854', Newman describes 'the late inauguration, as it may be called, of the Catholic University.' Details of the 4th June liturgical celebration are given, and the sermon by Dr Cullen, Newman relates, 'naturally terminated in a reference to the event of the day, and in a most touching address to the ecclesiastic in whom it was represented', that is, to himself. Archbishop Cullen concluded in terms reminiscent of Newman's own idea of a university as expressed in the 'Dublin Discourses' of two years earlier:

> ... And you, Very Reverend Father, to whom the execution of so great a work is committed by the Church of Ireland, allow me to exhort you to meet the difficulties and trials which you shall have to encounter, with courage and determination. You will have with you the blessing of the successor of St. Peter, the sanction and cooperation of the Church of Ireland, and the fervent prayers of the faithful.... Teach the young comitted to your care to cultivate every branch of learning, to scan the depths of every science, and to explore the mysteries of every art.... In all circumstances, and at all times, let it be your care to infuse a strong Catholic spirit, a true spirit of religion, into the tender minds of youths.... In this way your labours will tend to restore the ancient glories of this Island of Saints....[10]

[10] See also *My Campaign in Ireland*, p. 279.

III. THE OPENING OF THE CATHOLIC
UNIVERSITY, NOVEMBER, 1854

Then, on 3rd November 1854, feast of St. Malachy
O'More of Armagh (1095–1148), first papally canonized Irish saint, the Very Reverend Dr Newman,
having been officially installed as its Rector only five
months earlier, opened the doors of the University.
'And so, quietly and peacefully, without noise or ceremony, our Institution commenced its career.'[11]

As they settled into their living quarters that
weekend, the twenty or so newly matriculated
students were aware, perhaps anxiously so, that
lectures were to begin on Monday morning. To reas-
sure them and to confirm their tacit aspirations, as
much as to orient them to the purpose of their university career, Newman 'gave a *soirée*' that Sunday
evening, 5th November, in the Refectory of the
newly readied University House on St. Stephen's
Green. After each youth of sixteen had been introduced to him, he addressed his small cohort as
'gentlemen' and asked them if they knew what they
were there *for*. It was obvious, he said, that they were

[11] See the account of Robert Ornsby, Professor of Classical Literature,
who was one of the three administrators of the first entrance examinations and was present at the university's opening. He was editor,
after Newman, of the *Gazette* (*My Campaign in Ireland*, p. 319). Apart
from Newman's incomplete notes printed as 'Some Portions of the
Address to the Students on Opening the University' (*Campaign* pp.
313–324), Ornsby's eye-witness account, 'The Autumn Term, 1854'
(*University Gazette I*, p. 36: pp. 320 ff., partially contained in *Campaign*
pp. 319–324), is the only existing record of those first days. It was
published three months later in the *Gazette* of 1st February 1855,
contrary to W. P. Neville, editor, who says that Ornsby's report was
inserted as a Note in the *Gazette* 'twelve months later'
('Advertisement,' *Campaign*, p. xxxvi).

to prepare themselves for their respective professions in life, and a university could help with that preparation; but they might also be able to do that elsewhere. A university education was really intended for very much more. To illustrate what he meant by this, he would tell them about a conversation he had heard many years earlier.[12]

The conversation took place between a mother, who had been left a widow with seven children, and one of her sons, Charles, who had just been offered a position that he thought beneath him. Charles was about to turn down the offer, when his mother said to him: *It is not the place makes the man, but the man makes the place.* What the wise mother meant by this, Newman explained, is that a man who has a disciplined and cultivated mind, one who is gentleman-like and well-principled, will be honoured and respected, and will do well in life, no matter what the trade or profession in which he is engaged, provided it be honest work. On the other hand, he may have the best job around, with all of the professional training and know-how in the world, and may have wealth and property, but if he is unprincipled, undisciplined, and ungentleman-like, people will soon see the fellow for what he is, and will pass him by without notice or respect – for *it is the man makes the place, and not the place the man.*

So you see what is implied in this, the eminent Rector told his attentive young charges – 'a great truth'; namely, 'that there is an education necessary and desirable over and above that which may be called

---

[12] Newman and Ornsby, *Campaign*, pp. 313–324.

professional.' Professions differ, and those of you who will become physicians will need a different kind of education from that required for engineers, or for bankers. But the one kind of education which all of you should have in common and for which you especially come to the University is the kind which *makes the man*.

Newman then proposed to tell them *what* it is to be a *man*, by returning to the example of Charles and his mother. Let us suppose, he suggested, that Charles is indeed well-educated, filling any post in society we may wish, and being either well off or badly off. What we know is that he will meet all sorts of people, some in business, some in the family circle, some in times of recreation, and some in the world at large. Few of these people, except those in business with him, and they only partially, will care very much about what it is that he does for a trade or profession. What will matter to all of them, however, is what he is in himself. Does he have something to say for himself? Is he clear-headed, intelligent, articulate, yet modest and willing to learn? Is he flexible and well-mannered, and can he accept criticism? Is he balanced in his views and attitudes, respectful of others' opinions, and welcoming of adjustments to his own? Were Charles not found wanting in these highly regarded personal characteristics, his contemporaries would do well to consider him among those whose power of influence might sway both public and private affairs.

On the other hand, someone who grew up 'without learning to be a real man' would end up being a boy all his life, without any clear opinions, without views on things, without inner resources of his own. Because he never learned how to enjoy reading or thinking, he would not know how to amuse himself and would have nothing to talk about with friends or business associates. He would end up bored with them as well as with himself. A boy relies on others for his continuing instruction and amusement; a man is able to a great extent to be master of himself.

He told them about the young Romans putting on their *toga virilis*, and quoted St. Paul about putting aside childish things, while at the same time he assured them that anyone would be a fool not to remember that we are all children of the one Heavenly Father. They should make a good beginning, he said, and strive for manliness of mind. Then soon a *genius loci*, that is, a characteristic good spirit of the place, would abide among them all.

In this way, their Reverend Rector told them, they would fulfil the work for which they came on earth. And if they are religious men and good Catholics, they will be in a position to do a great deal of good for God and the Church, and for their Christian brethren, something another person could not do whose mind had not been cultivated and framed in this way. Up to this time, because of the circumstances of their country, Catholics in Ireland had not been able to avail themselves of this kind of education.[13] But the Holy See thought that this situation should come to an end, and that a Catholic university should be provided for young men from all over the world who

[13] For full affiliation with Trinity College Dublin (or, for that matter, with Oxford and Cambridge Universities), a young man had to subscribe to the Thirty-Nine Articles of the Church of Ireland (or of England). So, effectively, higher education was closed to the Catholic and Nonconformist population of Ireland.

speak the English language. Unlike the Queen's Colleges,[14] then, their own institution is a university, which means in part that it attracts students from all over the world, and to the very capital of the country – both provisions serving greatly to broaden and enrich their own education.

Newman then offered some remarks on the choice of St. Malachy's Day as the perfect time for opening the university, because that great saint had always been held with much reverence and devotion in Ireland. He concluded the *soirée* by speaking of their small number which, he said, may have disappointed some of them, but with which he himself was well pleased. There would come a time, he prophesied, when they would look back with great pleasure to St. Malachy's Day 1854, and be proud of their part in the founding of the University, which would by then be a great institution populated by many students. It reminded him, he said, of Shakespeare's *King Henry V*, before the battle of Agincourt. When some of the King's men became discouraged about the small number of his soldiers facing the overwhelming forces of the enemy, Henry bravely tells them that he would not wish for one man more:

[14] The Queen's Colleges, established in 1845 by the then Prime Minister Robert Peel's conciliatory act toward the Irish, were Parliament's solution to 'the Catholic problem' with respect to higher education. Non-denominational, or 'mixed', with no religious tests required for admission, degrees, or scholarships, and with no religion or theology taught in them, they quickly earned the sobriquet, 'the godless colleges'. Located in Limerick, Cork, and Belfast, they at first met with the approval of only a small number of Irish bishops. Subsequently, attendance at them by Catholics was banned by Rome in favour of establishing a Catholic university in Dublin.

> ... What's he that wishes so?
> My cousin Westmoreland? No, my fair cousin;
> The fewer men, the greater share of honour.
> This day is called the feast of Crispian:
> He that outlives this day and comes safe home,
> Will stand on tiptoe when this day is nam'ed.
> He that shall live this day, and see old age,
> Will yearly on the Vigil feast his neighbours,
> And say: To-morrow is Saint Crispian.
>   Then shall our names,
> Familiar in his mouth as household words, ...
> Be in their flowing cups freshly remember'd:
> This story shall the good man teach his son;
> And Crispin Crispian shall ne'er go by,
> From this day to the ending of the world,
> But we in it shall be remembered;
> We few, we happy few, we band of brothers.[15]

IV. THE TEXT – *RISE AND PROGRESS OF UNIVERSITIES*

The Idea and the Image

'I am investigating in the abstract,' Newman writes in the Introductory discourse of *The Idea of a University*; 'for the moment I know nothing, so to say, of history. ... I am here the advocate and the minister of a certain great principle.'[16] The abstract *idea* university-as-such is one thing; its living *image* in memory and imagination, in its

---

[15] Shakespeare, *King Henry V*, Act IV, Scene III, quoted by Newman. *My Campaign in Ireland*, p. 323.

[16] John Henry Newman, *The Idea of a University*, ed. I. T. Ker (Oxford, Clarendon Press, 1976), p. 24.

historical development, and in its real, institutional embodiments is quite another. It is the *university whole and entire*, in all its aspects and dimensions – that is, both the *idea* and the *image* taken together – that John Henry Newman was studying, writing, lecturing, teaching, preaching about, and actually living out, during that highly significant period of his life, the 1850s.

Always when he was preaching and teaching, and particularly, as will be see, in *Rise and Progress of Universities*, Newman employed images. Whether of King Henry V or of St. Paul, the portraits and actions of individual persons were Newman's best and most frequently used media of communication. He knew that images compel attention, that they impress themselves upon the mind – 'come home to' or 'lodge themselves in' the mind, he would say – more readily, more 'really', than abstract ideas.

For example, with the following words, an *image* is placed before our minds of one whose very soul resonated with the inmost thoughts and feelings of others:

> His mind was like some instrument of music, harp or viol, the strings of which vibrate, though untouched, by the notes which other instruments give forth, and he was ever, according to his own precept, 'rejoicing with them that rejoice, and weeping with them that wept.'[17]

It is the image of St. Paul, extolled in his characteristic gift of human sympathy, the subject of two of Newman's eight sermons preached before the Catholic University during the academic year of the

---

[17] John Henry Newman, *Sermons Preached on Various Occasions* (London, Longmans, Green & Co., 1904), p. 114.

opening of its new Church, 1856–1857.[18]

Put simply, Newman understood an idea or a notion to be a mental holding that is abstract and general, and an image to be a mental holding that is concrete and particular. 'King' is an idea, a notion; it is abstract and its meaning is commonly and generally understood. But 'Henry V of England', or 'a little touch of Harry in the night' as he walked about in disguise to hearten his troops, is concrete and particular, and impresses the mind with the vivid image of an individual person. The image of 'Harry' needs the idea of 'king,' or it remains idiosyncratic, not fully saying what is meant; the idea 'king' needs the concrete image of this particular Henry on the eve of the battle of Agincourt, or the idea is empty, floating, and 'unreal' to the imagination. It often takes many images to communicate or bring home to the mind a single idea. Only in the Christ, the Logos of God, do the idea and the image coincide in perfect unity and identity.

Newman's faith was deeply Trinitarian and Incarnational, rooted particularly in the theology of the Church of Antiquity, that is, of the centuries before the first ecumenical Council of Nicea (AD 325).[19]

---

[18] *Sermons Preached on Various Occasions*, Sermons VII and VIII.

[19] The *Logos* Christology of the Apologists, whose complete writings Newman first read in 1828, strongly influenced the Fathers of the anteNicene Church, particularly the Alexandrians, in whose writings Newman immersed himself, beginning in 1831, in preparation for what he initially thought would be a volume on the controversies of the Eastern or Greek Church, namely, those regarding the Trinity and the Incarnation. The work turned out in the long run to be Newman's first book, *The Arians of the Fourth Century* (1833).

For an important study of the influence of the Fathers, especially of Clement and Origen, on Newman's educational principles, see Vincent F. Blehl, S.J., 'Newman, the Fathers, and Education,' *Thought*, vol. xlv (Summer, 1970), pp. 196–212.

Accordingly, God's Idea is spoken or expressed eternally in God's Word, the *Logos*, and through the *Logos* all things come to be, marked with the imprint of their Maker. That eternal *Logos* was made flesh, given to the historical world and to human bodily sense, in Jesus Christ. In Christ, the Idea and the Image of God are one, for Christ is at once divine and human. With the whole of creation, humans bear in their very being the Image of their Creator, and in the body of Christ through baptism, they bear in their souls the Image of Jesus Christ. Through the working of the Holy Spirit, that Image of God can come to mirror ever more perfectly the eternal *Logos* of God, for the idea and the image belong together. 'It is the Image of Him who fulfils the one great need of human nature, the Healer of its wounds, the Physician of the soul, this Image it is which both creates faith, and then rewards it. . . . [T]his central Image [is] the vivifying idea both of the Christian body and of individuals in it. . . .'[20]

In his *Essay in Aid of a Grammar of Assent*, which he said he had been working on for 'thirty or forty years' before its 1870 publication (thus including the decade of the 1850s), Newman explicitly distinguished two ways of grasping or understanding statements or propositions.[21] These two ways he called 'notional' and 'real'. Notional apprehension is the way in which *ideas* attach to the mind. Real apprehension, on the other hand, is the personal and direct mode of understanding by which particular

---

[20] *An Essay in Aid of a Grammar of Assent*, (*Grammar*), ed. I. T. Ker (Oxford, Clarendon Press, 1985), p. 299.

[21] *Grammar*, especially Chapters I–IV.

things, individuals and persons compel the imagination and remain in memory through *images*.[22]

In their highest actualisation, notional and real apprehension work together and can be expressed simultaneously by the same mental act, as when a learned theologian prays in the evening to the personal God whose doctrine he has been studying all day, or when a lecturer in science intends by an experiment to enunciate it as an individual project in the laboratory and also as a general law of nature.[23] The more wholly one is intellectually, imaginatively and personally engaged by an object, the more likely it is that one's apprehension is a dynamic interplay of both the notional and the real, the conceptual and the imaginative, the abstract and the personal. Nonetheless, 'real apprehension has the precedence, as being the scope and end and the test of the notional.'[24]

In the *Grammar of Assent* Newman distinguished between the two modes of rational apprehension, the notional/conceptual and the real/imaginative, because he was concerned in that work to show the limitations of *merely* notional assent and of *merely* real assent in matters of religious faith. Assent that is only notional remains exclusively conceptual and content-oriented with no living faith in a personal God; assent that is exclusively imaginative tends toward excesses of emotion, even superstition, and has no interest in doctrine or dogma. Newman's intention was to describe the necessary synthesis

[22] *Grammar*, p. 63.
[23] *Grammar*, p. 14.
[24] *Grammar*, p. 30.

and integration of notional and real assent in the
mature and plenary act of religious faith.

It is obvious, then, that Newman's theological
and philosophical reflection, indeed his very faith,
were grounded in the principle of the profound
relation of the idea and the image, of the eternal
and the historical, and of the notional and the real.
By antecedent probability, then, and by analogy,
the same might be expected of his reflections on
university education. In brief, what Newman calls
the 'bare and necessary idea' of a university is an
abstract, general, ahistorical, even static notion of
what a university is in its essence, nature, or notion;
whereas the image of a university is the concrete,
historical, living embodiment of that idea as it was
anticipated, realised, or instantiated, however
imperfectly in relation to the ideal type, in a particular time and place. It cannot be overemphasised
that it was never Newman's intention that the
assemblage of his 'Dublin Discourses' as found in
The Idea of a University – often erroneously taken to
comprise *by itself* Newman's unqualified view of
university education – be considered in isolation
from what he himself saw as the *three companion
volumes* that together made up his one work on
university education.[25]

The first volume, published by Newman in 1852,

---

[25] In the 'Advertisement' to the 1859 edition of *The Idea of a University*
(*Idea*), Newman wrote that he 'removed from the text much
temporary, collateral, or superfluous matter, and has thus reduced it
to the size of *his two other volumes on University Teaching.*' See the
'Editor's Introduction' to Father Ker's critical edition of the *Idea*,
pp. xxxvi–xxxvii. [Emphases added.]

contained the 'Dublin Discourses' on the *idea* of a university. The second volume, published by him in 1859, comprised the occasional lectures and essays, which he saw as 'illustrations' of the *idea*. But it is the third volume, published by him in 1856, that is, *Rise and Progress of Universities*, as he renamed it in 1872, that is Newman's most engaging work on higher education.

The Idea of a University: Defined

But first things first. Newman attached a fifty-seven page Appendix to the 1852 publication of the 'Discourses', which he introduces by saying: 'The question before us is as to *the idea on the whole*, or *the formal conception*, of a University.'[26] Everything, Newman held, should be 'done on an idea'. Newman's *Idea* of a university, that is, its formal conception or abstract notion – its essence or 'type' – is of a centre of teaching and learning in which are studied all of the interconnected branches of the complete circle of knowledge. The metaphysical and theological premise of this idea is simply that the ultimate subject matter of knowledge is the great interconnected whole of God's creation. Because each branch of knowledge is, and is about, an integral part of this larger unity, each portion completes, corrects and balances every other part.

In the early 'Discourses' of the *Idea*, Newman argues that because the very notion or idea of a university includes within its compass the complete circle of knowledge, and because theology is a kind of knowledge and thus a portion of the circle, therefore

[26] *Idea*, '1852 Appendix', p. 435. [Emphases added.]

any university worthy of the name must teach theology. The systematic omission of theology, as of any other discipline, prejudices the accuracy and completeness of all knowledge, and accordingly distorts the basic idea of university education.

'Philosophy', in Newman's special sense of the word, is not a specific subject matter but enjoys a distinct and privileged perspective as the architectonic 'science of sciences'.[27] In its overarching view and commanding wisdom, it is not unlike in function what Aristotle called 'first philosophy', that is, metaphysics.[28] As if from outside the circle of knowledge, philosophy comprehends and orders the location, limitation, rank and bearing of each discipline in relation to the others and to the whole of knowledge. Its proper aim is the cultivation in students of a healthy, energised mind. It aims to develop in them 'a

---

[27] *The Idea of a University*, p. 57, pp. 103–105. See also A. Dwight Culler, *The Imperial Intellect* (New Haven, Yale University Press, 1955), pp. 182–86. In the (incomplete) Yale edition of *The Idea of a University*, ed. Frank M. Turner (New Haven, Yale University Press, 1966), several of the contributors' essays, including the editor's, mistakenly take Newman's 'science of sciences' to be theology (Turner, p. 259; Sara Castro-Klarén, p. 319) or religion (Martha McMackin Garland, pp. 278–80). George Marsden alone gets it right, magnificently (p. 304). With such a basic misconception of Newman's meaning, other problems were sure to follow. See review essay by Mary Katherine Tillman in the *Anglican Theological Review*, Vol. lxxx, No. 2 (Spring, 1998), pp. 276–286.

[28] See Aristotle, *Metaphysics*, 1003a21–25: 'There is a science which takes up the theory of being as being and of what "to be" means, taken by itself. It is identical with none of the sciences whose subjects are defined as special aspects of being. For none of them looks upon being on the whole or generally; but each, isolating some part, gets a view of the whole only incidentally.' See also Mary Katherine Tillman, '"Habit of Mind": Aristotle and Newman on the End of Liberal Education,' *Paideusis*, Vol. 3, No. 2 (Spring, 1990), pp. 17–27.

philosophical habit of mind' in just this sense of enabling them to 'map the Universe', that is, to comprehend the relative dispositions of things and of viewpoints.

In the fifth Discourse, the centerpiece of the *Idea*, and in the two following Discourses, Newman contrasts competing notions of the purpose of university education with his own. Not the mere acquisition of factual knowledge, 'the passive reception of scraps and details,' he says, but rather 'knowledge impregnated by thought,' appropriated and made a personal possession or habit; not useful knowledge in the sense of immediate training for a vocation or profession, but rather learning for its own sake, its own enjoyment and reward; not even useful knowledge in the sense of making students better morally or religiously, but simply, directly, and only, the cultivation of a healthy and illuminated intellect. Liberal education is a worthy and noble good entirely in itself, for it fulfils a direct need of our nature. The perfecting of the human intellect is, then, the *raison d'être* of a university in its 'bare and necessary idea', and this it is that constitutes the education of 'the gentleman'.

In the last two Discourses, however, Newman shifts into a wholly different register and radically qualifies the glorious ideal he has just set forth. The gentleman's education by itself, he warns, tends toward the absolutising of reason and of culture, tends toward a life of leisure for its own sake – certainly not the luxury of a Christian commanded to love and serve others. Knowledge is one thing, but virtue and religion involve much more than mere knowledge. An understanding of ideas and their relations may enlarge one's mind, but such understanding is no guarantee of goodness or devotion. 'Quarry the granite rock with razors, or moor the vessel with a thread of silk; then may you hope with such keen and delicate instruments as human knowledge and human reason to contend against those giants, the passion and the pride of man.'[29] In Newman's view, a merely philosophical morality and a religion of reason and culture provide no checks and balances for the bloated, prideful, and usurping intellect that makes itself its own centre and feeds on itself as sole arbiter and judge of all things.

Already on the first page of the *Idea*, in its Preface, Newman hints at what is to follow in more developed form in *Rise and Progress of Universities*: while the *essence* of the university is the cultivation of intellect 'independently of its relation to the Church,' he writes, 'practically speaking, ... the Church is necessary for its *integrity*.'[30] The 'integrity' of anything, writes Newman, though now in the *Gazette* articles, is what enables its continued existence and well-being. We may still be human beings if deprived of air and water, but we will not be human beings for long! The 'essence', that is, the definition or idea in itself, of a human being does not include the air we breathe and the water we drink, but these life-sustaining elements are absolutely necessary for the 'integrity' of human life, that is, for its completeness and well-being. 'Things are not content to be in fact just what we contemplate them in the abstract, and nothing more; they require something more than themselves, sometimes as necessary conditions of their being,

---

[29] *The Idea of a University*, (*Idea*), p. 111.
[30] *Idea*, p. 5. Also quoted in *Historical Sketches* (*HS*), Vol. III, p. 183.

sometimes for their well-being.'[31] At this point it becomes appropriate to speak of Newmans's living idea of *Catholic* higher education, of 'the Collegiate principle' as both antagonistic and complementary to 'the University principle,' and of the work of the college tutor as balancing and completing that of the university professor.

The idea of a university-in-itself does not include Catholicism any more than the essence or idea of a human being includes breathing. But the living university, as it has really developed through time and as it ought to be today, is given an added gift of sustenance and well-being by Catholicism, even as air gives vitality to human beings. As Newman sees it, the Church's main practical presence to a Catholic university resides in the university's historical development and particular tradition, and in the university's continuing exercise of ordering discipline – by means of its institutional structures, in its community and liturgical life, and in the individual lives of its members.

> When then I say, that a Great School or University consists in the communication of knowledge, in lecturers and hearers, that is, in the Professorial system, you must not run away with the notion that I consider personal influence enough for its well-being. It is indeed its essence, but something more is necessary than barely to get on from day to day; for its sure and comfortable existence we must look to law, rule, order; to religion, from which law proceeds; to the collegiate system, in which it is embodied; and to endowments, by which it is protected and

[31] *HS* III, pp. 73–74.

perpetuated. This is the part of the subject which my papers have not yet touched upon; nor could they well treat of what comes second, till they had done justice to what comes first.[32]

Newman begins his Chapter XV, on 'Professors and Tutors', by reinforcing the distinction between the essence of a thing and its 'integrity'. Referring to Aristotle's account of the nature of happiness, which is found in the *Nicomachean Ethics*, he quotes Aristotle's definition or idea of happiness as "the best and most noble and most delightful of energies according to virtue." But then he notes that Aristotle adds: "throughout the greater part of his life," and also that happiness "seems to stand in need of external goods," such as friends, wealth, and political power. In the same way, writes Newman: 'The Professorial system fulfils the strict idea of a University, and is sufficient for its *being*, but it is not sufficient for its *well-being*. Colleges constitute the *integrity* of a University.'[33]

The Idea of a University: Illustrated
The *image* of the university, necessary for the *realisation* of the idea, calls for a different though clearly related handling of the matter. In the introductory *Gazette* essay, Newman observes that many good people had misgivings about the new university, thinking the idea 'too noble ... to be possible'. The real difficulty, he argues, rests not so much in adverse facts, but in peoples' opinions about the facts. 'The despondence, with which the project is regarded by so many persons, is the

---

[32] *Historical Sketches*, Vol. III (*HS* III), p. 74.
[33] *HS* III, pp. 180–83.

offspring, not of their judgement, but mainly ... of their imagination. Public opinion especially acts upon the imagination; it does not convince, but it impresses....' Arguments are not fit weapons to assail a false imagination, he continues. 'The mind [in this case] has been misled by representations; it must be set right by representations.'[34] And so it is to the imaginations of the Irish people that he must appeal to gain their support for the new University. 'The heart is commonly reached not through reason, but through the imagination, by means of indirect impressions, by the testimony of persons, facts and events, by history, by descriptions.'[35] Newman uses the simple word 'illustrations' to include all of these ways of presenting images of the university, of trying to effect its realisation for the reader. In the *Grammar of Assent*, 'making an idea real' means the intensification of the idea by means of memory and imagination; 'realisation' involves taking seriously history, sources and authorities, concrete examples, and personal experiences. To make an idea real is to deepen the speculative vision of notional apprehension into a rich and compelling image.

In the 1852 Appendix, he offers 'illustrations of the main principles laid down in the foregoing Discourses.' These illustrations are mainly extracts and paraphrases of the various theories of liberal education from ancient and modern sources, from Latin, French, British and American authorities. But Newman says he is very aware of the 'meagreness' of these illustrations, which is due to his pressing duties at the time; they do not satisfy his own sense of what they ought to be.

[34] *HS* III, pp. 2–4.
[35] *An Essay in Aid of a Grammar of Assent*, pp. 65–66.

This presumed sparseness of illustrations begins to be filled in by Newman's *Lectures and Essays on University Subjects*, which are mainly the lectures he delivered on particular occasions to various assemblages of the university community and then printed in the *Catholic University Gazette*. In his 1858 Advertisement to this work, Newman says that he here 'pursued the illustration of one and the same important subject matter,' namely, that of the *Idea* made real. Here Newman illustrates his *Idea* in particular relation to the study of literature and to the study of science, the two traditional axes of liberal education, and he carries the idea quite practically into two of the actual commitments of the Catholic University of Ireland: medicine and preaching.

By means of the concrete applications, the varied voices and rich examples of these 'Occasional Lectures and Essays', the idea of a university takes more complete possession of the imagination and begins to live in the understanding. Here is no systematic argument deduced from a prepossessed idea, but rather an accumulation of concrete facts, personal examples, and unquestionable authorities which, taken altogether, serve to impress and persuade the imagination of the likely cogency of this great *Idea*.

The Image of a University: 'A Phantasia of Life'
What more could Newman add to the *Idea* of a university, now defined and illustrated? What he adds in his third and final volume of educational writings, stated quite simply, is *life*. Looking back on his campaign in Ireland, Newman says that he wrote the *Gazette* articles, which would become *Rise and Progress*

of Universities, in order to give 'a phantasia of life' to the idea of a university.[36] Accordingly, *Rise and Progress of Universities* in no way purports to be a history of how universities came to be.[37] It is, rather, a work of *historical imagination* – perhaps something like the creative cultural histories of Herodotus, where fact often gives way to enchanting description and embellished story-telling; or like the dramatic history of Thucydides, whose narrative of the Peloponnesian War develops so exquisitely through perfectly formed and paralleled dialogues, purportedly verbatim, of the military leaders. Or, this work of Newman's might be considered as something like Plato's celebrated story of the *idea* of a Republic: 'Come, then,' wrote Plato, 'let us create a city from the beginning, in our theory.' After all, Newman was a lifelong student of the Classics.

Newman's story in *Rise and Progress of Universities* is about the realisation of an ideal type, *universitas*; and each of its developments within history is used by him both as 'an anticipation of its type' – which is why he begins with Athens, Rome, and the Schools of Charlemagne, rather than with the medieval universities as such – and as 'an adumbration of the pattern of a University,' which is why he uses as exemplars such a variety of manifestations of his *idea*. Concluding one illustration, he writes:

> I take the account given us by Peter of Blois, merely as a *specimen* of the way in which the present

---

[36] See 'What I Aimed At,' *My Campaign in Ireland*, p. 294.

[37] In fact, the modern historian would find more than a few details in *Rise and Progress of Universities* to call into question *as history*.

fabric of knowledge was founded and reared, as a
picture in miniature of the great medieval revival,
whatever becomes of its historical truth. As a mere
legend, it is sufficient for my purpose; for historical
legends and fictions are made according to what is
probable, and after the pattern of precedents.[38]

Thus, the argument drawn from Newman's historical
imagination is not the comprehensive, theoretical, and
largely deductive argument of the 'Dublin Discourses';
rather, it is the complementary argument of concrete
reasoning from antecedent probabilities and of retro-
spective reasoning from pattern instances.

In the twenty articles he selected from his *Gazette*
publications for *Rise and Progress of Universities*, what
lies at the origin and core of the university is no
longer 'the bare and necessary idea' of the complete
circle of knowledge as appropriated by and integrated into the philosophically inclined mind; rather
it is the *living* means by which this always has been
and still is achieved, namely, the personal influence
of the distinguished professor. The near and far-
reaching power of *personal influence*, together with its
necessary check and ally, *discipline*, must be
conjoined and balanced if the university is to be
more than a simple idea or formal notion, that is, if
it is to flourish in full institutional good health and
actually enjoy continuing existence and development. *Rise and Progress of Universities* is the ingenious
story of the organic growth and historical development of what may be called 'the university venture'

[38] *Historical Sketches*, Vol. III, pp. 171–72.

in the West. And this story is told according to the shifting patterns and inflections of those two peremptory powers, influence and discipline.

We read the story of the university's birth (or, better, of the first 'anticipation of its type') in Athens and Rome, its survival of war and destruction, its cultivation in the monasteries and its protection by the popes, its maturation in medieval and modern Europe, and its struggle for survival and continued well-being in contemporary England. In tracing the development of the idea, Newman was hoping imaginatively and constructively to render the university-idea real to the minds of his readers. The *Rise and Progress of Universities* accomplishes the purpose of realizing the *idea* primarily through the vivid portraits of particular persons, of great institutions, and of flourishing cities and whole cultures.

Newman invites us to join him in imagination as he paints a composite picture of the wide-eyed 'freshman' upon his arrival at the Athenian port city of Piraeus:

So now let us fancy our Scythian, or Armenian, or African, or Italian, or Gallic student, after tossing on the Saronic waves, which would be his more ordinary course to Athens, at last casting anchor at Piraeus. He is of any condition or rank of life you please, and may be made to order, from a prince to a peasant. ... Perhaps he is some Cleanthes, who has been a boxer in the public games ... Or it is a young man of great promise as an orator ... called Cicero ... But see where comes from Alexandria (for we need not be very solicitous about anachro-

nisms), a young man . . . some say is a Christian . . .,
Gregory. . . .[39]

Our young man searches for lodgings and a teacher,
and Newman unfolds the physical loveliness in both
nature and art which made this sort of ideal land the
special seat of the Muses. Lowly abodes, narrow
streets, not a book-shop in sight! It was not ideas as
such, but what his senses brought home to his imagination that constituted his real education. '[I]t was
what the student gazed on, what he heard, what he
caught by the magic of sympathy, not what he read,
which was the education furnished by Athens.'[40]
Leaving the city behind, the young man mounts the
Acropolis to the right, or turns to the Areopagus on
the left; he studies sculpture at the Parthenon, painting at the temple, drama in the theatre; he turns
westward to the Agora and hears Lysias pleading or
Demosthenes haranguing; he passes through the city
gate to the tombs of the mighty dead, and there is
Pericles himself, converting a funeral oration into a
philosophical panegyric of the living. This is Athens,
the ideal site of the university, and here the student
imbibes 'the invisible atmosphere of genius and learns
by heart the oral traditions of taste.'[41]

At last the student comes to that celebrated
Academe, with its groves and statues, and the stream
of Cephissus flowing by. But wait, his eye and ear are
just now arrested and magnetically, irresistibly, drawn

---

[39] *Historical Sketches*, Vol. III (*HS* III), pp. 33–35.
[40] *HS* III, p. 40.
[41] *HS* III, p. 40.

by something – someone speaking: it is the great master Plato.

> What [the student] sees is a whole, complete in itself, not to be increased by addition, and greater than anything else. It will be a point in the history of his life; a stay for his memory to rest on, a burning thought in his heart, a bond of union with men of like mind, ever afterwards. Such is the spell which the living man exerts on his fellows, for good or for evil.[42]

In *Rise and Progress of Universities*, Newman places the personality of the great teacher at the birth of the entire university movement. In the 'Dublin Discourses', Newman had spoken abstractly of 'an intellectual tradition which is independent of particular teachers.' But now, of the living image of the university, he writes: 'An academical system without the personal influence of teachers upon pupils is an arctic winter; it will create an ice-bound, petrified, cast-iron, University, and nothing else.'[43] The general principles of any study may be learned at home from books; but the detail, colour and tone which bring an idea to life can only be 'caught' from those in whom it lives already. No books can get to the minute questions and felt difficulties, the special spirit and delicate peculiarities of its subject in the same and certain way that can come from the sympathy of mind with mind, through the eyes, the accent, the manner, the casual

[42] *HS* III, pp. 41–42.
[43] *HS* III, p. 74.

expression and unstudied turns of familiar conversation.

> If we wish to become exact and fully furnished in any branch of knowledge which is diversified and complicated, we must consult the living man and listen to his living voice. ... Till we have discovered some intellectual daguerreotype, which takes off the course of thought, and the form, lineaments, and features of truth, as completely and minutely, as the optical instrument reproduces the sensible object, we must come to the teachers of wisdom to learn wisdom, we must repair to the fountain, and drink there.[44]

It is in such assemblages of intellect – by means of lectures, discussions, arguments, speculations, all germinating, colliding, being tested, one with and by another – that books themselves, 'the masterpieces of human genius', are originated, that new explorations and mappings of knowledge are created, advanced and passed on. Newman strongly encourages research, writing and publication by university faculty, and their professional activity, such as participation in learned societies and periodic meetings. In these ways, personal influence extends beyond the university into the city and across national boundaries into the whole world. Personal influence, for Newman, is the direct source of the *advancement* of knowledge.[45]

The portraits of the Athenian freshman, of Plato

[44] *Historical Sketches*, Vol. III (*HS* III), pp. 8–9.
[45] For Newman's view of the advancement of knowledge through research and publication, see the last section of this Introduction.

and of Athens show but the birthplace, the precarious beginning and anticipation of the living idea of a university. Like St. Augustine, St. Thomas and Dante before him, however, Newman understood that the liberal arts, left to themselves, can be both powerful and dangerous. Always seeking balance and wholeness, he understood that the gift of an influential personality, either in popular teachers or talented students, brings with it the equally strong risk of pride of intellect, ambition and the intoxication of applause. Accordingly Newman devotes an entire article, or chapter, to the sobering portrait of the celebrated Abelard. 'Behold, the whole world is gone out after him.'[46]

Brilliant student and eloquent, attractive teacher, the young Abelard possessed an undisciplined self-will, ambition and contentiousness which, in Newman's view, became his downfall. Newman faults Abelard for his myopic devotion to the liberal art of logic, that 'gladiatorial wisdom' that was at once his greatest accomplishment, but also the cause for disrespectful treatment of his teachers and strenuous opposition to the reading of the classics. The young Abelard's impatient refusal to submit his mind and 'his one idea' to any author or authority outside himself illustrates the principle of personal influence run wild. 'In his popularity and in his reverses, in the criticisms of John of Salisbury on his method, and the protest of St. Bernard against his teaching, we read, as in a pattern specimen, what a University professes in its essence, and what it needs for its "integrity."'[47] For

[46] *HS* III, p. 202, from Chapter XVI.
[47] *HS* III, p. 192.

Newman, the *integrity* of the intellectual life and of higher education demands *discipline*.

The university's exercise of a balancing discipline in the moral and religious life of its members, Newman represents by Rome – both ancient, classical Rome and the Roman Catholic Church – and by the establishment of colleges to give equilibrium and stability to the university.

> As time has gone on, it has been found out that personal influence does not last for ever.... Accordingly, system has of necessity been superadded to individual action; a University has been embodied in a constitution, it has exerted authority, it has been protected by rights and privileges, it has enforced discipline, it has developed itself into Colleges and has admitted Monasteries into its territory.[48]

Ancient Rome, with its emphasis on the cultivation of civic virtue and its talent for organisation, formed a political framework and created establishments which were to last forever. In Rome, the elements of knowledge flourished in the Trivium and the Quadrivium, and the Law of the Empire provided for schools, and for the endowment of professors and their chairs in the Capital. Education was now institutionally established, assured of protection and propagation, even as it served the useful arts, developed a system of ethics and framed a code of laws. 'First the Greek, then the Macedonian and Roman; the Athenian created, the Imperialist organized and consolidated.'[49]

[48] *Historical Sketches*, Vol. III (*HS* III), pp. 77–78.
[49] *HS* III, p. 78.

For Newman, the intellect which, Athens-like, is noble, critical, proud and free, is by nature bound to conscience which, Rome-like, knows duty and devotion, sanction and rule. Without the formation and maturation of conscience, the cultivated intellect easily substitutes brilliance or legality or expedience for the gentle promptings within the deep heart's core. The happiness of the liberally educated 'gentleman' would only increase, writes Newman, 'were it not for the *memento* within him that books and gardens do not make a man immortal'.[50]

In educational institutions, colleges, the small residential communities of scholars and tutors living together, are the place of discipline – first of intellectual discipline, and also of moral and religious formation. Colleges take over where the institution of the family leaves off by providing all that is implied in the name of home – a refuge, a shelter, a place of companionship, prayer and instruction, 'the shrine of our best affections'. These second homes 'have no pretension indeed to be the essence of a University, but are conservative of that essence.'[51]

By discipline as the corrective and complement of personal influence, Newman means not only a life lived within the institutional authority and traditions of the university and the Church, but also the discipline or submission of a regular and ordered personal and social life, according to the dictates of the Image of God within oneself and others. 'Regularity, rule, respect for others, the eyes of friends and acquaintances, the absence from temptation, external

50 *HS* III, p. 63.
51 *HS* III, p. 189.

restraints generally, are of first importance in protecting us from ourselves.'[52]

The main instrument of seeing to the principle of
discipline in the colleges is, after the college dean, the
college tutor. Here too personal influence is crucial,
but it is influence tempered with the intimacy of
friendship. The work of a professor

> Is not sufficient by itself to form the pupil. The
> catechetical form of instruction and the closeness of
> work in a small class are needed besides. Without
> these, even supposing the Professor to be a man of
> genius and to interest his hearers, the acquirements
> carried away from him will often be very superfi-
> cial. No doubt, wherever the mind is really
> interested, it is also led in some degree to exert
> itself, and there is fruit; but if this is trusted to, the
> result will be undisciplined and unexercised minds,
> with a few notions, on which they are able to show
> off, but without any judgment or any solid powers.
> So that the principal making of men must be by the
> Tutorial system.[53]

The tutor selects his student's course of reading,
recommends the lectures he is to attend, and the
books and subjects which he is to present for examinations. Newman gives detailed directives of how the
tutor should handle, respectively, the more promising
students, the backward, and the idle, noting the
sustained solicitude and devotion required for this
post.

[52] *Historical Sketches*, Vol. III (*HS* III), pp. 189–90.
[53] *My Campaign in Ireland*, pp. 83–84.

The way to a young man's heart lies through his studies, certainly in the case of the more clever and diligent. He feels grateful towards the superior, who takes an interest in the things which are at the moment nearest to his heart, and he opens it to him accordingly.... Obscurities of thought, difficulties in philosophy, perplexities of faith, are confidentially brought out, sifted, and solved; and a pagan poet or theorist may thus become the occasion of Christian advancement.[54]

Newman sees in this idea of a college tutor the union of intellectual and moral influence, 'the separation of which is the evil of the age'. But just as the power of influence can be one-sidedly abused, as illustrated in the portrait of the young Abelard, so can discipline become, distortedly, an end in itself. In an autobiographical vignette, Newman recalls some of the 'dry old redtapists' of his student days, for whom law reigned without influence, system without personality, institutional establishment, regularity and tradition exclusively for their own sake.[55]

Even Rome, which Newman portrays as beautifully as he did Athens, as 'the noblest earthly power that ever was', eventually succumbed – first to the Goth, then the Hun, then the Lombard. And in the midst of this centuries-long destruction, it was the Church that preserved the ancient learning by its monasteries and schools, its educated clergy, its evangelising saints, and its learned and holy popes. The great medieval univer-

[54] *Campaign*, pp. 117–20.
[55] *HS* III, pp. 75–76.

sities – Christian all – rose out of the ancient culture preserved and spread by the Church. From the time of Charlemagne, and throughout the period of the Schools, Newman observes, 'Christianity which hitherto might be considered as a quality superinduced upon the face of society, now became the element out of which society grew into shape and reached its stature.'[56]

Whether attacked violently by the Goth and the Hun, whether usurped imperially by the single-minded logicians of the high Middle Ages, by the littérateurs of the Renaissance, the rationalists of the Enlightenment, or the English utilitarians of Newman's own day, the idea *University* would struggle to remain whole and integral, would be strengthened by the growth of its aspects and would survive and develop, just as the idea *State* and the idea *Church* have survived from antiquity until today – true to type, yet ever new.

The 'pattern specimens', which are continued by Newman to the Oxford and Paris of his own day, are sufficient to demonstrate that the continuing challenge to higher education has been the preservation of type by means of continual adaptation to historical and cultural circumstances. Only in its evolution and development, does the idea or notion discover its process of realisation. Though perhaps threatened with extinction in each variation and transformation, the species or formal idea perdures within the change, and is thereby preserved, strengthened and developed. As Newman said in his *Essay on the Development of*

[56] *Historical Sketches*, Vol. III, pp. 150–51.

Christian Doctrine of 1845, the thinking through and writing of which clearly had a powerful influence on his educational writings of the following decade: 'In proportion to the variety of aspects under which [a living idea] presents itself to various minds is its force and depth, and the argument for its reality. Ordinarily an idea is not brought home to the intellect as objective except through this variety.'[57]

The 'University principle,' then, is expansive *personal influence*, whereas the 'Collegiate principle' is concentrated *discipline*; the former defines, the latter completes. And in the flourishing university, both principles ideally work together in harmonious accord.

> A University embodies the principal of progress, and a College that of stability; the one is the sail, and the other the ballast; each is insufficient in itself for the pursuit, extension, and inculcation of knowledge; each is useful to the other. A University is the scene of enthusiasm of pleasurable exertion, of brilliant display, of winning influence, of diffusive and potent sympathy; and a College is the scene of order, of obedience, of modest and persevering diligence, of conscientious fulfilment of duty, of mutual private services, and deep and lasting attachments.... It would seem as if a University seated and living in Colleges, would be a perfect institution, as possessing excellences of opposite kinds.

> But such a union, such salutary balance and

---

[57] John Henry Newman, *An Essay on the Development of Christian Doctrine* (London, Longmans, Green & Co., 1897), pp. 34–35.

mutual complement of opposite advantages, is of
difficult and rare attainment.[58]

In the 'Dublin Discourses', Newman's presentation of
the idea, or formal notion, of a university was like the
large and sweeping strokes of a pencil sketch, showing
the outlines of the notion as a whole, and the perfectly
balanced relationships of parts to whole. In the illustrations of his 1852 Appendix and of the 'Occasional
Lectures and Essays', Newman filled in detail, dimen-
sion and colour – as if painting a portrait; and now, in
Rise and Progress of Universities, the idea *university*
comes fully to life in the imagination, and is set in
dramatic motion – almost like the protagonist of a
great epic.

V. BENEDICTINE ESSAYS

Newman begins this engaging pair of essays, 'The
Mission of St. Benedict' and 'The Benedictine
Schools',[59] from within his own broad philosophical

---

[58] *Historical Sketches*, Vol. III (*HS* III), pp. 228–29.

[59] The first of the two essays, 'Mission of St. Benedict', appeared in the
inaugural issue of the *Atlantis* in January, 1858, as 'The Mission of the
Benedictine Order'. It concluded with the words, 'To be continued'.
One year later, in January of 1859, the second essay, 'Benedictine
Schools', appeared under the title 'The Benedictine Centuries'. See
The Atlantis: A Register of Literature and Science, 4 vols. (London,
Longman, Brown, Green, Longmans, and Roberts; Dublin, John F.
Fowler: 1858–1870) I, 1: pp. 1–49; II, 3: pp. 1–43. Newman repub-
lished both Benedictine essays under their present titles in *Historical
Sketches*, II, pp. 363–430, pp. 431–487, to which correspond the page
numbers of the footnotes in this section of the Introduction, and in
the correlating Notes that follow the text.

habit of mind, one which truly possessed an expansive sense of the whole and delighted in mapping the universe in a rich variety of ways. As he so often did, so here too he draws that familiar analogy between the course of nature and the advance of human history: both, he says, are centered in axial fields of power and influence.

> As the physical universe is sustained and carried on in dependence on certain centres of power and laws of operation, so the course of the social and political world, and of that great religious organization called the Catholic Church, is found to proceed for the most part from the presence or action of definite persons, places, events and institutions, as the visible cause of the whole.[60]

Typically again, Newman then moves deductively toward that aspect of the whole which he will proceed to consider.

Dividing the history of education within Christianity into three periods – the ancient, the medieval, and the modern – Newman assigns to these epochs, respectively and successively, three of the prominent religious orders which 'represent the teaching given by the Catholic Church during the time of their ascendancy'. They are the orders of 'the three great Patriarchs of Christian teaching' of St. Benedict, who is distinguished by 'the element of Poetry', of St. Dominic, distinguished by 'the Scientific element', and of St. Ignatius, marked by 'Practical Sense'.[61]

[60] Historical Sketches, Vol. II (*HS* II), p. 365.
[61] *HS* II, pp. 365–67.

Newman takes pains to distinguish the large view he is sketching from one with which he has no sympathy at all, namely, the then-popular Positivist 'theory of progress', which also postulates three historical stages – an illusory 'theological' stage, an exclusively theoretical 'metaphysical' stage, and an empirical or 'scientific' stage – each one doing away with and superceding the preceding stage.[62] The crucial difference between this view and his own, Newman observes, is that the Catholic Church, in her educational progress from poetry through science to prudence, has never lost or left behind any one of these three elements.

> Instead of passing from one stage of life to another, she has carried her youth and middle age along with her, on to her latest time. She has not changed possessions, but accumulated them, and has brought out of her treasure-house, according to the occasion, things new and old. She did not lost Benedict by finding Dominic; and she has still both Benedict and Dominic at home, though she has become the mother of Ignatius. Imagination, Science, Prudence, all are good, and she has them all.[63]

Devoting little over one page to the Jesuits and their

---

[62] Although Newman does not mention 'Positivism' or its founder by name, Auguste Comte's influential six volume work, *Cours de philosophie positive* (1830–42), delineates precisely this threefold schema as the elements of his theory of progress. The work's influence in England is testified to by the critical analysis, shortly after Newman published the Benedictine essays, by John Stuart Mill in his book, *Auguste Comte and Positivism* (London, 1865).

[63] *Historical Sketches*, Vol. II, pp. 368–69.

founder, St. Ignatius of Loyola, Newman says that 'by common consent' the palm of religious Prudence, in Aristotle's broad sense of the word, belongs to them as the School of discretion, practical sense, and wise government.[64] And so he will confine his remarks to the Benedictines and the Dominicans. But then there is a note in Newman's text, which says that due to 'the temporary suspension of the *Atlantis*', the article on the Dominicans was not written.[65]

Indeed, there was a hiatus in the publication of the *Atlantis*, which appeared in 1858 and 1859 – each January volume containing one of the Benedictine essays – and then did not appear again until 1862 and 1863, after which it did not surface again until its last issue of 1870. But in addition to the Benedictine essays, Newman did write two other essays for the *Atlantis*, one of them on a theological formula of St. Cyril, which appeared in the July issue of 1858, and another article on the Roman Breviary, which appeared in the final volume of 1870. So presumably he could have published additional articles had he the time and desire to do so.[66]

But perhaps Newman was not as interested in

[64] See Aristotle, *Nicomachean Ethics*, Bk. VI.

[65] If one may judge by the extensive notes Newman worked up for each of the three Patriarchs and their religious orders, it seems clear that Newman intended also to write a third essay on the Jesuits, as well as to develop in greater detail an analogy between the three Patriarchs of Christian Education and the original Patriarchs of Judaism, Abraham, Isaac, and Jacob, respectively. See Birmingham Oratory Archives, B.2.9.

[66] Father Ker intimates that there was 'a criticism' of what Newman wrote on the Benedictines, and that Newman accordingly 'was afraid to write more about the religious orders without a great deal more research.' See Ian Ker, *John Henry Newman: A Biography* (Oxford, Oxford University Press, 1988), p. 457.

writing about the Dominicans and the Jesuits, as he was in writing about the Benedictines; for it is apparent, from what he had already written in *Rise and Progress of Universities*, that he was partial to the Benedictine *idea*, ethos, and spirit.

When he was writing the *Gazette* articles about the importance of *influence* and *discipline*, he noted that both principles ideally should be harmonised in a single institution by means of the combined professorial and the tutorial elements. Observing, however, that this complete integration is a difficult and rare achievement, he goes on to say that it is natural that the inclination toward one or the other, influence or discipline, may colour the unity and be dominant in a given institution – for better or for worse. Newman himself, interestingly, although not surprisingly, revealed in *Rise and Progress of Universities* that his sympathies resided more with the principle of personal influence as imaged in shining Athens, and also with his special patron, the 'Amabile Santo', Philip Neri, founder of the Congregation of the Oratory, of which he was a member.

> ... with my tenderness, on the one hand, for Athens ... and my devotion to a particular Catholic Institution on the other, I have ever thought I could trace a certain resemblance between Athens, as contrasted with Rome, and the Oratory of St. Philip, as viewed in contrast with the Religious Orders.[67]

---

[67] *Historical Sketches*, Vol. III (*HS* III), p. 86.

When Newman was in Rome, just after being received into the Catholic Church, he spent a good deal of time studying the histories and charisms of the various religious communities and visiting some of their houses, in order that he might discern the vocational direction of his own priestly life in concert with the companions who had joined him in his journey of conversion.[68] What appealed to him most was precisely the 'Greek' orientation of St. Philip Neri's Oratorians, in contrast to the 'Roman' characteristics he associated with the more traditional 'Regular Orders'. St. Philip, he observed,

> had no intention of forming any Congregation at all, but had formed it before he knew of it, from the beauty and the fascination of his own saintliness; and then, when he was obliged to recognize it and put it into shape, shrank from the severity of the Regular, would have nothing to say to vows, and forbade propagation and dominion; whose houses stand, like Greek colonies, independent of each other and complete in themselves; whose subjects in those several houses are allowed, like Athenian citizens, freely to cultivate their respective gifts and to follow out their own mission; whose one rule is Love, and whose own [one?] weapon Influence.[69]

---

[68] On Newman's careful choice of a priestly vocation, see Placid Murray, O.S.B., *Newman the Oratorian* (Leominster, Fowler Wright Books, 1980), especially Chap. 5. Father Murray observes: 'It would seem then that what Newman got hold of around Christmas 1846 and the following weeks in Rome, was the *idea* of the Oratory, rather than any practical existing model of an Oratory which could have been transplanted from Italy to a mid-nineteenth-century English town.' p. 90.

[69] *HS* III, p. 88.

Newman saw it as especially suitable – indeed, as having 'a providential fitness' – that the Congregation of the Oratory, 'in the person of one of its members', had undertaken 'the preparatory movements of the establishment of a great University'.

> Though to frame, to organize, and to consolidate, be the imperial gift of St. Dominic or St. Ignatius, and beyond his range, yet a son of St. Philip Neri may aspire without presumption to the preliminary task of breaking the ground and clearing the foundations of the Future.[70]

By omission, Newman thus implies that, in contrast to 'the imperial gift of St. Dominic or St. Ignatius', there remains the special charism of their predecessor, St. Benedict: to clear the forests, to break the ground, and to lay the foundation for what would follow. This omission in *Rise and Progress of Universities*, Newman supplies in the Benedictine essays.

The Idea of Monasticism
Like the *idea* University, and like the *idea* Church, Newman's *idea* of Monasticism governs and orders the whole of the subject matter at hand. But Newman's treatment of the *idea* of Monasticism in the *Benedictine Essays* is unlike his handling of the *idea* of a University in the 'Dublin Discourses', for the latter remains abstract and ahistorical by his expressed intention, and consequently requires illustrations and the historical essays of *Rise and Progress of Universities* in order to

---

[70] *Historical Sketches*, Vol. III, p. 89.

concretize the *idea* and make it real to his readers. Accordingly, the coherent body of thought that comprises Newman's one work on university education takes three companion volumes for its complete expression.

Quite different is his treatment of the *idea* of Monasticism. Here, in two relatively short essays, the *idea* or notion of Monasticism, and the *image*, that is, its historical realisations during the Benedictine centuries, are perfectly combined and integrated in one coherent whole. It would seem as though, in the *Benedictine Essays*, Newman finally achieved the unity of expression he had in mind, and perhaps sought, in writing his university volumes, though he did not have time to carry it out. Rhetorically and in substance, the *Benedictine Essays* attain that mastery of 'the twofold Logos of thought and speech', which Newman so admired in really great writers.[71]

According to Newman, St. Benedict, who is called the "Patriarch of the West", was, like Abraham, the "Father of many nations", in that he was the first to establish 'a perpetual Order of Regulars in Western Christendom'. As the representative of Latin monasticism for six centuries, 'while monachism was one', he was the source of the change from which new and independent monastic families arose. His Rule, like St. Basil's in the East, was the normal rule of the first age of the Church, and upon it would be based even the rules of many communities which did not owe their direct origin to him. Because his Rule was so

---

[71] See Newman's 1858 lecture on 'Literature' in the School of Philosophy and Letters, in *The Idea of a University*, especially pp. 232, 244.

uniformly expressive of 'the genius of monachism'
itinerant religious men were able to move freely from
one monastery to another, being at home in each and
all – for "in every place we are servants of one Lord
and soldiers of one King".[72]

> The unity of idea, which, as these words imply,
> is to be found in all monks in every part of
> Christendom, may be described as a unity of
> object, of state, and of occupation. Monachism
> was one and the same everywhere, because it was
> a reaction from that secular life, which has every-
> where the same structure and the same
> characteristics.[73]

Christianity had been born into 'an old, decayed, and
moribund world', which was especially heterogeneous, unsettled, and confused – at first the seat of
paganism, and then of hostile heresies – and so it was
natural that 'this encompassing, entangling system of
things' would generate from within itself a state that
was 'constant and unalterable'. Serious Christians,
weary of heart and laden of conscience, desired only
to be free of its vexations and sway.

> Their one idea then, their one purpose, was to be
> quit of it; too long had it enthralled them. It was
> not a question of this or that vocation, of the better
> deed, of the higher state, but of life and death. In
> later times a variety of holy objects might present

[72] *Historical Sketches*, Vol. II (*HS* II), pp. 370–73, concluding with a
passage from the Benedictine Rule.
[73] *HS* II, p. 373.

themselves for devotion to choose from, such as the
care of the poor, or of the sick, or of the young . . .;
but early monachism was flight from the world, and
nothing else.[74]

In its emphatic negation of the world, monasticism
was a 'mortification of sense, and a mortification of
reason'.

Newman is quick to expain that the monks were
'too good Catholics' to deny that these faculties are a
divine gift, and 'had too much common sense' to
think they could do without them. But they denied
themselves the many exercises and excitements of
reason – its combinations and complications, its analy-
ses and syntheses, its arguments and defenses, its
discoveries and inventions, and, perhaps above all, 'its
capacity to view things as a whole, whether for speculation or for action'. Instead of cultivating the mind,
in childlike simplicity they cultivated the earth, allow-
ing each work, each place, each occurrence to stand
by itself. They seemed more like citizens of eternity
than of time.

The monastic mortification, or silencing, of the
senses and of the intellect was for the sole purpose of
devotion. The monks sought out retirement, solitude,
and seclusion, in order that, in perfect peace and
quiet, they might consecrate themselves to divine
meditation. Any simple occupation would do: prayer,
fasting, choir, study, transcription, manual labour.
Newman takes on objections about differences
between the East and the West, and about exceptions

[74] *HS* II, pp. 374–75.

to the Rule, concerning this governing *idea* of monasticism. Nothing, he finds, detracts from its unity and universality. 'Such was their institution all over the world.'[75]

Monasticism is thus 'the most poetical' of religious disciplines, for herein the soul may be entirely quiet and at rest, free of all complications of intellect and of passion.

> It was a return to that primitive age of the world, of which poets have so often sung, the simple life of Arcadia or the reign of Saturn, when fraud and violence were unknown. It was a bringing back of those real, not fabulous, scenes of innocence and miracle, when Adam delved, or Abel kept sheep, or Noe planted the vine, and Angels visited them.[76]

Newman does not mean that monks were dreamy sentimentalists; rather 'their poetry was the poetry of hard work and hard fare, unselfish hearts and charitable hands.'[77]

Because his use of the word 'poetic' to describe the monastic state may seem somewhat problematic, Newman further clarifies his meaning by saying that poetry is always 'the antagonist to *science*'. Scientific knowledge is characterised by all of the intellectual activities of observation and investigation, and it results in system, whereas poetry 'delights in the indefinite' and the simple. 'As science makes progress in any subject-matter, poetry recedes from it.'

[75] *Historical Sketches*, Vol. II (*HS* II), pp. 375–85.
[76] *HS* II, p. 385.
[77] *HS* II, p. 398.

The aim of science is to grasp and handle and control things, to *master* them; and its mission is to do away with ignorance, doubt and illusion. The poetical frame of mind, on the other hand, demands a sense of being encompassed and comprehended by things, of being 'at their feet' – in awe and wonder, and almost in worship – rather that delineating and defining them as objects viewed from above.

It implies that we understand them to be vast, immeasurable, impenetrable, inscrutable, mysterious; so that at best we are only forming conjectures about them, not conclusions, for the phenomena which they present admit of many explanations, and we cannot know the true one.... The vague, the uncertain, the irregular, the sudden, are among its attributes or sources.[78]

So it is that the child's mind is more poetic than the old man's, nature more so than art, and history more than philosophy.

Newman finds that 'the family of St. Benedict' answers especially fittingly to this description of the poetical. While it is surely one in spirit and type, 'it is an organization, diverse, complex, and irregular, and variously ramified, rich rather than symmetrical, with many origins and centres and new beginnings and the action of local influences, like some great natural growth....'[79]

Example after historical example follows, of famous

[78] *HS* II, p. 387.
[79] *HS* II, p. 388.

monasteries and of sainted monks, and of authorities who have written on monasticism, with their praise and their criticism. Citing all of these images and real-isations of the singular *idea*, Newman emphasises, under the aspect of their poetry, the monks' utility to man and their service to God:

> How romantic then, as well as useful, how lively as well as serious, is their history, with its episodes of personal adventure and prowess, its pictures of squat-ter, hunter, farmer, civil engineer, and evangelist united in the same individual, with its supernatural colouring of heroic virtue and miracle![80]

Other special characteristics contained in the *idea* of Monasticism, in addition to poetic simplicity, are the gentleness and tenderness of heart of the monks; their works of penace, mercy, and charity; and their hospi-tality to high and low. Situated in the country and living for the day, 'doing works which cannot be cut short, for they are complete in every portion of them,' the monk leads a life that 'may be called emphatically Virgilian.'[81] By contrast, those whose duty lies in '*undertakings*,' that is, 'in sustained efforts of the intel-lect or elaborate processes of action – apologists, controversialists, disputants in the schools, professors in the chair, teachers in the pulpit, rulers in the

---

[80] *Historical Sketches*, Vol. II (*HS* II), p. 400.

[81] *HS* II, p. 409. After Virgil (70–19 BC), Newman's favourite Roman poet. See *HS* II, p. 407: 'Would that Christianity had a Virgil to describe the old monks at their rural labours, as it has had a Sacchi or a Domenichino to paint them!' See also *HS* II, pp. 467–470, for further discusion of the congeniality between 'the Benedictine idea, viewed in the abstract', and 'the spirit of the great Roman Poet' p. 453).

Church – have a noble and meritorious mission, but not so poetical a one.'[82]

The mission of St. Benedict was to restore the social and physical world, not structurally or systematically, but as a gradual and natural growth. 'By degrees the woody swamp became a hermitage, a religious house, a farm, an abbey, a village, a seminary, a school of learning, and a city.'[83] A further field of monastic manual labour, one directly ministering to and expressive of devotion, was the transcription, illumination, and binding of the words of inspired teachers – of Scripture, of the Fathers and Doctors of the Church. A method of instruction uniquely Benedictine in spirit and subject matter, this work was literary, quiet, unexciting – 'unequivocally a manual labour' – and it provided for the learning and edification of the monks who meditated upon it, as well as for the necessities of posterity.

The unique features of 'what may be especially called the Benedictine period, the five centuries between St. Gregory and St. Anselm', gradually came to expression in the compilation of chronicles and annals, and in the selection and arrangements of patristic texts according to special topics and doctrines, the latter serving to 'open the way to the intellectual exercises of the scholastic period'.[84]

In concluding his *Atlantis* essay on 'The Mission of St. Benedict', Newman returns full circle to an intimate, if serendipitous, link he sees between the Benedictines of antiquity and his own beloved

[82] *HS* II, p. 409.
[83] *HS* II, p. 410.
[84] *HS* II, pp. 416–418.

Oratorians. Observing that St. Bede is truly the pattern of a Benedictine – just as St. Thomas Aquinas is of a Dominican, and St. Francis Xavier of a Jesuit – Newman quotes at length 'from the letter of Cuthbert to Cuthwin', which narrates the holy death of Bede. Then, as if to give a finishing touch to the entire idea of monasticism, he discloses the 'remarkable' fact that St. Bede died on the very same day of the year as did St. Philip Neri, May 26. Bridging whole centuries in his robust and devout imagination, Newman declares: 'It was fitting that two saints should go to heaven together, whose mode of going thither was the same; both of them singing, praying, working, and guiding others, in joy and exultation, till their very last hour.'[85]

It is a slightly differing view of the history of Christendom that Newman takes up in the second of the *Atlantis* essays, 'The Benedictine Schools'. Confronted with 'the manifest tokens of an expiring world', the prevalent disposition of Christians living in the first centuries was to leave it, as did the monks, or to put up with it – but not to influence or challenge

---

[85] *Historical Sketches*, Vol. II (*HS* II), pp. 428–30. In *Newman the Oratorian*, Father Murray recounts Father Henry Tristram's query: 'I have often wondered why Newman did not become a Benedictine. It would have seemed the obvious thing, and yet it did not come up for consideration' – and answers it in the following terms. Despite his sympathetic portrayal of the Benedictines of antiquity in the *Atlantis* essays, Newman did not look to the English Benedictines of his day. From the marginal summaries of the *Atlantis* essays as they originally appeared, Father Murray deduces that Newman's interest in Benedictine learning was 'almost certainly motivated by the parallel with the writings of the Italian Oratory' (p. 82, note 40). Newman 'never had a monastic vocation, though he staked the whole working of the Oratory on one of the central ideas of cenobitic monasticism, viz. common life in a stable community' (p. 127).

or change it. However, by the ninth century, Newman observes, 'a singular change' must have occurred in 'the ecclesiastical position' of monks, for the upheavals in 'the moribund world' they had left behind, those which issued in the rule of Charlemagne, were beginning to affect their own home. They discovered that they themselves, artlessly and unwittingly, had created a whole new world.

> The old order of things died, sure enough; but then a new order took its place, and they themselves, by no will or expectation of their own, were in no small measure its very life. The lonely Benedictine rose from his knees and found himself a city. This was the case, not merely here or there, but everywhere; Europe was new mapped, and the monks were the principle of mapping.[86]

Entire cities had risen up around the monasteries, and the inmates found themselves pastors and school teachers, feudal lords, legislators, rulers, and royal counsellors. They realised that either they would again have to retreat from the world, remaining true to the original *idea* of monasticism, or they would have to find a way to remain faithful to St. Benedict while responding to the call of the Church and the world. As it turned out, both avenues were taken. Some returned to a more rigorous asceticism, as St. Romuald who founded the Camaldolese, and St. Bruno who founded the Carthusians; and some were overruled by the Church herself, which called them to

[86] *HS* II, p. 443.

active duties – to be priests, missionaries, bishops, teachers and controversialists – for at the time there were none but monks to fill these posts. The Church was responsible for requiring monks to leave their cloisters, and so 'such instances cannot fairly be taken, either as specimens of Benedictine work, or as modifications of the Benedictine idea.'[87] The new literary, pastoral, and political activity of the monks was imprinted with the living Benedictine *idea* and spirit, for 'whatever has life has in it a conservative principle, and a power of assimilation'.[88]

Newman's focus narrows to the monks of the Benedictine schools, which emerged during this new period of monastic activity. He restates his view of 'the Benedictine idea, *viewed in the abstract*' as poetical, and then immediately asks the reader, if this be so, to guess what the '*historical portrait*' filled out would look like – what books were studied and what sort of pupils were actually taught in the Benedictine schools.[89] He answers that because the Benedictine character was marked by simplicity, contentment, and patience, originating nothing, but living by tradition, it was fitting that Scripture should be the literature, and children should be the pupils, which St. Benedict taught. 'His convent was an infant school, a grammar school, and a seminary; it was not an academy.'[90]

For centuries, young boys, even infants, were brought to the monasteries and dedicated to God as oblates and monks. 'St. Boniface, Apostle of Germany,

---

[87] *Historical Sketches*, Vol. II (*HS* II), p. 446.
[88] *HS* II, p. 449.
[89] *HS* II, pp. 453–54. [Emphases added.]
[90] *HS* II, p. 456.

was a monk at the age of five; St. Bede came to Wiremouth at the age of seven; St. Paul of Verdun is said by an old writer to have left his cradle for the cloister; St. Robert entered it as soon as he was weaned...'[91] These children learned by gazing on what was about them, receiving the passive impressions of those solemn countenances and monastic services which surrounded them. By about the age of seven, they were taught to memorise the Psalter. Having mastered that, they entered the secular schoolroom to be introduced to the study of grammar, that is, to serious scholarship in Latin language, literature, and history. Eventually this extended to the study of all seven of the liberal arts of the Trivium and the Quadrivium. Newman finds this 'classical temperament of the Benedictines' to be in keeping with the genius and character of their institute.

> For they instinctively recognized in the graceful simplicity of Virgil or of Horace, in his dislike of the great world, of political contests and of ostentatious splendour, in his unambitious temper and his love of the country, an analogous gift to that of religious repose, that distaste for controversy, and that innocent cheerfulness which were the special legacy of St. Benedict to his children.[92]

In the devoted Benedictine educator, and in strong contrast with the schoolmen who followed, Newman saw a resemblance to 'the elegant scholar of a day which is now waning' – a resemblance to Oxford men

[91] *HS* II, p. 458.
[92] *HS* II, p. 467.

like Copleston or Keble – 'who thought little of science or philosophy by the side of the authors of Greece and Rome'. Nor is it too much to say, he continues, that in this respect of dutiful love of the Classics, 'the Colleges in the English Universities may be considered in matter of fact to be the lineal descendants or heirs of the Benedictine schools of Charlemagne.'[93]

Schooling by the Benedictines ended when the boys were about fourteen. Any higher education, beond 'the elements' of the Classics, would come from the 'public schools' founded by Charlemagne in the major cities throughout the empire. Newman notes, without further development here, that these cathedral schools of Charlemagne 'may be considered the shadow, and even the nucleus of the Universities which arose in a subsequent age'.[94] Years earlier, in *Rise and Progress of Universities*, Newman had devoted an entire chapter to 'The Schools of Charlemagne', saying:

> Here was the germ of the new civilization of Europe, which was to join together what man had divided, to adjust the claims of Reason and Revelation, and to fit men for this world while it trained them for another. Charlemagne has the glory of commencing this noble work; and, whether his school at Paris be called a University or not, he laid down principles of which a University is the result, in that he aimed at educating all classes, and undertook all subjects of teaching.[95]

[93] *Historical Sketches*, Vol. II (*HS* II), p. 466.
[94] *HS* II, p. 462.
[95] *Historical Sketches*, Vol. III (*HS* III), p. 152. See Chap. XIII.

Finally, Newman draws out a fundamental distinction between the Benedictine approach to theology, and the patristic and scholastic theology which preceded and followed it. For the liberally educated and mature monk, whose one devotion was the study of theology, this highest discipline meant a loving contemplation and straightforward exposition of Holy Scripture, according to the teaching of the Church Fathers. Loyal and devoted adherence to the past, and transmission of its treasures to future generations, were the hallmarks of Monasticism. The Benedictine 'seldom added anything original'. On the other hand, patristic theology which preceded it, as well as scholastic theology afterwards, involved intellectual creativity and originality.

> Origen, Tertullian, Athanasius, Chrysostom, Augustine, Jerome, Leo, are authors of powerful, original minds, and engaged in the production of original works. There is no greater mistake, surely, than to suppose that a revealed truth precludes originality in the treatment of it. The contrary is acknowledged in the case of secular subjects, in which it is the very triumph of originality, not to invent or discover what is not already known, but to make old things read as if they were new, from the novelty of aspect in which they are placed.... A reassertion of what is old with a luminousness of explanations which is new, is a gift inferior only to that of revelation itself.[96]

---

[96] *HS* II, pp. 475–76.

In the late Benedictine centuries, times were approaching when more was required than 'the rehearsal of what her champions had achieved and her sages had established in ages past'. At the time of Charlemagne, the intellect of society grew, the spirit of inquiry thrived, and new questions were raised, new difficulties proposed. 'Hard-headed objectors were not to be subdued by the reverence for antiquity and the amenities of polite literature.' All of the intellectual acumen that could be mustered was now to be employed in defending the doctrines of faith, in analysing and systematising them, and in entering into new scholarly researches that would advance theological understanding. 'And thus the period, properly Benedictine, ended', as religious orders of a different genius wielded new weapons against fresh opponents.[97]

Newman and Research

It is quite commonplace, and quite as mistaken, to criticise Newman for having no interest in research because of his outspoken commitment to liberal education in *The Idea of a University*.[98] This erroneous perception follows directly from wrongly concluding

---

[97] *Historical Sketches*, Vol. II, pp. 477–78, 486–87.

[98] For example, C. H. Holland says of Newman: 'This complicated man ... brought his liquid prose to bear against the pursuit of research in universities', in *Trinity College Dublin and the Idea of a University* (Dublin, Trinity College Press, 1991), p. 11. And J. M. Roberts writes: 'Of the deployment of university teaching (or research) with the aim of shaping society in any more direct way [than 'the formation of more individuals well equipped for life'], he does not speak.' See '*The Idea of a University* Revisited', in *Newman After a Hundred Years*, ed. Ian Ker and Alan G. Hill (Oxford, Clarendon Press, 1990), p. 210.

that the 'Dublin Discourses' in *The Idea of a University* constitute Newman's complete and final word on university education, when in fact, as has been shown, that work is but one of the three companion volumes on the topic, which he composed over a relatively concentrated period of three to four years, 1852–1856. Already drawn out have been Newman's clear distinctions, in *Rise and Progress of Universities*, between 'the University principle' and 'the Collegiate principle', and between the corresponding functions of both the professor and the tutor. In that work especially was found Newman's critical distinction between the *idea* or essence of a university (the cultivation in students, by professors, of an energised, healthy intellect) and the university's *integrity* or completeness (all of the 'institutions' not included in its essence – among them, its Catholicity, its colleges, and its faculty publication as a direct extension of professorial lecturing). Should any doubt remain, however, Newman's wholehearted justification for his scholarly register, the *Atlantis*, should lay the matter entirely to rest.

In his Introduction to the first number of the *Atlantis*,[99] Newman states unequivocally that it is a *duty* of professors to publish.

> It is natural that men, whose occupations are of an intellectual nature, should be led to record the speculations or the conclusions in which their labours have issued; and that, having taken this step, they should consider it even as a duty which we

[99] Reprinted as 'The *Atlantis* II' in *My Campaign in Ireland*, pp. 433–34, although not appearing in the bound Volume I of the *Atlantis*.

owe to society, to communicate to others what
they have thought it worth while to record. A periodical publication is the obvious mode of fulfilling
that duty.[100]

In order to attract distinguished professors to the
Catholic University and to provide for their particular
needs as professors, Newman established what he
called 'institutions', which, he said, 'have their value
intrinsically, whether students are present or not'.
Such would be the Medical School, the Irish
Archaeological Department, the science laboratories
and astronomical observatory, the various libraries and
museums, and the University Church. Such too was
the *Register of Literature and Science.*

Now, the *Atlantis* is one of these, and, in some
respects, the most important of all, because it is, in
a certain sense, the organ and the record of their
proceedings; and, again, because it is not of a local
nature, but world-wide in the most emphatic way,
increasing the 'celebrity' of the Professors of the
University, and making them useful to the literary
and scientific world....[101]

[100] '*The Atlantis II*,' *My Campaign in Ireland* (*Campaign*), p. 433.
[101] *Campaign*, LVII, pp. 371–72. One wonders, then, on what grounds
Martha McMackin Garland can write: 'Specialist professors might be
hired to instruct the students in the various disciplines of the liberal arts,
but providing the professors themselves with resources in order to
advance their scholarship was not part of Newman's plan, either in *The
Idea of a University* or in practice when he started setting up his institution.
If he had made a commitment to research, it would have been most
remarkable, inasmuch as this was such an alien concept within his own
experience.' See 'Newman in His Own Day' in the Yale edition of *The
Idea of a University*, ed. Frank M. Turner, p. 274.

Michael Tierney, who was from 1947–1964 the influential, if controversial, scholar-president of University College Dublin – the Catholic University's successor at St. Stephen's Green, after the Jesuits' inheritance of it – notes in particular Newman's contributions to Irish scientific studies and to early Irish history.[102] 'It would be hard to exaggerate the debt owed by this subject, with its very special national value, to Newman's conception of the functions of his "Catholic University of the English tongue."'[103] Eugene O'Curry, whom Newman appointed to the Chair of Irish History and Archaeology, and whose course of lectures Newman regularly attended, writes that the Catholic University 'was the first public establishment in the country spontaneously to erect a Chair of Irish History and Archaeology'.[104] Newman himself wrote proudly of the university's glad opening to O'Curry of a forum for the dissemination and publication to the world of his otherwise unknown and 'unrivalled treasures still extant of the antiquities of his country, for want of Catholic patronage'.[105]

When there were criticisms of the 'business-like tone and austere technicality' of the first number of the *Atlantis*, with some interested parties wishing 'somewhat of more indulgence to ordinary readers, by the introduction of matter less high and abstruse',

[102] See Donal McCartney's *UCD: A National Idea* (Dublin, Gill & Macmillan, 1999), especially the sections on 'Tierney and Newman,' pp. 141–58.

[103] Michael Tierney, 'Catholic University', in *A Tribute to Newman: Essays on Aspects of His Life and Thought*, ed. M. Tierney (Dublin, Browne and Nolan, 1945), p. 174.

[104] *Campaign*, pp. 310–312.

[105] *Campaign*, pp. 365–66.

Newman insisted that 'the very object of the publication is to record the successful diligence of the
Professors in their respective studies – not to write
eloquent reviews of essays, *currente calamo* [with
flowing pen], on curious or entertaining subjects.'

> Ornamental writing is about as much out of place
> in the *Atlantis*, as *ormolu* clocks, Dresden china, and
> Axminster carpets in Pump Court or Copthall
> Buildings. Scientific schools and circles abroad,
> where English is not vernacular, would not be
> impressed by fine periods, or edified by miscella-
> neous information.[106]

Newman was emphatically a friend, promoter, and
administrator, not only of faculty scholarship, but also
of faculty research and publication. To judge otherwise is to miss the marvellous integrity of his complete
work on university education.

Conclusion

If the Benedictine *idea* of the simple conservation of
tradition is in tension with the Dominican *idea* of
intellectual attainment; if the emblem of St. Bede
finds its contrariety in the emblem of St. Thomas
Aquinas; if the *idea* of Monasticism, in its poetic
elements, stands in stark contrast to the *idea* of
Scholasticism, in its scientific elements; and if there is
polarity between 'the Collegiate principle', with its
conscientious tutelage, and 'the University principle',
with its aim of cultivating the intellect and advancing

---

[106] *My Campaign in Ireland (Campaign)*, p. 374.

knowledge – well, then, Newman's *method* of coming to terms with all of these *ideas* is identical in every case: on the one hand, a philosophical approach to gleaning restrospectively the abstract essence of the *idea*, and, on the other, an historical approach to recounting the gradual realisation of each living *idea* through its developments and variations over the centuries.

Robert Ornsby was present at that remarkabe *soirée* on 5th November 1854, as the distinguished Rector spoke intimately with his small company of the newly enlisted. And Ornsby was obviously enchanted by what he witnessed: 'After this beautiful and animating discourse ... the youthful academics separated, highly delighted with their first evening in college.'[107]

We few, we happy few, we band of brothers.

Newman's heartening and unceremonious talk that evening, on which occasion his campaign in Ireland was at last really launched, is a perfect illustration of his consistent method, especially apparent both in *Rise and Progress of Universities* and in the *Benedictine Esssays*, of 'realising' an idea, making it real to his listeners or readers. Here, in a few minutes and on a few pages, Newman personally illuminates and conveys to these young men the otherwise abstract idea of a university by means of the concrete images of a conversation between a wise mother and her son, and between a

---

[107] *Campaign*, p. 324.

brave king and his soldiers facing battle. One might even say that the entire content of Newman's three-volumed 'one work' on universities is encountered here in miniature, by the deceptively simple means of 'a little touch of Newman in the night'.

UNIVERSITIES.

CHAPTER I.

INTRODUCTORY.

I HAVE it in purpose to commit to paper, time after time, various thoughts of my own, seasonable, as I conceive, when a Catholic University is under formation, and apposite in a publication, which is to be the record and organ of its proceedings. An anonymous person, indeed, like myself, can claim no authority for anything he advances; nor have I any intention of introducing or sheltering myself under the sanction of the Institution which I wish to serve. My remarks will stand amid weightier matters like the non-official portion of certain government journals in foreign parts; and I trust they will have their use, though they are but individual in their origin, and immethodical in their execution. When I say anything to the purpose, the gain is the University's; when I am mistaken or unsuccessful, the failure is my own.

The Prelates of the Irish Church are at present engaged in an anxious and momentous task, which has the inconvenience of being strange to us, if it be not novel. A University is not founded every day; and seldom indeed has it been founded under the peculiar circumstances which will now attend its establishment in

Catholic Ireland. Generally speaking, it has grown up out of schools, or colleges, or seminaries, or monastic bodies, which had already lasted for centuries; and, different as it is from them all, has been little else than their natural result and completion. While then it has been expanding into its peculiar and perfect form, it has at the same time been by anticipation educating subjects for its service, and has been creating and carrying along with it the national sympathy. Here, however, as the world is not slow to object, this great institution is to take its place among us without antecedent or precedent, whether to recommend or explain it. It receives, we are told, neither illustration nor augury from the history of the past, and requires to be brought into existence as well as into shape. It has to force its way abruptly into an existing state of society which has never duly felt its absence; and it finds its most formidable obstacles, not in anything inherent in the undertaking itself, but in the circumambient atmosphere of misapprehension and prejudice into which it is received. Necessary as it really is, it has to be carried into effect in the presence of a reluctant or perplexed public opinion, and that, without any counterbalancing assistance whatever, as has commonly been the case with Universities, from royal favour or civil sanction.

This is what many a man will urge, who is favourable to the project itself, viewed apart from the difficulties of the time; nor can the force of such representations be denied. On the other hand, such difficulties must be taken for what they are really worth; they exist, not so much in adverse facts, as in the opinion of the world about the facts. That opinion is the adverse fact. It would be absurd to deny, that grave and good men, zealous for religion, and experienced in the state of the country, have had serious misgivings on the subject, and have thought the vision of a Catholic University too noble, too desirable, to be possible. Still, making every admission on this score which can be required of me, I think it is true, after all, that our main adversary is to be found, not in the unfavourable judgments of particular persons, though such there are, but in the vague and diffusive influence of what is called Public Opinion.

I am not so irrational as to despise Public Opinion ; I have no thought of making light of a tribunal established in the conditions and necessities of human nature. It has its place in the very constitution of society ; it ever has existed, it ever will exist, whether in the commonwealth of nations, or in the humble and secluded village. But wholesome as it is as a principle, it has, in common with all things human, great imperfections, and makes many mistakes. Too often it is nothing else than what the whole world opines, and no one in particular. Your neighbour assures you that every one is of one way of thinking ; that there is but one opinion on the subject ; and while he claims not to be answerable for it, he does not hesitate to propound and spread it. In such cases, every one is appealing to every one else ; and the constituent members of a community one by one think it their duty to defer and succumb to the voice of that same community as a whole.

It would be extravagant to maintain that this is the adequate account of the sentiments which have for some time prevailed among us as to the establishment of our University ; but, so far as it holds good, this follows, viz.: that the despondency, with which the project is regarded by so many persons, is the offspring, not of their judgment, but mainly (I say it, as will be seen directly, without any disrespect) of their imagination. Public Opinion

especially acts upon the imagination ; it does not convince, but it impresses ; it has the force of authority,
rather than of reason ; and concurrence in it is, not an
intelligent decision, but a submission or belief.　This
circumstance at once suggests to us how we are to proceed in the case under consideration.　Arguments are
the fit weapons with which to assail an erroneous judgment, but assertions and actions must be brought to
bear upon a false imagination.　The mind in that case
has been misled by representations ; it must be set right
by representations.　What it asks of us is, not reasoning,
but discussion.　In works on Logic, we meet with a sophistical argument, the object of which is to prove that
motion is impossible ; and it is not uncommon, before
scientifically handling it, to submit it to a practical refutation ;—Solvitur ambulando.　Such is the sort of reply
which I think it may be useful just now to make to
public opinion, which is so indisposed to allow that a
Catholic University of the English tongue can be set in
motion.　I will neither directly prove that it is possible,
nor answer the allegations in behalf of its impossibility ;
I shall attempt a humbler, but perhaps a not less effica-
cious service, in employing myself to the best of my
ability, and according to the patience of the reader, in
setting forth what a University is.　I will leave the controversy to others ; I will confine myself to description
and statement, concerning the nature, the character, the
work, the peculiarities of a University, the aims with
which it is established, the wants it may supply, the
methods it adopts, what it involves and requires, what
are its relations to other institutions, and what has been
its history.　I am sanguine that my labour will not be
thrown away, though it aims at nothing very learned,
nothing very systematic ; though it should wander from

one subject to another, as each happens to arise, and gives no promise whatever of terminating in the production of a treatise.

And in attempting as much as this, while I hope I shall gain instruction from criticisms of whatever sort, I do not mean to be put out by them, whether they come from those who know more, or those who know less than myself;—from those who take exacter, broader, more erudite, more sagacious, more philosophical views than my own ; or those who have yet to attain such measure of truth and of judgment as I may myself claim. I must not be disturbed at the animadversions of those who have a right to feel superior to me, nor at the complaints of others who think I do not enter into or satisfy their difficulties. If I am charged with being shallow on the one part, or off-hand on the other, if I myself feel that fastidiousness at my own attempts, which grows upon an author as he multiplies his compositions, I shall console myself with the reflection, that life is not long enough to do more than our best, whatever that may be ; that they who are ever taking aim, make no hits ; that they who never venture, never gain ; that to be ever safe, is to be ever feeble ; and that to do some substantial good, is the compensation for much incidental imperfection.

With thoughts like these, which, such as they are, have been the companions and the food of my life hitherto, I address myself to my undertaking.

CHAPTER II

IF I were asked to describe as briefly and popularly as I could, what a University was, I should draw my answer from its ancient designation of a *Studium Generale*, or " School of Universal Learning." This description implies the assemblage of strangers from all parts in one spot ;—*from all parts ;* else, how will you find professors and students for every department of knowledge? and *in one spot ;* else, how can there be any school at all ? Accordingly, in its simple and rudimental form, it is a school of knowledge of every kind, consisting of teachers and learners from every quarter. Many things are requisite to complete and satisfy the idea embodied in this description ; but such as this a University seems to be in its essence, a place for the communication and circulation of thought, by means of personal intercourse, through a wide extent of country.

There is nothing far-fetched or unreasonable in the idea thus presented to us ; and if this be a University, then a University does but contemplate a necessity of our nature, and is but one specimen in a particular medium, out of many which might be adduced in others, of a provision for that necessity. Mutual education, in a large sense of the word, is one of the great and incessant occupations of human society, carried on partly with set purpose, and partly not. One generation forms another ; and the existing generation is ever acting and reacting upon itself in the persons of its individual members. Now, in this process, books, I need scarcely say, that is, the *litera scripta*, are one special instrument. It is true ; and emphatically so in this age. Considering the prodigious powers of the press, and how they are developed at this time in the never-intermitting issue of periodicals, tracts, pamphlets, works in series, and light literature, we must allow there never was a time which promised fairer for dispensing with every other means of information and instruction. What can we want more, you will say, for the intellectual education of the whole man, and for every man, than so exuberant and diversified and persistent a promulgation of all kinds of knowledge ? Why, you will ask, need we go up to knowledge, when knowledge comes down to us ? The Sibyl wrote her prophecies upon the leaves of the forest, and wasted them ; but here such careless profusion might be prudently indulged, for it can be afforded without loss, in consequence of the almost fabulous fecundity of the instrument which these latter ages have invented. We have sermons in stones, and books in the running brooks ; works larger and more comprehensive than those which have gained for ancients an immortality, issue forth every morning, and are projected onwards to the ends of the earth at the rate of hundreds of miles a day. Our seats are strewed, our pavements are powdered, with swarms of little tracts ; and the very bricks of our city walls preach wisdom, by informing us by their placards where we can at once cheaply purchase it.

I allow all this, and much more ; such certainly is our popular education, and its effects are remarkable. Nevertheless, after all, even in this age, whenever men are really serious about getting what, in the language of trade, is called "a good article," when they aim at something precise, something refined, something really luminous, something really large, something choice, they go to another market; they avail themselves, in some shape or other, of the rival method, the ancient method, of oral instruction, of present communication between man and man, of teachers instead of learning, of the personal influence of a master, and the humble initiation of a disciple, and, in consequence, of great centres of pilgrimage and throng, which such a method of education necessarily involves. This, I think, will be found to hold good in all those departments or aspects of society, which possess an interest sufficient to bind men together, or to constitute what is called "a world." It holds in the political world, and in the high world, and in the religious world; and it holds also in the literary and scientific world.

If the actions of men may be taken as any test of their convictions, then we have reason for saying this, viz. :—that the province and the inestimable benefit of the *litera scripta* is that of being a record of truth, and an authority of appeal, and an instrument of teaching in the hands of a teacher; but that, if we wish to become exact and fully furnished in any branch of knowledge which is diversified and complicated, we must consult the living man and listen to his living voice. I am not bound to investigate the cause of this, and anything I may say will, I am conscious, be short of its full analysis ;—perhaps we may suggest, that no books can get through the number of minute questions which it is possible to ask on any extended subject, or can hit upon the very difficulties which are severally felt by each reader in succession. Or again, that no book can convey the special spirit and delicate peculiarities of its subject with that rapidity and certainty which attend on the sympathy of mind with mind, through the eyes, the look, the accent, and the manner, in casual expressions thrown off at the moment, and the unstudied turns of familiar conversation. But I am already dwelling too long on what is but an incidental portion of my main subject. Whatever be the cause, the fact is undeniable. The general principles of any study you may learn by books at home ; but the detail, the colour, the tone, the air, the life which makes it live in us, you must catch all these from those in whom it lives already. You must imitate the student in French or German, who is not content with his grammar, but goes to Paris or Dresden: you must take example from the young artist, who aspires to visit the great Masters in Florence and in Rome. Till we have discovered some intellectual daguerreotype, which takes off the course of thought, and the form, lineaments, and features of truth, as completely and minutely, as the optical instrument reproduces the sensible object, we must come to the teachers of wisdom to learn wisdom, we must repair to the fountain, and drink there. Portions of it may go from thence to the ends of the earth by means of books ; but the fulness is in one place alone. It is in such assemblages and congregations of intellect that books themselves, the masterpieces of human genius, are written, or at least originated.

The principle on which I have been insisting is so obvious, and instances in point are so ready, that I should think it tiresome to proceed with the subject, except that one or two illustrations may serve to explain my own language about it, which may not have done justice to the doctrine which it has been intended to enforce.

For instance, the polished manners and high-bred bearing which are so difficult of attainment, and so

strictly personal when attained,—which are so much
admired in society, from society are acquired.   All that
goes to constitute a gentleman,—the carriage, gait,
address, gestures, voice; the ease, the self-possession,
the courtesy, the power of conversing, the talent of not
offending; the lofty principle, the delicacy of thought,
the happiness of expression, the taste and propriety, the
generosity and forbearance, the candour and consideration, the openness of hand;—these qualities, some of
them come by nature, some of them may be found
in any rank, some of them are a direct precept of
Christianity; but the full assemblage of them, bound
up in the unity of an individual character, do we expect
they can be learned from books? are they not necessarily
acquired, where they are to be found, in high society?
The very nature of the case leads us to say so; you
cannot fence without an antagonist, nor challenge all
comers in disputation before you have supported a thesis; and in like manner, it stands to reason, you cannot
learn to converse till you have the world to converse
with; you cannot unlearn your natural bashfulness, or
awkwardness, or stiffness, or other besetting deformity,
till you serve your time in some school of manners.
Well, and is it not so in matter of fact?   The metropolis,
the court, the great houses of the land, are the centres
to which at stated times the country comes up, as to
shrines of refinement and good taste; and then in due
time the country goes back again home, enriched with a
portion of the social accomplishments, which those very
visits serve to call out and heighten in the gracious dis-
pensers of them.   We are unable to conceive how the
" gentlemanlike " can otherwise be maintained; and
maintained in this way it is.

And now a second instance : and here too I am going

to speak without personal experience of the subject I am introducing. I admit I have not been in Parliament, any more than I have figured in the *beau monde;* yet I cannot but think that statesmanship, as well as high breeding, is learned, not by books, but in certain centres of education. If it be not presumption to say so, Parliament puts a clever man *au courant* with politics and affairs of state in a way surprising to himself. A member of the Legislature, if tolerably observant, begins to see things with new eyes, even though his views undergo no change. Words have a meaning now, and ideas a reality, such as they had not before. He hears a vast deal in public speeches and private conversation, which is never put into print. The bearings of measures and events, the action of parties, and the persons of friends and enemies, are brought out to the man who is in the midst of them with a distinctness, which the most diligent perusal of newspapers will fail to impart to them. It is access to the fountain-heads of political wisdom and experience, it is daily intercourse, of one kind or another, with the multitude who go up to them, it is familiarity with business, it is access to the contributions of fact and opinion thrown together by many witnesses from many quarters, which does this for him. However, I need not account for a fact, to which it is sufficient to appeal; that the Houses of Parliament and the atmosphere around them are a sort of University of politics.

As regards the world of science, we find a remarkable instance of the principle which I am illustrating, in the periodical meetings for its advance, which have arisen in the course of the last twenty years, such as the British Association. Such gatherings would to many persons appear at first sight simply preposterous.

Above all subjects of study, Science is conveyed, is propagated, by books, or by private teaching; experiments and investigations are conducted in silence; discoveries are made in solitude. What have philosophers to do with festive celebrities, and panegyrical solemnities with mathematical and physical truth? Yet on a closer attention to the subject, it is found that not even scientific thought can dispense with the suggestions, the instruction, the stimulus, the sympathy, the intercourse with mankind on a large scale, which such meetings secure. A fine time of year is chosen, when days are long, skies are bright, the earth smiles, and all nature rejoices; a city or town is taken by turns, of ancient name or modern opulence, where buildings are spacious and hospitality hearty. The novelty of place and circumstance, the excitement of strange, or the refreshment of well-known faces, the majesty of rank or of genius, the amiable charities of men pleased both with themselves and with each other; the elevated spirits, the circulation of thought, the curiosity; the morning sections, the outdoor exercise, the well-furnished, well-earned board, the not ungraceful hilarity, the evening circle; the brilliant lecture, the discussions or collisions or guesses of great men one with another, the narratives of scientific processes, of hopes, disappointments, conflicts, and successes, the splendid eulogistic orations; these and the like constituents of the annual celebration, are considered to do something real and substantial for the advance of knowledge which can be done in no other way. Of course they can but be occasional; they answer to the annual Act, or Commencement, or Commemoration of a University, not to its ordinary condition; but they are of a University nature; and I can well believe in their utility. They issue in the promotion of a certain living and, as it were, bodily communication of knowledge from one to another, of a general interchange of ideas, and a comparison and adjustment of science with science, of an enlargement of mind, intellectual and social, of an ardent love of the particular study, which may be chosen by each individual, and a noble devotion to its interests.

Such meetings, I repeat, are but periodical, and only partially represent the idea of a University. The bustle and whirl which are their usual concomitants, are in ill keeping with the order and gravity of earnest intellectual education. We desiderate means of instruction which involve no interruption of our ordinary habits ; nor need we seek it long, for the natural course of things brings it about, while we debate over it. In every great country, the metropolis itself becomes a sort of necessary University, whether we will or no. As the chief city is the seat of the court, of high society, of politics, and of law, so as a matter of course is it the seat of letters also ; and at this time, for a long term of years, London and Paris are in fact and in operation Universities, though in Paris its famous University is no more, and in London a University scarcely exists except as a board of administration. The newspapers, magazines, reviews, journals, and periodicals of all kinds, the publishing trade, the libraries, museums, and academies there found, the learned and scientific societies, necessarily invest it with the functions of a University ; and that atmosphere of intellect, which in a former age hung over Oxford or Bologna or Salamanca, has, with the change of times, moved away to the centre of civil government. Thither come up youths from all parts of the country, the students of law, medicine, and the fine arts, and the *employés* and *attachés* of literature. There they live, as

chance determines ; and they are satisfied with their
temporary home, for they find in it all that was promised
to them there.   They have not come in vain, as far as
their own object in coming is concerned.   They have not
learned any particular religion, but they have learned
their own particular profession well.   They have, moreover, become acquainted with the habits, manners, and
opinions of their place of sojourn, and done their part in
maintaining the tradition of them.   We cannot then be
without virtual Universities ; a metropolis is such : the
simple question is, whether the education sought and
given should be based on principle, formed upon rule,
directed to the highest ends, or left to the random succession of masters and schools, one after another, with a
melancholy waste of thought and an extreme hazard of
truth.

Religious teaching itself affords us an illustration of
our subject to a certain point.   It does not indeed seat
itself merely in centres of the world ; this is impossible
from the nature of the case.   It is intended for the many
not the few ; its subject matter is truth necessary for us,
not truth recondite and rare ; but it concurs in the principle of a University so far as this, that its great instrument, or rather organ, has ever been that which nature
prescribes in all education, the personal presence of a
teacher, or, in theological language, Oral Tradition.   It
is the living voice, the breathing form, the expressive
countenance, which preaches, which catechises.   Truth,
a subtle, invisible, manifold spirit, is poured into the
mind of the scholar by his eyes and ears, through his
affections, imagination, and reason ; it is poured into his
mind and is sealed up there in perpetuity, by propound-
ing and repeating it, by questioning and requestioning,
by correcting and explaining, by progressing and then

recurring to first principles, by all those ways which are implied in the word "catechising." In the first ages, it was a work of long time; months, sometimes years, were devoted to the arduous task of disabusing the mind of the incipient Christian of its pagan errors, and of moulding it upon the Christian faith. The Scriptures indeed were at hand for the study of those who could avail themselves of them; but St. Irenæus does not hesitate to speak of whole races, who had been converted to Christianity, without being able to read them. To be unable to read or write was in those times no evidence of want of learning: the hermits of the deserts were, in this sense of the word, illiterate; yet the great St. Anthony, though he knew not letters, was a match in disputation for the learned philosophers who came to try him. Didymus again, the great Alexandrian theologian, was blind. The ancient discipline, called the *Disciplina Arcani*, involved the same principle. The more sacred doctrines of Revelation were not committed to books but passed on by successive tradition. The teaching on the Blessed Trinity and the Eucharist appears to have been so handed down for some hundred years; and when at length reduced to writing, it has filled many folios, yet has not been exhausted.

But I have said more than enough in illustration; I end as I began;—a University is a place of concourse, whither students come from every quarter for every kind of knowledge. You cannot have the best of every kind everywhere; you must go to some great city or emporium for it. There you have all the choicest productions of nature and art all together, which you find each in its own separate place elsewhere. All the riches of the land, and of the earth, are carried up thither; there are the best markets, and there the best workmen. It is the centre of trade, the supreme court of fashion, the umpire of rival talents, and the standard of things rare and precious. It is the place for seeing galleries of first-rate pictures, and for hearing wonderful voices and performers of transcendent skill. It is the place for great preachers, great orators, great nobles, great statesmen. In the nature of things, greatness and unity go together ; excellence implies a centre. And such, for the third or fourth time, is a University ; I hope I do not weary out the reader by repeating it. It is the place to which a thousand schools make contributions ; in which the intellect may safely range and speculate, sure to find its equal in some antagonist activity, and its judge in the tribunal of truth. It is a place where in-quiry is pushed forward, and discoveries verified and perfected, and rashness rendered innocuous, and error exposed, by the collision of mind with mind, and knowledge with knowledge. It is the place where the professor becomes eloquent, and is a missionary and a preacher, displaying his science in its most complete and most winning form, pouring it forth with the zeal of enthusiasm, and lighting up his own love of it in the breasts of his hearers. It is the place where the catechist makes good his ground as he goes, treading in the truth day by day into the ready memory, and wedging and tightening it into the expanding reason. It is a place which wins the admiration of the young by its celebrity, kindles the affections of the middle-aged by its beauty, and rivets the fidelity of the old by its associations. It is a seat of wisdom, a light of the world, a minister of the faith, an Alma Mater of the rising generation. It is this and a great deal more, and demands a somewhat better head and hand than mine to describe it well.

Such is a University in its idea and in its purpose ;

such in good measure has it before now been in fact. Shall it ever be again? We are going forward in the strength of the Cross, under the patronage of the Blessed Virgin, in the name of St. Patrick, to attempt it.

CHAPTER III.

IF we would know what a University is, considered in its elementary idea, we must betake ourselves to the first and most celebrated home of European literature and source of European civilization, to the bright and beautiful Athens,—Athens, whose schools drew to her bosom, and then sent back again to the business of life, the youth of the Western World for a long thousand years. Seated on the verge of the continent, the city seemed hardly suited for the duties of a central metropolis of knowledge; yet, what it lost in convenience of approach, it gained in its neighbourhood to the traditions of the mysterious East, and in the loveliness of the region in which it lay. Hither, then, as to a sort of ideal land, where all archetypes of the great and the fair were found in substantial being, and all departments of truth explored, and all diversities of intellectual power exhibited, where taste and philosophy were majestically enthroned as in a royal court, where there was no sovereignty but that of mind, and no nobility but that of genius, where professors were rulers, and princes did homage, hither flocked continually from the very corners of the *orbis terrarum*, the many-tongued generation, just rising, or just risen into manhood, in order to gain wisdom.

Pisistratus had in an early age discovered and nursed the infant genius of his people, and Cimon, after the

Persian war, had given it a home. That war had established the naval supremacy of Athens ; she had become
an imperial state ; and the Ionians, bound to her by
the double chain of kindred and of subjection, were
importing into her both their merchandize and their
civilization. The arts and philosophy of the Asiatic
coast were easily carried across the sea, and there was
Cimon, as I have said, with his ample fortune, ready to
receive them with due honours. Not content with
patronizing their professors, he built the first of those
noble porticos, of which we hear so much in Athens, and
he formed the groves, which in process of time became
the celebrated Academy. Planting is one of the most
graceful, as in Athens it was one of the most beneficent,
of employments. Cimon took in hand the wild wood,
pruned and dressed it, and laid it out with handsome
walks and welcome fountains. Nor, while hospitable
to the authors of the city's civilization, was he ungrateful
to the instruments of her prosperity. His trees extended
their cool, umbrageous branches over the merchants,
who assembled in the Agora, for many generations.

Those merchants certainly had deserved that act of
bounty ; for all the while their ships had been carrying
forth the intellectual fame of Athens to the western
world. Then commenced what may be called her University existence. Pericles, who succeeded Cimon both
in the government and in the patronage of art, is said
by Plutarch to have entertained the idea of making
Athens the capital of federated Greece : in this he
failed, but his encouragement of such men as Phidias
and Anaxagoras led the way to her acquiring a far more
lasting sovereignty over a far wider empire. Little
understanding the sources of her own greatness, Athens
would go to war : peace is the interest of a seat of com-

merce and the arts ; but to war she went ; yet to her, whether peace or war, it mattered not. The political power of Athens waned and disappeared ; kingdoms rose and fell ; centuries rolled away,—they did but bring fresh triumphs to the city of the poet and the sage. There at length the swarthy Moor and Spaniard were seen to meet the blue-eyed Gaul ; and the Cappadocian, late subject of Mithridates, gazed without alarm at the haughty conquering Roman. Revolution after revolution passed over the face of Europe, as well as of Greece, but still she was there,—Athens, the city of mind,—as radiant, as splendid, as delicate, as young, as ever she had been.

Many a more fruitful coast or isle is washed by the blue Ægean, many a spot is there more beautiful or sublime to see, many a territory more ample ; but there was one charm in Attica, which in the same perfection was nowhere else. The deep pastures of Arcadia, the plain of Argos, the Thessalian vale, these had not the gift ; Bœotia, which lay to its immediate north, was notorious for its very want of it. The heavy atmosphere of that Bœotia might be good for vegetation, but it was associated in popular belief with the dulness of the Bœotian intellect : on the contrary, the special purity, elasticity, clearness, and salubrity of the air of Attica, fit concomitant and emblem of its genius, did that for it which earth did not ;—it brought out every bright hue and tender shade of the landscape over which it was spread, and would have illuminated the face even of a more bare and rugged country.

A confined triangle, perhaps fifty miles its greatest length, and thirty its greatest breadth ; two elevated rocky barriers, meeting at an angle ; three prominent mountains, commanding the plain,—Parnes, Pentelicus, and Hymettus ; an unsatisfactory soil ; some streams, not always full ;—such is about the report which the agent of a London company would have made of Attica. He would report that the climate was mild ; the hills were limestone ; there was plenty of good marble,; more pasture land than at first survey might have been expected, sufficient certainly for sheep and goats ; fisheries productive ; silver mines once, but long since worked out ; figs fair ; oil first-rate ; olives in profusion. But what he would not think of noting down, was, that that olive tree was so choice in nature and so noble in shape, that it excited a religious veneration ; and that it took so kindly to the light soil, as to expand into woods upon the open plain, and to climb up and fringe the hills. He would not think of writing word to his employers, how that clear air, of which I have spoken, brought out, yet blended and subdued, the colours on the marble, till they had a softness and harmony, for all their richness, which in a picture looks exaggerated, yet is after all within the truth. He would not tell, how that same delicate and brilliant atmosphere freshened up the pale olive, till the olive forgot its monotony, and its cheek glowed like the arbutus or beech of the Umbrian hills. He would say nothing of the thyme and thousand fragrant herbs which carpeted Hymettus ; he would hear nothing of the hum of its bees ; nor take much account of the rare flavour of its honey, since Gozo and Minorca were sufficient for the English demand. He would look over the Ægean from the height he had ascended ; he would follow with his eye the chain of islands, which, starting from the Sunian headland, seemed to offer the fabled divinities of Attica, when they would visit their Ionian cousins, a sort of viaduct thereto across the sea : but

that fancy would not occur to him, nor any admiration
of the dark violet billows with their white edges down
below ; nor of those graceful, fan-like jets of silver upon
the rocks, which slowly rise aloft like water spirits from
the deep, then shiver, and break, and spread, and shroud
themselves, and disappear, in a soft mist of foam ; nor
of the gentle, incessant heaving and panting of the
whole liquid plain ; nor of the long waves, keeping
steady time, like a line of soldiery, as they resound
upon the hollow shore,—he would not deign to notice
that restless living element at all, except to bless his
stars that he was not upon it.   Nor the distinct detail,
nor the refined colouring, nor the graceful outline and
roseate golden hue of the jutting crags, nor the bold
shadows cast from Otus or Laurium by the declining
sun ;—our agent of a mercantile firm would not value
these matters even at a low figure.   Rather we must
turn for the sympathy we seek to yon pilgrim student,
come from a semi-barbarous land to that small corner of
the earth, as to a shrine, where he might take his fill of
gazing on those emblems and coruscations of invisible
unoriginate perfection.   It was the stranger from a
remote province, from Britain or from Mauritania,
who in a scene so different from that of his chilly, woody
swamps, or of his fiery choking sands, learned at once
what a real University must be, by coming to understand the sort of country, which was its suitable home.

Nor was this all that a University required, and found
in Athens. No one, even there, could live on poetry. If
the students at that famous place had nothing better
than bright hues and soothing sounds, they would not
have been able or disposed to turn their residence there
to much account.   Of course they must have the means

of living, nay, in a certain sense, of enjoyment, if Athens was to be an Alma Mater at the time, or to remain afterwards a pleasant thought in their memory. And so they had : be it recollected Athens was a port, and a mart of trade, perhaps the first in Greece ; and this was very much to the point, when a number of strangers were ever flocking to it, whose combat was to be with intellectual, not physical difficulties, and who claimed to have their bodily wants supplied, that they might be at leisure to set about furnishing their minds. Now, barren as was the soil of Attica, and bare the face of the country, yet it had only too many resources for an elegant, nay luxurious abode there. So abundant were the imports of the place, that it was a common saying, that the productions, which were found singly elsewhere, were brought all together in Athens. Corn and wine, the staple of subsistence in such a climate, came from the isles of the Ægean ; fine wool and carpeting from Asia Minor ; slaves, as now, from the Euxine, and timber too ; and iron and brass from the coasts of the Mediterranean. The Athenian did not condescend to manufactures himself, but encouraged them in others ; and a population of foreigners caught at the lucrative occupation both for home consumption and for exportation. Their cloth, and other textures for dress and furniture, and their hardware—for instance, armour—were in great request. Labour was cheap ; stone and marble in plenty ; and the taste and skill, which at first were devoted to public buildings, as temples and porticos, were in course of time applied to the mansions of public men. If nature did much for Athens, it is undeniable that art did much more.

Here some one will interrupt me with the remark : ' By the bye, where are we, and whither are we going ?—

what has all this to do with a University? at least what
has it to do with education? It is instructive doubtless;
but still how much has it to do with your subject?"
Now I beg to assure the reader that I am most con-
scientiously employed upon my subject; and I should
have thought every one would have seen this: however,
since the objection is made, I may be allowed to pause
awhile, and show distinctly the drift of what I have been
saying, before I go farther. *What* has this to do with
my subject! why, the question of the *site* is the very
first that comes into consideration, when a *Studium
Generale* is contemplated; for that site should be a
liberal and noble one; who will deny it? All authorities agree in this, and very little reflection will be sufficient to make it clear. I recollect a conversation I once
had on this very subject with a very eminent man. I
was a youth of eighteen, and was leaving my University
for the Long Vacation, when I found myself in company
in a public conveyance with a middle-aged person, whose
face was strange to me. However, it was the great academical luminary of the day, whom afterwards I knew
very well. Luckily for me, I did not suspect it; and
luckily too, it was a fancy of his, as his friends knew, to
make himself on easy terms especially with stage-coach
companions. So, what with my flippancy and his condescension, I managed to hear many things which were
novel to me at the time; and one point which he was
strong upon, and was evidently fond of urging, was the
material pomp and circumstance which should environ a
great seat of learning. He considered it was worth the
consideration of the government, whether Oxford should
not stand in a domain of its own. An ample range, say
four miles in diameter, should be turned into wood and
meadow, and the University should be approached on

all sides by a magnificent park, with fine trees in groups and groves and avenues, and with glimpses and views of the fair city, as the traveller drew near it. There is nothing surely absurd in the idea, though it would cost a round sum to realise it. What has a better claim to the purest and fairest possessions of nature, than the seat of wisdom ? So thought my coach companion ; and he did but express the tradition of ages and the instinct of mankind.

For instance, take the great University of Paris. That famous school engrossed as its territory the whole south bank of the Seine, and occupied one half, and that the pleasanter half, of the city. King Louis had the island pretty well as his own,—it was scarcely more than a fortification ; and the north of the river was given over to the nobles and citizens to do what they could with its marshes ; but the eligible south, rising from the stream, which swept around its base, to the fair summit of St. Genevieve, with its broad meadows, its vineyards and its gardens, and with the sacred elevation of Montmartre confronting it, all this was the inheritance of the University. There was that pleasant Pratum, stretching along the river's bank, in which the students for centuries took their recreation, which Alcuin seems to mention in his farewell verses to Paris, and which has given a name to the great Abbey of St. Germain-des-Prés. For long years it was devoted to the purposes of innocent and healthy enjoyment ; but evil times came on the University ; disorder arose within its precincts, and the fair meadow became the scene of party brawls ; heresy stalked through Europe, and Germany and England no longer sending their contingent of students, a heavy debt was the consequence to the academical body. To let their land was the only resource left to them :

buildings rose upon it, and spread along the green sod, and the country at length became town. Great was the grief and indignation of the doctors and masters, when this catastrophe occurred. "A wretched sight," said the Proctor of the German nation, "a wretched sight, to witness the sale of that ancient manor, whither the Muses were wont to wander for retirement and pleasure. Whither shall the youthful student now betake himself, what relief will he find for his eyes, wearied with intense reading, now that the pleasant stream is taken from him?" Two centuries and more have passed since this complaint was uttered; and time has shown that the outward calamity, which it recorded, was but the emblem of the great moral revolution, which was to follow; till the institution itself has followed its green meadows, into the region of things which once were and now are not.

And in like manner, when they were first contemplating a University in Belgium, some centuries ago, "Many," says Lipsius, "suggested Mechlin, as an abode salubrious and clean, but Louvain was preferred, as for other reasons, so because no city seemed, from the disposition of place and people, more suitable for learned leisure. Who will not approve the decision? Can a site be healthier or more pleasant? The atmosphere pure and cheerful; the spaces open and delightful; meadows, fields, vines, groves, nay, I may say, a *rus in urbe.* Ascend and walk round the walls; what do you look down upon? Does not the wonderful and delightful variety smooth the brow and soothe the mind? You have corn, and apples, and grapes; sheep and oxen; and birds chirping or singing. Now carry your feet or your eyes beyond the walls; there are streamlets, the river meandering along; country-houses, convents, the superb fortress; copses or woods fill up the scene, and spots

for simple enjoyment." And then he breaks out into
poetry :

> Salvete Athenæ nostræ, Athenæ Belgicæ,
> Te Gallus, te Germanus, et te Sarmata
> Invisit, et Britannus, et te duplicis
> Hispaniæ alumnus, etc.

Extravagant, then, and wayward as might be the
thought of my learned coach companion, when, in the
nineteenth century, he imagined, Norman-wise, to turn
a score of villages into a park or pleasaunce, still, the
waywardness of his fancy is excused by the justness of
his principle ; for certainly, such as he would have made
it, a University ought to be. Old Antony-à-Wood, dis-
coursing on the demands of a University, had expressed
the same sentiment long before him ; as Horace in
ancient times, with reference to Athens itself, when he
spoke of seeking truth "in the *groves* of Academe."
And to Athens, as will be seen, Wood himself appeals,
when he would discourse of Oxford. Among "those
things which are required to make a University," he
puts down,—

"First, a good and pleasant site, where there is a
wholesome and temperate constitution of the air ; composed with waters, springs or wells, woods and pleasant
fields ; which being obtained, those commodities are
enough to invite students to stay and abide there. As
the Athenians in ancient times were happy for their
conveniences, so also were the Britons, when by a remnant of the Grecians that came amongst them, they or
their successors selected such a place in Britain to plant
a school or schools therein, which for its pleasant situation was afterwards called Bellositum or Bellosite, now
Oxford, privileged with all those conveniences before
mentioned."

By others the local advantages of that University have been more philosophically analyzed;—for instance, with a reference to its position in the middle of southern England; its situation on several islands in a broad plain, through which many streams flowed; the surrounding marshes, which, in times when it was needed, protected the city from invaders; its own strength as a military position; its easy communication with London, nay with the sea, by means of the Thames; while the London fortifications hindered pirates from ascending the stream, which all the time was so ready and convenient for a descent.

Alas! for centuries past that city has lost its prime honour and boast, as a servant and soldier of the Truth. Once named the second school of the Church, second only to Paris, the foster-mother of St. Edmund, St. Richard, St. Thomas Cantilupe, the theatre of great intellects, of Scotus the subtle Doctor, of Hales the irrefragible, of Occam the special, of Bacon the admirable, of Middleton the solid, and of Bradwardine the profound, Oxford has now lapsed to that level of mere human loveliness, which in its highest perfection we admire in Athens. Nor would it have a place, now or hereafter, in these pages, nor would it occur to me to speak its name, except that, even in its sorrowful depri vation, it still retains so much of that outward lustre, which, like the brightness on the prophet's face, ought to be a ray from an illumination within, as to afford me an illustration of the point on which I am engaged, viz.; what should be the material dwelling-place and appearance, the local circumstances, and the secular concomitants of a great University. Pictures are drawn in tales of romance, of spirits seemingly too beautiful in their fall to be really fallen, and the holy Pope at Rome,

Gregory, in fact, and not in fiction, looked upon the blue eyes and golden hair of the fierce Saxon youth in the slave market, and pronounced them Angels, not Angles ; and the spell which this once loyal daughter of the Church still exercises upon the foreign visitor, even now when her true glory is departed, suggests to us how far more majestic and more touching, how brimfull of indescribable influence would be the presence of a University, which was planted within, not without Jerusalem, —an influence, potent as her truth is strong, wide as her sway is world-wide, and growing, not lessening, by the extent of space over which its attraction would be exerted.

Let the reader then listen to the words of the last learned German, who has treated of Oxford, and judge for himself if they do not bear me out, in what I have said of the fascination which the very face and smile of a University possess over those who come within its range.

"There is scarce a spot in the world," says Huber, "that bears an historical stamp so deep and varied as Oxford ; where so many noble memorials of moral and material power, coöperating to an honourable end, meet the eye all at once. He who can be proof against the strong emotions which the whole aspect and genius of the place tend to inspire, must be dull, thoughtless, uneducated, or of very perverted views. Others will bear us witness, that, even side by side with the Eternal Rome, the Alma Mater of Oxford may be fitly named, as producing a deep, a lasting, and peculiar impression.

"In one of the most fertile districts of the Queen of the Seas, whom nature has so richly blessed, whom for centuries past no footstep of foreign armies has desecrated, lies a broad green vale, where the Cherwell and

the Isis mingle their full, clear waters. Here and there
primeval elms and oaks overshadow them ; while in
their various windings they encircle gardens, meadows,
and fields, villages, cottages, farm-houses, and country-
seats, in motley mixture. In the midst rises a mass of
mighty buildings, the general character of which varies
between convent, palace, and castle. Some few Gothic
church-towers and Romaic domes, it is true, break
through the horizontal lines ; yet the general impression
at a distance and at first sight, is essentially different
from that of any of the towns of the middle ages. The
outlines are far from being so sharp, so angular, so irregular, so fantastical ; a certain softness, a peculiar repose, reigns in those broader, terrace-like rising masses.
Only in the creations of Claude Lorraine or Poussin
could we expect to find a spot to compare with the
prevailing character of this picture, especially when lit
up by a favourable light. The principal masses consist
of Colleges, the University buildings, and the city
churches ; and by the side of these the city itself is lost
on distant view. But on entering the streets, we find
around us all the signs of an active and prosperous
trade. Rich and elegant shops in profusion afford a
sight to be found nowhere but in England ; but with all
this glitter and show, they sink into a modest, and, as it
were, a menial attitude, by the side of the grandly severe
memorials of the higher intellectual life, memorials which
have been growing out of that life from almost the beginning of Christianity itself. Those rich and elegant shops
are, as it were, the domestic offices of these palaces of
learning, which ever rivet the eye of the observer, while
all besides seems perforce to be subservient to them.
Each of the larger and more ancient Colleges looks like
a separate whole—an entire town, whose walls and monu-

ments proclaim the vigorous growth of many centuries; and the town itself has happily escaped the lot of modern beautifying, and in this respect harmonizes with the Colleges." *

There are those who, having felt the influence of this ancient School, and being smit with its splendour and its sweetness, ask wistfully, if never again it is to be Catholic, or whether at least some footing for Catholicity may not be found there. All honour and merit to the charitable and zealous hearts who so inquire! Nor can we dare to tell what in time to come may be the inscrutable purposes of that grace, which is ever more comprehensive than human hope and aspiration. But for me, from the day I left its walls, I never, for good or bad, have had anticipation of its future; and never for a moment have I had a wish to see again a place, which I have never ceased to love, and where I lived for nearly thirty years. Nay, looking at the general state of things at this day, I desiderate for a School of the Church, if an additional School is to be granted to us, a more central position than Oxford has to show. Since the age of Alfred and of the first Henry, the world has grown, from the west and south of Europe, into four or five continents; and I look for a city less inland than that old sanctuary, and a country closer upon the highway of the seas. I look towards a land both old and young; old in its Christianity, young in the promise of its future; a nation, which received grace before the Saxon came to Britain, and which has never quenched it; a Church, which comprehends in its history the rise and fall of Canterbury and York, which Augustine and Paulinus found, and Pole and

* Huber on English Universities. F. W. Newman's translation.

Fisher left behind them. I contemplate a people which has had a long night, and will have an inevitable day. I am turning my eyes towards a hundred years to come, and I dimly see the island I am gazing on, become the road of passage and union between two hemispheres, and the centre of the world. I see its inhabitants rival Belgium in populousness, France in vigour, and Spain in enthusiasm ; and I see England taught by advancing years to exercise in its behalf that good sense which is her characteristic towards every one else. The capital of that prosperous and hopeful land is situate in a beautiful bay and near a romantic region ; and in it I see a flourishing University, which for a while had to struggle with fortune, but which, when its first founders and servants were dead and gone, had successes far exceeding their anxieties. Thither, as to a sacred soil, the home of their fathers, and the fountain-head of their Christianity, students are flocking from East, West, and South, from America and Australia and India, from Egypt and Asia Minor, with the ease and rapidity of a locomotion not yet discovered, and last, though not least, from England,—all speaking one tongue, all owning one faith, all eager for one large true wisdom ; and thence, when their stay is over, going back again to carry over all the earth " peace to men of good will."

CHAPTER IV.

UNIVERSITY LIFE.

ATHENS.

HOWEVER apposite may have been the digression into which I was led when I had got about half through the foregoing Chapter, it has had the inconvenience of what may be called running me off the rails ; and now that I wish to proceed from the point at which it took place, I shall find some trouble, if I may continue the metaphor, in getting up the steam again, or if I may change it, in getting into the swing of my subject.

It has been my desire, were I able, to bring before the reader what Athens may have been, viewed as what we have since called a University ; and to do this, not with any purpose of writing a panegyric on a heathen city, or of denying its many deformities, or of concealing what was morally base in what was intellectually great, but just the contrary, of representing things as they really were ; so far, that is, as to enable him to see what a University is, in the very constitution of society and in its own idea, what is its nature and object, and what it needs of aid and support external to itself to complete that nature and to secure that object.

So now let us fancy our Scythian, or Armenian, or African, or Italian, or Gallic student, after tossing on the Saronic waves, which would be his more ordinary course to Athens, at last casting anchor at Piræus. He is of any condition or rank of life you please, and may be made to order, from a prince to a peasant. Perhaps he is some Cleanthes, who has been a boxer in the public games. How did it ever cross his brain to betake himself to Athens in search of wisdom? or, if he came thither by accident, how did the love of it ever touch his heart? But so it was, to Athens he came with three drachms in his girdle, and he got his livelihood by drawing water, carrying loads, and the like servile occupations. He attached himself, of all philosophers, to Zeno the Stoic,—to Zeno, the most high-minded, the most haughty of speculators; and out of his daily earnings the poor scholar brought his master the daily sum of an obolus, in payment for attending his lectures. Such progress did he make, that on Zeno's death he actually was his successor in his school; and, if my memory does not play me false, he is the author of a hymn to the Supreme Being, which is one of the noblest effusions of the kind in classical poetry. Yet, even when he was the head of a school, he continued in his illiberal toil as if he had been a monk; and, it is said, that once, when the wind took his pallium, and blew it aside, he was discovered to have no other garment at all;—something like the German student who came up to Heidelberg with nothing upon him but a great coat and a pair of pistols.

Or it is another disciple of the Porch,—Stoic by nature, earlier than by profession,—who is entering the city; but in what different fashion he comes! It is no other than Marcus, Emperor of Rome and philosopher. Professors long since were summoned from Athens for his service, when he was a youth, and now he comes, after his victories in the battle field, to make his acknowledgments at the end of life, to the city of wisdom, and to submit himself to an initiation into the Eleusinian mysteries.

Or it is a young man of great promise as an orator, were it not for his weakness of chest, which renders it necessary that he should acquire the art of speaking without over-exertion, and should adopt a delivery sufficient for the display of his rhetorical talents on the one hand, yet merciful to his physical resources on the other. He is called Cicero; he will stop but a short time, and will pass over to Asia Minor and its cities, before he returns to continue a career which will render his name immortal; and he will like his short sojourn at Athens so well, that he will take good care to send his son thither at an earlier age than he visited it himself.

But see where comes from Alexandria (for we need not be very solicitous about anachronisms), a young man from twenty to twenty-two, who has narrowly escaped drowning on his voyage, and is to remain at Athens as many as eight or ten years, yet in the course of that time will not learn a line of Latin, thinking it enough to become accomplished in Greek composition, and in that he will succeed. He is a grave person, and difficult to make out; some say he is a Christian, something or other in the Christian line his father is for certain. His name is Gregory, he is by country a Cappadocian, and will in time become preëminently a theologian, and one of the principal Doctors of the Greek Church.

Or it is one Horace, a youth of low stature and black hair, whose father has given him an education at Rome above his rank in life, and now is sending him to finish it at Athens; he is said to have a turn for poetry: a hero he is not, and it were well if he knew it; but he is caught by the enthusiasm of the hour, and goes off campaigning with Brutus and Cassius, and will leave his shield behind him on the field of Philippi.

Or it is a mere boy of fifteen : his name Eunapius ; though the voyage was not long, sea sickness, or confinement, or bad living on board the vessel, threw him into a fever, and, when the passengers landed in the evening at Piræus, he could not stand. His countrymen who accompanied him, took him up among them and carried him to the house of the great teacher of the day, Proæresius, who was a friend of the captain's, and whose fame it was which drew the enthusiastic youth to Athens. His companions understand the sort of place they are in, and, with the licence of academic students, they break into the philosopher's house, though he appears to have retired for the night, and proceed to make themselves free of it, with an absence of ceremony, which is only not impudence, because Proæresius takes it so easily. Strange introduction for our stranger to a seat of learning, but not out of keeping with Athens ; for what could you expect of a place where there was a mob of youths and not even the pretence of control ; where the poorer lived any how, and got on as they could, and the teachers themselves had no protection from the humours and caprices of the students who filled their lecture-halls? However, as to this Eunapius, Proæresius took a fancy to the boy, and told him curious stories about Athenian life. He himself had come up to the University with one Hephæstion, and they were even worse off than Cleanthes the Stoic ; for they had only one cloak between them, and nothing whatever besides, except some old bedding ; so when Proæresius went abroad, Hephæstion lay in bed, and practised himself in oratory ; and then Hephæstion put on the cloak, and Proæresius crept under the coverlet. At another time there was so fierce

a feud between what would be called " town and gown "
in an English University, that the Professors did not dare
lecture in public, for fear of ill treatment.

But a freshman like Eunapius soon got experience for
himself of the ways and manners prevalent in Athens.
Such a one as he had hardly entered the city, when he
was caught hold of by a party of the academic youth,
who proceeded to practise on his awkwardness and his
ignorance. At first sight one wonders at their childish-
ness ; but the like conduct obtained in the medieval
Universities ; and not many months have passed away
since the journals have told us of sober Englishmen,
given to matter-of-fact calculations, and to the anxieties
of money-making, pelting each other with snow-balls on
their own sacred territory, and defying the magistracy,
when they would interfere with their privilege of becoming
boys. So I suppose we must attribute it to something
or other in human nature. Meanwhile, there stands the
new-comer, surrounded by a circle of his new associates,
who forthwith proceed to frighten, and to banter, and to
make a fool of him, to the extent of their wit. Some
address him with mock politeness, others with fierceness ;
and so they conduct him in solemn procession across the
Agora to the Baths ; and as they approach, they dance
about him like madmen. But this was to be the end of
his trial, for the Bath was a sort of initiation ; he there-
upon received the pallium, or University gown, and was
suffered by his tormentors to depart in peace. One
alone is recorded as having been exempted from this
persecution ; it was a youth graver and loftier than even
St. Gregory himself : but it was not from his force of
character, but at the instance of Gregory, that he escaped. Gregory was his bosom-friend, and was ready in
Athens to shelter him when he came. It was another

Saint and Doctor; the great Basil, then, (it would appear,) as Gregory, but a catechumen of the Church.

But to return to our freshman. His troubles are not at an end, though he has got his gown upon him. Where is he to lodge? whom is he to attend? He finds himself seized, before he well knows where he is, by another party of men, or three or four parties at once, like foreign porters at a landing, who seize on the baggage of the perplexed stranger, and thrust half a dozen cards into his unwilling hands. Our youth is plied by the hangers-on of professor this, or sophist that, each of whom wishes the fame or the profit of having a housefull. We will say that he escapes from their hands,—but then he will have to choose for him·self where he will put up; and, to tell the truth, with all the praise I have already given, and the praise I shall have to give, to the city of mind, nevertheless, between ourselves, the brick and wood which formed it, the actual tenements, where flesh and blood had to lodge (always excepting the mansions of great men of the place), do not seem to have been much better than those of Greek or Turkish towns, which are at this moment a topic of interest and ridicule in the public prints. A lively picture has lately been set before us of Gallipoli. Take, says the writer,* a multitude of the dilapidated outhouses found in farm-yards in England, of the rickety old wooden tenements, the cracked, shutterless structures of planks and tiles, the sheds and stalls, which our bye lanes, or fish-markets, or river-sides can supply; tumble them down on the declivity of a bare bald hill; let the spaces between house and house, thus accidentally determined, be understood to form streets,

* Mr. Russell's Letters in the *Times* newspaper (1854).

winding of course for no reason, and with no meaning, up and down the town ; the roadway always narrow, the breadth never uniform, the separate houses bulging or retiring below, as circumstances may have determined, and leaning forward till they meet overhead ;— and you have a good idea of Gallipoli. I question whether this picture would not nearly correspond to the special seat of the Muses in ancient times. Learned writers assure us distinctly that the houses of Athens were for the most part small and mean ; that the streets were crooked and narrow ; that the upper stories projected over the roadway ; and that staircases, balustrades, and doors that opened outwards, obstructed it ; —a remarkable coincidence of description. I do not doubt at all, though history is silent, that that roadway was jolting to carriages, and all but impassable ; and that it was traversed by drains, as freely as any Turkish town now. Athens seems in these respects to have been below the average cities of its time. "A stranger," says an ancient, "might doubt, on the sudden view, if really he saw Athens."

I grant all this, and much more, if you will ; but, recollect, Athens was the home of the intellectual and, beautiful ; not of low mechanical contrivances, and material organization. Why stop within your lodgings counting the rents in your wall or the holes in your tiling, when nature and art call you away? You must put up with such a chamber, and a table, and a stool, and a sleeping board, any where else in the three continents; one place does not differ from another indoors ; your magalia in Africa, or your grottos in Syria are not perfection. I suppose you did not come to Athens to swarm up a ladder, or to grope about a closet : you came to see and to hear, what hear and see you could not elsewhere. What food for the intellect is it possible to procure indoors, that you stay there looking about you? do you think to read there? where are your books? do you expect to purchase books at Athens—you are much out in your calculations. True it is, we at this day, who live in the nineteenth century, have the books of Greece as a perpetual memorial; and copies there have been, since the time that they were written; but you need not go to Athens to procure them, nor would you find them in Athens. Strange to say, strange to the nineteenth century, that in the age of Plato and Thucydides, there was not, it is said, a bookshop in the whole place: nor was the book trade in existence till the very time of Augustus. Libraries, I suspect, were the bright invention of Attalus or the Ptolemies;* I doubt whether Athens had a library till the reign of Hadrian. It was what the student gazed on, what he heard, what he caught by the magic of sympathy, not what he read, which was the education furnished by Athens.

He leaves his narrow lodging early in the morning, and not till night, if even then, will he return. It is but a crib or kennel,—in which he sleeps when the weather is inclement or the ground damp; in no respect a home. And he goes out of doors, not to read the day's newspaper, or to buy the gay shilling volume, but to imbibe the invisible atmosphere of genius, and to learn by heart the oral traditions of taste. Out he goes; and, leaving the tumble-down town behind him, he mounts the Acropolis to the right, or he turns to the Areopagus on

* I do not go into controversy on the subject, for which the reader must have recourse to Lipsius, Morhof, Boeckh, Bekker, etc.; and this of course applies to whatever historical matter I introduce, or shall introduce.

the left. He goes to the Parthenon to study the sculptures of Phidias; to the temple of the Dioscuri to see the paintings of Polygnotus. We indeed take our Sophocles or Æschylus out of our coat-pocket; but, if our sojourner at Athens would understand how a tragic poet can write, he must betake himself to the theatre on the south, and see and hear the drama literally in action. Or let him go westward to the Agora, and there he will hear Lysias or Andocides pleading, or Demosthenes haranguing. He goes farther west still, along the shade of those noble planes, which Cimon has planted there; and he looks around him at the statues and porticos and vestibules, each by itself a work of genius and skill, enough to be the making of another city. He passes through the city gate, and then he is at the famous Ceramicus; here are the tombs of the mighty dead; and here, we will suppose, is Pericles himself, the most elevated, the most thrilling of orators, converting a funeral oration over the slain into a philosophical panegyric of the living.

Onwards he proceeds still; and now he has come to that still more celebrated Academe, which has bestowed its own name on Universities down to this day; and there he sees a sight which will be graven on his memory till he dies. Many are the beauties of the place, the groves, and the statues, and the temple, and the stream of the Cephissus flowing by; many are the lessons which will be taught him day after day by teacher or by companion; but his eye is just now arrested by one object; it is the very presence of Plato. He does not hear a word that he says; he does not care to hear; he asks neither for discourse nor disputation; what he sees is a whole, complete in itself, not to be increased by addition, and greater than anything else. It will be a point in the history of his life ; a stay for his memory to rest on, a burning thought in his heart, a bond of union with men of like mind, ever afterwards. Such is the spell which the living man exerts on his fellows, for good or for evil. How nature impels us to lean upon others, making virtue, or genius, or name, the qualification for our doing so ! A Spaniard is said to have travelled to Italy, simply to see Livy ; he had his fill of gazing, and then went back again home. Had our young stranger got nothing by his voyage but the sight of the breathing and moving Plato, had he entered no lecture-room to hear, no gymnasium to converse, he had got some measure of education, and something to tell of to his grandchildren.

But Plato is not the only sage, nor the sight of him the only lesson to be learned in this wonderful suburb. It is the region and the realm of philosophy. Colleges were the inventions of many centuries later ; and they imply a sort of cloistered life, or at least a life of rule, scarcely natural to an Athenian. It was the boast of the philosophic statesman of Athens, that his countrymen achieved by the mere force of nature and the love of the noble and the great, what other people aimed at by laborious discipline ; and all who came among them were submitted to the same method of education. We have traced our student on his wanderings from the Acropolis to the Sacred Way ; and now he is in the region of the schools. No awful arch, no window of many-coloured lights marks the seats of learning there or elsewhere; philosophy lives out of doors. No close atmosphere oppresses the brain or inflames the eyelid ; no long session stiffens the limbs. Epicurus is reclining in his garden ; Zeno looks like a divinity in his porch ; the restless Aristotle, on the other side of the city, as if in antagonism to Plato, is walking his pupils off their legs in his Lyceum by the Ilyssus. Our student has determined on entering himself as a disciple of Theophrastus, a teacher of marvellous popularity, who has brought together two thousand pupils from all parts of the world. He himself is of Lesbos; for masters, as well as students, come hither from all regions of the earth,—as befits a University. How could Athens have collected hearers in such numbers, unless she had selected teachers of such power? it was the range of territory, which the notion of a University implies, which furnished both the quantity of the one, and the quality of the other. Anaxagoras was from Ionia, Carneades from Africa, Zeno from Cyprus, Protagoras from Thrace, and Gorgias from Sicily. Andromachus was a Syrian, Proæresius an Armenian, Hilarius a Bithynian, Philiscus a Thessalian, Hadrian a Syrian. Rome is celebrated for her liberality in civil matters; Athens was as liberal in intellectual. There was no narrow jealousy, directed against a Professor, because he was not an Athenian; genius and talent were the qualifications; and to bring them to Athens, was to do homage to it as a University. There was a brotherhood and a citizenship of mind.

Mind came first, and was the foundation of the academical polity; but it soon brought along with it, and gathered round itself, the gifts of fortune and the prizes of life. As time went on, wisdom was not always sentenced to the bare cloak of Cleanthes; but, beginning in rags, it ended in fine linen. The Professors became honourable and rich; and the students ranged themselves under their names, and were proud of calling themselves their countrymen. The University was divided into four great nations, as the medieval anti· quarian would style them; and in the middle of the fourth century, Proæresius was the leader or proctor of the Attic, Hephæstion of the Oriental, Epiphanius of the Arabic, and Diophantus of the Pontic. Thus the Professors were both patrons of clients, and hosts and *proxeni* of strangers and visitors, as well as masters of the schools : and the Cappadocian, Syrian, or Sicilian youth who came to one or other of them, would be encouraged to study by his protection, and to aspire by his example.

Even Plato, when the schools of Athens were not a hundred years old, was in circumstances to enjoy the *otium cum dignitate.* He had a villa out at Heraclea ; and he left his patrimony to his school, in whose hands it remained, not only safe, but fructifying, a marvellous phenomenon in tumultuous Greece, for the long space of eight hundred years. Epicurus too had the property of the Gardens where he lectured ; and these too became the property of his sect. But in Roman times the chairs of grammar, rhetoric, politics, and the four philosophies, were handsomely endowed by the State ; some of the Professors were themselves statesmen or high functionaries, and brought to their favourite study senatorial rank or Asiatic opulence.

Patrons such as these can compensate to the freshman, in whom we have interested ourselves, for the poorness of his lodging and the turbulence of his companions. In every thing there is a better side and a worse ; in every place a disreputable set and a respectable, and the one is hardly known at all to the other. Men come away from the same University at this day, with contradictory impressions and contradictory statements, according to the society they have found there ; if you believe the one, nothing goes on there as it should be : if you believe the other, nothing goes on as it should *not.* Virtue, however, and decency are at least in the minority every where, and under some sort of a cloud or disadvantage ; and this being the case, it is so much gain whenever an Herodes Atticus is found, to throw the influence of wealth and station on the side even of a decorous philosophy. A consular man, and the heir of an ample fortune, this Herod was content to devote his life to a professorship, and his fortune to the patronage of literature. He gave the sophist Polemo about eight thousand pounds, as the sum is calculated, for three declamations. He built at Athens a stadium six hundred feet long, entirely of white marble, and capable of admitting the whole population. His theatre, erected to the memory of his wife, was made of cedar wood curiously carved. He had two villas, one at Marathon, the place of his birth, about ten miles from Athens, the other at Cephissia, at the distance of six ; and thither he drew to him the *élite*, and at times the whole body of the students. Long arcades, groves of trees, clear pools for the bath, delighted and recruited the summer visitor. Never was so brilliant a lecture-room as his evening banqueting-hall ; highly connected students from Rome mixed with the sharp-witted provincial of Greece or Asia Minor ; and the flippant sciolist, and the nondescript visitor, half philosopher, half tramp, met with a reception, courteous always, but suitable to his deserts. Herod was noted for his repartees ; and we have instances on record of his setting down, according to the emergency, both the one and the other.

A higher line, though a rarer one, was that allotted to the youthful Basil. He was one of those men who seem by a sort of fascination to draw others around them even without wishing it. One might have deemed that his gravity and his reserve would have kept them at a distance ; but, almost in spite of himself, he was the centre of a knot of youths, who, pagans as most of them were, used Athens honestly for the purpose for which they professed to seek it ; and, disappointed and displeased with the place himself, he seems nevertheless to have been the means of their profiting by its advantages. One of these was Sophronius, who afterwards held a high office in the State : Eusebius was another, at that time the bosom-friend of Sophronius, and afterwards a Bishop. Celsus too is named, who afterwards was raised to the government of Cilicia by the Emperor Julian. Julian himself, in the sequel of unhappy memory, was then at Athens, and known at least to St. Gregory. Another Julian is also mentioned, who was afterwards commissioner of the land tax. Here we have a glimpse of the better kind of society among the students of Athens ; and it is to the credit of the parties composing it, that such young men as Gregory and Basil, men as intimately connected with Christianity, as they were well known in the world, should hold so high a place in their esteem and love. When the two saints were departing, their companions came around them with the hope of changing their purpose. Basil persevered ; but Gregory relented, and turned back to Athens for a season.

CHAPTER V.

WHEN the Catholic University is mentioned, we hear people saying on all sides of us,—" Impossible! how can you give degrees? what will your degrees be worth? where are your endowments? where are your edifices? where will you find students? what will government have to say to you? who wants you? who will acknowledge you? what do you expect? what is left for you?"

Now, I hope I may say without offence, that this surprise on the part of so many excellent men, is itself not a little surprising. When I look around at what the Catholic Church now is in this country of Ireland, and am told what it was twenty or thirty years ago; when I see the hundreds of good works, which in that interval have been done, and now stand as monuments of the zeal and charity of the living and the dead; when I find that in those years new religious orders have been introduced, and that the country is now covered with convents; when I gaze upon the sacred edifices, spacious and fair, which during that time have been built out of the pence of the poor; when I reckon up the multitude of schools now at work, and the sacrifices which gave them birth; when I reflect upon the great political exertions and successes which have made the same period memorable in all history to come; when I contrast what was then almost a nation of bondsmen, with the intelligence, and freedom of thought, and hope for the future, which is its present characteristic ; when I meditate on the wonderful sight of a people springing again fresh and vigorous from the sepulchre of famine and pestilence ; and when I consider that those bonds of death which they have burst, are but the specimen and image of the adamantine obstacles, political, social, and municipal, which have all along stood in the way of their triumphs, and how they have been carried on to victory by the simple energy of a courageous faith ; it sets me marvelling to find some of those very men, who have been heroically achieving impossibilities all their lives long, now beginning to scruple about adding one little sneaking impossibility to the list, and I feel it to be a great escape for the Church that they did not insert the word "impossible" into their dictionaries and encyclopedias at a somewhat earlier date.

However, this by the way : as to the objection itself, which has led to this not unnatural reflection, perhaps the reader may have observed, if he has taken the trouble to follow me, that in what I have said above I have already been covertly aiming at it ; and now I propose to handle it avowedly, at least as far as my limits will allow in one Chapter.

He will recollect, perhaps, that in former Chapters I have already been maintaining, that a University consists, and has ever consisted, in demand and supply, in wants which it alone can satisfy and which it does satisfy, in the communication of knowledge, and the relation and bond which exists between the teacher and the taught. Its constituting, animating principle is this moral attraction of one class of persons to another ; which is prior in its nature, nay commonly in its history, to any other tie whatever ; so that, where this is wanting, a University is alive only in name, and has lost its true essence, whatever be the advantages, whether of position or of affluence, with which the civil power or private benefactors contrive to encircle it. I am far indeed from undervaluing those external advantages ; a certain share of them is necessary to its well-being : but on the whole, as it is with the individual, so will it be with the body :—it is talents and attainments which command success. Consideration, dignity, wealth, and power, are all very proper things in the territory of literature ; but they ought to know their place ; they come second, not first ; they must not presume, or make too much of themselves, or they had better be away. First intellect, then secular advantages, as its instruments and as its rewards ; I say no more than this, but I say no less.

Nor am I denying, as I shall directly show, that, under any circumstances, professors will ordinarily lecture, and students ordinarily attend them, with a view, in some shape or other, to secular advantage. Certainly ; few persons pursue knowledge simply for its own sake. But though remuneration of some sort, both to the teachers and to the taught, may be inseparable from the fact of a University, still it may be separable from its idea. Much less am I forgetting (to view the subject on another side), that intellect is helpless, because ungovernable and self-destructive, unless it be regulated by a moral rule and by revealed truth. Nor am I saying anything in disparagement of the principle, that establishments of literature and science should be in subordination to ecclesiastical authority.

I would not make light of any of these considerations ; some I shall even assume at once, as necessary for the purpose ; of some I shall say more hereafter ; here, however, I am merely suggesting to the reader's better judgment what constitutes a University, what is just enough to constitute it, or what a University consists in, viewed in its essence. What this is, seems to me most simply explained and ascertained, as I noticed in a former Chapter, by the instance of metropolitan centres. It would appear as if the very same kinds of need, social and moral, which give rise to a metropolis, give rise also to a University; nay, that every metropolis *is* a University, as far as the rudiments of a University are concerned. Youths come up thither from all parts, in order to better themselves gene-rally;—not as if they necessarily looked for degrees in their own several pursuits, and degrees recognized by the law; not as if there were to be any competition for fellowships in chemistry, for instance, or engineering,—but they come to gain that instruction which will turn most to their account in after life, and to form good and serviceable connexions, and that, as regards the fine arts, literature, and science, as well as in trade and the professions. I do not see why it should be more diffi-cult for Ireland to trade, if I may use the term, upon the field of knowledge, than for the inhabitants of San Fran-cisco or of Melbourne to make a fortune by their gold fields, or for the North of England by its coal. If gold is power, wealth, influence; and if coal is power, wealth, influence; so is knowledge.

> " When house and lands are gone and spent,
>   Then learning is most excellent" ;

and, as some men go to the Antipodes for the gold, so others may come to us here for the knowledge. And it is as reasonable to expect students, though we have no charter from the State, provided we hold out the inducement of good teachers, as to expect a crowd of Britishers, Yankees, Spaniards, and Chinamen at the diggings, though there are no degrees for the successful use of the pickaxe, sieve, and shovel.

And history, I think, corroborates this view of the matter. In all times there have been Universities; and in all times they have flourished by means of this profession of teaching and this desire of learning. They have needed nothing else but this for their existence. There has been a demand, and there has been a supply; and there has been the supply necessarily before the demand, though not before the need. This is how the University, in every age, has made progress. Teachers have set up their tent, and opened their school, and students and disciples have flocked around them, in spite of the want of every advantage, or even of the presence of every conceivable discouragement. Years, nay, centuries perhaps, passed along of discomfort and disorder: and these, though they showed plainly enough that, for the well-being and perfection of a University, something more than the desire for knowledge is required, yet they showed also how irrepressible was that desire, how reviviscent, how indestructible, how adequate to the duties of a vital principle, in the midst of enemies within and without, amid plague, famine, destitution, war, dissension, and tyranny, evils physical and social, which would have been fatal to any other but a really natural principle naturally developed.

Do not let the reader suppose, however, that I am anticipating for Dublin at this day such dreary periods or such ruinous commotions, as befel the schools of the medieval period. Such miseries were the accidents of the times; and this is why we hear so much then of protectors of learning—the Charlemagnes and Alfreds,—as the compensation of those miseries. It may be asked, whether royal protectors do not tell against the inherent vitality, on which I have been insisting, of Universities; but in truth, powerful sovereigns, such as they, did but clear and keep the ground, on which Universities were to build. Learning in the middle ages had great foes and great friends; we too, were we setting up a school of learning in a rude period of society, should have to expect perils on the one hand, and to court protectors on the other; as it is, however, we can afford to treat with comparative unconcern the prospect both of the one and of the other. We may hope, and we may be content, to be just let alone; or, if we must be anxious about the future, we may reasonably use the words of the proverb, "Save me from my friends." Charlemagne was indeed a patron of learning, but he was its protector far more; it is our happiness, for which we cannot be too thankful to the Author of all good, that we need no protector; for it is our privilege just now, whatever comes of the morrow, to live in the midst of a civilization, the like of which the world never saw before. The descent of enemies on our coasts, the forays of indigenous marauders, the sudden rise of town mobs, the unbridled cruelty of rulers, the resistless sweep of pestilence, the utter insecurity of life and property, and the recklessness which is its consequence, all that deforms the annals of the medieval Universities, is to us for the present but a matter of history. The statesman, the lawyer, the soldier, the policeman, the reformer, the economist, have most of them seriously wronged and afflicted us Catholics in other ways, national, social, and religious; but, on the side on which I have here to view them, they are acting in our behalf as a blessing from heaven. They are giving us that tranquillity for which the Church so variously

and so anxiously prays ; that real freedom, which enables us to consult her interests, to edify her holy
house, to adorn her sanctuary, to perfect her discipline,
to inculcate her doctrines, and to enlighten and form
her children, " with all confidence," as Scripture speaks,
" without prohibition." We are able to set up a *Studium
Generale*, without its concomitant dangers and inconveniences ; and the history of the past, while it adum-
brates for us the pattern of a University, and supplies
us with a specimen of its good fruits, conveys to us no
presage of the recurrence of those melancholy conflicts,
in which the cultivated intellect was in those times engaged, sometimes with brute force, and sometimes, alas !
with Revealed Religion.

Charlemagne then was necessary, but not so much for
the University, as against its enemies ; he was confessedly a patron of letters, effectual as well as munificent, but he could not any how have dispensed with his
celebrated professors, and they, as the history of literature, both before and after him, shows, could probably
have dispensed with him. Whether we turn to the
ancient world or to the modern, in either case we have
evidence in behalf of this position : we have the spec-
tacle of the thirst of knowledge acting for and by itself,
and making its own way.

Here I shall confine myself to ancient history : both
in Athens and in Rome, we find it pushing forward, in
independence of the civil power. The professors of
literature seated themselves in Athens without the
favour of the government ; and they opened their
mission in Rome in spite of its state traditions. It was
the rising generation, it was the mind of youth un-
fettered by the conventional ideas of the ruling politics
which in either instance became their followers. The ex-

citement they created in Athens is described by Plato in one of his Dialogues, and has often been quoted. Protagoras came to the bright city with the profession of teaching "the political art"; and the young flocked around him. They flocked to him, be it observed, not because he promised them entertainment or novelty, such as the theatre might promise, and a people proverbially fickle and curious might exact; nor, on the other hand, had he any definite recompense to hold out,—a degree, for instance, or a snug fellowship, or an India writership, or a place in the civil service. He offered them just the sort of inducement, which carries off a man now to a conveyancer, or a medical practitioner, or an engineer,—he engaged to prepare them for the line of life which they had chosen as their own, and to prepare them better than Hippias or Prodicus, who were at Athens with him. Whether he was really able to do this, is another thing altogether; or rather it makes the argument stronger, if he were unable; for, if the very promise of knowledge was so potent a spell, what would have been its real possession?

But now let us hear the state of the case from the mouth of Hippocrates himself,—the youth, who in his eagerness woke Socrates, himself a young man at the time, while it was yet dark, to tell him that Protagoras was come to Athens. "When we had supped, and were going to bed,"* he says, "then my brother told me that Protagoras was arrived, and my first thought was to come and see you immediately; but afterwards it appeared to me too late at night. As soon, however, as sleep had refreshed me, up I got, and came here." "And I," continued Socrates, giving an account of the conversation, "knowing his earnestness and excitability,

* Carey's translation is followed almost verbatim.

said : 'What is that to you? does Protagoras do you
any harm?' He laughed and said : 'That he does,
Socrates ; because he alone is wise, and does not make
me so.' 'Nay,' said I, 'do you give him money enough,
and he will make you wise too.' 'O Jupiter and ye
gods,' he made answer, 'that it depended upon that,
for I would spare nothing of my own, or of my friends'
property either ; and I have now come to you for this
very purpose, to get you to speak to him in my behalf.
For, besides that I am too young, I have never yet seen
Protagoras, or heard him speak ; for I was but a boy
when he came before. However, all praise him, Socrates,
and say that he has the greatest skill in speaking. But
why do we not go to him, that we may find him at
home?'"

They went on talking till the light ; and then they
set out for the house of Callias, where Protagoras, with
others of his own calling, was lodged. There they
found him pacing up and down the portico, with his
host and others, among whom, on one side of him, was
a son of Pericles (his father being at this time in power),
while another son of Pericles, with another party, was
on the other. A party followed, chiefly of foreigners,
whom Protagoras had " bewitched, like Orpheus, by his
voice." On the opposite side of the portico sat Hippias,
with a bench of youths before him, who were asking him
questions in physics and astronomy. Prodicus was still in
bed, with some listeners on sofas round him. The house is
described as quite full of guests. Such is the sketch
given us of this school of Athens, as there represented.
I do not enter on the question, as I have already said,
whether the doctrine of these Sophists, as they are called,
was true or false ; more than very partially true it could
not be, whether in morals or in physics, from the cir-

cumstances of the age ; it is sufficient that it powerfully interested the hearers. We see what it was that filled the Athenian lecture-halls and porticos ; not the fashion of the day, not the patronage of the great, not pecuniary prizes, but the reputation of talent and the desire of knowledge,—ambition, if you will, personal attachment, but not an influence, political or other, external to the School. "Such Sophists," says Mr. Grote, referring to the passage in Plato, " had *nothing to recommend them* except superior *knowledge* and *intellectual fame*, combined with an imposing *personality*, making itself felt in the lectures and conversation."

So much for Athens, where Protagoras had at least this advantage, that Pericles was his private friend, if he was not publicly his patron ; but now when we turn to Rome, in what is almost a parallel page in her history, we shall find that literature, or at least philosophy, had to encounter there the direct opposition of the ruling party in the state, and of the hereditary and popular sentiment. The story goes, that when the Greek treatises which Numa had had buried with him, were accidentally brought to light, the Romans had burned them, from the dread of such knowledge coming into fashion. At a later date decrees passed the Senate for the expulsion from the city, first of philosophers, then of rhetoricians, who were gaining the attention of the rising generation. A second decree was passed some time afterwards to the same effect, assigning, in its vindication, the danger, which existed, of young men losing, by means of these new studies, their taste for the military profession.

Such was the nascent conflict between the old rule and policy of Rome, and the awakening intellect, at the time of that celebrated embassy of the three philosophers, Diogenes the Stoic, Carneades the Academic, and Critolaus the Peripatetic, sent to Rome from Athens on a political affair. Whether they were as skilful in diplomacy as they were zealous in their own particular line, need not here be determined ; any how, they lengthened out their stay at Rome, and employed themselves in giving lectures. "Those among the youth," says Plutarch, "who had a taste for literature went to them, and became their constant and enthusiastic hearers. Especially, the graceful eloquence of Carneades, which had a reputation equal to its talent, secured large and favourable audiences, and was noised about the city. It was reported that a Greek, with a perfectly astounding power both of interesting and of commanding the feelings, was kindling in the youth a most ardent emotion, which possessed them, to the neglect of their ordinary indulgences and amusements, with a sort of rage for philosophy." Upon this, Cato took up the matter upon the traditionary ground ; he represented that the civil and military interests of Rome were sure to suffer, if such tastes became popular ; and he exerted himself with such effect, that the three philosophers were sent off with the least possible delay, "to return home to their own schools, and in future to confine their lessons to Greek boys, leaving the youth of Rome, as heretofore, to listen to the magistrates and the laws." The pressure of the government was successful at the moment ; but ultimately the cause of education prevailed. Schools were gradually founded ; first of grammar, in the large sense of the word, then of rhetoric, then of mathematics, then of philosophy, and then of medicine, though the order of their introduction, one with another, is not altogether clear. At length the Emperors secured the interests of letters by an establishment, which has lasted to this day in the Roman University, now called *Sapienza*.

Here are two striking instances in very different countries, to prove that it is the thirst for knowledge, and not the patronage of the great, which carries on the cause of literature and science to its ultimate victory ; and all that can be said against them is, that I have gone back a great way to find them. But a general truth is made up of particular instances, which cannot be brought forward all at once, nor crowded into half a dozen pages of a work like this. I shall continue the subject some future time ; meanwhile I will but observe that, while these ancient instances teach us that a University is *founded* on principles *sui generis* and proper to itself, so do they coincidently suggest that it may boldly *appeal* to those principles before they are yet brought into exercise, and may, or rather must, take the initiative in its own success. It must be set up before it can be sought ; and it must offer a supply, in order to create a demand. Protagoras and Carneades needed nothing more than to advertise themselves in order to gain disciples ; if we have a confidence that we have that to offer to Irishmen, to Catholics, which is good and great, and which at present they have not, our success may be tedious and slow in coming, but ultimately come it must.

Therefore, I say, let us set up our University ; let us only set it up, and it will teach the world its value by the fact of its existence. What ventures are made, what risks incurred by private persons in matters of trade ! What speculations are entered on in the departments of building or engineering ! What boldness in innovation or improvement has been manifested by statesmen during the last twenty years ! Mercantile undertakings indeed may be ill-advised, and political measures may be censurable in themselves, or fatal in their results. I am not considering them here in their motive or their object, in their expedience or their justice, but in the manner in which they have been carried out. What largeness then of view, what intrepidity, vigour, and resolution are implied in the Reform Bill, in the Emancipation of the Blacks, in the finance changes, in the Useful Knowledge movement, in the organization of the Free Kirk, in the introduction of the penny postage, and in the railroads! This is an age, if not of great men, at least of great works; are Catholics alone to refuse to act on faith? England has faith in her skill, in her determination, in her resources in war, in the genius of her people; is Ireland alone to fail in confidence in her children and her God? *Fortes fortuna adjuvat;* so says the proverb. If the chance concurrence of half a dozen of sophists, or the embassy of three philosophers, could do so much of old to excite the enthusiasm of the young, and to awaken the intellect into activity, is it very presumptuous, or very imprudent, in us at this time, to enter upon an undertaking, which comes to us with the authority of St. Peter, the blessing of St. Patrick, the coöperation of the faithful, the prayers of the poor, and all the ordinary materials of success, resources, intellect, pure intention, and self devotion, to bring it into effect? Shall it be said in future times, that the work needed nought but good and gallant hearts, and found them not?

CHAPTER VI.

DISCIPLINE AND INFLUENCE.

I HAVE had some debate with myself, whether what are called myths and parables, and similar compositions of a representative nature, are in keeping with this work; yet, considering that the early Christians recognized the *Logi* of the classical writers as not inconsistent with the gravity of their own literature, not to mention the precedent afforded by the sacred text, I think I may proceed, without apology to myself or others, to impart to the reader in confidence, while it is fresh on my mind, a conversation which I have just had with an intimate English friend, on the general subject to which these columns are devoted. I do not say that it was of a very important nature; still to those who choose to reflect, it may suggest more than it expresses. It took place only a day or two ago, on occasion of my paying him a flying visit.

My friend lives in a spot as convenient as it is delightful. The neighbouring hamlet is the first station out of London of a railroad; while not above a quarter of a mile from his boundary wall flows the magnificent river, which moves towards the metropolis through a richness of grove and meadow of its own creation. After a liberal education, he entered a lucrative business; and, making a competency in a few years, exchanged

New Broad Street for the "fallentis semita vitæ." Soon after his marriage, which followed this retirement, his wife died, and left him solitary. Instead of returning to the world, or seeking to supply her place, he gave himself to his garden and his books; and with these companions he has passed the last twenty years. He has lived in a largish house, the "monarch of all he surveyed;" the sorrows of the past, his creed, and the humble chapel not a stone's throw from his carriage-gate, have saved him from the selfishness of such a sovereignty, and the oppressiveness of such a solitude; yet not, if I may speak candidly, from some of the inconveniences of a bachelor life. He has his own fixed views, from which it is difficult to move him, and some people say that he discourses rather than converses, though, somehow, when I am with him, from long familiarity, I manage to get through as many words as he.

I do not know that such peculiarities can in any case be called moral defects; certainly not, when contrasted with the great mischiefs which a life so enjoyable as his might have done to him, and has not. He has indeed been in possession of the very perfection of earthly happiness, at least as I view things;—mind, I say of "earthly;" and I do not say that earthly happiness is desirable. On the contrary, man is born for labour, not for self; what right has any one to retire from the world and profit no one? He who takes his ease in this world, will have none in the world to come. All this rings in my friend's ears quite as distinctly as I may fancy it does in mine, and has a corresponding effect upon his conduct; who would not exchange consciences with him? but still the fact remains, that a life such as his is in itself dangerous, and that, in proportion to its attractiveness. If indeed there were no country beyond the grave, it would be our wisdom to make of our present dwelling-place as much as ever we could ; and this would be done by the very life which my friend has chosen, not by any absurd excesses, not by tumult, dissipation, excitement, but by the "moderate and rational use," as Protestant sermons say, "of the gifts of Providence."

Easy circumstances, books, friends, literary connexions, the fine arts, presents from abroad, foreign correspondents, handsome appointments, elegant simplicity, gravel walks, lawns, flower beds, trees and shrubberies, summer houses, strawberry beds, a greenhouse, a wall for peaches, "hoc erat in votis";—nothing out of the way, no hot-houses, graperies, pineries,—"Persicos odi, puer, apparatus,"—no mansions, no parks, no deer, no preserves ; these things are not worth the cost, they involve the bother of dependants, they interfere with enjoyment. One or two faithful servants, who last on as the trees do, and cannot change their place :—the ancients had slaves, a sort of dumb waiter, and the real article ; alas ! they are impossible now. We must have no one with claims upon us, or with rights ; no incum-brances ; no wife and children ; they would hurt our dignity. We must have acquaintance within reach, yet not in the way ; ready, not troublesome or intrusive. We must have something of name, or of rank, or of ancestry, or of past official life, to raise us from the dead level of mankind, to afford food for the imagination of our neighbours, to bring us from time to time strange visitors, and to invest our home with mystery. In con-sequence we shall be loyal subjects, good conservatives, fond of old times, averse to change, suspicious of novelty, because we know perfectly when we are well off, and that in our case "progredi *est* regredi." To a life such as this, a man is more attached, the longer he lives ;

and he would be more and more happy in it too, were it not for the *memento* within him, that books and gardens do not make a man immortal ; that, though they do not leave him, he at least must leave them, all but "the hateful cypresses," and must go where the only book is the book of doom, and the only garden the Paradise of the just.

All this has nothing to do with our University, but nevertheless they are some of the reflections which came into my mind, as I left the station I have spoken of, and turned my face towards my friend's abode. As I went along, on the lovely afternoon of last Monday, which had dried up the traces of a wet morning, and as I fed upon the soothing scents and sounds which filled the air, I began to reflect how the most energetic and war-like race among the descendants of Adam, had made, by contrast, this Epicurean life, the " otium cum dignitate," the very type of human happiness. A life in the country in the midst of one's own people, was the dream of Roman poets from Virgil to Juvenal, and the reward of Roman statesmen from Cincinnatus to Pliny. I called to mind the Corycian old man, so beautifully sketched in the fourth Georgic, and then my own fantastic protesta-tion in years long dead and gone, that, if I were free to choose my own line of life, it should be that of a gardener in some great family, a life without care, without excite-ment, in which the gifts of the Creator screened off man's evil doings, and the romance of the past coloured and illuminated the matter-of-fact present.

" Otium divos," I suppose the reader will say. Smiling myself at the recollection of my own absurdity, I passed along the silent avenues of solemn elms, which, belong-ing to a nobleman's domain, led the way towards the humbler dwelling for which I was bound ; and then I recurred to the Romans, wandering in thought, as in a time of relaxation one is wont ; and I contrasted, or rather investigated, the respective aspects, one with another, under which a country life, so dear to that conquering people nationally, presented itself severally to Cicero, to Virgil, to Horace, and to Juvenal, and I asked myself under which of them all was my friend's home to be regarded.   Then suddenly the scene changed, and I was viewing it in my own way; for I had known him since I was a schoolboy, in his father's time ; and I recollected with a sigh how I had once passed a week there of my summer holidays, and what I then thought of persons and things I met there, of its various inmates, father, mother, brothers, and sisters, all of them, except himself and me, now numbered with the departed.   Thus Cicero and Horace glided off from my field of view, like the rounds of a magic lantern ; and my ears, no longer open to the preludes of the nightingales around me, who were preparing for their nightly concert, heard nothing but

The voices of the dead, and songs of other years.

Thus, deep in sad thoughts, I reached the well-known garden gate, and unconsciously opened it, and was upon the lower lawn, advancing towards the house, before I apprehended shrubberies and beds, which were sensibly before me, otherwise than through my memory.   Then suddenly the vivid past gave way, and the actual present flowed in upon me, and I saw my friend pacing up and down on the side furthest from me, with his hands behind him, and a newspaper or some such publication in their grasp.

It is an old-fashioned place ; the house may be of the date of George the Second ; a square hall in the middle, and in the centre of it a pillar, and rooms all around. The servants' rooms and offices run off on the right; a rookery covers the left flank, and the drawing-room opens upon the lawn. There a large plane tree, with its massive branches, whilome sustained a swing, when there were children on that lawn, blithely to undergo an exercise of head, at the very thought of which the grown man sickens. Three formal terraces gradually conduct down to one of the majestic avenues, of which I have already spoken; the second and third, intersected by grass walks, constitute the kitchen-garden. As a boy, I used to stare at the magnificent cauliflowers and large apricots which it furnished for the table; and how difficult it was to leave off, when once one got among the gooseberry bushes in the idle morning!

I had now got close upon my friend; and, in return for the schoolboy reminiscences and tranquil influences of the place, was ungrateful enough to begin attacking him for his epicurean life. "Here you are, you old pagan," I said, "as usual, fit for nothing so much as to be one of the interlocutors in a dialogue of Cicero's."

"*You* are a pretty fellow," he made answer, "to accuse me of paganism, who have yourself been so busily engaged just now in writing up Athens;" and then I saw that it was several numbers of the *Gazette*, which he had in his hand, and which perhaps had given energy to his step.

After giving utterance to some general expressions of his satisfaction at the publication, and the great interest he took in the undertaking to which it was devoted, he suddenly stopped, turned round upon me, looked hard in my face, and taking hold of a button of my coat, said abruptly: "But what on earth possessed you, my good friend, to have anything to do with this Irish University? what was it to you? how did it fall in your way?"

I could not help laughing out ; " O I see," I cried, " you consider me a person who cannot keep quiet, and must ever be in one scrape or another."

" Yes, but seriously, tell me," he urged, " what *had* you to do with it ? what was Ireland to you? you had your own line and your own work ; was not that enough ?"

" Well, my dear Richard," I retorted, " better do **too** much than too little."

" A *tu quoque* is quite unworthy of you," he replied ; " answer me, charissime, what had you to do with an Irish undertaking ? do you think they have not clever men enough there to work it, but you must meddle ?"

" Well," I said, " I do not think it *is* an Irish under-taking, that is, in such a sense that it is not a Catholic undertaking, and one which intimately and directly interests other countries besides Ireland."

" Say England," he interposed.

"Well, I say and mean England : I think it most intimately concerns England ; unless it was an affair of England, as well as of Ireland, I should have sympa-thized in so grand a conception, I should have done what I could to aid it, but I should have had no call, as you well say, I should have considered it presumption in me, to take an active part in its execution."

He looked at me with a laughing expression in his eye, and was for a moment silent ; then he began again :

" You must think yourself a great genius," he said, " to fancy that place is not a condition of capacity. You are an Englishman; your mind, your habits are English; you have hitherto been acting only upon Englishmen, with Englishmen ; do you really anticipate that you will be able to walk into a new world, and to do any good service there, because you have done it here ? *Ne sutor ultra crepidam.* I would as soon believe that you could shoot your soul into a new body, according to the Eastern tale, and make it your own."

I made him a bow ; " I thank you heartily," I said, " for the seasonable encouragement you give me in a difficult undertaking ; you are determined, Richard, that I shall not get too much refreshment from your shrubberies."

" I beg your pardon," he made answer, " do not mistake me ; I am only trying to draw you out ; I am curious to know how you came to make this engagement ; you know we have not had any talk together for some time."

" It may be as you say," I answered ; " that is, I may be found quite unequal to what I have attempted ; but, I assure you, not for want of zealous and able assistance, of sympathizing friends,—not because it is in Ireland, instead of England, that I have to work."

" They tell me," he replied, " that they don't mean to let you have any Englishmen about you if they can help it."

" You seem to know a great deal more about it here than I do in Ireland," I answered : " I have not heard this ; but still, I suppose, in former times, when men were called from one country to another for a similar purpose, as Peter from Ireland to Naples, and John of Melrose to Paris, they did in fact go alone."

" Modest man !" he cried, " to compare yourself to the sages and doctors of the Middle Age ! But still the fact is not so : far from going alone, the very number they could and did spare from home is the most remarkable evidence of the education of the Irish in those times. Moore, I recollect, emphatically states, that it was abroad that the Irish sought, and abroad that they found, the rewards of their genius. If any people ought to suffer foreigners to come to them, it is they who have, with so much glory to themselves, so often gone to foreigners. In the passage I have in my eye, Moore calls it 'the peculiar fortune of Ireland, that both in talent and in fame her sons have prospered more signally abroad than at home ; that not so much those who confined their labours to their native land, as those who carried their talents and zeal to other lands, won for their country the high title of the Island of the Holy and the Learned.' But, not to insist on the principle of reciprocity, jealousy of foreigners among them is little in keeping with that ancient hospitality of theirs, of which history speaks as distinctly."

" Really," I made answer, " begging your pardon, you do not quite know what you are talking about. You never were in Ireland, I believe ; am I likely to know less than you ? If there be a nation, which in matters of intellect does not want 'protection,' to use the political word, it is the Irish. A stupid people would have a right to claim it, when they would set up a University ; but, if I were you, I would think twice before I paid so bad a compliment to one of the most gifted nations of Europe, as to suppose that it could not keep its ground, that it would not take the lead, in the intellectual arena, though competition was perfectly open. If their 'grex philosophorum' spread in the medieval time over Europe, in spite of the perils of sea and land, will they not be sure to fill the majority of chairs in their own University in an age like this, from the sheer claims of talent, though those chairs were open to the world ? No ; a monopoly would make the cleverest people idle ; it would sink the character of their undertaking, and Ireland herself would be the first to exclaim against the places of a great school of learning becoming mere pieces of patronage and occasions for jobbing, like the sees of the Irish Establishment."

My friend did not reply, but looked grave ; at length he said that he was not stating what ought to be, but what would be ; Irishmen boasted, and justly, that in ancient times they went to Melrose, to Malmesbury, to Glastonbury, to East Anglia, to Oxford ; that they established themselves in Paris, Ratisbon, Padua, Pavia, Naples, and other continental schools ; but there was in fact no reciprocity now ; Paris had not been simply for Frenchmen, nor Oxford simply for Englishmen, but Ireland must be solely for the Irish.

"Really, in truth," I made answer, " to speak most seriously, I think you are prejudiced and unjust, and I should be very sorry indeed to have to believe that you expressed an English sentiment. I am sure you do not. However, you speak of what you simply do not know. In Ireland, as in every country, there is of course a wholesome jealousy towards persons placed in important posts, such as my own, lest they should exercise their power unfairly ; there is a fear of jobs, not a jealousy of English ; and I don't suppose you think I am likely to turn out a jobber. This is all I can grant you at the utmost, and perhaps I grant too much. But I do most solemnly assure you, that, as far as I have had the means of bearing witness, there is an earnest wish in the promoters and advocates of this great undertaking to get the best men for its execution, wherever they are to be found, in England, or in France, or in Belgium, or in Germany, or in Italy, or in the United States ; though there is an anticipation too, which is far from unreasonable, that for most of the Professorships of the University the best men *will* be found in Ireland. Of course in particular cases, there ever will be a difference of opinion who is the best man ; but this does not interfere at all, as is evident, with the honest desire on all sides, to make the Institution a real honour to Ireland and a defence of Ireland's faith."

My companion again kept silence, and so we walked on ; then he suddenly said : "Come let us have some tea, since you tell me," (I had told him by letter,) "that you cannot take a bed ; the last train is not over-late."

As we walked towards the house, " The truth is," he continued, speaking slowly, " I had another solution of my own difficulty myself. I cannot help thinking that your *Gazette* makes more of *persons* than is just, and does not lay stress enough upon order, system, and rule, in conducting a University. This is what I have said to myself. 'After all, suppose there *be* an exclusive system, it does not much matter ; a great institution, if well organized, moves of itself, independently of the accident of its particular functionaries.' . . . Well now, is it not so ?" he added briskly ; " you have been laying too much stress upon *persons ?* "

I hesitated how best I should begin to answer him, and he went on :—"Look at the Church herself ; how little she depends on individuals ; in proportion as she can develop her system, she dispenses with them. In times of great confusion, in countries under conversion, great men are given to her, great Popes, great Evangelists ; but there is no call for Hildebrands or Ghislieris in the nineteenth century, or for Winfrids or Xaviers in modern Europe. It is so with states ; despotisms require great monarchs, Turkish or Russian ; constitutions manage to jog on without them ; this is the meaning of the famous saying, 'Quantulâ sapientiâ regitur mundus !' What a great idea again, to use Guizot's ex·

pression, is the Society of Jesus! what a creation of genius is its organization; but so well adapted is the institution to its object, that for that very reason it can afford to crush individualities, however gifted; so much so, that, in spite of the rare talents of its members, it has even become an objection to it in the mouth of its enemies, that it has not produced a thinker like Scotus or Malebranche. Now, I consider your papers make too much of persons, and put system out of sight; and this is the sort of consolation which occurs to me, in answer to the misgivings which come upon me, about the exclusiveness with which the University seems to me to be threatened."

"You know," I answered, "these papers have not got half through their subject yet. I assure you I do not at all forget, that something more than able Professors are necessary to make a University."

"Still," said he, "I should like to be certain you were sufficiently alive to the evils which spring from over-valuing them. You have talked to us a great deal about Platos, Hephæstions, Herods, and the rest of them, sophists one and all, and very little about a constitution. All that you have said has gone one way. You have professed a high and mighty independence of state patronage, and a conviction that the demand and supply of knowledge is all in all; that the supply must be pro-vided before the demand in order to create it; and that great minds are the instruments of that supply. You have founded your ideal University on individuals. Then, I say, on this hypothesis, be sure you have for your purpose the largest selection possible; do not pro-claim that you mean to have the tip-top men of the age, and then refuse to look out beyond one country for them, as if any country, though it be Ireland, had a

monopoly of talent.   Observe, I say this on your hypothesis ; but I confess I am disposed to question its
soundness, and it is in that way I get over my own misgiving about you.   I say that, may be, your University
need not have the best men ; it may fall back on a jog-
trot system, a routine, and perhaps it ought to do so."

" Forbid it ! " said I ; " you cannot suppose that what
you have said is new to me, or that I do not give it due
weight.   Indeed I could almost write a dissertation on
the subject which you have started, that is, on the functions
and mutual relations, in the conduct of human affairs, of
Influence and Law.   I should begin by saying that these
are the two moving powers which carry on the world,
and that in the supernatural order they are absolutely
united in the Source of all perfection.   I should observe
that the Supreme Being is both,—a living, individual
Agent, as sovereign as if an Eternal Law were not ; and
a Rule of right and wrong, and an Order fixed and
irreversible, as if He had no will, or supremacy, or
characteristics of personality.   Then I should say that
here below the two principles are separated, that each
has its own function, that each is necessary for the
other, and that they ought to act together ; yet that it
too often happens that they become rivals of one another, that this or that acts of itself, and will encroach
upon the province, or usurp the rights of the other ; and
that then every thing goes wrong.   Thus I should start,
and would you not concur with me ?   Would it not be
sufficient to give you hope that I am not taking a one-
sided view of the subject of University education ? "

He answered, as one so partial to me was sure to
answer ; that he had no sort of suspicion that I was
acting without deliberation, or without viewing the
matter as a whole ; but still he could not help saying

that he thought he saw a bias in me which he had not expected, and he would be truly glad to find himself mistaken. "Do you know," he said, "I am surprised to find that you, of all men in the world, should be taking the intellectual line, and should be advocating the professorial system. Surely it was once far otherwise; I thought our line used to be, that knowledge without principle was simply mischievous, and that Professors did but represent and promote that mischievous knowledge. This used to be our language: and, beyond all doubt, a great deal may be said in justification of it. What is heresy in ecclesiastical history but the action of personal influence against law and precedent? and what were such heterodox teachers as the Arian leaders in primitive times, or Abelard in the middle ages, but the eloquent and attractive masters of philosophical schools? And what again were Arius and Abelard but the forerunners of modern German professors, a set of clever charlatans, or subtle sophists, who aim at originality, show, and popularity, at the expense of truth? Such men are the *nucleus* of a system, if system it may be called, of which disorder is the outward manifestation, and scepticism the secret life. This you used to think; but now you tell us that demand and supply are all in all, and that supply must precede demand;—and that this is a University in a nutshell."

I laughed, and said he was unfair to me, and rather had not understood me at all. "We are neither of us theologians or metaphysicians," said I; "yet I suppose we know the difference between a direct cause and a *sine quâ non*, and between the essence of a thing and its integrity. Things are not content to be in fact just what we contemplate them in the abstract, and nothing more; they require something more than themselves, sometimes as necessary conditions of their being, some-times for their well-being. Breath is not part of man ; it comes to him from without ; it is merely the surround-ing air, inhaled, and then exhaled ; yet no one can live without breathing. Place an animal under an exhausted receiver, and it dies : yet the air does not enter into its definition. When then I say, that a Great School or University consists in the communication of knowledge, in lecturers and hearers, that is, in the Professorial system, you must not run away with the notion that I consider personal influence enough for its well-being. It is indeed its essence, but something more is necessary than barely to get on from day to day ; for its sure and comfortable existence we must look to law, rule, order ; to religion, from which law proceeds ; to the collegiate system, in which it is embodied ; and to endowments, by which it is protected and perpetuated. This is the part of the subject which my papers have not yet touched upon ; nor could they well treat of what comes second, till they had done justice to what comes first."

I thought that here he seemed disposed to interrupt me, so I interposed : " Now, please, let me bring out what I want to say, while I am full of it. I say then, that the personal influence of the teacher is able in some sort to dispense with an academical system, but that the system cannot in any sort dispense with personal in-fluence. With influence there is life, without it there is none ; if influence is deprived of its due position, it will not by those means be got rid of, it will only break out irregularly, dangerously. An academical system without the personal influence of teachers upon pupils, is an arctic winter ; it will create an ice-bound, petrified, cast-iron University, and nothing else. You will not call this any new notion of mine ; and you will not suspect, after what happened to me a long twenty-five years ago, that I can ever be induced to think otherwise. No! I have known a time in a great School of Letters, when things went on for the most part by mere routine, and form took the place of earnestness. I have experienced a state of things, in which teachers were cut off from the taught as by an insurmountable barrier; when neither party entered into the thoughts of the other; when each lived by and in itself; when the tutor was supposed to fulfil his duty, if he trotted on like a squirrel in his cage, if at a certain hour he was in a certain room, or in hall, or in chapel, as it might be; and the pupil did his duty too, if he was careful to meet his tutor in that same room, or hall, or chapel, at the same certain hour; and when neither the one nor the other dreamed of seeing each other out of lecture, out of chapel, out of academical gown. I have known places where a stiff manner, a pompous voice, coldness and condescension, were the teacher's attributes, and where he neither knew, nor wished to know, and avowed he did not wish to know, the private irregularities of the youths committed to his charge.

" This was the reign of Law without Influence, System without Personality. And then again, I have seen in this dreary state of things, as you yourself well know, while the many went their way and rejoiced in their liberty, how that such as were better disposed and aimed at higher things, looked to the right and to the left, as sheep without a shepherd, to find those who would exert that influence upon them which its legitimate owners made light of; and how, wherever they saw a little more profession of strictness and distinctness of creed, a little more intellect, principle, and devotion, than was ordinary, thither they went, poor youths, like

St. Anthony when he first turned to God, for counsel and encouragement; and how, as this feeling, without visible cause, mysteriously increased in the subjects of that seat of learning, a whole class of teachers gradually arose, unrecognised by its authorities, and rivals to the teachers whom it furnished, and gained the hearts and became the guides of the youthful generation, who found no sympathy were they had a claim for it. And then moreover, you recollect, as well as I, how, as time went on and that generation grew up and came into University office themselves, then, from the memory of their own past discomfort, they tried to mend matters, and to unite Rule and Influence together, which had been so long severed, and how they claimed from their pupils for themselves that personal attachment which in their own pupillage they were not invited to bestow; and then, how in consequence a struggle began between the dry old red-tapists, as in politics they are called, and—"

Here my friend, who had been unaccountably impatient for some time, fairly interrupted me. " It seems very rude," he said, "very inhospitable; it is against my interest; perhaps you will stay the night; but if you must go, go at once you must, or you will lose the train." An announcement like this turned the current of my thoughts, and I started up. In a few seconds we were walking, as briskly as elderly men walk, towards the garden entrance. Sorry was I to leave so abruptly so sweet a place, so old and so dear to me; sorry to have disturbed it with controversy instead of drinking in its calm. When we reached the lofty avenue, from which I entered, Richard shook my hand, and wished me God-speed,

" portâque emittit eburnâ."

CHAPTER VII.

ATHENIAN SCHOOLS:

INFLUENCE.

TAKING Influence and Law to be the two great principles of Government, it is plain that, historically speaking, Influence comes first, and then Law. Thus Orpheus preceded Lycurgus and Solon. Thus Deioces the Mede laid the foundations of his power in his personal reputation for justice, and then established it in the seven walls by which he surrounded himself in Ecbatana. First we have the "virum pietate gravem," whose word "rules the spirits and soothes the breasts" of the multitude;—or the warrior;—or the mythologist and bard;—then follow at length the dynasty and constitution. Such is the history of society: it begins in the poet, and ends in the policeman.

Universities are instances of the same course: they begin in Influence, they end in System. At first, whatever good they may have done, has been the work of persons, of personal exertions; of faith in persons, of personal attachments. Their Professors have been a sort of preachers and missionaries, and have not only taught, but have won over or inflamed their hearers. As time has gone on, it has been found out that personal influence does not last for ever; that individuals get past their work, that they die, that they cannot always be depended on, that they change; that, if they are to be the exponents of a University, it will have no abidance, no steadiness; that it will be great and small again, and will inspire no trust. Accordingly, system has of necessity been superadded to individual action; a University has been embodied in a constitution, it has exerted authority, it has been protected by rights and privileges, it has enforced discipline, it has developed itself into Colleges, and has admitted Monasteries into its territory. The details of this advance and consummation are of course different in different instances; each University has a career of its own; I have been stating the process in the logical, rather than in the historical order; but such it has been on the whole, whether in ancient or medieval times. Zeal began, power and wisdom completed: private enterprise came first, national or governmental recognition followed; first the Greek, then the Macedonian and Roman; the Athenian created, the Imperialist organized and consolidated. This is the subject I am going to enter upon to-day.

Now as to Athens, I have already shown what it did, and implied what it did not do; and I shall proceed to say something more about it. I have another reason for dwelling on the subject; it will lead me to direct attention to certain characteristics of Athenian opinion, which are not only to my immediate purpose, but will form an introduction to something I should like to say on a future occasion, if I could grasp my own thoughts, about the philosophical sentiments of the present age, their drift, and their bearing on a University. This is another matter; but I mention it because it is one out of several reasons which will set me on a course, in which I shall seem to be ranging very wide of my mark, while all the time I shall have a meaning in my wanderings.

Beginning then the subject very far back, I observe that the guide of life, implanted in our nature, discriminating right from wrong, and investing right with authority and sway, is our Conscience, which Revelation does but enlighten, strengthen, and refine. Coming from one and the same Author, these internal and external monitors of course recognize and bear witness to each other ; Nature warrants without anticipating the Supernatural, and the Supernatural completes without superseding Nature. Such is the divine order of things ; but man,— not being divine, nor over partial to so stern a reprover within his breast, yet seeing too the necessity of some rule or other, some common standard of conduct, if Society is to be kept together, and the children of Adam to be saved from setting up each for himself with every one else his foe, —as soon as he has secured for himself some little cultivation of intellect, looks about him how he can manage to dispense with Conscience, and find some other principle to do its work. The most plausible and obvious and ordinary of these expedients, is the Law of the State, human law; the more plausible and ordinary, because it really comes to us with a divine sanction, and necessarily has a place in every society or community of men. Accordingly it is very widely used instead of Conscience, as but a little experience of life will show us ; "the law says this ;" "would you have me go against the law ?" is considered an unanswerable argument in every case ; and, when the two come into collision, it follows of course that Conscience is to give way, and the Law to prevail.

Another substitute for Conscience is the rule of Expediency : Conscience is pronounced superannuated and retires on a pension, whenever a people is so far advanced in illumination, as to perceive that right and wrong can to a certain extent be measured and determined by the useful on the one hand, and by the hurtful on the other; according to the maxim, which embodies this principle, that " honesty is the best policy."

Another substitute of a more refined character is, the principle of Beauty :—it is maintained that the Beautiful and the Virtuous mean the same thing, and are convertible terms.   Accordingly Conscience is found out to be but slavish ; and a fine taste, an exquisite sense of the decorous, the graceful, and the appropriate, this is to be our true guide for ordering our mind and our conduct, and bringing the whole man into shape.   These are great sophisms, it is plain ; for, true though it be, that virtue is always expedient, always fair, it does not therefore follow that every thing which is expedient, and every thing which is fair, is virtuous.   A pestilence is an evil, yet may have its undeniable uses ; and war, " glorious war," is an evil, yet an army is a very beautiful object to look upon ; and what holds in these cases, may hold in others ; so that it is not very safe or logical to say that Utility and Beauty are guarantees for Virtue.

However, there are these three principles of conduct, which may be plausibly made use of in order to dispense with Conscience ; viz., Law, Expedience, and Propriety ; and (at length to come to our point) the Athenians chose the last of them, as became so exquisite a people, and professed to practise virtue on no inferior consideration, but simply because it was so praiseworthy, so noble, and so fair.   Not that they discarded Law, not that they had not an eye to their interest ; but they boasted that " grass-hoppers " like them, old of race and pure of blood, could be influenced in their conduct by nothing short of a fine and delicate taste, a sense of honour, and an elevated, aspiring spirit.   Their model man, like the pattern of chivalry, was a gentleman, καλοκἀγαθός ;—a word which has hardly its equivalent in the sterner language of Rome, where, on the contrary,

> Vir bonus est quis?
> Qui consulta patrum, qui leges juraque servat.

For the Romans deified Law, as the Athenians deified the Beautiful.

This being the state of the case, Athens was in truth a ready-made University. The present age, indeed, with that solidity of mind for which it is indebted to Christianity, and that practical character which has ever been the peculiarity of the West, would bargain that the True and Serviceable as well as the Beautiful should be made the aim of the Academic intellect and the business of a University ;—of course,—but the present age, and every age, will bargain for many things in its schools which Athens had not, when once we set about summing up her *desiderata.* Let us take her as she was, and I say, that a people so speculative, so imaginative, who throve upon mental activity as other races upon mental repose, and to whom it came as natural to think, as to a barbarian to smoke or to sleep, such a people were in a true sense born teachers, and merely to live among them was a cultivation of mind. Hence they took their place in this capacity forthwith, from the time that they emancipated themselves from the aristocratic families, with which their history opens. We talk of the "republic of letters," because thought is free, and minds of whatever rank in life are on a level. The Athenians felt that a democracy was but the political expression of an intellectual isonomy, and, when they had obtained it, and taken the Beautiful for their Sovereign, instead of king or tyrant, they came forth as the civilizers, not of Greece only, but of the European world.

A century had not passed from the expulsion of the Pisistratidæ, when Pericles was able to call Athens the " schoolmistress " of Greece. And ere it had well run out, the old Syracusan, who, upon her misfortunes in Sicily, pleaded in behalf of her citizens, conjured his fellow-citizens, " in that they had the gift of Reason," to have mercy upon those, who had opened their land, as " a common school," to all men ; and he asks, " To what foreign land will men betake themselves for liberal education, if Athens be destroyed ? " And the story is well known, when, in spite of his generous attempt, the Athenian prisoners were set to work in the stone-quarries, how that those who could recite passages from Euripides, found this accomplishment serve them instead of ransom, for their liberation. Such was Athens on the coast of the Ægean and in the Mediterranean ; and it was hardly more than the next generation, when her civilization was conveyed by means of the conquests of Alexander into the very heart of further Asia, and was the life of the Greek kingdom which he founded in Bactriana. She became the centre of a vast intellectual propagandism, and had in her hands the spell of a more wonderful influence than that semi-barbarous power which first conquered and then used her. Wherever the Macedonian phalanx held its ground, thither came a colony of her philosophers ; Asia Minor and Syria were covered with her schools, while in Alexandria her children, Theophrastus and Demetrius, became the life of the great literary undertakings which have immortalized the name of the Ptolemies.

Such was the effect of that peculiar democracy, in which Pericles glories in his celebrated Funeral Oration. It made Athens in the event politically weak, but it was her strength as an ecumenical teacher and civilizer. The love of the Beautiful will not conquer the world, but, like the voice of Orpheus, it may for a while carry it away captive. Such is that "divine Philosophy," in the poet's words,

> " Not harsh and crabbed, as dull fools suppose,
> But musical, as is Apollo's lute,
> And a perpetual feast of nectared sweets,
> Where no crude surfeit reigns."

The Athenians then exercised Influence by discarding Law. It was their boast that they had found out the art of living well and happily, without working for it. They professed to do right, not from servile feeling, not because they were obliged, not from fear of command, not from belief of the unseen, but because it was their nature, because it was so truly pleasant, because it was such a luxury to do it. Their political bond was good will and generous sentiment. They were loyal citizens, active, hardy, brave, munificent, from their very love of what was high, and because the virtuous was the enjoyable, and the enjoyable was the virtuous. They regulated themselves by music, and so danced through life.

Thus, according to Pericles, while, in private and personal matters, each Athenian was suffered to please himself, without any tyrannous public opinion to make him feel uncomfortable, the same freedom of will did but unite the people, one and all, in concerns of national interest, because obedience to the magistrates and the laws was with them a sort of passion, to shrink from dishonour an instinct, and to repress injustice an indulgence. They could be splendid in their feasts and spectacles without extravagance, because the crowds whom they attracted from abroad, repaid them for the outlay ; and such large hospitality did but cherish in them a frank, unsuspicious, and courageous spirit, which better protected them than a pile of state secrets and exclusive laws. Nor did this joyous mode of life relax them, as it might relax a less noble race, for they were warlike without effort, and expert without training, and rich in resource by the gift of nature, and, after their fill of pleasure, they were only more gallant in the field, and more patient and enduring on the march. They cultivated the fine arts with too much taste to be expensive, and they studied the sciences with too much point to become effeminate ; debate did not blunt their energy, nor foresight of danger chill their daring ; but, as their tragic poet expresses it, " the loves were the attendants upon wisdom, and had a share in the acts of every virtue."

Such was the Athenian according to his own account of himself, and very beautiful is the picture ; very original and attractive ; very suitable, certainly, to a personage, who was to be the world-wide Professor of the humanities and the philosophic Missionary of mankind. Suitable, if he could be just what I have been depicting him, and nothing besides ; but, alas ! when we attentively consider what the above conception was likely in fact to turn out, as soon as it came to be carried into execution, we shall feel no surprise, on passing from panegyric to experience, that he looks so different in history, from what he promised to be in the glowing periods of the orator. The case, as I have already remarked, is very simple : if beautifulness was all that was needed to make a thing right, then nothing graceful and pleasant could be wrong ; and, since there is no abstract idea but admits of being embellished and dressed up, and made pleasant and graceful, it followed as a matter of course that any thing whatever is permissible. One sees at once, that, taking men as they are, the love of the Beautiful would be nothing short of the love of the Sensual ; nor was the anticipation falsified by the event : for in Athens genius and voluptuousness ever went hand in hand, and their literature, as it has come down to us, is no sample or measure of their actual mode of living.

Their literature indeed is of that serene and severe beauty, which has ever been associated with the word "classical ; " and it is grave and profound enough for ancient Fathers to have considered it a preparation for the gospel; but we are concerned here, not with the writings, but with the social life of Athens. I have been speaking of her as a living body, as an intellectual home, as the pattern school of the Professorial system ; and we now see where the hitch lay. She was of far too fine and dainty a nature for the wear and tear of life ;—she needed to be " of sterner stuff," if she was to aspire to the charge of the young and inexperienced. Not all the zeal of the teacher and devotion of the pupil, the thirst of giving and receiving, the exuberance of demand and supply, will avail for a University, unless some provision is made for the maintenance of authority and of discipline, unless the terrors of the Law are added to the persuasives of the Beautiful. Influence was not enough without command. This too is the reason why Athens, with all her high gifts, was at fault, not only as a University, but as an Empire. She was proud, indeed, of her imperial sway, in the season of her power, and ambitious of its extension ; but, in matter of fact, she was as ill adapted to reign in the cities of the earth, as to rule in its schools. In this world no one rules by mere love ; if you are but amiable, you are no hero ; to be powerful, you must be strong, and to have dominion you must have a genius for organizing. Macedon and

Rome were, as in politics, so in literature, the necessary complement of Athens.

Yet there is something so winning in the idea of Athenian life, which Pericles sets before us, that, acknowledging, as, alas! I must acknowledge, that that life was inseparable from the gravest disorders, in the world as it is, and much more in the pagan world, and that at best it is only ephemeral, if attempted, still, since I am now going to bid farewell to Athens and her schools, I am not sorry to be able to pay her some sort of compliment in parting. I think, then, her great orators have put to her credit a beautiful idea, which, though not really fulfilled in her, has literally and unequivocally been realized within the territory of Christianity. I am not speaking of course of the genius of the Athenians, which was peculiar to themselves, nor of those manifold gifts in detail, which have made them the wonder of the world, but of that profession of philosophical democracy, so original and so refined in its idea, of that grace, freedom, nobleness, and liberality of daily life, of which Pericles, in his oration, is specially enamoured; and, with my tenderness, on the one hand, for Athens (little as I love the radical Greek character), and my devotion to a particular Catholic Institution on the other, I have ever thought I could trace a certain resemblance between Athens, as contrasted with Rome, and the Oratory of St. Philip, as viewed in contrast with the Religious Orders.

All the creations of Holy Church have their own excellence and do their own service; each is perfect in its kind, nor can any one be measured against another in the way of rivalry or antagonism. We may admire one of them without disparaging the rest; again, we may specify its characteristic gift, without implying thereby that it has not other gifts also. Whereas then, to take up the language which my friend Richard has put into my mouth, there are two great principles of action in human affairs, Influence and System, some ecclesiastical institutions are based upon System, and others upon Influence. Which are those which flourish and fulfil their mission by means of System? Evidently the Regular Bodies, as the very word "regular" implies; they are great, they are famous, they spread, they do exploits, in the strength of their Rule. They are of the nature of imperial states. Ancient Rome, for instance, had the talent of organization; and she formed a political framework to unite to herself and to each other the countries which she successively conquered. She sent out her legions all over the earth to secure and to govern it. She created establishments which were fitted to last for ever; she brought together a hundred nations into one, and she moulded Europe on a model, which it retains even now;—and this not by a sentiment or an imagination, but by wisdom of policy, and the iron hand of Law. Establishment is the very idea, which the name of Imperial Rome suggests. Athens, on the other hand, was as fertile, indeed, in schools, as Rome in military successes and political institutions; she was as metropolitan a city, and as frequented a capital, as Rome; she drew the world to her, she sent her literature into the world; but still men came and went, in and out, without constraint; and her preachers went to and fro, as they pleased; she sent out her missions by reason of her energy of intellect, and men came on pilgrimage to her from their love for philosophy.

Observe, I am all along directing attention, not to the mental gifts of Athens, which belonged to her nature, but to what is separable from her, her method and her instruments. I repeat, that, contrariwise to Rome, it was the method of Influence : it was the absence of rule, it was the action of personality, the intercourse of soul with soul, the play of mind upon mind, it was an admirable spontaneous force, which kept the schools of Athens going, and made the pulses of foreign intellects keep time with hers.

Now, I say, if there be an Institution in the Catholic Church, which in this point of view has caught the idea of this great heathen precursor of the Truth, and has made the idea Christian,—if it proceeds from one who has even gained for himself the title of the " Amabile Santo,"—who has placed the noblest aims before his children, yet withal the freest course ; who always drew them to their duty, instead of commanding, and brought them on to perform before they had yet promised ; who made it a man's praise that he " potuit transgredi, et non est transgressus, facere mala, et non fecit ; " who in his humility had no intention of forming any Congregation at all, but had formed it before he knew of it, from the beauty and the fascination of his own saintliness ; and then, when he was obliged to recognize it and put it into shape, shrank from the severity of the Regular, would have nothing to say to vows, and forbade propagation and dominion ; whose houses stand, like Greek colonies, independent of each other and complete in themselves ; whose subjects in those several houses are allowed, like Athenian citizens, freely to cultivate their respective gifts and to follow out their own mission ; whose one rule is Love, and whose own weapon Influence ;—I say, if all this is true of a certain Congregation in the Church, and if it so happens that that Congregation, in the person of one of its members, finds itself at the present moment in contact with the preparatory movements of

the establishment of a great University, then surely I
may trust, without fancifulness and without impertinence,
that there is a providential fitness discernible in the circumstance of the traditions of that Congregation flowing
in upon the first agitation of that design ; and, though
to frame, to organize, and to consolidate, be the imperial
gift of St. Dominic or St. Ignatius, and beyond his
range, yet a son of St. Philip Neri may aspire without
presumption to the preliminary task of breaking the
ground and clearing the foundations of the Future, of introducing the great idea into men's minds, and making
them understand it, and love it, and have hope in it, and
have faith in it, and show zeal for it ;—of bringing many
intellects to work together for it, and of teaching them to
understand each other, and bear with each other, and go on
together, not so much by rule, as by mutual kind feeling
and a common devotion,—after the conception and in
the spirit of that memorable people, who, though they
could bring nothing to perfection, were great (over and
above their supreme originality) in exciting a general interest, and in creating an elevated taste, in the various
subject-matters of art, science, and philosophy.

But here I am only in the middle of my subject, and
at the end of my paper ; so I must reserve the rest of
what I have to say for the next Chapter.

CHAPTER VIII.

MACEDONIAN AND ROMAN SCHOOLS :
DISCIPLINE.

LOOKING at Athens as the preacher and missionary of Letters, and as enlisting the whole Greek race in her work, who is not struck with admiration at the range and multiplicity of her operations ? At first, the Ionian and Æolian cities are the principal scene of her activity; but, if we look on a century or two, we shall find that she forms the intellect of the colonies of Sicily and Magna Græcia, has penetrated Italy, and is shedding the light of philosophy and awakening thought in the cities of Gaul by means of Marseilles, and along the coast of Africa by means of Cyrene. She has sailed up both sides of the Euxine, and deposited her literary wares where she stopped, as traders nowadays leave samples of foreign merchandize, or as war steamers land muskets and ammunition, or as agents for religious societies drop their tracts or scatter their versions. The whole of Asia Minor and Syria resounds with her teaching ; the barbarians of Parthia are quoting fragments of her tragedians ; Greek manners are introduced and perpetuated on the Hydaspes and Acesines ; Greek coins, lately come to light, are struck in the capital of Bactriana; and so charged is the moral atmosphere of the East with Greek civilization, that, down to this day, those tribes are said to show to most advantage, which can claim relation of place or kin with Greek colonies established there above two thousand years ago. But there is one city, which, though Greece and Athens have no longer any memorial in it, has in this point of view a claim, beyond the rest, upon our attention ; and that, not only from its Greek origin, and the memorable name which it bears, but because it introduces us to a new state of things, and is the record of an advance in the history of the education of the intellect ;—I mean, Alexandria.

Alexander, if we must call him a Greek, which the Greeks themselves would not permit, did that which no Greek had done before ; or rather, because he was no thorough Greek, though so nearly a Greek by descent and birthplace and by tastes, he was able, without sacrificing what Greece was, to show himself to be what Greece was not. The creator of a wide empire, he had talents for organization and administration, which were foreign to the Athenian mind, and which were absolutely necessary if its mission was to be carried out. The picture, which history presents of Alexander, is as beautiful as it is romantic. It is not only the history of a youth of twenty, pursuing conquests so vast, that at the end of a few years he had to weep that there was no second world to subjugate, but it is that of a beneficent prince, civilizing, as he went along, both by his political institutions and by his patronage of science. It is this union of an energetic devotion to letters with a genius for sovereignty, which places him in contrast both to Greek and Roman. Cæsar, with all his cultivation of mind, did not conquer in order to civilize, any more than Hannibal; he must add Augustus to himself, before he can be an Alexander. The royal pupil of Aristotle and Callisthenes started, where aspiring statesmen or generals end ; he professed to be more ambitious of a name for knowledge than for power, and he paid a graceful homage to the city of intellect by confessing, when he was in India, that he was doing his great acts to gain the immortal praise of the Athenians. The classic poets and philosophers were his recreation ; he preferred the contest of song to the palæstra ; of medicine he had more than a theoretical knowledge ; and his ear for music was so fine, that Dryden's celebrated Ode, legendary as may be its subject, only does justice to its sensitiveness. He was either expert in fostering, or quick in detecting, the literary tastes of those around him; and two of his generals have left behind them a literary fame. Eumenes and Ptolemy, after his death, engaged in the honourable rivalry, the one in Asia Minor, the other in Egypt, of investing the dynasties which they respectively founded, with the patronage of learning and of its professors.

Ptolemy, upon whom, on Alexander's death, devolved the kingdom of Egypt, supplies us with the first great instance of what may be called the establishment of Letters. He and Eumenes may be considered the first founders of public libraries. Some authors indeed allude to the Egyptian king, Osymanduas, and others point to Pisistratus, as having created a precedent for their imitation. It is difficult to say what these pretensions are exactly worth : or how far those personages are entitled to more than the merit of a conception, which obviously would occur to various minds before it was actually accomplished. There is more reason for referring it to Aristotle, who, from his relation to Alexander, may be considered as the head of the Macedonian literary movement, and whose books, together with those of his wealthy disciple, Theophrastus, ultimately came into the possession of the Ptolemies ; but Aristotle's idea, to whatever extent he realized it, was carried out by the two Macedonian dynasties with a magnificence of execution, which kings alone could project, and a succession of ages secure. For the first time, a great system was set on foot for collecting together in one, and handing down to posterity, the oracles of the world's wisdom In the reign of the second Ptolemy the number of volumes rescued from destruction, and housed in the Alexandrian Library, amounted to 100,000, as volumes were then formed ; in course of time it grew to 400,000 ; and a second collection was commenced, which at length rose to 300,000, making, with the former, a sum total of 700,000 volumes. During Cæsar's military defence of Alexandria, the former of these collections was unfortunately burned ; but, in compensation, the library received the 200,000 volumes of the rival collection of the kings of Pergamus, the gift of Antony to Cleopatra. After lasting nearly a thousand years, this noblest of dynastic monuments was deliberately burned, as all the world knows, by the Saracens, on their becoming masters of Alexandria.

A library, however, was only one of two great conceptions brought into execution by the first Ptolemy ; and as the first was the embalming of dead genius, so the second was the endowment of living. Here again the Egyptian priests may be said in a certain sense to have preceded him ; moreover, in Athens itself there had grown up a custom of maintaining in the Prytaneum at the public cost, or of pensioning, those who had deserved well of the state, nay, their children also. This had been the privilege, for instance, conferred on the family of the physician Hippocrates, for his medical services at the time of the plague ; yet I suppose the provision of a home or residence was never contemplated in its idea. But as regards literature itself, to receive money for teaching, was considered to degrade it to an illiberal purpose, as had been felt in the instance of the Sophists; even the Pythian prize for verse, though at first gold or silver, became nothing more than a crown of leaves, as soon as a sufficient competition was secured. Kings, indeed, might lavish precious gifts upon the philosophers or poets whom they kept about them ; but such practices did not proceed on rule or by engagement, nor imply any salary settled on the objects of their bounty. Ptolemy, however, prompted, or at least encouraged, by the cele- brated Demetrius of Phalerus, put into execution a plan for the formal endowment of literature and science. The fact indeed of the possession of an immense library seemed sufficient to render Alexandria a University; for what could be a greater attraction to the students of all lands, than the opportunity afforded them of intellectual converse, not only with the living, but with the dead, with all who had any where at any time thrown light upon any subject of inquiry ? But Ptolemy determined that his teachers of knowledge should be as stationary and as permanent as his books ; so, resolving to make Alexandria the seat of a *Studium Generale*, he founded a College for its domicile, and endowed that College with ample revenues.

Here, I consider, he did more than has been com- monly done, till modern times. It requires considerable knowledge of medieval Universities to be entitled to give an opinion; as regards Germany, for instance, or Poland, or Spain ; but, as far as I have a right to speak, such an en- dowment has been rare down to the sixteenth century, as well as before Ptolemy. The University of Toulouse, I think, was founded in a College ; so was Orleans ; so has been the Protestant University of Dublin ; other Universities have yearly salaries from the Government ; but even the University of Oxford to this day, viewed as a University, is a poor body. Its Professors have for the most part a scanty endowment and no house of residence ; and it subsists mainly on fees received from year to year from its members. Such too, I believe, is the case with the University of Cambridge. The University founded in Dublin in John the Twenty-second's time, fell for lack of funds. The University of Paris could not be very wealthy, even in the ninth century of its existence, or it would not have found it necessary to sell its beautiful Park or Pratum. As for ourselves at present, it is commonly understood, that we are starting with ample means already, while large contributions are still expected ; a sum equal perhaps to a third of what has already been collected is to be added to it from the United States ; as to Ireland herself, the overflowing, almost miraculous liberality of her poorest classes makes no anticipation of their prospective contributions extravagant. Well, any how, if money made a University, we might expect ours to last as long as the Ptolemies' ; and, I suppose, any one of us would be content that an institution, which he helped to found, should live through a thousand years.

But to return to the Alexandrian College. It was called the Museum,—a name since appropriated to another institution connected with the seats of science. Its situation affords an additional instance in corroboration of remarks I have already made upon the sites of Universities. There was a quarter of the city so distinct from the rest in Alexandria, that it is sometimes spoken of as a suburb. It was pleasantly situated on the water's edge, and had been set aside for ornamental buildings, and was traversed by groves of trees. Here stood the royal palace, here the theatre and amphitheatre ; here the gymnasia and stadium ; here the famous Serapeum. And here it was, close upon the Port, that Ptolemy placed his Library and College. As might be supposed, the building was worthy of its purpose; a noble portico stretched along its front, for exercise or conversation, and opened upon the public rooms devoted to disputations and lectures. A certain number of Professors were lodged within the precincts, and a handsome hall, or refectory, was provided for the common meal. The Prefect of the house was a priest, whose appointment lay with the government. Over the Library a dignified person presided, who, if his jurisdiction extended to the Museum also, might somewhat answer to a medieval or modern Chancellor; the first of these functionaries being the celebrated Athenian who had so much to do with the original design. As to the Professors, so liberal was their maintenance, that a philosopher of the very age of the first foundation called the place a " bread basket," or a " bird coop;" yet, in spite of accidental exceptions, so careful on the whole was their selection, that even six hundred years afterwards, Ammianus describes the Museum under the title of "the lasting abode of distinguished men." Philostratus, too, about a century before, calls it " a table gathering together celebrated men :" a phrase which merits attention, as testifying both to the high character of the Professors, and to the means by which they were secured. In some cases, at least, they were chosen by *concursus* or competition, in which the native Egyptians are said sometimes to have surpassed the Greeks. We read too of literary games or contests, apparently of the same nature. As time went on, new Colleges were added to the original Museum ; of which one was a foundation of the Emperor Claudius, and called after his name.

It cannot be thought that the high reputation of these

foundations would have been maintained, unless Ptolemy had looked beyond Egypt for occupants of his chairs; and indeed he got together the best men, wherever he could find them. On these he heaped wealth and privileges; and so complete was their naturalization in their adopted country, that they lost their usual surnames, drawn from their place of birth, and, instead of being called, for instance, Apion of Oasis, or Aristarchus of Samothracia, or Dionysius of Thrace, received each simply the title of "the Alexandrian." Thus Clement of Alexandria, the learned father of the Church, was a native of Athens.

A diversity of teachers secured an abundance of students. "Hither," says Cave, "as to a public emporium of polite literature, congregated, from every part of the world, youthful students, and attended the lectures in Grammar, Rhetoric, Poetry, Philosophy, Astronomy, Music, Medicine, and other arts and sciences;" and hence proceeded, as it would appear, the great Christian writers and doctors, Clement, whom I have just been mentioning, Origen, Anatolius, and Athanasius. St. Gregory Thaumaturgus, in the third century, may be added; he came across Asia Minor and Syria from Pontus, as to a place, says his namesake of Nyssa, "to which young men from all parts gathered together, who were applying themselves to philosophy."

As to the subjects taught in the Museum, Cave has already enumerated the principal; but he has not done justice to the peculiar character of the Alexandrian school. From the time that science got out of the hands of the pure Greeks, into those of a power which had a talent for administration, it became less theoretical, and bore more distinctly upon definite and tangible objects. The very conception of an endowment is a specimen of this change. Without yielding the palm of subtle speculation to the Greeks, philosophy assumed a more masculine and vigorous character. Dreamy theorists, indeed, they could also show in still higher perfection than Athens, where there was the guarantee of genius that abstract investigation would never become ridiculous. The Alexandrian Neo-platonists certainly have incurred the risk of this imputation; yet, Potamo, Ammonius, Plotinus, and Hierocles, who are to be numbered among them, with the addition perhaps of Proclus, in spite of the frivolousness and feebleness of their system, have a weight of character, taken together, which would do honour to any school. And the very circumstance that they originated a new philosophy is no ordinary distinction in the intellectual world : and that it was directly intended to be a rival and refutation of Christianity, while no great recommendation to it certainly in a religious judgment, marks the practical character of the Museum even amid its subtleties. So much for their philosophers : among their poets was Apollonius of Rhodes, whose poem on the Argonauts carries with it, in the very fact of its being still extant, the testimony of succeeding ages either to its merit, or to its antiquarian importance. Egyptian Antiquities were investigated, at least by the disciples of the Egyptian Manetho, fragments of whose history are considered to remain ; while Carthaginian and Etruscan had a place in the studies of the Claudian College. The Museum was celebrated, moreover, for its grammarians ; the work of Hephæstion *de Metris* still affords matter of thought to a living Professor of Oxford ; * and Aris-

---

* Dr. Gaisford, since dead. For the Alexandrian Grammarians, vid, Fabric. Bibl. Græc., t. vi., p. 353.

tarchus, like the Athenian Priscian, has almost become the nick-name for a critic.

Yet, eminent as is the Alexandrian school in these departments of science, its fame rests still more securely upon its proficiency in medicine and mathematics. Among its physicians is the celebrated Galen, who was attracted thither from Pergamus ; and we are told by a writer of the fourth century,* that in his time the very fact of a physician having studied at Alexandria, was an evidence of his science which superseded further testimonial. As to mathematics, it is sufficient to say, that, of four great ancient names, on whom the modern science is founded, three came from Alexandria. Archimedes indeed was a Syracusan ; but the Museum may boast of Apollonius of Perga, Diophantus, a native Alexandrian, and Euclid, whose country is unknown. Of these three, Euclid's services to Geometry are known, if not appreciated, by every school-boy ; Apollonius is the first writer on Conic Sections ; and Diophantus the first writer on Algebra. To these illustrious names, may be added, Eratosthenes of Cyrene, to whom astronomy has obligations so considerable ; Pappus ; Theon ; and Ptolemy, said to be of Pelusium, whose celebrated system, called after him the Ptolemaic, reigned in the schools till the time of Copernicus, and whose Geography, dealing with facts, not theories, is in repute still.

Such was the celebrated *Studium* or University of Alexandria ; for a while, in the course of the third and fourth centuries, it was subject to reverses, principally from war. The whole of the Bruchion, the quarter of the city in which it was situated, was given to the flames ; and, when Hilarion came to Alexandria, the

* Ammianus.

holy hermit, whose rule of life did not suffer him to
lodge in cities, took up his lodgment with a few solitaries among the ruins of its edifices. The schools,
however, and the library continued ; the library was
reserved for the Caliph Omar's famous judgment; as
to the schools, even as late as the twelfth century, the
Jew, Benjamin of Tudela, gives us a surprising report of
what he found in Alexandria. "Outside the city," he
says, a mode of speaking which agrees with what has
been above said about the locality of the Museum, "is
the Academy of Aristotle, Alexander's preceptor; a
handsome pile of buildings, which has twenty Colleges,
whither students betake themselves from all parts of
the world to learn his philosophy. The marble columns
divide one College from another."

Though the Roman schools have more direct bearing
on the subsequent rise of the medieval Universities, they
are not so exact an anticipation of its type, as the
Alexandrian Museum. They differ from the Museum,
as being for the most part, as it would appear, devoted
to the education of the very young, without any reference
to the advancement of science. No list of writers or
of discoveries, no local or historical authorities, can be
adduced, from the date of Augustus to that of Justinian,
to rival the fame of Alexandria ; we hear on the contrary much of the elements of knowledge, the Trivium
and Quadrivium ; and the Law of the Empire provided,
and the Theodosian Code has recorded, the discipline
necessary for the students. Teaching and learning was
a department of government ; and schools were set up
and professors endowed, just as soldiers were stationed
or courts opened, in every great city of the East and
West. In Rome itself the seat of education was placed

in the Capitol; ten chairs were appointed for Latin Grammar, ten for Greek; three for Latin Rhetoric, five for Greek; one, some say three, for Philosophy; two or four for Roman Law. Professorships of Medicine were afterwards added. Under Grammar (if St. Gregory's account of Athens in Roman times may be applied to the Roman schools generally), were included knowledge of language and metre, criticism, and history. Rome, as might be expected, and Carthage, were celebrated for their Latin teaching; Roman Law is said to have been taught in three cities only, Rome itself, Constantinople, and Berytus; but this probably was the restriction of a later age.

The study of grammar and geography was commenced at the age of twelve, and apparently at the private school, and was continued till the age of fourteen. Then the youths were sent to the public academy for oratory, philosophy, mathematics, and law. The course lasted five years; and, on entering on their twentieth year, their education was considered complete, and they were sent home. If they studied the law, they were allowed to stay, (for instance, in Berytus,) till their twenty-fifth year; a permission, indeed, which was extended in that city to the students in polite literature, or, as we should now say, in Arts.

The number of youths, who went up to Rome for the study of the Law, was considerable; chiefly from Africa and Gaul. Originally the Government had discouraged foreigners in repairing to the metropolis, from the dangers it naturally presented to youth; when their residence there became a necessary evil, it contented itself with imposing strict rules of discipline upon them. No youth could obtain admission into the Roman schools, without a certificate signed by the magistracy of his

province.   Next, he presented himself before the
Magister Censûs, an official who was in the department
of the Præfectus Urbis, and who, besides his ordinary
duties, acted as Rector of the Academy.   Next, his
name, city, age, and qualifications were entered in a
public register; and a specification, moreover, of the
studies he proposed to pursue, and of the lodging-house
where he proposed to reside.   He was amenable for his
conduct to the Censuales, as if they had been Proctors ;
and he was reminded that the eyes of the world were
upon him, that he had a character to maintain, and that
it was his duty to avoid clubs, of which the Government was jealous, riotous parties, and the public shows,
which were of daily occurrence and of most corrupting
nature.   If he was refractory and disgraced himself,
he was to be publicly flogged, and shipped off at once
to his country.   Those who acquitted themselves well,
were reported to the Government, and received public
appointments.   The Professors were under the same
jurisdiction as the students, and were sometimes made to
feel it.

Of the schools planted through the Empire, the most
considerable were the Gallic and the African, of which
the latter had no good reputation, while the Gallic
name stood especially high.   Marseilles, one of the
oldest of the Greek colonies, was the most celebrated
of the schools of Gaul for learning and discipline.   For
this reason, and from its position, it drew off numbers,
under the Empire, who otherwise would have repaired
to Athens.   It was here that Agricola received his education ; "a school," says his biographer, "in which
Greek politeness was happily blended and tempered
with provincial strictness."   The schools of Bourdeaux
and Autun also had a high name ; and Rheims received

the title of a new Athens. This appellation was also bestowed upon the school of Milan. Besides these countries, respectful mention is made of the schools of Britain. As to Spain, the colonies there established are even called, by one commentator on the Theodosian code, " literary colonies ; " a singular title when Rome is concerned; and, in fact, a considerable number of writers of reputation came from Spain. Lucan, the Senecas, Martial, perhaps Quintilian, Mela, Columella, and Hyginus, are its contribution in the course of a century.

It will be seen that the Roman schools, as little as Athens itself, answer to the precise idea of a modern University. The Roman schools were for boys, or, at least, *adolescentuli :* Agricola came to Marseilles when a child, " parvulus." On the other hand, a residence at Athens corresponded rather to seeing the world, as in touring and travelling, and was often delayed till the season of education was over. Cicero went thither, after his public career had begun, with a view to his health, as well as to his oratory. St. Basil had already studied at the schools of Cæsarea and Cappadocia. Sometimes young men on campaign, when quartered near Athens, took the opportunity of attending her schools. However, the case was the same with Rome so far as regards the departments of jurisprudence and general cultivation. We read both of Rusticus, the correspondent of St. Jerome, and of St. Germanus of Auxerre, coming to Rome, after attending the Gallic schools ;—the latter expressly in order to study the law ; the former, for the same general purpose as might take a student to Athens, to polish and perfect his style of conversation and writing.

All this suggests to us, what of course must ever be borne in mind, that while the necessities of human society and the nature of the case are guarantees to us that such Schools of general education will ever be in requisition, still they will be modified in detail by the circumstances, and marked by the peculiarities, of the age to which they severally belong.

CHAPTER IX.

DOWNFALL **AND** REFUGE OF ANCIENT CIVILIZATION.

THE LOMBARDS.

THERE never was, perhaps, in the history of this tumultuous world, prosperity so great, so far-spreading, so lasting, as that which began throughout the vast Empire of Rome, at the time when the Prince of Peace was born into it. Preternatural as was the tyranny of certain of the Cæsars, it did not reach the mass of the population; and the reigns of the Five good Emperors, who succeeded them, are proverbs of wise and gentle government. The sole great exception to this universal happiness was the cruel persecution of the Christians; the sufferings of a whole world fell and were concentrated on them, and the children of heaven were tormented, that the sons of men might enjoy their revel. Their Lord, while His shadow brought peace upon earth, foretold that in the event He came to send "not peace but a sword;" and that sword was first let loose upon His own people. "Judgment commenced with the House of God;" and though, as time went on, it left Jerusalem behind, and began to career round the world and sweep the nations as it travelled on, nevertheless, as if by some paradox of Providence, it seemed at first, that truth and wretchedness had "met together," and sin and prosperity had "kissed one another." The more the heathens enjoyed themselves, the more they scorned,

hated, and persecuted their true Light and true Peace.
They persecuted Him, for the very reason that they had
little else to do ; happy and haughty, they saw in Him
the sole drawback, the sole exception, the sole hinder-
ance, to a universal, a continual sunshine ; they called
Him "the enemy of the human race:" and they felt
themselves bound, by their loyalty to the glorious and
immortal memory of their forefathers, by their traditions
of state, and their duties towards their children, to
trample upon, and, if they could, to stifle that teaching, which was destined to be the life and mould of a
new world.

But our immediate subject here is, not Christianity,
but the world that passed away ; and before it passed, it
had, I say, a tranquillity great in proportion to its former
commotions. Ages of trouble terminated in two centuries of peace. The present crust of the earth is said
to be the result of a long war of elements, and to have
been made so beautiful, so various, so rich, and so useful,
by the discipline of revolutions, by earthquake and
lightning, by mountains of water and seas of fire ; and
so in like manner, it required the events of two thousand years, the multiform fortunes of tribes and populations, the rise and fall of kings, the mutual collision of
states, the spread of colonies, the vicissitudes and the
succession of conquests, and the gradual adjustment and
settlement of innumerous discordant ideas and interests,
to carry on the human race to unity, and to shape and
consolidate the great Roman Power.

And when once those unwieldy materials were welded
together into one mass, what human force could split
them up again ? what "hammer of the earth" could
shiver at a stroke a solidity which it had taken ages to
form ? Who can estimate the strength of a political

establishment, which has been the slow birth of time? and what establishment ever equalled pagan Rome? Hence has come the proverb, "Rome was not built in a day:" it was the portentous solidity of its power that forced the gazer back upon an exclamation, which was the relief of his astonishment, as being his solution of the prodigy. And, when at length it was built, Rome, so long in building, was "Eternal Rome:" it had been done once for all; its being was inconceivable beforehand, and its not being was inconceivable afterwards. It had been a miracle that it was brought to be; it would take a second miracle that it should cease to be. To remove it from its place was to cast a mountain into the sea. Look at the Palatine Hill, penetrated, traversed, cased with brickwork, till it appears a work of man, not of nature; run your eye along the cliffs from Ostia to Terracina, covered with the debris of masonry; gaze around the bay of Baiæ, whose rocks have been made to serve as the foundations and the walls of palaces; and in those mere remains, lasting to this day, you will have a type of the moral and political strength of the establishments of Rome. Think of the aqueducts making for the imperial city, for miles across the plain; think of the straight roads stretching off again from that one centre to the ends of the earth; consider the vast territory round about it strewn to this day with countless ruins; follow in your imagination its suburbs, extending along its roads, for as much, at least in some directions, as forty miles; and number up its continuous mass of population, amounting, as grave authors say, to almost six million; and answer the question, how was Rome ever to be got rid of? why was it not to progress? why was it not to progress for ever? where was that ancient civilization to end? Such were the questionings and anticipations of thoughtful minds, not specially proud or fond of Rome. "The world," says Tertullian, "has more of cultivation every day, and is better furnished than in times of old. All places are opened up now ; all are familiarly known ; all are scenes of business. Smiling farms have obliterated the notorious wilderness ; tillage has tamed the forest land; flocks have put to flight the beasts of prey. Sandy tracts are sown ; rocks are put into shape ; marshes are drained. There are more cities now, than there were cottages at one time. Islands are no longer wild ; the crag is no longer frightful ; everywhere there is a home, a population, a state, and a livelihood." Such was the prosperity, such the promise of progress and permanence, in which the Assyrian, the Persian, the Greek, the Macedonian conquests had terminated.

Education had gone through a similar course of difficulties, and had a place in the prosperous result. First, carried forth upon the wings of genius, and disseminated by the energy of individual minds, or by the colonizing missions of single cities, Knowledge was irregularly extended to and fro over the spacious regions, of which the Mediterranean is the common basin. Introduced, in course of time, to a more intimate alliance with political power, it received the means, at the date of Alexander and his successors, both of its cultivation and its propagation. It was formally recognized and endowed under the Ptolemies, and at length became a direct object of the solicitude of the government under the Cæsars. It was honoured and dispensed in every considerable city of the Empire ; it tempered the political administration of the conquering people ; it civilized the manners of a hundred barbarian conquests ; it gradually reconciled uncongenial, and associated distant countries, with each other; while it had ever ministered to the fine arts, it now proceeded to subserve the useful. It took in hand the reformation of the world's religion; it began to harmonize the legends of discordant worships; it purified the mythology by making it symbolical; it interpreted it, and gave it a moral, and explained away its idolatry. It began to develope a system of ethics, it framed a code of laws: what might not be expected of it, as time went on, were it not for that illiberal, unintelligible, fanatical, abominable sect of Galileans? If they were allowed to make play, and get power, what might not happen? There again Christians were in the way, as hateful to the philosopher, as to the statesman. Yet in truth it was not in this quarter that the peril of civilization lay: it lay in a very different direction, over against the Empire to the North and North-East, in a black cloud of inexhaustible barbarian populations: and when the storm mounted overhead and broke upon the earth, it was those scorned and detested Galileans, and none but they, the men-haters and God-despisers, who, returning good for evil, housed and lodged the scattered remnants of that old world's wisdom, which had so persecuted them, went forth valiantly to meet the savage destroyer, tamed him without arms, and became the founders of a new and higher civilization. Not a man in Europe now, who talks bravely against the Church, but owes it to the Church, that he can talk at all.

But what was to be the process, what the method, what the instruments, what the place, for sheltering the treasures of ancient intellect during the convulsion, of bridging over the abyss, and of linking the old world to the new? In spite of the consolidation of its power, Rome was to go, as all things human go, and vanish for

ever.   In the words of inspiration, "Great Babylon came
in remembrance before God, and every island fled away,
and the mountains were not found."   All the fury of the
elements was directed against it ; and, as a continual
dropping wears away the stone, so blow after blow, and
revolution after revolution, sufficed at last to heave up,
and hurl down, and smash into fragments, the noblest
earthly power that ever was.   First came the Goth, then
the Hun, and then the Lombard.   The Goth took possession, but he was of noble nature, and soon lost his
barbarism.   The Hun came next ; he was irreclaimable,
but did not stay.   The Lombard kept both his savage-
ness and his ground ; he appropriated to himself the
territory, not the civilization of Italy, fierce as the Hun,
and powerful as the Goth, the most tremendous scourge
of Heaven.   In his dark presence the poor remains of
Greek and Roman splendour died away, and the world
went more rapidly to ruin, material and moral, than it
was advancing from triumph to triumph in the time of
Tertullian.   Alas ! the change between Rome in the
hey-day of her pride, and in the agony of her judgment !
Tertullian writes while she is exalted ; Pope Gregory
when she is in humiliation.   He was delivering homilies
upon the Prophet Ezekiel, when the news came to Rome
of the advance of the Lombards upon the city, and in the
course of them he several times burst out into lamenta-
tions at the news of miseries, which eventually obliged
him to cut short his exposition.

"Sights and sounds of war," he says, "meet us on
every side.   The cities are destroyed ; the military
stations broken up ; the land devastated ; the earth
depopulated.   No one remains in the country ; scarcely
any inhabitants in the towns ; yet even the poor remains
of human kind are still smitten daily and without inter-

mission.   Before our eyes some are carried away captive,
some mutilated, some murdered.   She herself, who once
was mistress of the world, we behold how Rome fares :
worn down by manifold and incalculable distresses, the
bereavement of citizens, the attack of foes, the reiteration
of overthrows, where is her senate ?   where are her
people ?   We, the few survivors, are still the daily prey
of the sword and of other innumerable tribulations.
Where are they who in a former day revelled in her
glory ? where is their pomp, their pride, their frequent
and immoderate joy ?—youngsters, young men of the
world, congregated here from every quarter, where they
aimed at a secular advancement.   Now no one hastens
up to her for preferment ; and so it is with other cities
also ; some places are laid waste by pestilence, others
are depopulated by the sword, others are tormented by
famine, and others are swallowed up by earthquakes."

These words, far from being a rhetorical lament, are
but a meagre statement of some of the circumstances of
a desolation, in which the elements themselves, as St.
Gregory intimates, as well as the barbarians, took a
principal part.   In the dreadful age of that great Pope,
a plague spread from the lowlands of Egypt to the Indies
on the one hand, along Africa across to Spain on the
other, till, reversing its course, it reached the eastern
extremity of Europe.   For fifty-two years did it retain
possession of the infected atmosphere, and, in Constantinople, during three months, five thousand, and at
length ten thousand persons, are said to have died daily.
Many cities of the East were left without inhabitants ;
and in several districts of Italy there were no labourers
to gather either harvest or vintage.   A succession of
earthquakes accompanied for years this heavy calamity.
Constantinople was shaken for above forty days.   Two

hundred and fifty thousand persons are said to have
perished in the earthquake of Antioch, crowded, as the
city was, with strangers for the festival of the Ascension.
Berytus, the Eastern school of Roman jurisprudence,
called, from its literary and scientific importance, the eye
of Phœnicia, shared a similar fate. These, however,
were but local visitations. Cities are indeed the homes
of civilization, but the wide earth, with her hill and dale,
open plain and winding valley, is its refuge. The barbarian invaders, spreading over the country, like a flight
of locusts, did their best to destroy every fragment of
the old world, and every element of revival. Twenty-
nine public libraries had been founded at Rome ; but,
had these been destroyed, as in Antioch, or Berytus, by
earthquakes or by conflagration, yet a large aggregate
of books would have still survived. Such collections
had become a fashion and a luxury in the latter Empire,
and every colony and municipium, every larger temple,
every prætorium, the baths, and the private villas, had
their respective libraries. When the ruin swept across
the country, and these various libraries were destroyed,
then the patient monks had begun again, in their quiet
dwellings, to bring together, to arrange, to transcribe
and to catalogue ; but then again the new visitation of
the Lombards fell, and Monte Cassino, the famous
metropolis of the Benedictines, not to mention monasteries of lesser note, was sacked and destroyed.

Truly was Christianity revenged on that ancient civilization for the persecutions which it had inflicted on
Christianity. Man ceased from the earth, and his works
with him. The arts of life, architecture, engineering,
agriculture, were alike brought to nought. The waters
were let out over the face of the country ; arable and
pasture lands were drowned ; landmarks disappeared.

Pools and lakes intercepted the thoroughfares ; whole districts became pestilential marshes; the strong stream, or the abiding morass, sapped and obliterated the very site of cities. Here the mountain torrent cut a channel in the plain ; there it elevated ridges across it ; elsewhere it disengaged masses of rock and earth in its precipitous passage, and, hurrying them on, left them as islands in the midst of the flood. Forests overspread the land, in rivalry of the waters, and became the habitation of wild animals, of wolves, and even bears. The dwindled race of man lived in scattered huts of mud, where best they might avoid marauder, and pestilence, and inundation ; or clung together for mutual defence in cities, where wretched cottages, on the ruins of marble palaces, over-balanced the security of numbers by the frequency of conflagration.

In such a state of things, the very mention of education was a mockery, the very aim and effort to exist was occupation enough for mind and body. The heads of the Church bewailed a universal ignorance, which they could not remedy ; it was a great thing that schools remained sufficient for clerical education, and this education was only sufficient, as Pope Agatho informs us, to enable them to hand on the traditions of the Fathers, without scientific exposition or polemical defence. In that Pope's time, the great Council of Rome, in its letter to the Emperor of the East, who had asked for Episcopal legates of correct life and scientific knowledge of the Scriptures, made answer, that, if by science was meant knowledge of revealed truth, the demand could be supplied ; not, if more was required ; " since," continue the Fathers, " in these parts, the fury of our various heathen foes is ever breaking out, whether in conflicts, or in inroads and rapine. Hence our life is simply one of

anxiety of soul and labour of body ; of anxiety, because
we are in the midst of the heathen; of labour, because the
maintenance, which used to come to us as ecclesiastics,
is at an end ; so that faith is our only substance, to live
in its possession our highest glory, to die for it our
eternal gain." The very profession of the clergy is the
knowledge of letters : if even these lost it, would others
retain it in their miseries, to whom it was no duty ?
And what then was the hope and prospect of the world
in the generations which were to follow ?

"What is coming ? what is to be the end ?" Such was
the question, that weighed so heavily upon the august
line of Pontiffs, upon whom rested " the solicitude of all
the churches," and whose failure in vigilance and decision in that miserable time would had been the loss of
ancient learning, and the indefinite postponement of new
civilization. What could be done for art, science, and
philosophy, when towns had been burned up, and country
devastated ? In such distress, islands, or deserts, or the
mountain-top have commonly been the retreat, to which
in the last instance the hopes of humanity have been
conveyed. Thus the monks of the fourth century had
preserved the Catholic faith from the tyranny of Arianism
in the Egyptian desert ; and so the inhabitants of Lombardy had taken refuge from the Huns in the shallows
of the Adriatic ; so too just then the Christian Goths
were biding their time to revenge themselves on the
Saracens, in the mountains of Asturias. Where should
the Steward of the Household deposit the riches, which
his predecessors had inherited from Jew and heathen, the
things old as well as new, in an age, in which each succeeding century threatened them with woes worse than
the centuries which had gone before ! Pontiff after Pontiff
looked out from the ruins of the Imperial City which

were to be his ever-lasting, ever-restless throne, if per-
chance some place was to be found, more tranquil than
his own, where the hope of the future might be lodged.
They looked over the Earth, towards great cities and
far provinces, and whether it was Gregory, or Vitalian,
or Agatho, or Leo, their eyes had all been drawn in one
direction, and fixed upon one quarter for that purpose,—
not to the East, from which the light of knowledge had
arisen, not to the West, whether it had spread,—but to
the North.

High in the region of the North, beyond the just
limits of the Roman world, though partly included in
its range, so secluded and secure in their sea-encircled
domain, that they have been thought to be the fabulous
Hesperides, where heroes dwelt in peace, lay two sister
islands,—whose names and histories, warned by my
diminished space, I must reserve for another Chapter.

CHAPTER X.

THE TRADITION OF CIVILIZATION.

THE ISLES OF THE NORTH.

WHATEVER were the real causes of the downfall of the ancient civilization, its immediate instrument was the fury of the barbarian invasions, directed again and again against the institutions in which it was embodied. First one came down upon the devoted Empire, and then another ; and " that which the palmer worm left, the locust ate ; and what the locust left, the mildew destroyed." Nay, this succession of assaults did not merely carry on and finish the process of destruction, but rather undid the promise and actual prospect of recovery. In the interval between blow and blow, there was a direct tendency to a revival of what had been trodden down, and a restoration of what had been defaced ; and that, not only from any such reaction as might take place in the afflicted population itself, when the crisis was over, but from the incipient domestication of the conqueror, and the introduction of a new and vigorous element into the party and cause of civilization. The fierce soldier was vanquished by the captive of his sword and bow. The beauty of the southern climate, the richness of its productions, the material splendour of its cities, the majesty of the imperial organization, the spontaneous precision of a routine administration, the influence of religion upon the imagination and the affections, antiquity, rule, name, prescription, and territory, presented to him in visible and recognized forms,—in a word, the conservative power proper to establishments,— awed, overcame, and won, the sensitive and noble savage. "Order is heaven's first law," and bears upon it the impress of divinity; and it has an especial power over those minds which have had least experience of it. The Goth not only took pay, and sought refuge, from the Empire, but, still more, when, instead of dependent, he was lord and master, he found himself absorbed into and assimilated with the civilization, upon which he had violently thrust himself. Had he been left in possession, great revolutions certainly, but not dissolution, would have been the destiny of the social framework; and the tradition of science and of the arts of life would have been unbroken.

Thus, in the midst of the awful events which were then in progress, there were intervals of respite and of hope. The day of wrath seemed to be passing away; things began to look up, and the sun was on the point of coming out again. Statesmen, who watched the signs of the times, perhaps began to say, that at last they did think that the worst was over, and that there were good grounds for looking hopefully at the state of affairs. Adolphus, the successor of Alaric, took on himself the obligations of a Roman general, assumed the Roman dress, accepted the Emperor's sister in marriage, and opposed in arms the fiercer barbarians who had overrun Spain. The sons of Theodoric the Visigoth were taught Virgil and Roman Law in the schools of Gaul. Theodoric, the Ostrogoth, anxiously preserved the ancient monuments of Rome, and ornamented the cities of Italy with new edifices; he revived agriculture, promoted commerce, and patronized literature. But the

Goth was not to retain the booty which the Roman had been obliged to relinquish ; he had soon, in company with his former foe, to repel the Vandal, the Hun, or the Frank ; or, weakened from within, to yield to the younger assailants who were to succeed him.   Then the whole work of civilization had to begin again—if indeed there was to be a new begining ; or rather there was not life enough left in its poor remains, to vivify the fresh mass of barbarism which fell heavily upon it, or even to save itself from a final extinction.   As great Cæsar fell, not under one, but under twenty strokes ; so it was only by many a cleaving, many a shattering blow, " scalpri frequentis ictibus et tunsione plurimâ," that the existing fabric of the old world, to which Cæsar, more than any other, had given name and form, was battered down.   It was the accumulation, the reiteration of calamities, in every quarter and through a long period, by " the rain falling, and the floods coming, and the winds blowing and breaking upon that house," that it fell, "and great was the fall thereof."

The judgments of God were upon the earth, and " the clouds returned after the rain ;" and as a thunder cloud careers around the sky, and condenses suddenly here or there, and repeats its violence when it seems to have been spent, so was it with the descent of the North upon the South.   There was scarcely a province of the great Empire, but twice or thrice had to sustain attack, invasion, or occupation, from the barbarian.   Till the termination of the reign of the Antonines, for a hundred and fifty years, the long peace continued, which the Prince of Peace brought with Him ; then a fitful century of cloud and sunshine, hope and fear, suspense and affliction ; till at length, just at the middle of the third century of our era, the trumpet sounded, and the time of visitation began. The tremendous period opened in a great pestilence, and in an eruption of the barbarians both on the East and on the West. The pestilence lasted for fifteen years ; and, though sooner brought to an end than that more awful pestilence in St. Gregory's day with which the season of judgment closed, yet in that fifteen years it made its way into every region and city of the Empire. Many cities were emptied ; Rome at one time lost 5,000 inhabitants daily, Alexandria lost half her population. As to the barbarians, the Franks on the West descended into Spain ; and the Goths on the East into Asia Minor.

Asia Minor had had a long peace of three hundred years, a phenomenon almost solitary in the history of the world, and difficult for the imagination to realize. Its cities were unwalled; military duties had been abolished ; the taxes were employed on the public buildings and the well-being and enjoyments of life ; the face of the country was decorated and diversified by the long growth and development of vegetation, by the successive accumulations of art, and by the social memorials and reminiscences of nine peaceful generations. Its parks and groves, its palaces and temples, were removed further by a hundred years from the injuries of warfare, than England is now from the ravages of the Great Rebellion. Down came the Goths from Prussia, Poland, and the Crimea ; they sailed along the Euxine, ravaged Pontus and Bithynia, sacked the wealthy Trebizond and Chalcedon, and burned the imperial Nicæa and Nicomedia, and other great cities of the country ; then they fell upon Cyzicus and the cities on the coast, and finally demolished the famous temple of Diana at Ephesus, the wonder of the world. Then they passed over to the opposite continent, sacked Athens, and spread dismay and confusion, if not conflagration, through both upper Greece and the Peloponnese. At the same solemn era, the Franks fell upon Spain, and ran through the whole of it, destroying flourishing cities, whose ruins lay on the ground for centuries, nor stopped till they had crossed into Africa.

A second time, at a later date, was Spain laid waste by the Vandals and their confederates, with an utter desolation of its territory. Famine became so urgent, that human flesh was eaten ; pestilence so rampant, that the wild beasts multiplied among the works of man. Passing on to Africa, these detestable savages cut down the very fruit-trees, as they went, in the wantonness of their fury ; and the inhabitants of the plundered cities fled away with such property as they could save beyond sea. A new desolation of Africa took place two centuries later, when the Saracens passed in a contrary direction from Egypt into Spain.

Nor were the Greek and Asiatic provinces, more than the West, destined to be protected against successive invasions. Scarcely a hundred years had passed since the barbarian Goth had swept so fiercely each side of the Egean, when additional blows fell upon Europe and Asia from fresh enemies. In Asia the Huns poured down upon Cappadocia, Cilicia, and Syria, scaring the pagans of Antioch, and the monks and pilgrims of Palestine, silencing at once the melody of immodest song and of holy chant, till they came to the entrance of Egypt. In Europe it was the Goths again, who descended with fire and sword into Greece, desolated the rich lands of Phocis and Bœotia, destroyed Eleusis and its time-honoured superstitions, and passing into the Peloponnese, burned its cities and enslaved its population. About the same time the fertile and cultivated tract, stretching from the Euxine to the Adriatic, was devastated by the same reckless invaders, even to the destruction of the brute creation. Sixty years afterwards the same region was overrun by the still more terrible Huns, who sacked as many as seventy cities, and carried off their inhabitants. This double scourge, of which Alaric and Attila are the earlier and later representatives, travelled up the country northwards, and thence into Lombardy, pillaging, burning, exterminating, as it went along.

What Huns and Goths were to the South, such were Germans, Huns, and Franks to Gaul. That famous country, though in a less favoured climate, was as cultivated and happy as Asia Minor after its three centuries of peace. The banks of the Rhine are said to have been lined with villas and farms ; the schools of Marseilles, Autun, and Bordeaux, vied with those of the East, and even with that of Athens ; opulence had had its civilizing effect upon their manners, and familiarity with the Latin classics upon their native dialect. At the time that Alaric was carrying his ravages from Greece into Lombardy, the fierce Burgundians and other Germans, to the number of 200,000 fighting men, fell upon Gaul ; and, to use the words of a well-known historian, " the scene of peace and plenty was suddenly changed into a desert, and the prospect of the smoking ruins could alone distinguish the solitude of nature from the work of man." The barbarian torrent, sweeping away cities and inhabitants, spread from the banks of the Rhine to the Atlantic and the Pyrenees. Fifty years later a great portion of the same region was devastated with like excesses by the Huns ; and in the intervals between the two visitations, destructive inroads, or rather permanent occupations, were effected by the Franks and Burgundians.

As to Italy, with Rome as a centre, its multiplied

miseries are too familiarly known to require illustration. I need not enlarge upon the punishments inflicted on it by German, Goth, Vandal, Hun, and Byzantine, who in those same centuries overspread the country, or upon the destruction of cities, villas, monasteries, of every place where literature might be stored, or civilization transmitted to posterity. Barbarians occupied the broad lands of nobles and senators ; mercenary bands infested its roads, and tyrannized in its towns and its farms; even the useful arts were gradually forgotten, and the ruins of its cities sufficed for the remnant of its citizens. Such was the state of things, when, after the gleam of prosperity and hope which accompanied the Gothic ascendency, at length the Lombards came down in the age of St. Gregory, a more fatal foe than any before, to complete the desolation of the garden of Europe.

Encompassed then by such calamities, present and hereditary, through such a succession of centuries and in such a multitude of countries, where should the Roman Pontiff look for a refuge of learning, sacred and profane, when the waters were out all over the earth ? What place shall he prepare, what people shall he choose, with a view to a service, the more necessary in proportion as it was difficult ? I know where it must be ; doubtless in the old citadel of science, which hitherto had been safe from the spoiler,—in Alexandria. The city and country of the Ptolemies was inviolate as yet ; the Huns had stopped on its eastern, the Vandals at its western boundary ; and though Athens and Rhodes, Carthage and Madaura, Cordova and Lerida, Marseilles and Bordeaux, Rheims and Milan, had been overrun by the barbarian, yet the Museum, the greatest of all schools, and the Serapeum, the largest of all libraries, had recovered from the civil calamities which had pressed upon

them in a past century, and were now far away from the
Lombard, who was the terror of the age. It would have
been a plausible representation in the age of St. Gregory
and his immediate successors, if human wisdom had been
their rule of judgment, that they must strengthen their
alliance, since they could not with ambitious and
schismatical Constantinople, at least with Alexandria.
Yet to Alexandria they did not turn, and in fact, before
another century had passed, Alexandria itself was taken,
and her library burned by an enemy, more hostile to religion, if not to philosophy, even than the Lombard.
The instinctive sagacity of Popes, when troubled about
the prospective fortunes of the human race, did not look
for a place of refuge to a city which had done great
services to science and literature in its day, but was soon
to fall for ever.

The weak and contemptible things of this world are
destined to bring to nought and to confound the strong
and noble. High up in the North, above the continent
of Europe, lay two sister islands, ample in size, happy in
soil and climate, and beautiful in the face of the country.
Alas ! that the passions of man should alienate from one
another, those whom nature and religion had bound together ! So far away were they from foreign foes, that
one of them the barbarians had never reached, and though
a solitary wave of their invasion has passed over the
other, it was not destined to be followed by a second for
some centuries. In those days the larger of the two
was called Britannia, the lesser Hibernia. The latter
was then the seat of a flourishing Church, abounding
in the fruits of sanctity, learning, and zeal ; the former, at least its southern half, had formed part of the
Empire, had partaken both of its civilization and its
Christianity, but had lately been occupied, with the ex-

termination of its population, by the right wing of the great barbaric host which was overrunning Europe. I need but allude to a well-known history ; we all recollect how some of those pagan invaders of Britain were brought for sale in the slave-market at Rome, and were taken as samples of their brethren by the great Saint so often mentioned in these pages, who succeeded at length in buying the whole race, not for any human master, but for Christ.

St. Gregory, who, amid his troubles at Rome, engaged in this sacred negotiation, was led by his charity towards a particular people, to do a deed which resulted in surpassing benefits on the whole of Christendom. Here lay the answer to the prayers and questionings of himself and other holy Popes, and the solution of the great problem which had so anxiously perplexed their minds. The old world was to pass away, and its wealth and wisdom with it ; but these two islands were to be the storehouse of the past and the birthplace of the future. A divine purpose ruled his act of love towards the Anglo-Saxon race ; or, if we ascribe it to the special prescience proper to Popes, then we may say that it was inspired by what he saw already realized in his own day, in the instance of the remarkable people planted from time immemorial on the sister island. For the Celt, it cannot be denied, preceded the Anglo-Saxon, not only in his Christianity, but in his cultivation and custody of learning, religious and secular, and again in his special zeal for its propagation ; and St. Gregory, in evangelizing England, was but following the example of St. Celestine. Let us on this point hear the words of an historian, who has high claims on the respect and gratitude of this generation :—

" During the sixth and seventh centuries," says Dr.

Döllinger, " the Church of Ireland stood in the full beauty of its bloom. The spirit of the gospel operated amongst the people with a vigorous and vivifying power ; troops of holy men, from the highest to the lowest ranks of society, obeyed the counsel of Christ, and forsook all things, that they might follow Him. There was not a country of the world, during this period, which could boast of pious foundations or of religious communities equal to those that adorned this far distant island. Among the Irish, the doctrines of the Christian Religion were preserved pure and entire ; the names of heresy or of schism were not known to them ; and in the Bishop of Rome they acknowledged and venerated the Supreme Head of the Church on earth, and continued with him, and through him with the whole Church, in a never interrupted communion. The schools in the Irish cloisters were at this time the most celebrated in all the West ; and in addition to those which have been already mentioned, there flourished the Schools of St. Finian of Clonard, founded in 530, and those of Cataldus, founded in 640. Whilst almost the whole of Europe was desolated by war, peaceful Ireland, free from the invasions of external foes, opened to the lovers of learning and piety a wel- come asylum. The strangers, who visited the island, not only from the neighbouring shores of Britain, but also from the most remote nations of the Continent, received from the Irish people the most hospitable re- ception, a gratuitous entertainment, free instruction, and even the books that were necessary for their studies. Thus in the year 536, in the time of St Senanus, there arrived at Cork, from the Continent, fifteen monks, who were led thither by their desire to perfect themselves in the practices of an ascetic life under Irish directors, and to study the Sacred Scriptures in the school established near that city. At a later period, after the year 650, the Anglo-Saxons in particular passed over to Ireland in great numbers for the same laudable purposes. On the other hand, many holy and learned Irishmen left their own country to proclaim the faith, to establish or to reform monasteries in distant lands, and thus to become the benefactors of almost every nation in Europe."

Such was St. Columba, who is the Apostle of the Northern Picts in the sixth century; such St. Fridolin in the beginning of the same century, who, after long labours in France, established himself on the Rhine; such the far-famed Columbanus, who, at its end, was sent with twelve of his brethren to preach in France, Burgundy, Switzerland, and Lombardy, where he died. All these great acts and encouraging events had taken place, ere yet the Anglo-Saxon race was converted to the faith, or at least while it was still under education for its own part in extending it; and thus in the contemporary or previous labours of the Irish the Pope found an encouragement, as time went on, boldly to prosecute that conversion and education of the English, which was beginning with such good promise,—and not only in the labours of the Irish missionaries elsewhere, for in England itself, as the writer I have quoted intimates, they had already commenced their evangelical work.

"The foundation of many of the English sees," he says, "is due to Irishmen; the Northumbrian diocese was for many years governed by them, and the abbey of Lindisfarne, which was peopled by Irish monks and their Saxon disciples, spread far around it its all-blessing influence. These holy men served God and not the world; they possessed neither gold nor silver, and all that they received from the rich, passed through their hands into the hands of the poor. Kings and nobles visited them from time to time, only to pray in their churches, or to listen to their sermons ; and as long as they remained in the cloisters, they were content with the humble food of the brethren. Wherever one of these ecclesiastics or monks came, he was received by all with joy; and whenever he was seen journeying across the country, the people streamed around him to implore his benediction and to hearken to his words. The priests entered the villages only to preach or to administer the sacraments ; and so free were they from avarice, that it was only when compelled by the rich and noble, that they would accept lands for the erection of monasteries. Thus has Bede described the Irish bishops, priests, and monks of Northumbria, although so displeased with their custom of celebrating Easter. Many Anglo-Saxons passed over to Ireland, where they received a most hospitable reception in the monasteries and schools. In crowds, numerous as bees, as Aldhelm writes, the English went to Ireland, or the Irish visited England, where the Archbishop Theodore was surrounded by Irish scholars. Of the most celebrated Anglo-Saxon scholars and saints, many had studied in Ireland ; among these were St. Egbert, the author of the first Anglo-Saxon mission to the pagan continent, and the blessed Willebrod, the Apostle of the Frieslanders, who had resided twelve years in Ireland. From the same abode of virtue and of learning, came forth two English priests, both named Ewald, who in 690, went as messengers of the gospel to the German Saxons, and received from them the crown of martyrdom. An Irishman, Mailduf, founded, in the year 670, a school, which afterwards grew into the famed Abbey of Malmesbury ; among his scholars was St. Aldhelm, afterwards Abbot of Malmesbury, and first bishop of Sherburne or Salisbury, and whom, after two centuries, Alfred pronounced to be the best of the Anglo-Saxon poets."

The seventh and eighth centuries are the glory of the Anglo-Saxon Church, as are the sixth and seventh of the Irish. As the Irish missionaries travelled down through England, France, and Switzerland, to lower Italy, and attempted Germany at the peril of their lives, converting the barbarian, restoring the lapsed, encouraging the desolate, collecting the scattered, and founding churches, schools, and monasteries, as they went along ; so, amid the deep pagan woods of Germany and round about, the English Benedictine plied his axe and drove his plough, planted his rude dwelling and raised his rustic altar upon the ruins of idolatry, and then settling down as a colonist upon the soil, began to sing his chants and to copy his old volumes, and thus to lay the slow but sure foundations of the new civilization. Distinct, nay antagonistic, in character and talent, the one nation and the other, Irish and English, the one more resembling the Greek, the other the Roman, open from the first perhaps to jealousies as well as rivalries, they consecrated their respective gifts to the Almighty Giver, and, labouring together for the same great end, they obliterated whatever there was of human infirmity in their mutual intercourse by the merit of their common achievements. Each by turn could claim preëminence in the contest of sanctity and of learning. In the schools of science England has no name to rival Erigena in origin-ality, or St. Virgil in freedom of thought ; nor among its canonized women any saintly virgin to compare with St. Bridget ; nor, although it has 150 saints in its calendar, can it pretend to equal that Irish multitude which the Book of Life alone is large enough to contain. Nor can Ireland, on the other hand, boast of a doctor such as St. Bede, or of an Apostle equal to St. Boniface, or of a Martyr like St. Thomas,—or of so long a catalogue of royal devotees as that of the thirty male or female Saxons who in the course of two centuries resigned their crowns, or as the roll of twenty-three kings, and sixty queens and princes, who, between the seventh and the eleventh centuries, gained a place among the saints. Yet, after all, the Irish, whose brilliancy of genius has sometimes been considered, like the Greek, to augur fickleness and change, have managed to persevere to this day in the science of the saints, long after their ancient rivals have lost the gift of faith.

But I am not writing a history of the Church, nor of England or Ireland ; but tracing the fortunes of literature. When Charlemagne arose upon the Continent, the special mission of the two islands was at an end ; and accordingly Ragnor Lodbrog with his Danes then began his descents upon their coasts. Yet they were not superseded, till they had formally handed over the tradition of learning to the schools of France, and had written their immortal names on one and the same page of history. The Anglo-Saxon Alcuin was the first Rector, and the Irish Clement the second, of the Studium of Paris. In the same age the Irish John was sent to found the school of Pavia ; and, when the heretical Claudius of Turin exulted over the ignorance of the devastated Churches of the Continent, and called the Synod of Bishops, who summoned him, " a congregation of asses," it was no other than the Irish Dungall, a monk of St. Denis, who met and overthrew the presumptuous railer.

CHAPTER XI.

A CHARACTERISTIC OF THE POPES.

ST. GREGORY THE GREAT.

DETACHMENT, as we know from spiritual books, is a rare and high Christian virtue; a great Saint, St. Philip Neri, said that, if he had a dozen really detached men, he should be able to convert the world. To be detached is to be loosened from every tie which binds the soul to the earth, to be dependent on nothing sublunary, to lean on nothing temporal; it is to care simply nothing what other men choose to think or say of us, or do to us; to go about our own work, because it is our duty, as soldiers go to battle, without a care for the consequences; to account credit, honour, name, easy circumstances, comfort, human affections, just nothing at all, when any religious obligation involves the sacrifice of them. It is to be as reckless of all these goods of life on such occasions, as under ordinary circumstances we are lavish and wanton, if I must take an example, in our use of water,—or as we make a present of our words without grudging to friend or stranger,—or as we get rid of wasps or flies or gnats, which trouble us, without any sort of compunction, without hesitation before the act, and without a second thought after it.

Now this "detachment" is one of the special ecclesiastical virtues of the Popes. They are of all men most exposed to the temptation of secular connections; and,

as history tells us, they have been of all men least subject
to it. By their very office they are brought across every
form of earthly power ; for they have a mission to high
as well as low, and it is on the high, and not the low,
that their maintenance ordinarily depends. Cæsar
ministers to Christ ; the framework of society, itself a
divine ordinance, receives such important aid from the
sanction of religion, that it is its interest in turn to uphold
religion, and to enrich it with temporal gifts and honours.
Ordinarily speaking, then, the Roman Pontiffs owe their
exaltation to the secular power, and have a great stake
in its stability and prosperity. Under such circumstances,
any men but they would have had a strong leaning towards what is called "Conservatism;" and they have been,
and are, of course Conservatives in the right sense of
the word ; that is, they cannot bear anarchy, they think
revolution an evil, they pray for the peace of the world
and the prosperity of all Christian States, and they
effectively support the cause of order and good government. The name of Religion is but another name for
law on the one hand, freedom on the other ; and at this
very time, who are its professed enemies, but Socialists,
Red Republicans, Anarchists, and Rebels ? But a Conservative, in the political sense of the word, commonly
signifies something else, which the Pope never is, and
cannot be. It means a man who is at the top of the tree,
and knows it, and means never to come down, whatever
it may cost him to keep his place there. It means a
man who upholds government and society and the existing state of things,—not because it exists,—not because
it is good and desirable, because it is established, because it
is a benefit to the population, because it is full of promise
for the future,—but rather because he himself is well off
in consequence of it, and because to take care of number

one is his main political principle. It means a man who defends religion, not for religion's sake, but for the sake of its accidents and externals ; and in this sense Conservative a Pope can never be, without a simple betrayal of the dispensation committed to him. Hence at this very moment the extreme violence against the Holy See, of the British legislature and constituency and their newspapers and other organs, mainly because it will not identify the cause of civil government with its own, because, while it ever benefits this world, it ever contemplates the world unseen.

So much, however, is intelligible enough ; but there is a more subtle form of Conservatism, by which ecclesiastical persons are much more likely to be tempted and overcome, and to which also the Popes are shown in history to be superior. Temporal possessions and natural gifts may rightly be dedicated to the service of religion; however, since they do not lose their old nature by being invested by a new mission or quality, they still possess the pabulum of temptation, and may be fatal to ecclesiastical "detachment." To prefer the establishment of religion to its purity, is Conservatism, though in a plausible garb. It was once of no uncommon occurrence for saintly Bishops, in the time of famine or war, to break up the Church plate and sell it, in order to relieve the hungry or to redeem the captives by the sums which it brought them. Now this proceeding was not unfrequently urged against them in their day as some great offence; but the Church has always justified them. Here we see, as in a typical instance, both the wrong Conservatism, of which I am speaking, and its righteous repudiation. This fault is an over-attachment to the ecclesiastical establishment, as such ;—to the seats of its power, to its holy places, its sanctuaries, churches, and palaces,

—to its various national hierarchies, with their several prescriptions, privileges, and possessions,—to traditional lines of policy, precedent, and discipline,—to rules and customs of long standing. But a great Pontiff must be detached from everything save the deposit of faith, the tradition of the Apostles, and the vital principles of the divine polity. He may use, he may uphold, he may and will be very slow to part with, a hundred things which have grown up, or taken shelter, or are stored, under the shadow of the Church; but, at bottom, and after all, he will be simply detached from pomp and etiquette, secular rank, secular learning, schools and libraries, Basilicas and Gothic cathedrals, old ways, old alliances, and old friends. He will be rightly jealous of their loss, but still he will "know nothing but" Him whose Vicar he is; he will not stake his fortunes, he will not rest his cause, upon any one else :—this is what he will do, and what he will not do, as in fact the great Popes of history have shown, in their own particular instances, on so many and various occasions.

Take the early Martyr-Popes, or the Gregories and the Leos; whether they were rich or poor, in power or in persecution, they were simply detached from every earthly thing save the Rock of Peter. This was their adamantine foundation, their starting-point in every enterprise, their refuge in every calamity, the point of leverage by which they moved the world. Secure in this, they have let other things come and go, as they would; or have deliberately made light of what they had, in order that they might gain what they had not. They have known, in the fulness of an heroic faith, that, while they were true to themselves and to their divinely appointed position, they could not but "inherit the earth," and that, if they lost ground here, it was only to make progress elsewhere. Old men usually get fond of old habits; they cannot imagine, understand, relish any thing to which they are not accustomed. The Popes have been old men; but, wonderful to say, they have never been slow to venture out upon a new line, when it was necessary, and had ever been looking about, sounding, exploring, taking observations, reconnoitring, attempting, even when there was no immediate reason why they should not let well alone, as the world would say, or even when they were hampered with difficulties at their door so great, that you would think that they had no time or thought to spare for anything in the distance. It is but a few years ago that a man of eighty, of humble origin, the most Conservative of Popes, as he was considered, with disaffection and sedition upheaving his throne, was found to be planning missions for the interior of Africa, and, when a moment's opportunity was given him, made the most autocratical of Emperors, the very hope of Conservatives, the very terror of Catholics, quail beneath his glance. And, thus independent of times and places, the Popes have never found any difficulty, when the proper moment came, of following out a new and daring line of policy (as their astonished foes have called it), of leaving the old world to shift for itself and to disappear from the scene in its due season, and of fastening on and establishing themselves in the new.

I am led to this line of thought by St. Gregory's behaviour to the Anglo-Saxon race, on the break-up of the old civilization. I am not mentioning our people for their own sake, but because they furnish an instance of that remarkable trait in the character of Popes, of which I have been speaking. One would have thought that in the age of St. Gregory, a Pope had enough to do in living on from day to day, without troubling himself about the future; that, with the Lombard at his doors, he would not have had spirit to set about converting the English; and that, if he was anxious about the preservation of learning, he would have looked elsewhere than to the Isles of the North, for its refuge in the evil day. Why, I repeat, was it not easier, safer, and more feasible for him to have made much of the prosperous, secure, and long established schools of Alexandria, when the enemy went about him plundering and burning? He was not indeed on the best terms with Constantinople; Antioch was exposed to other enemies, and had suffered from them already; but Alexandria was not only learned and protected, but was a special ally of the Holy See; yet Alexandria was put aside for England and Ireland.

With what pertinacity of zeal does Gregory send his missionaries to England! with what an appetite he waits for the tidings of their progress! with what a relish he dwells over the good news, when they are able to send it! He wrote back to Augustine in words of triumph:—"'Gloria in excelsis Deo,'" he says, "'et in terrâ pax hominibus bonæ voluntatis!' for the Grain of corn died and was buried in the earth, that It might reign with a great company in Heaven,—by whose death we live, by whose weakness we are strengthened, by whose sufferings we escape suffering, by whose love we are seeking in Britain brothers whom we know not of, by whose gift we find those whom, not knowing, we were seeking. Who can describe the joy, which was caused in the hearts of all the faithful here, on the news that the English nation, by the operation of the grace of the Omnipotent God, and by your labours, my brother, had been rescued from the shades of error and overspread with the light of holy faith! If on one penitent there is great joy in heaven, what, think we, does it become, when a whole people has turned from its error, and has betaken itself to faith, and condemned the evil it has done by repenting of the doing! Wherefore in this joy of Heaven and Angels, let me say once more the very Angels' words, ' Gloria in excelsis Deo, et in terrâ pax hominibus bonæ voluntatis.'"

What were these outer barbarians to Gregory? how could they relieve him or profit him? What compensation could they make for what the Church was then losing, or might lose in future? Yet he corresponds with their king and queen, urges them to complete what they had so happily begun, reminds Bertha of St. Helena, and what St. Helena did for the Romans, and Ethelbert, of the great Constantine; informs them of the satisfaction which their conversion had given to the Imperial Court at Constantinople, and sends them sacred presents from the Apostle Peter. Nay he cannot keep from talking of these savages, apropos of anything whatever, for they have been running in his head from the day he first saw them in the slave market; and he makes the learned Church of Alexandria the special partner of his joy upon this contemptible victory. The Patriarch Eulogius had been telling him of his own success in reclaiming the heretics of Alexandria, and he sends him a piece of good news in return:—" As I am well aware," he says, " that in the midst of your own good deeds, you rejoice in those of others, I will repay you for the kindness of your tidings by telling you something of the same sort." And then he goes on to speak of the conversion of the English, " who are situated in a corner of the world," as if their gain was comparable to that of the educated and wealthy persons whom Eulogius had been reconciling to the Church. Nay, lest he should take too much credit for his own success, and grow vain upon it, he attributes it to the prayers of the Alexandrians, or at least of their Bishop, all that way off, as if the Angles and Jutes were anything at all to the city of the Ptolemies! " On Christmas Day," he says, " more than 10,000 of them were baptized. I tell you of it, that you may know, that, while your words avail for your own people, your prayers avail for the ends of the earth. For you are by prayer where you are not, while you manifest yourself by holy labours where you are."

Time went on, and the Popes showed less and less disposition to cling to past associations, or to confide in existing establishments, or to embarrass themselves in political engagements. When they were in trouble, their old friends could not, or would not, help them. Rome was almost deserted ; no throng of pilgrims mounted to the threshold of the Apostles ; no students flocked to the schools. The Pope sat in the Lateran desolate, till at length news was brought him that one foreigner had made his appearance. Whence did he come ? from the north ; from beyond the sea ; he was one of those barbarians whom his Holiness's predecessor, Gregory of blessed memory, had converted. The pilgrim came, and he went. An interval, and then, I think, a second pilgrim-student came : and who was he ? Why, he was an Englishman too. A fact to remember ! one of these young barbarians is worth a thousand of those time-servers of Constantinople. Our predecessor must have acted under some special guidance, when, at the beginning of this century, he set his heart upon the worshippers of Thor and Woden ! So, when a vacancy occurs in the see of Canterbury, Pope Vitalian determines to place in it a man of his own choosing, one whom so faithful a people deserves. The Irish, says the Pope, have done much for England, but teachers it still needs. Moreover, local teaching, even the best, and though saints be its organs, is apt to have something in it of local flavour, and needs from time to time to be refreshed from the founts of apostolical tradition. We will pick out, says he, the best specimens of learning and science, which the length and breadth of southern Christendom can furnish, and send them thither, uniting the excellence of different lands, under the immediate sanction of Rome. In this eclecticism, he did but follow St. Gregory himself, who, when Augustine represented to him, that, while faith was one, customs were so various, made answer, "I wish that, wherever you find anything especially pleasing to Almighty God, whether in the Roman, or Gallic, or any other Church, you would be at pains to select it, and introduce it into the English Church, as yet new in the faith."

This line of proceeding in ecclesiastical matters was carried on by Vitalian into the province of learning. The Greek colonies of Syria and Asia Minor, and the Roman settlements upon the African coast, had been, almost from their first formation, flourishing schools of education; and now that they were perishing under the barbarism of the Saracens, they were abandoned, by such professors and students as remained, for the cities of Italy. In a convent near Naples lived Adrian, an African; at Rome there was a monk, named Theodore, from Tarsus in Cilicia; both of them were distinguished for their classical, as well as their ecclesiastical attainments; and while Theodore had been educated in Greek usages, Adrian represented the more congenial and suitable traditions of the West. Of these two, Theodore, at the age of sixty-six, was made Primate of England, while Adrian was placed at the head of the monastery of Canterbury. Passing through France, in their way to their post of duty, they delayed there a while at the command of the Pope, to accustom themselves to the manners of the North ; and at length they made their appearance in England, with a collection of books, Greek classics, and Gregorian chants, and what-- ever other subjects of study may be considered to fill up the interval between those two. They then proceeded to found schools of secular, as well as of sacred learning throughout the south of the island ; and we are assured by St. Bede, that many of their scholars were as well acqainted with Latin and Greek, as with their native tongue. One of these schools in Wiltshire, as the legend goes, was, on that account, called "Greeklade," since corrupted into Cricklade, and, migrating afterwards to Oxford, was one of the first elements of its University. Meanwhile, one of those Saxon pilgrims, who had been so busy at Rome, having paid, it is said, as many as five visits to the Apostles, went up to the north of the country. Before the coming of the two foreign teachers, Benedict Biscop had been Abbot of Canterbury ; but, making way for Adrian, he took himself and his valuable library, the fruit of his travels, to Wearmouth in Northumberland, where he founded a Church and monastery.

These details are not out of place in the history of Universities ; but I introduce them here as illustrating a point, much to be remarked, in the character of the Popes. It is a common observation of Protestants, that, curiously enough, the Holy See is weakest at home when it is strongest abroad, and they derive some consolation to themselves, I do not know what, from the fact. So it is ; this weakness is an alleviation of the annoyance which they feel at the sight of a world suc-

cumbing to the See of Peter.   They say, that after all, if
the world has its mortifications, Peter, on the other hand,
has his discomforts too.   True, the gates of hell do not
prevail against him, but then he is driven about from
place to place, thrown into prison, and, if he escapes the
sword of Herod, it is only that Nero may inflict upon
him the more cruel death of crucifixion.   What then is
Peter's but a hollow power, which profits the possessor
nothing, though it be ecumenical?   Does it secure him
health, strength, wealth, comfort, ease, that he is revered
by millions whom he never saw?   He inherits the earth,
but is not certain of a roof to sleep under, or a grave
to be buried in.   How is he better off, because his name
is mentioned in Mass in the Brazils, and his briefs are
read in the Churches of Cochin China?

   This taunt does but supply a boast to the Catholic,
and has a moral for the philosopher.   Certainly Popes
are unlike any other old and infirm men that ever were.
To clutch at what is within their reach, to keep tight
hold of what they have, to believe what they see, to care
that things should last their own time, to let posterity
shift for itself, to hate disturbance and turmoil, to com-
pound for present peace, to be sceptical about improve-
ments, to be averse to new plans, in a word, to live in
sense, not in imagination, is the characterstic of old
statesmen, old lawyers, and old traders.   They cannot
throw their minds into new ideas; they cannot realize
the views of others; they cannot move out of their life-
long position, nor advance one inch towards any other.
Were such a person,—sound, safe, sensible, sagacious,
experienced,—at the elbow of Pope Gregory, or his successors of the seventh century, he would have advised
him to fall back upon Constantinople, to come to an
understanding with the Imperial Court, to link his

fortunes with those of an effete civilization, and to allow the encroachments of an ambitious hierarchy; as to Franks, and Frisons, and Westphalians, and Saxons, and Burgundians, and Visigoths, and Scots, to leave them to themselves. I need not take an imaginary instance; not many years have passed since a *Nuncio* of the Holy See passed through England in his way from Portugal to Rome, and had an interview with a great warrior now no more, a man of preternatural sagacity in his own sphere of thought,—which was not Catholic and divine. When the ecclesiastic in question asked the great man's advice what the then Pope's policy should be, the Duke abruptly replied, "Let him catch hold of the coat-tail of Austria, and hang on as hard as he can." Yes, and the able statesmen of each age would have said the same to Gregory the First, to the Second, the Third, and the Seventh, as well as to Gregory the Sixteenth,—to Julius, Silverian, and Martin; they would have counselled the Vicar of Christ a safe and pleasant course, "fallentis semita vitæ," which would have ended in some uninhabitable desert, or some steep precipice, far from the haunts of man.

When Pius the Ninth, foiled in his attempt to better the civil condition of his states, from the worthlessness both of his materials and his instruments, was a fugitive and exile at Gaeta, the Protestant public jeered and mocked at him, as one whose career was over and whose candle was put out. Yet he has but supplied a fresh and the latest instance, later there cannot be, of the heroic detachment of Popes, and has carried down the tradition of St. Peter into the age of railroads and newspapers. But we are entering upon a new part of the subject, which our present limits will not admit, and which we cannot perhaps treat without freedom.

CHAPTER XII.

MORAL OF THAT CHARACTERISTIC OF THE POPES.
PIUS THE NINTH.

A GREAT personage, within the last fifteen years, sent his advice to the Pope "to make sure of the coat-tail of Austria, and hold on." Austria is a great and religious power; she inherits the prerogatives of the German Empire and the titles of the Cæsars. There must ever be relations of a very peculiar kind between the Holy See and the Holy Roman Empire. Nevertheless, when the time came for taking advantage of his advice, the Pope did just the reverse. He made light of this master of political wisdom, and showed his independence of Austria;—not that he did not honour Austria, but that he honoured the Rock of Peter more. And what has been the consequence? he has simply gained by his fidelity to his position. Austria has been far more truly the friend and protector, the child and servant of the Pope than before; she has repealed the Josephine statutes, so injurious to the Church, and has opened her territories to the full religious influences of the Holy See. Here is an instance of what I have called "ecclesiastical detachment," and of its working.

Again, a revolution breaks out in Europe, and a deep scheme is laid to mix up the Pope in secular politics of a contrary character. He is to be the head of Italy, to range himself against the sovereigns of Europe, and to

carry all things before him in the name of Religion.
He steadily refuses to accept the insidious proposal;
and at length he is driven out of his dominions, because,
while he would ameliorate their condition, he would do
so as a Father and a Prince, and not as the tool of a
conspiracy. However, not many months pass, and the
party of disorder is defeated, and he goes back to Rome
again. Rome is his place; but it is little to him
whether he is there or away, compared with the duty of
fidelity to his Trust.

Once more, the power which restores him to his
country, presumes; and insists upon his modelling his
temporal polity upon the unecclesiastical principles of a
foreign code. France, too, as Austria, is a great Catholic
power; the eldest-born of the Church; the representative of the coming civilization, as Austria is the heir of
the past; but France was not likely to gain for the
Code of a dead Emperor, what that Emperor, in the
plenitude of his living genius and authority, could not
compass for it. The Pope refuses to subject himself to
France, as he had refused to subject himself to Austria;
and what is the consequence? It is the old story;
a new Emperor arises, with the name, and without the
religious shortsightedness, of his great predecessor. He
has the wisdom to run a race with Austria in doing
honour to the Church, and France professes Catholicity
with an ardour unknown to her since the reign of Louis
the Fourteenth.

These are times of peculiar difficulty and delicacy for
the Church. It is not as in the middle ages, or as in
the ante-Nicene period, when right and wrong were
boldly marked out, and there was a broad line between
them, and little chance of mistaking one for the other.
In such times detachment was another name for faith;

it was scarcely a virtue, substantive and *sui generis ;* for attachment to any temporal possession or advantage then was practically nothing else than apostasy. Things are otherwise now ; it has not, therefore, fallen to the lot of many Popes, to have such opportunities as Pius the Ninth, of resisting temptation, of resigning himself to the political weakness incident to the Holy See, of falling back calmly upon its traditionary principles, of rejecting the arguments for innovating upon its true position, and in consequence of attaining so rapid a triumph after deplorable reverses. When Pius was at Gaeta and Portici, the world laughed on hearing that he was giving his attention to the theological bearings of the doctrine of the Immaculate Conception. Little fancying what various subject-matters fall all at once under a Pope's contemplation, and are successively carried out into effect, as circumstances require ; little dreaming of the intimate connexion of these matters with each other, even when they seem most heterogeneous ; or that a belief touching the Blessed Virgin might have any influence upon the fortunes of the Holy See ; the wise men of the day concluded from the Pope's Encyclical about that doctrine, that he had, what they called, given up politics in disgust, and had become a harmless devotee or a trifling school-divine. But soon they heard of other acts of the Holy Father ; they heard of his interposition in the East ; of his success in Spain· of his vigilant eye directed towards Sardinia and Switzerland in his own neighbourhood, and towards North and South America in another hemisphere ; of his preachers spreading through Germany ; of his wonderful triumphs, already noticed, in Austria and France ; of his children rising as if out of the very earth in England ; and of their increasing moral strength in Ireland, in proportion to her past extraordinary sufferings ; of the hierarchies of England and Holland, and of the struggle going forward on the Rhine ; and then they exchanged contempt for astonishment and indignation, saying that it was intoler-able that a potentate who could not keep his own, and whose ease and comfort at home were not worth a month's purchase, should be so blind to his own interests as to busy himself with the fortunes of Religion at the ends of the earth.

And an additional feeling arose, which it is more to our purpose to dwell upon. They were not only angry, but they began to fear. It may strike one at first with surprise, that, in the middle of the nineteenth century, in an age of professed light and liberality, so determined a spirit of persecution should have arisen, as we expe-rience it, in these countries, against the professors of the ancient faith. Catholics have been startled, irritated, and depressed, at this unexpected occurrence ; they have been frightened, and have wished to retrace their steps ; but after all, far from suggesting matter for alarm or despondency, it is nothing more or less than a confession on the part of our adversaries, how strong we are, and how great our promise. It is the expression of their profound misgiving that the Religion which existed long before theirs, is destined to live after it. This is no mere deduction from their acts ; it is their own avowal. They have seen that Protestantism was all but extinct abroad ; they have confessed that its last refuge and for-tress was in England ; they have proclaimed aloud, that, if England was supine at this moment, Protestantism was gone. Twenty years ago England could afford, as much in contempt as in generosity, to grant to Catholics political emancipation.* Forty or fifty years ago it was

* It is not meant that contempt was the feeling towards Ireland at the

a common belief in her religious circles, that the great Emperor, with whom she was at war, was raised up to annihilate the Popedom. But from the very grave of Pius the Sixth, and from the prison of Pius the Seventh, from the very moment that they had an opportunity of showing to the world their familiarity with that ecclesiastical virtue of which I have said so much, the Catholic movement began. In proportion to the weakness of the Holy See at home, became its influence and its success in the world. The Apostles were told to be prudent as serpents, and simple as doves. It has been the simplicity of the Sovereign Pontiffs which has been their prudence. It is their fidelity to their commission, and their detachment from all secular objects, which has given them the possession of the earth.

I am not pursuing the line of thought which has engaged me in my last chapter and my present without a drift. It bears directly upon the subject which leads me to write at all ; and it has an important bearing, intelligible even to the historian and philosopher, so that reason and experience would be able to extort from him what faith could not obtain. Even a pagan ought to be able to prophecy that our University is destined for great things. I look back at the early combats of Popes Victor and Stephen ; I go on to Julius and Celestine, Leo and Gregory, Boniface and Nicholas ; I pass along the Middle Ages, down to Paul the Third and Pius the Fifth ; and thence to the two Popes of the same name, who occupy the most eventful fifty years, since Christianity was ; and I cannot shut my eyes to the fact, that the Sovereign Pontiffs have had a gift, proper to them-

time, which influenced Sir Robert Peel, or of the Government of the day, but that it was the feeling of the Peelite and Whig parties towards Catholicism as such. *Vide* infr. ch. xix. p. 231.

selves, of understanding what is good for the Church, and what Catholic interests require. And in the next place, I find that this gift exercises itself in an absolute independence of secular politics, and a detachment from every earthly and temporal advantage, and pursues its end by uncommon courses, and by unlikely instruments, and by methods of its own. I see that it shines the brightest, and is the most surprising in its results, when its possessors are the weakest in this world and the most despised ; that in them are most vividly exemplified the Apostle's words, in the most beautiful and most touching of his Epistles, "We have this treasure in earthen vessels, that the excellency may be of the power of God, and not of us ; as needy, yet enriching many, as having nothing, and possessing all things."

I get these two points of history well into my mind ; and then I shut my book, and look at the world before my eyes. I see an age of transition, the breaking up of the old and the coming in of the new ; an old system shattered some sixty years ago, and a new state of things scarcely in its rudiments as yet, to be settled perhaps some centuries after our time. And it is a special circumstance in these changes, that they extend beyond the past historical platform of human affairs ; not only is Europe broken up, but other continents are thrown open, and the new organization of society aims at embracing the world. It is a day of colonists and emigrants ;— and, what is another most pertinent consideration, the language they carry with them is English, which consequently, as time goes on, is certain, humanly speaking, to extend itself into every part of the world. It is already occupying the whole of North America, whence it threatens to descend upon South ; already is it the language of Australia, a country large enough in the course of centuries to rival Europe in population; already it has become the speech of a hundred marts of commerce, scattered over the East, and, even where not the mother tongue, it is at least the medium of intercourse between nations. And, lastly, though the people who own that language is Protestant, a race preëminently Catholic has adopted it, and has a share in its literature; and this Catholic race is, at this very time, of all tribes of the earth, the most fertile in emigrants both to the West and the South. These are the manifest facts of the day, which would be before our eyes, whether the Pope had anything to say to them or no. The English language and the Irish race are overrunning the world.

When then I consider what an eye the Sovereign Pontiffs have for the future ; and what an independence in policy and vigour in action have been the characteristics of their present representative ; and what a flood of success, mounting higher and higher, has lifted up the Ark of God from the beginning of this century ; and then, that the Holy Father has definitely put His finger upon Ireland, and selected her soil as the seat of a great Catholic University, to spread religion, science, and learning, wherever the English language is spoken; when I take all these things together,—I care not what others think, I care not what others do, God has no need of men,—oppose who will, shrink who will, I know and cannot doubt that a great work is begun. It is no great imprudence to commit oneself to a guidance which never yet has failed ; nor is it surely irrational or fanatical to believe, that, whatever difficulties or disappointments, reverses or delays, may be our lot in the prosecution of the work, its ultimate success is certain, even though it seemed at first to fail,—just as the greatest measures in former times have been the most tardy in execution, as Athanasius triumphed though he passed away before Arianism, and Hildebrand died in exile, that his successors might enter into his labours.

CHAPTER XIII.

SCHOOLS OF CHARLEMAGNE.

PARIS.

AS nations are inscrutably brought within the sacred fold, and inscrutably cast without it, so are they used, while within it, in this way or that, according to the supreme will and for the greater glory of Him, who has brought them into being from some common ancestor, and holds them together by unity of government or by traditionary ideas. One Catholic nation is high in the world, another low ; one rises and expands into an Empire, another is ever in the position of subject or even dependent. England and Ireland were, in the darkest age of Christian history, the conservators of sacred and profane knowledge : not, however, for any merit of their own, but according to the good pleasure of their Maker : (and, when the time came, in His counsels, for the revival of learning on the Continent, then He dispensed with their ministry, and put them aside.) It is a remarkable fact, to which I have already alluded, that the appearance of the Danes off the coasts of England and Ireland, the destroyers in both islands of religion and science, synchronizes with the rise of Charlemagne, the founder of modern civilization.

Christianity, which hitherto might be considered as a quality superinduced upon the face of society, now became the element, out of which society grew into shape and reached its stature. The Church had battled with the Roman Empire, and had eventually vanquished it; but, while she succeeded in teaching it the new song of the Saints, she did not demand of it that flexibility of the organs of speech which only exists in the young. It was the case of an old man learning a foreign tongue; its figure, gait, attitudes, and gestures, and in like manner its accent, belonged to an earlier time. Up to the point at which a change was imperative, its institutions were suffered to remain just as they had been in paganism; christianized just so far as to enable them to work christian-wise, however cumbrously or circuitously. And as to the system of education in particular, I suppose the primary, or, as they may be better called, the grammar schools, as far as they were not private speculations, were from first to last in the hands of the State; state-institutions, first of pagan, then of mixed education. I do not mean to say that there are no traces in Christian antiquity of a higher pattern of education, in which religion and learning were brought together,—as in the method of teaching which St. Basil and St. Gregory brought into Asia Minor from Alexandria, and in the Benedictine Schools of Italy; but I am speaking of what the Christian Empire did, and again of what the Church exacted from it. She for the most part confined herself to the education of the clergy, and their ecclesiastical education; the laity and secular learning seem to have been still, more or less, in the charge of the State;—not, however, as if this were the best way of doing things, as the attempts I have spoken of bore testimony, but, because she found things in a certain state, and used them as best she could. Her aim was to make the Empire Christian, not to revolutionize it; and, without a revolution of society, the typical form of a Christian polity could not have been

given to the institutions of Rome. But, when society
was broken up, and had to be constructed over again,
the case was different; it would have been as preposterous,
under such circumstances, not to build it up upon Catholicity, as it would have been to attempt to do so before.
Henceforth, as all government, so all education, was to
be founded on Revealed Truth. Secular teaching was
to be united to sacred ; and the Church had the super-
vision both of lay students and of profane learning.

The new state of things began in the Frankish Empire;
but it is observable how Rome after all strikes the key note
of the movement. Charlemagne indeed betook himself
to the two Islands of the North for a tradition ; Alcuin,
an Englishman, was at the head of his educational establishments ; he came to France, not with sacred learning
only, but with profane ; he set up schools for laity as
well as clergy ; but whence was it that he in turn got the
tradition which he brought ? His history takes us back
to that earlier age, when Theodore of Tarsus, Primate of
England, brought with him thither from Rome the
classics, and made Greek and Latin as familiar to the
Anglo-Saxons as their native tongue. Alcuin was the
scholar of Bede and Egbert ; Egbert was educated in
the York school of Theodore, and Bede in that of Benedict Biscop and of John precentor of the Vatican Basilica.
Here was the germ of the new civilization of Europe,
which was to join together what man had divided, to
adjust the claims of Reason and of Revelation, and to fit
men for this world while it trained them for another.
Charlemagne has the glory of commencing this noble
work ; and, whether his school at Paris be called a University or not, he laid down principles of which a University is the result, in that he aimed at educating all
classes, and undertook all subjects of teaching.

In the first place, however, he turned his attention to the Episcopal Seminaries, which seem to have been institutions of the earliest times of Christianity, though they had been in great measure interrupted amid the dissolution of society consequent upon the barbarian inroads, as various passages in these Essays have already suggested. His restoration lasted for four centuries, till Universities rose in their turn, and indirectly interfered with the efficiency of the Seminaries, by absorbing them into the larger institution. This inconvenience was set right at a later period by the Council of Trent, whose wise regulations were in turn the objects of the jealousy of the Josephism of the last century, which used or rather abused the University system to their prejudice. The present policy of the Church in most places has been to return to the model both of the first ages and of Charlemagne.

To these Seminaries he added, what I have spoken of as his characteristic institution, grammar and public schools, as preparatory both to the Seminaries and to secular professions. Not that they were confined to grammar, for they recognized the *trivium* and *quadrivium* ; but grammar, in the sense of literature, seems to have been the principle subject of their teaching. These schools were established in connexion with the Cathedral or the Cloister ; and they received ecclesiastics and the sons of the nobility, though not to the exclusion of the poorer class.

Charlemagne probably did not do much more than this ; though it was once the custom to represent him as the actual founder of the University of Paris. But great creations are not perfected in a day ; without doing everything which had to be done, he did many things, and opened the way for more. It will throw light upon his position in the history of Christian education, to quote a passage from the elaborate work of Bulæus, on the University of Paris, though he not unnaturally clsims the great Emperor as its founder, maintaining that he established, not only the grammar or public schools already mentioned, but the higher *Studia Generalia.* This assumption, well founded or not, will not make his account less instructive, if, as I have supposed, Charlemagne certainly introduced ideas and principles, of which the University was the result.

"It is observable," says Bulæus, "that Charles, in seeking out masters, had in view, not merely the education of his own family, but of his subjects generally, and of all lovers of the Christian Religion ; and wished to be of service to all students and cultivators of the liberal arts. It is indeed certain that he sought out learned men and celebrated teachers from all parts of the world, and induced them to accept his invitation by rewards and honours, on which Alcuin lays great stress. 'I was well aware, my Lord David,' he says, 'that it has been your praiseworthy solicitude ever to love and to extol wisdom ; and to exhort all men to cultivate it, nay, to incite them by means of prizes and honours ; and out of divers parts of the world to bring together its lovers as the helpers of your good purpose ; among whom you have taken pains to secure even me, the meanest slave ef that holy wisdom, from the extremest boundaries of Britain.'

"It is evident hence, that Charles's intention was not to found any common sort of schools, such, that is, as would have required only a few instructors, but public schools, open to all, and possessing all kinds of learning. Hence the necessity of a multiplicity of Professors, who from their number and the remoteness of their homes might seem a formidable charge, not only to the court, or to one city, but even to his whole kingdom. Such is the testimony of Eginhart, who says : ' Charles loved foreigners and took great pains to support them; so that their number was a real charge, not to the Palace alone, but even to the realm. Such, however, was his greatness of soul, that the burden of them was no trouble to him, because even of great inconveniences the praise of munificence is a compensation.'

" Charles had in mind to found two kinds of schools, less and greater. The less he placed in Bishops' palaces, canons' cloisters, monasteries, and elsewhere ; the greater, however, he established in places which were public, and suitable for public teaching ; and he intended them, not only for ecclesiastics, but for the nobility and their children, and on the other hand for poor scholars too ; in short, for every rank, class, and race.

" He seems to have had two institutions before his mind, when he contemplated this object; the first of them was the ancient schools. Certainly, a man of so active and inquiring a mind as Charles, with his intercourse with learned persons and his knowledge of mankind, must have been well aware that in former ages these two kinds of schools were to be found everywhere ; the one kind few in number, public, and of great reputation, possessed moreover of privileges, and planted in certain conspicuous and central sites. Such was the Alexandrian in Egypt, the Athenian in Greece ; such under the Roman Emperors, the schools of Rome, of Constantinople, of Berytus, which are known to have been attended by multitudes, and amply privileged by Theodosius, Justinian, and other princes ; whereas the other kind of schools, which were far more numerous, were to be found up and down the country, in cities, towns, villages, and were remarkable neither in number of students nor in name.

" The other pattern which was open to Charles was to be found in the practice of monasteries, if it really existed there.   The Benedictines, from the very beginning of their institution, had applied themselves to the profession of literature, and it has been their purpose to have in their houses two kinds of school, a greater or a less, according to the size of the house ; and the greater they wished to throw open to all students, at a time when there were but few laymen at all who could teach, so that externs, seculars, laymen, as well as clerics, might be free to attend to them.   However, true as it was that boys, who were there from childhood intrusted to the monks, bound themselves by no vow, but could leave when they pleased, marry, go to court, or enter the army, still a great many of the cleverest of them were led, either by the habits which they acquired from their intercourse with their teachers, or by their persuasion, to embrace the monastic life.   And thus, while the Church in consequence gained her most powerful supports, the State, on the other hand, was wanting in men of judgment, learning, and experience, to conduct its affairs.   This led very frequently to kings choosing monks for civil administration, because no others were to be found capable of undertaking it.

" Charles then, consulting for the common good, made literature in a certain sense secular, and transplanted it from the convents to the royal palace ; in a word, he established in Paris a Universal School like that at Rome.

" Not that he deprived Monks of the license to teach and profess, though he certainly limited it, from a clear view that that variety of sciences, human and profane, which secular academies require, is inconsistent with the profession and devotion of ascetics ; and accordingly in conformity to the spirit of their institute, it was his wish that the lesser schools should be set up or retained in the Bishops' palaces and monasteries, while he prescribed the subjects which they were to teach. The case was different with the schools which are higher and public, which, instead of multiplying, he confined to certain central and celebrated spots, not more than to three in his whole empire—Paris, and in Italy, Pavia and Bologna."

Such certainly was the result, in which his reforms ended, even though they did not reach it ; and they may be said to have directly tended to it, considering that it was their characteristic, in contrast with the previous schools, to undertake the education of laity as well as clergy, and secular studies as well as religious. But, after all, it was not in an Emperor's power, though he were Charlemagne, to carry into effect in any case, by the resources peculiar to himself, so great an idea as a University. Benefactors and patrons may supply the framework of a Studium Generale ; but there must be a popular interest and sympathy, a spontaneous coöperation of the many, the concurrence of genius, and a spreading thirst for knowledge, if it is to live. Centuries passed before these conditions were supplied, and then at length about the year 1200 a remarkable intellectual movement took place in Christendom ; and to it must be ascribed the development of Universities, out of the public or grammar schools, which I have already described. No such movement could happen, without the rise of some deep and comprehensive philosophy ; and, when it rose, then the existing Trivium and Quadrivium became the subjects, and the existing seats of learning the scene, of its victories ; and next the curiosity and enthusiasm, which it excited, attracted larger and

larger numbers to places which were hitherto but local
centres of education. Such a gathering of students,
such a systematizing of knowledge, are the notes of a
University.

The increase of members and the multiplication of
sciences both involved changes in the organization of
the Schools of Charlemagne ; and of these the increase
of members came first. Hitherto there had been but
one governor over the students, who were but few at the
most, and came from the neighbourhood ; but now the
academic body was divided into Nations, according to
the part of Europe from which they joined it, and each
Nation had a head of its own, under the title of Procu-
rator or Proctor. There were traces of this division, as
we have seen in a former Chapter, in Athens ; where the
students were arranged under the names of Attic,
Oriental, Arab, and Pontic, with a protector for each
class. In like manner, in the University of Paris, there
were four nations, first, the French, which included the
middle and south of France, Spain, Italy, and Greece ,
secondly, the English, which, besides the two British
islands, comprehended Germany and Scandinavia ;
thirdly, the Norman ; and fourthly, the Picards, who
carried with them the inhabitants of Flanders and Bra-
bant. Again, in the University of Vienna, there were
also four nations,—Austria, the Rhine, Hungary, and
Bohemia. Oxford recognized only two Nations ; the
north English, which comprehended the Scotch ; and
the South English, which comprehended the Irish and
Welsh. The Proctors of the Nations both governed
and represented them ; the double office is still traceable,
unless the recent Act of Parliament has destroyed it, in
the modern constitution of Oxford, in which the two
Proctors on the one hand represent the Masters of

Arts in the Hebdomadal Board, and on the othei have in their hands the discipline of the University.

And as Nations and their Proctors arose out of the metropolitan character of a University, to which students congregated from the farthest and most various places, so are Faculties and Deans of Faculties the consequence of its encyclopedic profession. According to the idea of the institutions of Charlemagne, each school had its own teacher, who was called Rector, or Master. In Paris, however, where the school was founded in St. Genevieve's, the Chancellor of that Church became the Rector, and he kept his old title of Chancellor in his new office. Elsewhere the head of the University was called Provost. However, it was not every one who would be qualified to profess even the Seven Sciences, of which the old course of instruction consisted, though the teaching was only elementary, and to become the Rector, Chancellor, or Provost, of the University ; but, when these sciences became only parts of a whole system of instruction, which demanded in addition a knowledge of philosophy, scholastic theology, civil and canon law, medicine, natural history, and the Semitic languages, no one person was equal to the undertaking. The Rector fell back from the position of a teacher to that of a governor ; and the instruction was divided among a board of Doctors, each of whom represented a special province in Science. This is the origin of Deans of Faculties ; and, inasmuch as they undertook among themselves one of those departments of academical duty, which the Chancellor or Rector had hitherto fulfilied, they naturally became his Council. In some places the Proctors of the Nations were added. Thus, in Vienna the Council consisted of the Four Deans of Faculties, and the Four Proctors.

As Nations preceded Faculties, we may suppose that Degrees, which are naturally connected with the latter, either did not enter into the original provisions of a University, or had not the same meaning as afterwards. And this seems to have been the case. At first they were only testimonials that a resident was fit to take part in the public teaching of the place ; and hence, in the Oxford forms still observed, the Vice-Chancellor admits the person taking a degree to the "lectio" of certain books. Degrees would not at that time be considered mere honours or testimonials, to be enjoyed by persons who at once left the University and mixed in the world. The University would only confer them for its own purposes ; and to its own subjects, for the sake of its own subjects. It would claim nothing for them external to its own limits ; and, if so, only used a power obviously connate with its own existence. But of course the recognition of a University by the State, not to say by other Universities, would change the import of degrees, and, since such recognition has commonly been granted from the first, degrees have seldom been only what they were in their original idea ; but the formal words by which they are denoted, still preserve its memory. As students on taking degrees are admitted "legere et disputare," so are they called "Magistri," that is, of the *schools ;* and "Doctors," that is, teachers, or in some places "Professors," as the letters S.T.P. show, used instead of D.D.

It will be observed that the respective distributions into Faculties and into Nations are cross-divisions. Another cross-division, on which I shall not now enter, is into Colleges and Halls.

I conclude by enumerating the characteristic distinctions, laid down by Bulæus, between the public or grammar schools founded by Charlemagne, and the Universities into which eventually some of them grew, or, as he would say, which Charlemagne also founded.

First, he says, they differ from each other *ratione disciplinæ.* The Scholæ Minores only taught the Trivium (*viz.,* Grammar, Logic, Rhetoric,) and the Quadrivium, (*viz.,* Geometry, Astronomy, Arithmetic, and Music,) the seven liberal Arts ; whereas the Scholæ Majores added Medicine, Law, and Theology.

Next, *ratione loci ;* for the Minores were many and everywhere, but the Majores only in great cities, and few in number. I have already remarked on the physical and social qualifications necessary for a place which is to become the seat of a great school of learning : Bulæus observes, that the Muses were said to inhabit mountains, Parnassus or Helicon, spots high and healthy and secured against the perils of war, and that the Academy was a grove; though of course he does not forget that the place must be accessible too, and in the highway of the world. "That the city of Paris," he says, "is ample in size, largely frequented, healthy and pleasant in site, there can be no doubt." Frederic the Second spoke the general sentiment, when he gave as a reason for establishing a University at Naples, the convenience of the sea coast and the fertility of the soil. We are informed by Matamorus, in his account of the Spanish Universities,* that Salamanca was but the second site of its University, which was transferred thither from Palencia on account of the fertility of the neighbourhood, and the mildness of its climate. And Mr. Prescott speaks of Alcala being chosen by Cardinal Ximenes as the site for his celebrated foundations, because " the salubrity of the air, and the sober, tranquil complexion of the scenery, on the beautiful

* Hispan. Illustr. t. 2, p. 801.

borders of the Henares, seemed well suited to academic study and meditation."

The third difference between the greater and lesser schools lies *ratione fundatorum.* Popes, Emperors, and Kings, are the founders of Universities ; lesser authorities in Church and State are the founders of Colleges and Schools.

Fourthly, *ratione privilegiorum.* The very notion of a University, I believe, is, that it is an institution of privilege. I think it is Bulæus who says, "Studia Generalia cannot exist without privileges, any more than the body without the soul. And in this all writers on Universities agree." He reduces those privileges to two heads, "Patrocinium" and "Præmium ;" and these, it is obvious, may be either of a civil or an ecclesiastical nature. There were formerly five Universities endowed with singular privileges : those of Rome, of Paris, of Bologna, of Oxford, and of Salamanca ; but Antony à Wood quotes an author who seems to substitute Padua for Rome in this list.

Lastly, the greater and lesser schools differ *ratione regiminis.* The head of a College is one ; but a University is a " respublica litteraria "

CHAPTER XIV.

SUPPLY AND DEMAND:

THE SCHOOLMEN.

IT is most interesting to observe how the foundations of the present intellectual greatness of Europe were laid, and most wonderful to think that they were ever laid at all. Let us consider how wide and how high is the platform of our knowledge at this day, and what openings in every direction are in progress,—openings of such promise, that, unless some convulsion of society takes place, even what we have attained, will in future times be nothing better than a poor beginning ; and then on the other hand, let us recollect that, seven centuries ago, putting aside revealed truths, Europe had little more than that poor knowledge, partial and uncertain, and at best only practical, which is conveyed to us by the senses. Even our first principles now are beyond the most daring conjectures then ; and what has been said so touchingly of Christian ideas as compared with pagan, is true in its way and degree of the progress of secular knowledge also in the seven centuries I have named.

> " What sages would have died to learn,
> [Is] taught by cottage dames."

Nor is this the only point in which the revelations of science may be compared to the supernatural revelations of Christianity. Though sacred truth was delivered once for all, and scientific discoveries are progressive, yet there is a great resemblance in the respective histories of Christianity and of Science. We are accustomed to point to the rise and spread of Christianity as a miraculous fact, and rightly so, on account of the weakness of its instruments, and the appalling weight and multiplicity of the obstacles which confronted it. To clear away those obstacles was to move mountains ; yet this was done by a few poor, obscure, unbefriended men, and their poor, obscure, unbefriended followers. No social movement can come up to this marvel, which is singular and archetypical, certainly ; it is a divine work, and we soon cease to admire it in order to adore. But there is more in it than its own greatness to contemplate ; it is so great as to be prolific of greatness. Those whom it has created, its children who have become such by a supernatural power, have imitated, in their own acts, the dispensation which made them what they were ; and, though they have not carried out works simply miraculous, yet they have done exploits sufficient to bespeak their own unearthly origin, and the new powers which had come into the world. The revival of letters by the energy of Christian ecclesiastics and laymen, when everything had to be done, reminds us of the birth of Christianity itself, as far as a work of man can resemble a work of God.

Two characteristics, as I have already had occasion to say, are generally found to attend the history of Science:—first, its instruments have an innate force, and can dispense with foreign assistance in their work ; and secondly, these instruments must exist and must begin to act, before subjects are found who are to profit by their action. In plainer language, the teacher is strong, not

in the patronage of great men, but in the intrinsic value
and attraction of what he has to communicate ; and next,
he must come forward and advertise himself, before he
can gain hearers.   This I have expressed before, in saying that a great school of learning lived in demand and
supply, and that the supply must be before the demand.
Now, what is this but the very history of the preaching
of the Gospel ? who but the Apostles and Evangelists
went out to the ends of the earth without patron, or
friend, or other external advantage which could insure
their success ? and again, who among the multitude they
enlightened, would have called for their aid unless they
had gone to that multitude first, and offered to it blessings which up to that moment it had not heard of?
They had no commission, they had no invitation, from
man ; their strength lay neither in their being sent, nor
in their being sent for ; but in the circumstances that
they had that with them, a divine message, which they
knew would at once, when it was uttered, thrill through
the hearts of those to whom they spoke, and make for
themselves friends in any place, strangers and outcasts
as they were when they first came.   They appealed to
the secret wants and aspirations of human nature, to its
laden conscience, its weariness, its desolateness, and its
sense of the true and the divine ; nor did they long wait
for listeners and disciples, when they announced the
remedy of evils which were so real.

Something like this were the first stages of the process
by which in medieval Christendom the structure of our
present intellectual elevation was carried forward. From
Rome as from a centre, as the Apostles from Jerusalem,
went forth the missionaries of knowledge, passing to and
fro all over Europe ; and, as metropolitan sees were the
record of the presence of Apostles, so did Paris, Pavia,

and Bologna, and Padua, and Ferrara, Pisa and Naples, Vienna, Louvain, and Oxford, rise into Universities at the voice of the theologian or the philosopher. Moreover, as the Apostles went through labours untold, by sea and land, in their charity to souls ; so, if robbers, shipwrecks, bad lodging, and scanty fare are trials of zeal, such trials were encountered without hesitation by the martyrs and confessors of science. And as Evangelists had grounded their teaching upon the longing for happiness natural to man, so did these securely rest their cause on the natural thirst for knowledge : and again as the preachers of Gospel peace had often to bewail the ruin which persecution or dissension had brought upon their flourishing colonies, so also did the professors of science often find or flee the ravages of sword or pestilence in those places, which they themselves perhaps in former times had made the seats of religious, honourable, and useful learning. And lastly, as kings and nobles have fortified and advanced the interests of the Christian faith without being necessary to it, so in like manner we may enumerate with honour Charlemagne, Alfred, Henry the First of England, Joan of Navarre, and many others, as patrons of the schools of learning, without being obliged to allow that those schools could not have progressed without such countenance.

These are some of the points of resemblance between the propagation of Christian truth and the revival of letters ; and, to return to the two points, to which I have particularly drawn attention, the University Professor's confidence in his own powers, and his taking the initiative in the exercise of them, I find both these distinctly recognized by Mr. Hallam in his history of Literature. As to the latter point, he says, " The schools of Charlemagne were designed to lay the basis of a learned education,

for which there was at that time no sufficient desire" :—
that is, the supply was prior to the demand. As to the
former : " In the twelfth century," he says, " the *im-
petuosity* with which men *rushed* to that source of what
they deemed wisdom, the great University of Paris,
*did-not depend upon academical privileges or eleemosynary
stipends,* though these were undoubtedly very effectual
in keeping it up. The University *created patrons, and
was not created by them ":*—that is, demand and supply
were all in all.

A story of the age of Charlemagne will serve in
illustration. We are told that two wandering Irish
students were brought by British traders to the coast of
France. There, observing the eagerness with which
those hawkers of perishable merchandize were surrounded by the populace, they imitated them by crying
out, " Who wants wisdom ? here is wisdom on sale ! this
is the store for wisdom ! " till a sensation was created, and
they were sent for and taken into favour by the great
Emperor.

The professors of Greece and Rome, though pursuing
the same course, had an easy time of it, compared with
the duties, which, at least in the earlier periods or in
certain localities, fell upon the medieval missionaries of
knowledge. The pagan teachers might indeed be told
to quit the city, whither they had come, on their outrag-
ing its religious sentiments or arousing its political
jealousy ; but still they were received as superior beings
by the persons in immediate contact with them, and
what they lost in one place they regained in another.
On the contrary, as the cloister alone gave birth to the
revivers of knowledge, so the cloister alone prepared them
for their work. There was nothing selfish in their aim,
nothing cowardly in their mode of operation. It was

generosity which sent them out upon the public stage ;
it was ascetic practice which prepared them for it.
Afterwards, indeed, they received the secular rewards of
their exertions ; but even then the general character of
the intellectual movement remained as before. " The
Doctors," says Fleury in his Discourses, " being sure of
finding in a certain town occupation with recompense
for their labours, established themselves there of their
own accord ; and students, in like manner, sure to find
there good masters with all the commodities of life,
assembled there in crowds from all parts, even from
distant countries. Thus they came to Paris from
England, from Germany and all the North, from Italy,
from Spain."

Bec, a poor monastery of Normandy, set up in the
eleventh century by an illiterate soldier, who sought the
cloister, soon attracted scholars to its dreary clime from
Italy, and transmitted them to England. Lanfranc, afterwards Archbishop of Canterbury, was one of these, and
he found the simple monks so necessitous, that he opened
a school of logic to all comers, in order, says William of
Malmesbury, " that he might support his needy monastery by the pay of the students." The same author
adds, that " his reputation went into the most remote
parts of the Latin world, and Bec became a great and
famous; Academy of letters." Here is an instance of a
commencement without support, without scholars, in
order to attract scholars, and in them to find support.
William of Jumièges, too, bears witness to the effect,
powerful, sudden, wide spreading, and various, of
Lanfranc's advertisement of himself. The fame of Bec
and Lanfranc, he says, quickly penetrated through the
whole world ; and " clerks, the sons of dukes, the most
esteemed masters of the Latin schools, powerful laymen,

high nobles, flocked to him." What words can more strikingly attest the enthusiastic character of the movement which he began, than to say that it carried away with it all classes ; rich as well as poor, laymen as well as ecclesiastics, those who were in that day in the habit of despising letters, as well as those who might wish to live by them ?

It was about a century after Lanfrac that from this same monastery of Bec came forth another Abbot, and he another Lombard, to begin a second movement, in a new science, in these same northern regions, especially in England. This was the celebrated Vacarius, or Bacalareus, who from the proximity of his birthplace to Bologna, seems to have gained that devotion to the study of the Law which he ultimately kindled in Oxford. Lanfranc had lectured in logic; Vacarius lectured in law. Bologna, which is celebrated in history for its cultivation of this august science, was one of the earliest, if not the earliest, of Universities, as far as historical evidence is to decide the question. Its University was commenced a little later than the first years of the School of Bec ; and affords us an observable instance, first, of the self-originating, independent character of the scientific movement, —then, of the influence and attraction it exerted on the people,—and lastly, of the incidental difficulties through which it slowly advanced in the course of many years to its completion. There Irnerius, or Warner, according to Muratori, is found at the end of the eleventh century, and opened a school of civil law. In the next century canon law was added; in the first years of the thirteenth, the school of grammar and literature ; and a few years later, those of theology and medicine. Fifty years later, it had ten thousand students under its teaching, numbers of whom had come all across sea and mountain from England; so strong and encompassing was the sentiment.

And as Englishmen at that time sought Italy, so in turn, I say, did Vacarius a native of Italy, seek England. Selden completes the parallel between him and Lanfranc, by making him Archbishop of Canterbury, after which he retired again to Bec. However, to England he came, and to Oxford; and there, he effected a revolution in the studies of the place, and that on the special ground of the definite drift and direct usefulness of the science in which he was a proficient. As in the case of Lanfranc, not one class of persons, but "rich and poor," says Wood, "gathered around him." The professors of Arts were thrown into the shade. Their alarm was increased by the rival zeal with which the medical science was prosecuted, and the aspect of things got in course of years so threatening, that the Holy See was obliged to interfere. If knowledge is power, it also may be honour and wealth; hence the couplet, expressive of the feeling of the day,

> " Dat Galenus opes, dat Justinianus honores,
> Sed Genus et Species, cogitur ire pedes."

It was indeed the Faculty of Arts which constituted the staple, as it may be called, of a University; Arts, as seems to be commonly allowed, constituted a University; and by Arts are understood the studies comprised in the Trivium and Quadrivium, that is, (as I have said before), Grammar, Rhetoric, Logic, Arithmetic, Geometry, Astronomy, and Music. These were inherited from the ancient world, and were the foundation of the system which was then in course of formation. But the life of Universities lay in the new sciences, not indeed superseding, but presupposing Arts, viz., those of

Theology, Law, Medicine, and in subordination to them, of Metaphysics, Natural History, and the languages. I have been speaking of the law movement, as it may be called ; now, about the same time that Vacarius came to Oxford, Robert Pullus or Pulleyne came thither too from Exeter, just about the time of St. Anselm, and gave the same sort of impulse to biblical learning, which Vacarius gave to law. "From his teaching," says the Osney Chronicle, "the Church both in England and in France gained great profit." Leland says, that he lectured daily, "and left no stone unturned to make the British youth flourish in the sacred tongues." "Multitudes" are said to have come to hear him, and his fame spread to Rome, whither Pope Innocent the Second sent for him. Celestine the Second made him a Cardinal, and Lucius the Second his Chancellor. He was an intimate friend of St. Bernard's, and his influence extended to Cambridge as well as to Paris.

At Cambridge the intellectual movement had already commenced, and with similar phenomena in its course. These points, indeed, are so enveloped in obscurity, and on the other hand have so intimate a bearing on the sensibilities, now as keen as ever, of rival schools, that I, who look on philosophically, a member neither of Cambridge nor of Oxford nor of Paris, "turbantibus æquora ventis," find it necessary to state that, in what I shall say, I am determining nothing to the prejudice of the antiquity or precedence of any of those seats of learning. I take the account given us by Peter of Blois, merely as a *specimen* of the way in which the present fabric of knowledge was founded and reared, as a picture in miniature of the great medieval revival, whatever becomes of its historical truth. As a mere legend, it is sufficient for my purpose ; for historical legends and fictions are made ac-

cording to what is probable, and after the pattern of
precedents.

The author, then, to whom I have referred, says, that
Jeoffred, or Goisfred, had studied at Orleans ; thence he
came to Lincolnshire, and became Abbot of Croyland ;
whence he sent to his manor of Cotenham, near Cambridge, four of his French fellow-students and monks,
one of them to be Professor of sacred learning, the rest
teachers in Philosophy, in which they were excellently
versed.   At Cambridge they hired a common barn, and
opened it as a School of the high Sciences.   They
taught daily.   By the second year the number of
hearers was so great, from town and country, " that
not the biggest house and barn that was," says Wood,
" nor any church whatsoever, sufficed to hold them."
They accordingly divided off into several schools, and
began an arrangement of classes, some of which are
enumerated.   " Betimes in the morning, brother Odo, a
very good grammarian and satirical poet, read grammar
to the boys, and those of the younger sort, according to
the doctrine of Priscian ;" at one o'clock " a most acute
and subtle Sophist taught the elder sort of young men
Aristotle's Logic ;" at three o'clock, " brother William
read a lecture on Tully's Rhetoric and Quintilian's
Flores ;"—such was the beginning of the University of
Cambridge.   And " Master Gislebert upon every Sunday and Holyday, preached the Word of God to the
people ;"—such was the beginning of its University
Church.

It will be observed, that in these accounts, Scripture
comment is insisted on, and little or nothing is said of
Theology, properly so called.   Indeed, it was not till
the next (the thirteenth) century, that Theology took
that place, which Law assumed about a century before

it. Then it was that the Friars, especially the Dominicans, were doing as much for Theology, as Irnerius,
Vacarius, and the Bolognese Professors did for Law.
They raised it (if I may so speak of what is divine) to
the dignity of a science. "They had such a succinct
and delightful method," says Wood, speaking of them
at Oxford, "in the whole course of their discipline, quite
in a manner different from the sophistical way of the
Academicians, that thereby they did not only draw to
them the Benedictines and Carthusians, to be sometimes their constant auditors, but also the Friars of St.
Augustine."

Here we have another exemplification of the same
great principles of the movement which we have noticed
elsewhere; its teachers came from afar, and they depended, not on kings and great men for their support,
but on the enthusiasm they created. "The reputation
of the school of Paris," says Fleury, "increased consider-
ably at the commencement of the twelfth century under
William of Champeaux and his disciples at St. Victor's.
At the same time Peter Abelard came thither and taught
them with great *éclat* the humanities and the Aristotelic
philosophy. Alberic of Rheims taught there also; and
Peter Lombard, Hildebert, Robert Pullus, the Abbot
Rupert, and Hugh of St. Victor; Albertus Magnus
also, and the Angelic Doctor." How few of these professors at Paris were fellow-countrymen! Albert was
from Germany, St. Thomas from Naples, Peter Lombard from Novara, Robert Pullus from Exeter in England. The case had been the same three centuries
before in the same great school. Charlemagne brought
Peter of Pisa from Pavia for Grammar; Alcuin from
England for Rhetoric and Logic; Theodore and Benedict from Rome for Music; John of Melrose, who was

afterwards at the head of the schools at Pavia, and Claudius Clemens, two Scots, from Ireland. Ireland, indeed, contributed a multitude of teachers to the continental schools, and the more, because, great as was the fame of its earlier schools, it had now no University of its own. The names of its professors have not commonly been preserved, though Erigena and Scotus by their very titles show their origin : but we find that, when the Emperor Frederick the Second would set up the University of Naples, he sent all the way to Ireland for the learned Peter to be its first Rector ; and an author, quoted in Bulæus, speaks of " the whole of Ireland, with its *family* of philosophers, despising the dangers of the sea," and migrating to the south. Such was the famous Richard of St. Victor, whose very title marks his connexion with the great school of Paris.

There is a force in the words, " despising the dangers of the sea." We in this degenerate age sometimes shrink from the passage between Holyhead and Kingstown, when duty calls for it ; yet before steam-boats, almost before seaworthy vessels, we find those zealous scholars, both Irish and English, voluntarily exposing themselves to the winds and waves, from their desire of imparting and acquiring knowledge. Not content with one teacher, they went from place to place, according as in each there was preëminence in a particular branch of knowledge. We have in St. Athanasius's life of St. Antony a beautiful account of the diligence with which the young hermit went about " like the bee," as his great biographer says, in quest of superiority in various kinds of virtue. From one holy man, he says (I quote from memory), the youth gained courtesy and grace, from another gentleness, from another mortification, from another humility ; and in a similar way did the knights errant of science go about, seeking indeed sometimes rivals to encounter, but more frequently patterns and instructors to follow. As then the legendary St. George or St. Denys wandered from place to place to achieve feats of heroism, as St. Antony or Sulpicius Severus went about on pilgrimage to holy hermits, as St. Gregory Nazianzen visited Greece, or St. Jerome traversed Europe, and became, the one the most accomplished theologian, the other the first Biblical scholar of his age, so did the medieval Doctors and Masters go the round of Universities in order to get the best instruction in every school.

The famous John of Salisbury (as Mr. Sharon Turner tells us) went to Paris for the lectures of Abelard just on the death of Henry the First, and with him he studied logic. Then for dialectics he went to Alberic and to the English Robert for two years. Then for three years to William de Conchia for grammar; afterwards to Richard Bishop for a renewed study of grammar and logic, going on to the Quadrivium; and to the German Harduin. Next he restudied rhetoric, which he had learned from Theodoric, and more completely from Father Elias. Meanwhile, he supported himself by teaching the children of noble persons, and became intimate with Adam, an Englishman, a stout Aristotelian, and returned to logic with William of Soissons and Gilbert. Lastly, he studied theology with Robert Pulleyne or Pullus, already mentioned, and Simon de Poissy. Thus he passed as many as twelve years. Better instances, however, than his, as introducing a wider extent of travel, are those already referred to, of St. Thomas, or Vacarius, or Lanfranc, or St. Anselm, or John of Melrose.

The ordinary course of study, however, lay between

the schools of Paris and Oxford, in which was almost centered the talent of the age, and which were united by the most intimate connexion. Happy age, whatever its other inconveniences, happy so far as this, that religion and science were then a bond of union, till the ambition of monarchs and the rivalry of race dissolved it! Wood gives us a list of thirty-two Oxford professors of name, who in their respective times went to teach in Paris, among whom were Alexander Hales, and the admirable St. Edmund, afterwards Archbishop of Canterbury,—St. Edmund, who, as St. Anselm and St. Thomas, shows us how sanctity is not inconsistent with preëminence in the schools. On the other hand, Bulæus recites the names of men, even greater, viewed as a body, who went from Oxford to Paris, not to teach, but to be taught ; such as St. Thomas of Canterbury, St. Richard, St. Gilbert of Sempringham, Giraldus Cambrensis, Gilbert the Universal, Haimo, Richard de Barry, Nicholas Breakspeare, afterwards Pope, Nekam, Morley, and Galfredus de Vinsalfe. So intimate, or to use the word, so *thick* were Paris and Oxford at this time, as to give occasion to this couplet,

> " Et procul et propius jam Francus et Anglicus æquè,
> Norunt Parisiis quid feceris, Oxoniæque."

And this continued till the time of Edward the Third, when came the wretched French wars and the Lollards, and then adieu to familiar intercourse down to this day.

I have not found the number of students in Paris; but from what I have said, one is led to expect two things of it, first, that it would be very great, next, that it would be very variable : and these inferences are confirmed by what is told us of the numbers at Oxford. In that University we read of Scotch, Irish, Welsh, French, Spanish, German, Bohemian, Hungarian, and Polish Students ; and, when it is considered, as a modern writer tells us, that they would bring with them, or require for their uses, a number of dependents in addition, such as parchment-preparers, bookbinders, stationers, apothecaries, surgeons, and laundresses, it may be understood that the whole number of matriculated persons was sometimes even marvellous, and as fluctuating in a long period as excessive at particular dates. We are told that there were in Oxford in 1209 three thousand members of the University, in 1231 thirty thousand, in 1263 fifteen thousand, in 1350 between three and four thousand, and in 1360 six thousand. This ebbing and flowing, moreover, suggests what it is all along very much to my purpose to observe, and on which, if I have the opportunity, I shall have more to say presently ; first, that the zeal for study and knowledge is sufficient indeed in itself for the being of a University ; but secondly, that it is not sufficient for its well being, or what is technically called its *integrity*.

The era of the French wars, which put an end to this free intercourse of France and England, seems for various reasons to have been the beginning of a decline in the ecumenical greatness of Universities. They lost some advantages, they gained others ; they became national bodies ; they gained much in the way of good order and in comfort ; they became rich and honourable establishments. Each age has its own character and its own wants : and we trust that in each a loving Providence shapes the institutions of the Church as they may best subserve the objects for which she has been sent into the world. We cannot tell exactly what the Catholic University ought to be at this era ; doubtless neither the

University of Scotus, nor that of Gerson, in matters of detail ; but, if we keep great principles before us, and feel our way carefully, and ask guidance from above for every step we take, we may trust to be able to serve the cause of truth in our day and according to our measure, and in that way which is most expedient and most profitable, as our betters did in ages past and gone.

CHAPTER XV.

PROFESSORS AND TUTORS.

I MAY seem in the foregoing Chapter to have relapsed into the tone of thought which created some surprise when I was speaking of Athens and the Sophists; and my good friend Richard, the Epicurean, may be upon me again, for my worship, as he will consider it, of the intellect, and my advocacy of the Professorial System. This is an additional call on me to go forward with my subject, if I can do so without wearying the reader. I say "without wearying," for I beg to assure him, if he has not already found it out for himself, that it is very difficult for any one to discuss points of ancient usage or national peculiarity, as I am doing, and to escape the dry, dull tone of an antiquarian. This is so acknowledged an inconvenience, that every now and then you find an author attempting to evade it by turning his book of learned research into a novel or a poem. I will say nothing of Thalaba or Kehama, though the various learning displayed in the notes appended to those pleasing fables, certainly suggests the idea, that the poetry may have grown out of the notes, instead of the notes being the illustration of the poetry. However, I believe it is undoubted, that Morier converted his unsaleable quarto on Persia into his amusing Hadji Baba; while Palgrave has poured out his medieval erudition by the channels of Friar Bacon and Marco Polo, and Bekker has insinuated archeology in the persons of Charicles and Gallus. Were I to attempt to do the same, whether for the grouping of facts or the relief of abstract discussion, I have reason to believe I should not displease men of great authority and judgment; but for success in such an undertaking there would be demanded a very considerable stock of details, and no small ability in bringing them to bear on principles, and working them up into a narrative. On the whole, then, I prefer to avail myself, both as counsel and as comfort, of the proverb, " Si gravis, brevis ; " and to make it a point, that, weary as my reader may be, he shall not have time to go to sleep. And to-day especially, since I mean to be particularly heavy in the line of abstract discussion, I mean also to be particularly short.

I purpose, then, to state here what is the obvious safeguard of a University from the evils to which it is liable if left to itself, or what may be called, to use the philosophical term, its *integrity*. By the "integrity" of anything is meant a gift superadded to its nature, without which that nature is indeed complete, and can act, and fulfil its end, but does not find itself, if I may use the expression, in easy circumstances. It is in fact very much what easy circumstances are in relation to human happiness. This reminds me of Aristotle's account of happiness, which is an instance in point. He specifies two conditions, which are required for its integrity ; it is indeed a state of *mind*, and in its nature independent of externals, yet he goes on (inconsistently we might say, till we make the distinction I am pointing out), he goes on, I say, after laying down that " man's chief good is an energy of the soul according to virtue," to add, " besides this, *throughout the greater part of life*,—for, as neither one swallow, nor one day, makes a spring, so neither does one day, nor a short time, make a man blessed and happy." Here then is one condition, which in some sense may be said to fall under the notion of "integrity ;" but, whether this be so or not, a second condition, which he proceeds to mention, seems altogether to answer to it. After repeating that "happiness is the best and most noble and most delightful of energies according to virtue," he adds : "at the same time *it seems to stand in need of external goods*, for it is impossible, or at least not easy, to perform praiseworthy actions without external means, for many things are performed, as it were by instruments, by friends, and wealth, and political power. But men deprived of some things, as of noble birth, fine progeny, a fine form, have a flaw in their happiness ; for he is not altogether capable of happiness, who is deformed in his body, or of mean birth, or deserted and childless ; and still less so, perhaps, if he have vicious children, or if they were dear and dutiful, and have died. Therefore it seems to demand such prosperity as this ; whence some arrange good fortune in the same class with happiness ; but others virtue."

This then is how we may settle the dispute which my Epicurean introduced, and which has been carried on at intervals in the British Universities for the last fifty years. It began in the pages of the Edinburgh Review, which at that time might in some sense be called the organ of the University of Edinburgh. Twenty years later, if my memory does not play me false, it was renewed in the same quarter; then it was taken up at Cambridge, and lately it was going on briskly between some of the most able members of the University of Oxford. Now what has been the point of dispute between the combatants ? This,—whether a University should be conducted on the system of Professors, or on the system of Colleges and College Tutors. By a College was understood something

more than the Museum of Alexandria, or such corporations among ourselves, as are established for Medicine,
Surgery, Engineering, or Agriculture.   It was taken to
mean a place of residence for the University student,
who would there find himself under the guidance and
instruction of Superiors and Tutors, bound to attend to
his personal interests, moral and intellectual.   The party
of the North and of progress have ever advocated the
Professorial system, as it has been called, and have pointed
in their own behalf to the practice of the middle ages
and of modern Germany and France ; the party of the
South and of prescription have ever stood up for the
Tutorial or collegiate system, and have pointed to
Protestant Oxford and Cambridge, where it has almost
or altogether superseded tne Professorial.   Now I have
on former occasions said enough to show that I am for
both views at once, and think neither of them complete
without the other.   I admire the Professor, I venerate
the College.   The Professorial system fulfils the strict
idea of a University, and is sufficient for its *being*, but it
is not sufficient for its *well-being*.   Colleges constitute
the *integrity* of a University.

This view harmonizes with what I said in a former
Chapter, about Influence and Law ; for though Professors
may be and have been utterly without personal weight
and persuasiveness, and Colleges utterly forgetful of moral
and religious discipline, still, taking a broad view of history, we shall find that Colleges are to be accounted the
maintainers of order, and Universities the centres of movement.   It coincides, too, with what I have lately said in a
Treatise on University Education,* in which a *Studium
Generale* is considered first in its own nature, then as it

---

* Discourses on the Scope and Nature of University Education

exists within the pale of Catholicism. "It is," I there say, "a place of teaching universal knowledge. Such is a University in its *essence* and independently of its relation to the Church. But, practically speaking, it can-not fulfil its object duly without the Church's assistance, or the Church is necessary for its *integrity ;* not that its main characters are changed by this incorporation ; it still has the office of intellectual education ; but the Church steadies it in the performance of that office." I say this passage coincides with the statements I have been making, because Colleges are the direct and special instruments, which the Church *uses* in a University, for the attainment of her sacred objects,—as other passages of the same Volume incidentally teach.

Let us then bring the real state of the case before our minds. A University is "a school of knowledge of every kind, consisting of teachers and learners from every quarter." Two or three learned men, with little or no means, make their way to some great city. They come with introductions to the Bishop, if there is no University there yet, and receive his sanction, or they get the necessary leave, and then on their own respon-sibility they open a school. They may, or they may not be priests ; but, any how, they are men of correct principles, in earnest, set on their work, and not careful of their own ease and interest. They do not mind where they lodge, or how they live, and their learning, zeal, and eloquence soon bring hearers to them, not only natives, but strangers to the place, travelling thither from considerable distances, on the report of the teachers who have there congregated. If the professors have but scanty means, the pupils have not more abundant ; and, in spite of their thirst for knowledge, whatever it may be, they cannot have the staidness and gravity of

character, or the self-command, which years and experience have given to their teachers. They have difficulty
in finding food or lodging, and are thrown upon shifts,
and upon the world, for both the one and the other.

Now, it must be an extraordinary devotion to science
which can save them from the consequences of a trial such
as this. They lodge in garrets or cellars, or they share
a room with others ; they mix with the inhabitants of
the place, who, if not worse, at least will not be better
than the run of mankind. A man must either be a saint
or an enthusiast to be affected in no degree by the dis-
advantages of such a mode of living. There are few
people whose minds are not unsettled on being thrown
out of habits of regularity ; few who do not suffer, when
withdrawn from the eye of those who know them, or
from the scrutiny of public opinion. How often does a
religious community complain, on finding themselves in
a new home, of the serious inconvenience, in a spiritual
point of view, which attaches to the mere circumstance
that they have not an habitation suited to the rule which
they are bound to observe ! Without elbow room,
without order, without tranquillity, they grieve to find
that recollection and devotion have not fair play. What,
then, will be the case with a number of youths of un-
formed minds, so little weaned from the world that
their very studies are perhaps the result of their ambition, and who are under no definite obligation to be
better than their neighbours, only bound by that general
Christian profession, which those neighbours share with
them ? The excitement of novelty or emulation does
not last long ; and then the mind is commonly left a
prey to its enemies, even when there is no disarrange-
ment of daily life such as I have been describing.
It is not to be expected that the Professor, whom they

attend, necessitous himself, can exercise a control over such a set of pupils, even if he has any jurisdiction, or can bring his personal influence to bear upon any great number of them; or that he can see them beyond the hours in which the schools are open, or, indeed, can do much more than deliver lectures in their presence. It is certain then, that, in proportion to the popularity, whether of the Professor or the place itself, granting there will be numerous exceptions to the contrary, a mob of lawless youths will gradually be formed, after the pattern of the rioters whom Eunapius encountered and St. Basil escaped, at Athens. Nor will the state of things be substantially different, even if we suppose that, instead of the indigence I have described, the frequenters of the schools have a competency for their maintenance; much less, if they have superfluity of means.

To these disorders, which are of certain occurrence, others may easily be added. A popular Professor will be carried away by his success, and, in proportion as his learning is profound, his talents ready, and his elocution attractive, will be in danger of falling into some extravagance of doctrine, or even of being betrayed into heresy. The teacher has his own perils, as well as the taught; there are in his path such enemies as the pride of intellect, the aberrations of reasoning, and the intoxication of applause. The very advantages of his position are his temptation. I have spoken in a former Chapter of the superiority of oral instruction to books, in the communication of knowledge; the following passage from an able controversialist of the day, which is intended to illustrate that superiority, incidentally suggests to us also, that, first, the speaker may suffer from the popularity of his gift, and, then, the hearer from its fascination.

" While the type," he says, " is so admirable a contrivance for perpetuating knowledge, it is certainly more expensive, and in some points of view less effective as a means of communication, than the lecture.   The type is a poor substitute for the human voice.   It has no means of arousing, moderating, and adjusting the attention. It has no emphasis except Italics, and this meagre notation cannot finely graduate itself to the need of the occasion.   It cannot in this way mark the heed which should be specially and chiefly given to peculiar passages or words.   It has no variety of manner and intonation, to show by their changes how the words are to be accepted, or what comparative importance is to be attached to them.   It has no natural music to take the ear, like the human voice ; it carries with it no human eye to range, and to rivet the student when on the verge of truancy, and to command his intellectual activity by an appeal to the courtesies of life.   Half the symbolism of a living language is thus lost, when it is committed to paper ; and that symbolism is the very means by which the forces of the hearer's mind can be best economized or most pleasantly excited.   The lecture, on the other hand, as delivered, possesses all these instruments to win, and hold, and harmonize attention ; and above all, it imparts to the whole teaching a human character, which the printed book can never supply.   The Professor is the science or subject, vitalized and humanized in the student's presence.   He sees him kindle into his subject ; he sees reflected and exhibited in him, his manner, and his earnestness, the general power of the science to engage, delight, and absorb a human intelligence.   His natural sympathy and admiration attract or impel his tastes and feelings and wishes for the moment into the same currents of feeling, and his mind is naturally and rapidly and insensibly strung and attuned to the strain of truth which is offered to him."*

It needs not this elegant panegyric of an Oxford Professor to inform us of the influence which eloquence can exert over an audience; I quote it rather for its able analysis of that influence. I quote it, because it forcibly suggests to the mind how fitted the talent is, first to exalt the possessor in his own eyes, and then through him to mislead his hearers. I will *cap* it, if I may use the expression, with the following histories or legends of the thirteenth century;—" Simon of Tournay, a famous Parisian doctor, one day proved in a lecture by such powerful arguments, the divinity of Christianity, that his school burst out into admiration of his ability. On this he cried out, ' Ha, good Jesus; I could, if I chose, refute Thee quite as well.' " The story goes on to say that he was instantly struck dumb. A disciple of Silo, a professor of theology, died; after a while he returned to his master from the grave, invested in a cope of fire, inscribed all over with philosophical theses. A drop of his sweat fell upon the professor's hand, and burned it through. This cope lay on him as a punishment for intellectual pride." †

Considerations such as this, are sufficiently suggestive of the dangers of the Professorial system; it is obvious, however, to mention one additional evil. We are supposing a vast influx and congregation of young men, their own masters, in a strange city, from countries various, of different traditions, politics, and manners, and which have often been at war with each other. And they have come to attend lecturers, whom they are to choose out of a number of able men, themselves of various countries

* Professor Vaughan
+ Vide Fr. Dalgairns's article in the British Critic, Jan. 1843.

and characters too. Some of these professors are their own countrymen respectively, others are not ; and all of them are more or less in rivalry one with another, so far as their department of teaching is the same. They will have their respective gatherings, their respective hostilities ; many will puff them, many run them down ; their countrymen, for the sake of "la belle France," or "merry England," will range themselves on their side, and fight in their behalf. Squabbles, conflicts, feuds, will be the consequence ; the peace of the University will be broken, the houses will be besieged, the streets will be impassable. Accustomed to brawls with each other, they are not likely to be peaceable with any third party ; they will find themselves a match for the authority of Chancellor and Rector ; nor will they scruple at compromising themselves with the law, or even with the government ; nay, with the Church, if her authorities come in their way ; with the townspeople of course—a sort of ready-made opponent. The bells of St. Mary's and St. Martin's will ring ; out will rush from their quarters the academic youth ; and the smart blackguard of the city, and the stout peasant from the neighbourhood, will answer to the challenge. The worse organized is a country, the greater of course will be the disorder ; intolerable of course in the middle ages ; in times such as these, the magistracy or police would to a very considerable extent keep under such manifestations ; yet, in Germany, we are told that at least duels and party skirmishes are not uncommon, and even within the very home and citadel of Order, town-and-gown rows are not yet matters of history in the English Universities.

Now, I have said quite enough for the purpose of showing that, taking human nature as it is, the thirst of knowledge and the opportunity of quenching it, though

these be the real life of a great school of philosophy and
science, will not be sufficient in fact for its establishment ;
that they will not work to their ultimate end, which is
the attainment and propagation of truth, unless surrounded by influences of a different sort, which have no
pretension indeed to be the essence of a University, but
are conservative of that essence. The Church does not
think much of any "wisdom," which is not "*desursum,*"
that is, revealed ; nor unless, as the Apostle proceeds,
it is "primum quidem *pudica,* deinde *pacifica.*" These
may be called the three vital principles of the Christian
student, faith, chastity, love ; because their contraries,
viz., unbelief or heresy, impurity, and enmity, are just the
three great sins against God, ourselves, and our neighbour, which are the death of the soul :—now, these are
also just the three imputations which I have been bringing against the incidental action of what may be called
the Professorial system.

And lastly, obvious as are the deficiencies of that
system, as obvious surely is its remedy, as far as
human nature admits of one. I have been saying
that regularity, rule, respect for others, the eye of friends
and acquaintances, the absence from temptation,
external restraints generally, are of first importance
in protecting us against ourselves. When a boy
leaves his home, when a peasant leaves his country,
his faith and morals are in great danger, both because he is in the world, and also because he is among
strangers. The remedy, then, of the perils which a
University presents to the student, is to create within it
homes, "altera Trojæ Pergama," such as those, or better
than those, which he has left behind. Small communities must be set up within its precincts, where his better
thoughts will find countenance, and his good resolutions

support ; where his waywardness will be restrained, his heedlessness forewarned, and his prospective deviations anticipated. Here, too, his diligence will be steadily stimulated ; he will be kept up to his aim ; his progress will be ascertained, and his week's work, like a labourer's, measured. It is not easy for a young man to determine for himself whether he has mastered what he has been taught ; a careful catechetical training, and a jealous scrutiny into his power of expressing himself and of turning his knowledge to account, will be necessary, if he is really to profit from the able Professors whom he is attending ; and all this he will gain from the College Tutor.

Moreover, it has always been considered the wisdom of lawgivers and founders, to find a safe outlet for natural impulses and sentiments, which are sure to be found in their subjects, and which are hurtful only in excess ; and to direct, and moderate, and variously influence what they cannot extinguish. The story is familiarly told, when a politician was advocating violently repressive measures upon some national crisis, of a dissentient friend who was present, proceeding to fasten down the lid of the kettle, which was hissing on his fire, and to stop up its spout. Here, in like manner, the subdivision of the members of a University, while it breaks up the larger combination of parties, and makes them more manageable, answers also the purposes of providing a safe channel for national, or provincial, or political feeling, and for a rivalry which is wholesome when it is not inordinate. These small societies, pitted, as it were, one against another, give scope to the exertion of an honourable emulation ; and this, while it is a stimulus on the literary exertions of their respective members, is changed from a personal and self-ish feeling, into a desire for the reputation of the body.

Patriotic sentiment, too, here finds its home ; one college has a preponderance of members from one race or district, another from another ; the "Nations" no longer fight on the academic scene, like the elements in chaos ; they are submitted to a salutary organization ; and the love of country, without being less intense, becomes purer, and more civilized, and more religious.

My object at present is not to prove what I have been saying, either by argument or from history, but to suggest views to the reader which he will pursue for himself. It may be said that small bodies may fall into a state of decay or irregularity, as well as large. It is true ; but that is not the question ; but whether in themselves smaller bodies of students are not easier to manage on the long run, than large ones. I should not like to do either, but, if I must choose between the two, I would rather drive four-in-hand, than the fifty wild cows which were harnessed to the travelling wagon of the Tartars.

CHAPTER XVI.

THE STRENGTH AND WEAKNESS OF UNIVERSITIES.
ABELARD.

WE can have few more apposite illustrations of at once the strength and weakness of what may be called the University principle, of what it can do and what it cannot, of its power to collect students, and its impotence to preserve and edify them, than the history of the celebrated Abelard. His name is closely associated with the commencement of the University of Paris; and in his popularity and in his reverses, in the criticisms of John of Salisbury on his method, and the protest of St. Bernard against his teaching, we read, as in a pattern specimen, what a University professes in its essence, and what it needs for its "integrity." It is not to be supposed, that I am prepared to show this here, as fully as it might be shown; but it is a subject so pertinent to the general object of these Essays, that it may be useful to devote even a few pages to it.

The oracles of Divine Truth, as time goes on, do but repeat the one message from above which they have ever uttered, since the tongues of fire attested the coming of the Paraclete; still, as time goes on, they utter it with greater force and precision, under diverse forms, with fuller luminousness, and a richer ministration of thought, statement, and argument. They meet the varying wants, and encounter the special resistance of each successive age ; and, though prescient of coming errors and their remedy long before, they cautiously reserve their new enunciation of the old Truth, till it is imperatively demanded. And, as it happens in kings' cabinets, that surmises arise, and rumours spread, of what is said in council, and is in course of preparation, and secrets perhaps get wind, true in substance or in direction, though distorted in detail ; so too, before the Church speaks, one or other of her forward children speaks for her, and, while he does anticipate to a certain point what she is about to say or enjoin, he states it incorrectly, makes it error instead of truth, and risks his own faith in the process. Indeed, this is actually one source, or rather concomitant, of heresy, the presence of some misshapen, huge, and grotesque foreshadow of true statements which are to come. Speaking under correction, I would apply this remark to the heresy of Tertullian or of Sabellius, which may be considered a reaction from existing errors, and an attempt, presumptuous, and therefore unsuccessful, to meet them with those divinely-appointed correctives which the Church alone can apply, and which she will actually apply, when the proper moment comes. The Gnostics boasted of their intellectual proficiency before the time of St. Irenæus, St. Athanasius, and St. Augustine ; yet, when these doctors made their appearance, I suppose they were examples of that knowledge, true and deep, which the Gnostics professed. Apollinaris anticipated the work of St Cyril and the Ephesine Council, and became a heresiarch in consequence ; and, to come down to the present times, we may conceive that writers, who have impatiently fallen away from the Church, because she would not adopt their views, would have found, had they but trusted her, and waited, that she knew how to profit by them, though she never could have need to borrow her enunciations from them; for their writings contained, so to speak, truth *in the ore*, truth which they themselves had not the gift to disengage from its foreign concomitants, and safely use, which she alone could use, which she would use in her destined hour, and which became their stone of stumbling simply because she did not use it faster. Now, applying this principle to the subject before us, I observe, that, supposing Abelard to be the first master of scholastic philosophy, as many seem to hold, we shall have still no difficulty in condemning the author, while we honour the work. To him is only the glory of spoiling by his own self-will what would have been done well and surely under the teaching and guidance of Infallible Authority.

Nothing is more certain, than that some ideas are consistent with one another, and others inconsistent; and, again, that every truth must be consistent with every other truth;—hence, that all truths of whatever kind form into one large body of Truth, by virtue of the consistency between one truth and another, which is a connecting link running through them all. The science which discovers this connection, is logic; and, as it discovers the connection when the truths are given. so, having one truth given and the connecting principle, it is able to go on to ascertain the other. Though all this is obvious, it was realized and acted on in the middle age with a distinctness unknown before; all subjects of knowledge were viewed as parts of one vast system, each with its own place in it, and from knowing one, another was inferred. Not indeed always rightly inferred, because the art might be less perfect than the science, the instrument than the theory and aim; but I am speaking of the principle of the scholastic method, of which Saints and Doctors were the teachers;—such

I conceive it to be, and Abelard was the ill-fated logician who had a principal share in bringing it into operation.

Others will consider the great St. Anselm and the school of Bec, as the proper source of Scholasticism ; I am not going to discuss the question ; any how, Abelard, and not St. Anselm, was the Professor at the University of Paris, and it is of Universities that I am speaking ; any how, Abelard illustrates the strength and the weakness of the principle of advertising and communicating knowledge for its own sake, which I have called the University principle, whether he is, or is not, the first of scholastic philosophers or scholastic theologians. And, though I could not speak of him at all without mentioning the subject of his teaching, yet, after all, it is of him and of his teaching itself, that I am going to speak, whatever that might be which he actually taught.

Since Charlemagne's time the schools of Paris had continued, with various fortunes, faithful, as far as the age admitted, to the old learning, as other schools elsewhere, when, in the eleventh century, the famous school of Bec began to develop the powers of logic in forming a new philosophy. As the inductive method rose in Bacon, so did the logical in the medieval schoolmen ; and Aristotle, the most comprehensive intellect of Antiquity, as the one who had conceived the sublime idea of mapping the whole field of knowledge, and subjecting all things to one profound analysis, became the presiding master in their lecture halls. It was at the end of the eleventh century that William of Champeaux founded the celebrated Abbey of St. Victor under the shadow of St. Geneviève, and by the dialectic methods which he introduced into his teaching, has a claim to have commenced the work of forming the University out of the Schools of Paris. For one at least, out of the two characteristics of a University, he prepared the way ; for, though the schools were not public till after his day, so as to admit laymen as well as clerks, and foreigners as well as natives of the place, yet the logical principle of constructing all sciences into one system, implied of course a recognition of all the sciences that are comprehended in it. Of this William of Champeax, or de Campellis, Abelard was the pupil ; he had studied the dialectic art elsewhere, before he offered himself for his instructions ; and, in the course of two years, when as yet he had only reached the age of twenty-two, he made such progress, as to be capable of quarrelling with his master, and setting up a school for himself.

This school of Abelard was first situated in the royal castle of Melun ; then at Corbeil, which was nearer to Paris, and where he attracted to himself a considerable number of hearers. His labours had an injurious effect upon his health ; and at length he withdrew for two years to his native Britanny. Whether other causes coöperated in this withdrawal, I think, is not known ; but, at the end of the two years, we find him returning to Paris, and renewing his attendance on the lectures of William, who was by this time a monk. Rhetoric was the subject of the lectures he now heard ; and after awhile the pupil repeated with greater force and success his former treatment of his teacher. He held a public disputation with him, got the victory, and reduced him to silence. The school of William was deserted, and its master himself became an instance of the vicissitudes incident to that gladiatorial wisdom (as I may style it) which was then eclipsing the old Benedictine method of the Seven Arts. After a time, Abelard found his reputation sufficient to warrant him in setting up a school himself on Mount St. Geneviève ; whence he waged incessant war against the unwearied logician, who by this time had rallied his forces to repel the young and ungrateful adventurer who had raised his hand against him.

Great things are done by devotion to one idea ; there is one class of geniuses, who would never be what they are, could they grasp a second. The calm philosophical mind, which contemplates parts without denying the whole, and the whole without confusing the parts, is notoriously indisposed to action ; whereas single and simple views arrest the mind, and hurry it on to carry them out. Thus, men of one idea and nothing more, whatever their merit, must be to a certain extent narrow-minded ; and it is not wonderful that Abelard's devotion to the new philosophy made him undervalue the Seven Arts out of which it had grown. He felt it impossible so to honour what was now to be added, as not to dishonour what existed before. He would not suffer the Arts to have their own use, since he had found a new instrument for a new purpose. So he opposed the reading of the Classics. The monks had opposed them before him ; but this is little to our present purpose ; it was the duty of men, who abjured the gifts of this world on the principle of mortification, to deny themselves literature just as they would deny themselves particular friendships or figured music. The doctrine which Abelard introduced and represents was founded on a different basis. He did not recognize in the poets of antiquity any other merit than that of furnishing an assemblage of elegant phrases and figures ; and accordingly he asks why they should not be banished from the city of God, since Plato banished them from his own commonwealth. The *animus* of this language is clear, when we turn to the pages of John of Salisbury and Peter of Blois, who were champions of the ancient learning. We find them complaining that the careful "getting up," as we now call it, " of books," was growing out of fashion. Youths once studied critically the text of poets or philosophers; they got them by heart; they analyzed their arguments; they noted down their fallacies; they were closely examined in the matters which had been brought before them in lecture; they composed. But now, another teaching was coming in; students were promised truth in a nutshell; they intended to get possession of the sum-total of philosophy in less than two or three years; and facts were apprehended, not in their substance and details, by means of living and, as it were, personal documents, but in dead abstracts and tables. Such were the reclamations to which the new Logic gave occasion.

These, however, are lesser matters; we have a graver quarrel with Abelard than that of his undervaluing the Classics. As I have said, my main object here is not what he taught, but why and how, and how he lived. Now it is certain, his activity was stimulated by nothing very high, but something very earthly and sordid. I grant there is nothing morally wrong in the mere desire to rise in the world, though Ambition and it are twin sisters. I should not blame Abelard merely for wishing to distinguish himself at the University; but when he makes the ecclesiastical state the instrument of his ambition, mixes up spiritual matters with temporal, and aims at a bishopric through the medium of his logic, he joins together things incompatible, and cannot complain of being censured. It is he himself, who tells us, unless my memory plays me false, that the circumstance of William of Champeaux being promoted to the see of Chalons, was an incentive to him to pursue the same path with an eye to the same reward. Accordingly, we next hear of his attending the theological lectures of a certain master of William's, named Anselm, an old man, whose school was situated at Laon. This person had a great reputation in his day ; John of Salisbury, speaking of him in the next generation, calls him the doctor of doctors ; he had been attended by students from Italy and Germany ; but the age had advanced since he was in his prime, and Abelard was disappointed in a teacher, who had been good enough for William. He left Anselm, and began to lecture on the prophet Ezekiel on his own resources.

Now came the time of his great popularity, which was more than his head could bear ; which dizzied him, took him off his legs, and whirled him to his destruction. I spoke in my foregoing Chapter of those three qualities of true wisdom, which a University, absolutely and nakedly considered, apart from the safeguards which constitute its integrity, is sure to compromise. Wisdom, says the inspired writer, is *desursum*, is *pudica*, is *pacifica*, " from above, chaste, peaceable." We have already seen enough of Abelard's career to understand that his wisdom, instead of being " pacifica," was ambitious and contentious. An Apostle speaks of the tongue both as a blessing and as a curse. It may be the beginning of a fire, he says, a " Universitas iniquitatis ; " and alas ! such did it become in the mouth of the gifted Abelard. His eloquence was wonderful ; he dazzled his contemporaries, says Fulco, " by the brilliancy of his genius, the sweetness of his eloquence, the ready flow of his language, and the subtlety of his knowledge." People came to him from all quarters ;—from Rome, in spite of mountains and robbers ; from England, in spite of the sea ; from Flanders and Germany ; from Normandy, and the remote districts of France ; from Angers and

Poitiers ; from Navarre by the Pyrenees, and from Spain, besides the students of Paris itself ; and among those, who sought his instructions now or afterwards, were the great luminaries of the schools in the next generation. Such were Peter of Poitiers, Peter Lombard, John of Salisbury, Arnold of Brescia, Ivo, and Geoffrey of Auxerre. It was too much for a weak head and heart, weak in spite of intellectual power ; for vanity will possess the head, and worldliness the heart, of the man, however gifted, whose wisdom is not an effluence of the Eternal Light.

True wisdom is not only "pacifica," it is "pudica ; " chaste as well as peaceable. Alas for Abelard ! a second disgrace, deeper than ambition, is his portion now. The strong man,—the Samson of the schools in the wildness of his course, the Solomon in the fascination of his genius,—shivers and falls before the temptation which overcame that mighty pair, the most excelling in body and in mind.

> Desire of wine, and all delicious drinks,
> Which many a famous warrior overturns,
> Thou couldst repress ; nor did the dancing ruby
> Sparkling outpour'd, the flavour or the smell,
> Or taste that cheers the heart of gods and men,
> Allure thee from the cool crystalline stream.
> But what avail'd this temperance, not complete,
> Against another object more enticing ?
> What boots it at one gate to make defence,
> And at another to let in the foe,
> Effeminately vanquished ?

In a time when Colleges were unknown, and the young scholar was commonly thrown upon the dubious hospitality of a great city, Abelard might even be thought careful of his honour, that he went to lodge with an old ecclesiastic, had not his host's niece Eloisa lived with him. A more subtle snare was laid for him than beset the heroic champion or the all-accomplished monarch of Israel; for sensuality came upon him under the guise of intellect, and it was the high mental endowments of Eloisa, who became his pupil, speaking in her eyes, and thrilling on her tongue, which were the intoxication and the delirium of Abelard. . . . .

He is judged, he is punished;—but he is not reclaimed. True wisdom is not only "pacifica," not only "pudica;" it is "desursum" too. It is a revelation from above; it knows heresy as little as it knows strife or licence. But Abelard, who had run the career of earthly wisdom in two of its phases, now is destined to represent its third.

It is at the famous Abbey of St. Denis that we find him languidly rising from his dream of sin, and the suffering that followed. The bad dream is cleared away; clerks come to him, and the Abbot,—begging him to lecture still, for love now, as for gain before. Once more his school is thronged by the curious and the studious; but at length a rumour spreads, that Abelard is exploring the way to some novel view on the subject of the Most Holy Trinity. Wherefore is hardly clear, but about the same time the monks drive him away from the place of refuge he had gained. He betakes himself to a cell, and thither his pupils follow him. "I betook myself to a certain cell," he says, "wishing to give myself to the schools, as was my custom. Thither so great a multitude of scholars flocked, that there was neither room to house them, nor fruits of the earth to feed them," such was the enthusiasm of the student, such the attraction of the teacher, when knowledge was advertised freely, and its market opened.

Next he is in Champagne, in a delightful solitude near Nogent in the diocese of Troyes. Here the same phenomenon presents itself, which is so frequent in his history. " When the scholars knew it," he says, " they began to crowd thither from all parts ; and, leaving other cities and strongholds, they were content to dwell in the wilderness. For spacious houses they framed for themselves small tabernacles, and for delicate food they put up with wild herbs. Secretly did they whisper among themselves : ' Behold, the whole world is gone out after him ! ' When, however, my Oratory could not hold even a moderate portion of them, then they were forced to enlarge it, and to build it up with wood and stone." He called the place his Paraclete, because it had been his consolation.

I do not know why I need follow his life further. I have said enough to illustrate the course of one, who may be called the founder, or at least the first great name, of the Parisian Schools. After the events I have mentioned he is found in Lower Britanny ; then, being about forty-eight years of age, in the Abbey of St. Gildas ; then with St. Geneviève again. He had to sustain the fiery eloquence of a Saint, directed against his novelties ; he had to present himself before two Councils ; he had to burn the book which had given offence to pious ears. His last two years were spent at Clugni on his way to Rome. The home of the weary, the hospital of the sick, the school of the erring, the tribunal of the penitent, is the city of St. Peter. He did not reach it ; but he is said to have retracted what had given scandal in his writings, and to have made an edifying end. He died at the age of sixty-two, in the year of grace 1142.

In reviewing his career, the career of so great an intellect so miserably thrown away, we are reminded of the famous words of the dying scholar and jurist, which are a lesson to us all : " Heu, vitam perdidi, operosè nihil agendo " A happier lot be ours !

CHAPTER XVII.

THE ANCIENT UNIVERSITY OF DUBLIN.

THE most prominent distinction between the primitive and the medieval schools, as I have already many times said, was, that the latter had a range and system in their subjects and the manner of their teaching, which were unknown to the former. The primitive schools, for instance, lectured from Scripture with the comments of the Fathers; but the medieval schools created the science of theology. The primitive schools collected and transmitted the canonical rules and traditions of the Church; the medieval schools taught the science of canon law. And so as regards secular studies, the primitive schools professed the three sciences of grammar, rhetoric, and logic, which make up the Trivium, and the four branches of the mathematics, arithmetic, geometry, astronomy, and music, which make up the Quadrivium. On the other hand, the medieval schools recognized philosophy as a science of sciences, which included, located, connected, and used all kinds and modes of knowledge; they enlarged the sphere and application of logic; and they added civil law, natural history, and medicine to the curriculum. It followed, moreover, from this, that while, on the one hand, they were led to divide their work among a number of Professors, they opened their doors on the other to laity as well as clergy, and to foreigners as well as natives.

Of schools founded on this magnificent idea and answering to a profession so comprehensive and so engrossing, there could be but a few specimens ; for instance, Paris, Oxford, and Bologna.   These, too, owed their characteristic splendour in no small measure to the zeal and learning of the Friars, especially the Dominicans ; accordingly, their great era was the thirteenth century.   But various causes came into operation to modify the University type, as I have described it, or at least its applications and manifestations, when that century had passed away. The first movements of new agents, both in the physical and social world, are commonly more energetic and more successful than those which follow ; and this remark includes both Universities themselves, and the religious bodies which were their prominent supporters. New orders of religion commonly achieve their greatest works in their first fervour.   The very success too of the experiment would tend to impair the University type by multiplying copies of it ; for an imperial power (and a University was such in the intellectual world) must be solitary to be imperial.   As, then, the utility of the new schools was recognized, they became more numerous and their respective territories less extensive.   Moreover, it was natural, that, as country after country woke up into existence and assumed an individuality, each in turn should desire a University of its own, that is, an institution indigenous and national.   Peace between states could not always be maintained ; the elements were beyond the traveller's control ; and a safe-conduct did not secure the pilgrim scholar from bandits and pirates.   The mutual divergence and distinctive formation of languages and of national character, national histories, national pride, national antipathies, would all carry forward the course of events in the same direction ; and the Collegiate system, of which I shall presently speak, coöperated in making a University a local institution, and in embodying it among the establishments of the nation. Hence it came to pass, that Oxford, for instance, in course of time, was not exactly the Oxford of the thirteenth century. Not that the great and primary idea of a University was not sufficiently preserved ; it was still a light set upon a hill, or a sort of ecumenical doctor on all subjects of knowledge, human and divine ; but it was directed and coloured by the political and social influences to which it was accidentally exposed. This change began about the commencement of the fourteenth century ; however, I am not going to dwell upon it here ; for the foregoing reference to it is only introductory to a short notice, which I propose now to give, of the ancient University of Dublin or of Ireland, set up at this very era,—a subject to which the mind naturally reverts just at this moment, when we are now on the point of laying down the rudiments of its revival or reconstruction upon the old foundations, on a grander scale, and, as we trust and believe, with a happier prospect for the future.

If by " University " is meant a large national School, conducted on the basis of the old Roman education, it was impossible that such should not have existed in a people so literary as the Irish, from the very time that St. Patrick brought among them Christianity and civilization. Accordingly, we hear of great seats of learning of this description in various parts of the country. The school of Armagh is said at one time to have numbered as many as seven thousand students ; and tradition assigns a University town to the locality where the Seven Churches still preserve the memory of St. Kevin. Foreigners, at least Anglo-Saxons, frequented such schools, and, so far, they certainly had a University character ; but that

they offered to their pupils more than the glosses on the
sacred text and the collections of canons, and the Trivium and the Quadrivium, which were the teaching of
the schools of the Continent, it is difficult to suppose ;
or that the national genius for philosophizing, which
afterwards anticipated or originated the scholastic period,
should at this era have come into exercise. When that
period came, the Irish, so far having its characteristic
studies already domiciled among them, were forced to
go abroad for their prosecution. They went to Paris or
to Oxford for the living traditions, which are the ordinary
means by which religion and morals, science and art, are
diffused over communities, and propagated from land
to land. In Oxford, indeed, there was from the earliest
time even a street called " Irishman's Street," and the
Irish were included there under the " Nation " of the
Southern English ; but they gained what they sought in
that seat of learning, at the expense of discomforts which
were the serious drawback of the first age of Universities. Lasting feuds and incessant broils marked the
presence of Irish, Welsh, Scotch, English, and French in
one place, at a time when the Collegiate System was
not formed. To this great evil was added the very circumstance that home was far away, and the danger of
the passage across the channel; which would diminish
the number, while it illustrated the literary zeal, of the
foreign students. And an additional source of discon-
tent was found in the feeling of incongruity, that Ireland,
with her literary antecedents, should be without a University of her own ; and, moreover, as time went on, in
the feeling which existed at Rome, in favour of the multiplication of such centres of science and learning.

   Another perfectly distinct cause was in operation, to
which I was just now referring. The Dominicans, and

other Orders of the age, had had a preëminent place in the history of the Universities of Paris and Oxford, and had done more than any other teachers to give the knowledge taught in them their distinctive form. When then these Orders came into Ireland, it was only to be expected that they should set about the same work there, which had marked their presence in England and France. Accordingly, at the end of the thirteenth century, the question of a University in Ireland had been mooted, and its establishment was commenced in the first years of the fourteenth.

This was the date of the foundation of the Universities of Avignon and Perugia, which was followed by that of Cahors, Grenoble, Pisa, and Prague. It was the date at which Oxford in consequence lost its especial preëminence in science ; and it was the date, I say, at which the University of Dublin was projected and begun. In 1311 or 1312, John Lech or Leach, Archbishop of Dublin, obtained of Clement the Fifth a brief for the undertaking ; in which, as is usual in such documents, the Pope gives the reasons which have induced him to decide upon it. He begins by setting forth the manifold, or rather complex, benefits of which a University is the instrument ; as father of the faithful, he recognizes it as his office to nurture learned sons, who, by the illumination of their knowledge, may investigate the divine law, protect justice and truth, illustrate the faith, promote good government, teach the ignorant, confirm the weak, and restore the fallen. This office he is only fulfilling, in receiving favourably the supplication of his venerable brother, John de Lecke, who has brought before him the necessities of his country, in which, as well as in Scotland, Man, and Norway, the countries nearest to Ireland, a " Universitas Scholarum," or " Generale Studium," is not to be found ;—the consequence being, that though there are in Ireland some doctors and bachelors in theology, and other graduates in grammar, these are, after all, few in comparison of the number which the country might fairly produce. The Pope proceeds to express his desire, that from the land itself should grow up men skilled and fruitful in the sciences, who would make it to be a well-watered garden, to the exaltation of the Catholic faith, the honour of Mother Church, and the advantage of the faithful population. And with this view he erects in Dublin a *Studium Generale* in every science and faculty, to continue for " perpetual times."

And, I suppose no greater benefit could have been projected for Ireland at that date, than such a bond of union and means of national strength, as an Irish University. But the parties, who had originated the undertaking, had also to carry it out : and at the moment of which I am speaking, by the fault neither of Prelate nor laity, nor by division, nor by intemperance or jealousy, nor by wrong-headedness within the fold, nor by malignant interference from without, but by the will of heaven and the course of nature, the work was suspended ;—for John de Lecke fell ill and died the next year, and his successor, Alexander de Bicknor, was not in circumstances to take up his plans at the moment, where de Lecke had left them.

Seven years passed ; and then Bicknor turned his mind to their prosecution. Acting under the authority of the brief of Clement, and with the sanction and confirmation of the reigning Pontiff, John the Twenty-second, he published an instrument, in which he lays down on his own authority the provisions and dispositions which he had determined for the nascent University. He addresses himself to "the Masters and Scholars of our

University," and that "with the consent and assent of our chapters of Holy Trinity and St. Patrick." I think I am correct in saying, though I write without book, that he makes no mention of a Rector. If not, the Chancellor probably, whom he does mention, took his place, or was his synonyme, as in some other Universities. This Chancellor the Regent Masters were to have the privilege of choosing, with a *proviso* that he was a "Doctor in sacrâ paginâ," or in "jure canonico," with a preference of members of the two chapters. He was to take the oath of fidelity to the Archbishop. The Regent Masters elected the Proctors also, who were two in number, and who supplied the place of the Chancellor in his absence. The Chancellor was invested with jurisdiction over the members of the University, and had a court, to which causes belonged in which they were concerned. There was, moreover, a University chest, supplied by means of the fines which were the result of his decisions. Degrees were to be conferred upon certificate of the Masters of the Faculty, in which the candidate was proceeding. Statutes were to be passed by the Chancellor, in council of Masters Regent and Nonregent, subject to the confirmation of the Archbishop. The Schools of the Friars Preachers (or Dominicans) and of the Minorites (or Franciscans) were recognized in their connection with the University, the Archbishop reserving to himself the right of appointing a Lecturer in Holy Scripture.

Such was the encouraging and hopeful start of the University ; the Dean of St. Patrick was advanced to the Doctorate in Canon Law, and was created its first Chancellor ; its first Doctors in Theology were two Dominicans and one Franciscan. The Canons of the Cathedral seem to have been its acting members, and

filled the offices of a place of education without pre-
judicing their capitular duties. However, it soon appeared that there was somewhere a hitch, and the work
did not make progress. It has been supposed with
reason, that under the unhappy circumstances of the
time, the University could not make head against the
necessary difficulties of a commencement. Another
and more definite cause which is assigned for the
failure, is the want of funds. The Irish people were
poor, and unable to meet the expenses involved in the
establishment of a great seat of learning, at a time when
other similar institutions already existed. The time
had passed when Universities grew up out of the enthusiasm of teachers and the curiosity and eagerness of
students ; or, if these causes still were in operation, they
had been directed and flowed in upon seats of learning
already existing in other countries. It was the age of
national schools, of colleges and endowments ; and,
though the civil power appeared willing to take its part
in endowments in furtherance of the new undertaking,
it did not go much further than to enrich it now
and then with a stray lectureship, and wealthy prelates
or nobles were not forthcoming in that age, capable of
conceiving and executing works in the spirit of Ximenes
two centuries afterwards in Spain.

Yet down to the very time of Ximenes, and beyond
it, continual and praiseworthy efforts were made, on the
part both of the Church and of the State, to accomplish
a work which was important in proportion to its difficulty. In 1358 the clergy and scholars of Ireland represented to Edward the Third the necessity under which
they lay of cultivating theology, canon law, and the other
clerical sciences, and the serious impediments in the
way of these studies which lay in the expense of travel

and the dangers of the sea to those who had no University of their own. In answer to this request, the king seems to have founded a lectureship in theology ; and he indirectly encouraged the University schools by issuing his letters-patent, giving special protection and safe-conduct to English as well as Irish, of whatever degree, with their servants and attendants, their goods and habiliments, in going, residing, and returning. A few years later, in 1364, Lionel, Duke of Clarence, founded a preachership and lectureship in the Cathedral, to be held by an Augustinian.

A further attempt in behalf of a University was made a century later. In 1465, the Irish Parliament, under the presidency of Thomas Geraldine, Earl of Desmond, Vicegerent of George, Duke of Clarence, Lieutenant of the English King, had erected a University at Drogheda, and endowed it with the privileges of the University of Oxford. This attempt, however, in like manner was rendered abortive by the want of funds ; but it seems to have suggested a new effort in favour of the elder institution at Dublin, which at this time could scarcely be said to exist. Ten years after the Parliament in question, the Dominican and other friars preferred a supplication to Pope Sixtus the Fourth, in which they represent that in Ireland there is no University to which Masters, Doctors of Law, and Scholars may resort ; that it is necessary to go to England at a great expense and peril ; and consequently they ask for leave to erect a University in the metropolitan city. The Pope granted their request, and, though nothing followed, the attempt is so far satisfactory, as evidencing the perseverance of the Irish clergy in aiming at what they felt to be a benefit of supreme importance to their country.

Nor was this the last of such attempts, nor were the

secular behind the regular clergy in zeal for a University. As late as the reign of Henry the Seventh, in the year 1496, Walter Fitzsimon, Archbishop of Dublin, in provincial Synod, settled an annual contribution to be levied for seven years in order to provide salaries for the Lecturers. And, though we have no record, I believe, of the effect of this measure, yet, when the chapter was reëstablished in the reign of Philip and Mary, the allusion made in the legal instrument to the loss which the youthful members of society had sustained in its suppression, may be taken to show, that certain scholastic benefits had resulted from its stalls though the education which they provided was not of that character which the name of a University demanded.

Times are changed since these attempts were made ; and, while the causes no longer exist which operated in their failure, the object towards which they were directed has attained a moment, both in itself and in its various bearings, which could never have been predicted in the fourteenth or the sixteenth century. Ireland is no longer the conquered possession of a foreign king ; it is, as in the primitive times, the centre of a great Catholic movement and of a world-wide missionary enterprise. Nor does the Holy See simply lend an ear to the project of others : it originates the undertaking.

CHAPTER XVIII.

COLLEGES THE CORRECTIVE OF UNIVERSITIES.

OXFORD.

COLLEGES, and Colleges for the advancement of science, were not altogether a medieval idea. To say nothing else, it is obvious to refer to the Museum of the Ptolemies at Alexandria, of which I spoke in an earlier Chapter. The Saracens too founded Colleges for learned education at Cordova, Granada, and Malaga; and these obtained a great reputation. Yet it is an idea, which has been brought out and familiarized in history, and recognized in political institutions, and completed in its parts, during the era of Universities, with a fulness which almost allows us to claim it as belonging to the new civilization. By a College, I suppose, is meant, not merely a body of men living together in one dwelling, but belonging to one establishment. In its very notion, the word suggests to us position, authority, and stability; and again, these attributes presuppose a foundation; and that foundation consists either in public recognition, or in the possession of revenues, or in some similar advantage. If two or three individuals live together, the community is not at once called a College; but a charter, or an endowment, some legal *status*, or some ecclesiastical privilege, is necessary to erect it into the Collegiate form. However, it does, I suppose, imply a community or *convitto* too ; and, if so, it must be of a certain definite size : for, as soon as it exceeds in point of numbers, non-residence may be expected to follow. It is then a household, and offers an abode to its members, and requires or involves the same virtuous and paternal discipline which is proper to a family and home. Moreover, as no family can subsist without a maintenance, and as children are dependent on their homes, so it is not unnatural that an endowment, which is, as I have said, suggested by the very idea of a College, should ordinarily be necessary for its actual carrying out. Still more necessary are buildings, and buildings of a prominent character ; for, whereas every family must have its dwelling, a family which has a recognized and official existence, must live in a sort of public building, which satisfies the eye, and is the enduring habitation of an enduring body.

This view of a College, which I have not been attempting to prove but to delineate, suggests to us the objects which a College is adapted to fulfil in a University. It is all, and does all, which is implied in the name of home. Youths, who have left the paternal roof, and travelled some hundred miles for the acquisition of knowledge, find an " altera Troja" and " simulata Pergama" at the end of their journey and in their place of temporary sojourn. Home is for the young, who know nothing of the world, and who would be forlorn and sad, if thrown upon it. It is the refuge of helpless boyhood, which would be famished and pine away, if it were not maintained by others. It is the providential shelter of the weak and inexperienced, who have still to learn how to cope with the temptations which lie outside of it. It is the place of training for those who are not only ignorant, but have not yet learned how to learn, and who have to be taught, by careful individual trial, how to set about profiting by the lessons of a teacher. And it is the school of elementary studies, not of advanced; for such studies alone can boys at best apprehend and master. Moreover, it is the shrine of our best affections, the bosom of our fondest recollections, a spell upon our after life, a stay for world-weary mind and soul, wherever we are cast, till the end comes. Such are the attributes or offices of home, and like to these, in one or other sense and measure, are the attributes and offices of a College in a University.

We may consider, historically speaking, that Colleges were but continuations, *mutatis mutandis*, of the schools which preceded the rise of Universities. These schools indeed were monastic or at least clerical, and observed a religious or an ecclesiastical rule; so far they were not simple Colleges, still they were devoted to study, and, at least sometimes, admitted laymen. They had two courses of instruction going on at once, attended by the inner classes and the outer; of which the latter were filled by what would now be called *externs*. Thus even in that early day the school of Rheims educated a certain number of noble youths; and the same arrangement is reported of Bec also.

And in matter of fact these monastic schools remained within the limits of the University, when it was set up, as they had been before, only of course more exclusively religious; for, as soon as the reception of laymen was found to be a part of the academical idea, the monasteries seemed to be relieved of the necessity of receiving lay students within their walls. At first, those Orders only would have a place in the University which were already there; but in process of time nearly every religious fraternity found it its interest to provide a College for its

own subjects, and to have representatives in the Academical body. Thus in Paris, as soon as the Dominicans and
Franciscans had thrown themselves into the new system,
and had determined that their vocation did not hinder
them from taking degrees, the Cistercians, under the
headship of an Englishman, founded a College near St
Victor's ; and the Premonstrants followed their example.
The Carmelites, being at first at a distance from St.
Geneviève, were planted by a king of France close under
her hill.   The Benedictines were stationed in the famous
Abbey of St. German, near the University Pratum ; the
monks of Cluni and of Marmoutier had their respective
houses also, and the former provided lecturers within
their walls for the students.   And in Oxford, in like
manner, the Benedictines founded Durham Hall for
their monks of the North of England, and Gloucester
Hall for their monks of the South, on the respective sites
of the present Trinity and Worcester Colleges.   The
Carmelites (to speak without book,) were at Beaumont,
the site of Henry the First's palace ; and St. John's and
Wadham Colleges are also on the sites of monastic
establishments.   Besides these, there were in Oxford
houses of Dominicans, Franciscans, Cistercians, and
Augustinians.

These several foundations, indeed, are of very different
eras; but, looking at the course of the history as a whole,
we shall find that such houses as were monastic preceded
the rest.   And if the new changes had stopped there, lay
education would have suffered, not gained, by the rise
of Universities ; for it had the effect of multiplying, indeed, monastic halls, but of shutting their doors against
all but monks more rigidly than before.   The solitary
strangers, who came up to Paris or Oxford from a far
country, must have been stimulated by a most uncommon

thirst for knowledge, to persevere in spite of the discouragements by which they were surrounded. Some attempt indeed was made by the Professors to meet so obvious and so oppressive an evil. The former scholastic type had recognized one master, and one only, in a school, who professed in consequence the whole course of instruction without any assistant Tutors. The tradition of this system continued ; and led in many instances to the formation of halls, inns, courts, or hostels, as they were variously called. That is, the Professor of the school kept house, and boarded his pupils. Thus we read of Torald schools in Oxford in the reign of Henry the Third, which had belonged previously to one Master Richard Bacum, who had fitted up a large tenement, partly for lodging house, partly for lecture rooms. In like manner, early in the twelfth century, Theobald had as many as from sixty to a hundred scholars under his tuition, for whom he would necessarily be more or less answerable. A similar custom was pointed out in Athens, in an early Chapter of these sketches, where it was the occasion of a great deal of rivalry and canvassing between the Professorial housekeepers, each being set upon obtaining as many lodgers as possible. And apparently a similar inconvenience had to be checked at Paris in the thirteenth century, though, whatever might be that incidental inconvenience, the custom itself, under the circumstances of the day, was as advantageous to the cause of study, as it was natural and obvious.

But still lodging keepers, though Professors, must be paid, and how could poor scholars find the means of fulfilling so hard a condition ? And the length of time then required for a University course hindered an evasion of its difficulties by such shifts and expedients, as serve for passing a mere trying crisis, or weathering a threatening season. The whole course, from the termination of the grammatical studies to the licentiate, extended originally through twenty years ; though afterwards it was reduced to ten. If we are to consider the six years of the course in Arts to have been in addition to this long space, the residence at the University is no longer a sojourn at the seat of learning, but becomes a sort of naturalization, yet without offering a home.

The University itself has little or no funds, to meet the difficulty withal. At Oxford, it had no buildings of its own, but rented such as were indispensable for academical purposes, and these were of a miserable description. It had little or no ground belonging to it, and no endowments. It had not the means of being an Alma Mater to the young men who came thither for education. Some verses are quoted by Antony à Wood, apropos of the poor scholar, which describe both his enthusiastic love of study and the trial to which it was put. The following is a portion of them :—

> Parva domus, res ipsa minor, contraxit utrumque
> Immensus tractusque diu sub Pallade fervor,
> Et logices jucundus amor &c., &c.   .   .   .   .
> Pauperies est tota domus, desuevit ad illos
> Ubertas venisse lares ; nec visitat ægrum
> Copia Parnassum ; sublimior advolat aulas,
> His ignota casis.

Accordingly, one of the earliest movements in the University, almost as early as the entrance into it of the monastic bodies, was that of providing maintenance for poor scholars. The authors of such charity hardly aimed at giving more than the bare necessaries of life,—food, lodging, and clothing,—so as to make a life of study possible. Comfort or animal satisfaction can hardly be

said to have entered into the scope of their benefactions ;
and we shall gain a lively impression of the sufferings of
the student, before the era of endowments, by considering his rude and hardy life even when a member of a
College. From an account which has been preserved in
one of the colleges of Cambridge, we are able to extract
the following *horarium* of a student's day. He got up
between four and five ; from five to six he assisted at
Mass, and heard an exhortation. He then studied or
attended the schools till ten, which was the dinner hour.
The meal, which seems also to have been a breakfast,
was not sumptuous ; it consisted of beef, in small messes
for four persons, and a pottage made of its gravy and
oatmeal. From dinner to five p.m., he either studied, or
gave instruction to others, when he went to supper, which
was the principal meal of the day, though scarcely more
plentiful than dinner. Afterwards, problems were dis-
cussed and other studies pursued, till nine or ten ; and
then half an hour was devoted to walking or running
about, that they might not go to bed with cold feet ;—
the expedient of hearth or stove for the purpose was
out of the question.

However, poor as was the fare, the collegiate life was
a blessing in many other ways far more important than
meat and drink ; and it was the object of pious benefactions for centuries. Hence the munificence of Robert
Capet, as early as 1050, even before the canons of St.
Geneviève and the monks of St. Victor had commenced
the University of Paris. His foundation was sufficient for
as many as one hundred poor clerks. Another was St.
Catherine in the Valley, founded by St. Louis, in consequence of a vow, which his grandfather, Philip Augustus,
had died before executing. Another and later was the
Collegium Bonorum Puerorum, which is assigned to the

year 1245. Such too, in its original intention, was the Harcurianum, or Harcourt College, the famous College of Navarre, the more famous Sorbonne, and the Montague College.

These Colleges, as was natural, were often provincial or diocesan, being founded by benefactors of a particular district for their own people. Sometimes too they were connected with one or other of the Nations of the University; I think the Harcurianum, just mentioned, was founded for the Normans; such too was the Dacian, founded for the Danes; and the Swedish; to which may be added the Burses provided for the Italians, the Lombards, the Germans, and the Scotch. In Bologna there was the greater College of St. Clement for the Spaniards, and the Collegio Sondi for the Hungarians. As to Diocesan or Provincial Colleges, such was Laon College, for poor scholars of the diocese of Laon; the College of Bayeux for scholars of the dioceses of Mons and Angers; the Colleges of Narbonne, of Arras, of Lisieux, and various others. Such too in Oxford at present are Queen's College, founded in favour of north countrymen, and Jesus College for the Welsh. Such are the fellowships, founded in various Colleges, for natives of particular counties; and such the fellowships or scholarships for founder's kin. In Paris, in like manner, Cardinal de Dormans founded a College for more than twenty students, with a preference in favour of his own family. A Society of a peculiar kind was founded in the very beginning of the thirteenth century. Baldwin, Count of Flanders, at that time Emperor of Constantinople, is said to have established a Greek College with a view to train up the youth of Constantinople in devotion to the Holy See.

When I said that there were graver reasons than

the need of maintenance, for establishing Colleges and Burses for poor scholars, it may be easily understood that I alluded to the moral evils, of which a University, without homes and guardians for the young, would infallibly be the occasion and the scene. These are so intelligible, and so much a matter of history, and so often illustrated, whether from the medieval or the modern continental Universities, that they need not occupy our attention here. Whatever licentiousness of conduct there is at Oxford and Cambridge now, where the Collegiate system is in force, does but suggest to us how fatal must be the strength of those impulses to disorder and riot when unrestrained, which are so imperfectly controlled even when submitted to an anxious discipline. Leaving this head of the subject, I think it better to turn to the consideration of an important innovation on the character and drift of academical foundations, which took place in the fifteenth century, when political changes in the nations of Europe brought with them corresponding changes in their Universities.

I have lately alluded to these changes in introducing the subject of the ancient University of Ireland. I said that the multiplication of Universities, the growth of nationalism, the increasing appreciation of peace and of the conveniences of life, the separation of languages, the Collegiate system itself, and similar and cognate causes, tended to give these institutions a local, political, and, I may now add, aristocratic character. At first Universities were almost democracies : Colleges tended to break their anarchical spirit, introduced ranks and gave the example of laws, and trained up a set of students, who, as being morally and intellectually superior to other members of the academical body, became the depositaries

of academical power and influence. Moreover, learning
was no longer thought unworthy of a gentleman ; and,
while the nobles of an earlier period had not disdained
to send their sons to Lanfranc or Vacarius, now it even
became a matter of custom, that young men of rank
should have a University education. Thus, in the
charter of the 29th of Edward the Third, we even read
that "to the University a multitude of nobles, gentry,
strangers, and others continually flock ; " and towards
the end of the century, we find Henry of Monmouth,
afterwards the Fifth, as a young man, a sojourner at
Queen's College, Oxford. But it was in the next century, of which Henry has made the first years glorious,
that Colleges were provided, not for the poor, but for the
noble. Many Colleges too, which had been originally
for the poor, opened their gates to the rich, not as fellows
or foundation-students, but as simple lodgers, or what
are now called independent members, such as monasteries
might have received in a former age. This was especially
the case with the College of Navarre at Paris ; and the
change has continued remarkably impressed upon Oxford and Cambridge even down to this day, with this
additional peculiarity, that, while the influence of
aristocracy upon those Universities is not less than it
was, the influence of other political classes has been introduced into the academic cloisters also. Never has
learned institution been more directly political and
national than the University of Oxford. Some of its
Colleges represent the talent of the nation, others its
rank and fashion, others its wealth ; others have been
the organs of the government of the day ; while others,
and the majority, represent one or other division, chiefly
local, of the country party. That all this has rather
destroyed, than subserved, the University itself, which

Colleges originally were instituted to complete, I will not take upon myself to deny ; but good comes out of many things which are in the way to evil, and this antagonism of the Collegiate to the University principle was not worked out, till Colleges had first rendered signal service to the University, and that, not only by completing it in those points where the University was weak, but even corroborating it in those in which it was strong. The whole nation, brought into the University by means of the Colleges, gave the University itself a vigour and a stability which the abundant influx of foreigners had not been able to secure.

As in the twelfth and thirteenth centuries French, German, and Italian students had flocked to the University of Oxford, and made its name famous in distant lands, so in the fifteenth, all ranks and classes of the nation furnished it with pupils, and what was wanting in their number or variety, compared with the former era, was compensated by their splendour or political importance. At that time nobles moved only in state, and surrounded themselves with retainers and servants, with an ostentation which has now quite gone out of fashion. A writer, whom I have from time to time used, Huber, informs us, that, before the wars of the Roses, and when the aristocracy were more powerful than the king, each noble family sent up at least one son to Oxford with an ample retinue of followers. Nor were the towns in that age, less closely united to the University than the upper classes, by reason of the numerous members of it that belonged to the clerical order, the popular character of that institution, and its intimate connection, as now, with the seat of learning. Thus town and country, high and low, north and south, had a common stake in the academical institutions, and took a personal interest in the academical proceedings. The degree possessed a sort of indelible *character*, which all classes understood; and the people at large were more or less partakers of a cultivation which the aristocracy were beginning to appreciate. And, though railroad travelling certainly did not then exist, communication between the students and their homes occurred with a frequency which could not be when they came from abroad; and Oxford became in a peculiar way a national and political centre. Not only in vacations and term-time was there a stated ebbing and flowing of the academical youth, but messengers posted to and fro between Oxford and all parts of the country in all seasons of the year. So intimate was this connection, that Oxford became a sort of selected arena for the conflicts of the various interests of the nation, and a serious University strife was received far and wide as the presage of civil war.

> " Chronica si penses, cum pugnant Oxonienses,
>   Post paucos menses, volat ira per Angligenenses."

But one may admire the position of a University, as a national centre, without any desire of renewing, in this day or in Ireland, the particular mode in which that position was in former times manifested in England. Such an united action of the Collegiate and of the National principle, far from being prejudicial, was simply favourable to the principle of a University. It was a later age which sacrificed the University to the College. We must look to the last two or three centuries, if we would witness the ascendency of the College idea in the English Universities, to the extreme prejudice, not indeed of its own peculiar usefulness (for that it has retained), but of the University itself. Huber, who gives us this account of Oxford, and who is neither Catholic on the one hand, nor innovator on the existing state of things on the other, warming yet saddening at his own picture, ends by observing : " Those days never can return ; for the plain reason that then men learned and taught by the living word, but now by the dead paper."

What has been here drawn out from the history of Oxford, admits of ample illustration from the parallel history of Paris. We find Chancellor Gerson on one occasion remonstrating in the name of his University with the French king. " Shall the University," he says, " being what she is, shut her eyes and be silent ? What would all France say, whose population she is ever exhorting, by means of her members, to patience and good obedience to the king and rulers ? Does not she represent the universal realm, nay, the whole world ? She is the vigorous seminary of the whole body politic, whence issue men of every kind of excellence. Therefore in behalf of the whole of France, of all states of men, of all her friends, who cannot be present here, she ought to expostulate and cry, ' Long live the king.' "

There is one other historical peculiarity attached to Colleges, to which I will briefly allude before concluding. If Colleges, with their endowments and local interests, provincial or county, are necessarily, when compared with Universities, of a national character, it follows that the education which they will administer, will also be national, and adapted to all ranks and classes of the community. And if so, then again it follows, that they will be far more given to the study of the Arts than to the learned professions, or to any special class of pursuits at all ; and such in matter of fact has ever been the case. They have inherited under changed circumstances the position of the monastic teaching founded by Charlemagne, and have continued its primitive tradition, through, and in spite of, the noble intellectual developments, to which Universities have given occasion. The historical link between the Monasteries and the Colleges have been the Nations, as some words of Antony à Wood about the latter suggest, and as the very name of " Nation" makes probable ; and indeed the Colleges were hardly more than the Nations formally established and endowed, with Provosts and Wardens in the place of Proctors.

Bulæus has some remarks on the subject of Colleges, which illustrate the points I have last insisted on, and several others which have previously come before us. He says : " The College system had no slight influence in restoring Latin composition. Indeed Letters were publicly professed in Colleges, and that, not only by persons on the foundation, but by others also who lived within the walls, though external to the body, and who were admitted to the schools of the Masters and to the classes in a fixed order and by regulated steps. On the contrary, we find that all the ancient Colleges were established for the education and instruction of poor scholars, members of the foundation ; but in the fifteenth century other ranks were gradually introduced also. By this means the lecturer was stimulated by the largeness of the classes, and the pupil by emulation, while the opportunities of a truant life were removed. Accordingly laws were frequently promulgated and statutes passed, with a view of bringing the Martinets and wandering scholars within the walls of the Colleges. We do not know exactly when this practice began ; it is generally thought that the College of Navarre, which was reformed in the year 1464, was the first to open its gates to these public professors of letters. It is certain, that in former ages the teachers of grammar and rhetoric had schools of their own, or hired houses and hostels, where they received pupils ; but in this century teachers of grammar, or of rhetoric, or of philosophy, began to teach within the Colleges." He adds that in the time of Louis the eleventh, the Professors who lectured on literature, rhetoric, and philosophy in the town, were generally left by the students for those who had taken up their abodes in the Colleges.

This is rather an enumeration of some characteristics of Colleges, than a sufficient sketch of their relation to the University ; but it may suggest points of inquiry to those who would know more. I will but add, that at Paris there seem to have been as many as fifty Colleges ; at Oxford at present there are from twenty to twenty-four ; as many, I believe, were at Salamanca ; at Cambridge not so many ; at Toulouse, eight. As to Louvain, I have been told that if a bird's-eye view be taken of the city, the larger and finer buildings which strike the beholder throughout it, will be found at one time to have belonged to the University.

CHAPTER XIX.

IF what has been said in former Chapters of this
volume upon the relation of a University to its
Colleges, be in the main correct, the difference between
the two institutions, and the use of each, is very clear.
A University embodies the principal of progress, and a
College that of stability ; the one is the sail, and the
other the ballast; each is insufficient in itself for the
pursuit, extension, and inculcation of knowledge ; each
is useful to the other. A University is the scene of
enthusiasm, of pleasurable exertion, of brilliant display,
of winning influence, of diffusive and potent sympathy ;
and a College is the scene of order, of obedience, of
modest and persevering diligence, of conscientious fulfilment of duty, of mutual private services, and deep and
lasting attachments. The University is for the world,
and the College is for the nation. The University is for
the Professor, and the College for the Tutor ; the University is for the philosophical discourse, the eloquent
sermon, or the well contested disputation ; and the
College for the catechetical lecture. The University is
for theology, law, and medicine, for natural history, for
physical science, and for the sciences generally and their
promulgation ; the College is for the formation of character, intellectual and moral, for the cultivation of the

mind, for the improvement of the individual, for the study of literature, for the classics, and those rudimental sciences which strengthen and sharpen the intellect. The University being the element of advance, will fail in making good its ground as it goes ; the College, from its Conservative tendencies, will be sure to go back, because it does not go forward. It would seem as if an University seated and living in Colleges, would be a perfect institution, as possessing excellences of opposite kinds.

But such a union, such salutary balance and mutual complement of opposite advantages, is of difficult and rare attainment. At least the present day rather gives us instances of the two antagonistic evils, of naked Universities and naked Colleges, than of their alliance and its benefits. The great seats of learning on the Continent, to say nothing of those in Scotland, show us the need of Colleges to complete the University ; the English, on the contrary, show us the need of a University to give life to an assemblage of Colleges. The evil of a University, standing by itself, as in Germany, is often insisted on and may readily be apprehended ; and therefore, leaving that part of the subject alone, I will say a few words on the state of things in England, where the action of the University is suspended, and the Colleges have supreme and sovereign authority.

At the Reformation, the State not only made itself the head of the Anglican Church, but resolved to suppress, or nearly so, its legal existence. It not only ignored the idea of a central authority in Christendom ; but it went very far towards ignoring the existence of a Church in England itself. I believe I am right in saying that the Church of England, as such, scarcely has a legal *status*. Its Bishops indeed are Peers of Parliament, its chapters have charters, its Rectors are corporations sole, its ministers are officers of the law, its fabrics have special rights, its courts have a civil position and functions, its Prayer-book is (as has been observed) an Act of Parliament; but, as far as I know, there is no corporation of the United Church of England and Ireland, though that title itself be a legal one. The Protestant Church, as such, holds no property, and exercises no functions. It is an aggregate of many thousand corporations professing one object, and moulded on a common rule. The nearest approach to corporate power lay in its Convocations, which were at least three in number, not one,—those of Canterbury, of York, and of Dublin; and these have been virtually long obsolete. The Protestant Church would be an *imperium in imperio,* considering the immense wealth, power, and influence of its constituent members, were it itself a corporation.

The same spirit which destroyed the legal incorporation of the religious principle, was the jealous enemy also of the incorporation of the intellectual; and the civil power could as little bear a University as it bore a Church. Accordingly, Oxford and Cambridge shared the fate of the Hierarchy; the component parts of those Universities were preserved, but they themselves were superseded; and there would be almost as great difficulties now in Protestant England, in restoring its Universities to their proper place, as in restoring its Church. It is true, that the Colleges themselves are important political bodies, independent of the civil power; but at the same time they are national bodies; they represent not the human mind, but sections of the political community; and the civil power is itself nothing else than an expression of national power in one or other of its aspects ; whereas a University is an intellectual power, as such, just as the Church is a religious power. Intellect, as well as Faith and Conscience, are authorities simply independent of State and Nation ; State and Nation are but different aspects of one and the same power : and thus the State and Nation will endure chapters and colleges, as they bear city companies and municipalities, but not a Church, not a University. On the other hand, considering the especially popular character of the English constitution, and how congenial to it is the existence of organs of public opinion and of representative bodies, it is not wonderful that the Collegiate system has not merely remained in these later centuries, but has been cherished and advanced.

I am not denying this political value of the Colleges as counterpoises to the government of the day. The greatest weight has actually been given to their acts and decisions in this point of view. Oxford has been made the stage on which political questions have been tried, and political parties have carried on their contests. This was particularly instanced at the time of that famous Session of Parliament, in which Catholic Emancipation was granted. It is well known that the king then on the throne was averse to the measure ; and it was felt that an adhesion to it on the part of the University would exert a material influence on his feelings ; and the question to be determined was what opinion had the University upon it. In the summer of 1828, Sir Robert Peel is said to have consulted* those who were most intimately in his confidence in Oxford, as to the effect which would be produced upon

* Since this was written, Sir. R. Peel's narrative has been given to the world, and seems to contain nothing inconsistent with it.

its members by a ministerial project in favour of
Catholics. His friends belonged to a section of the
University, who lived very much in their own circle ;
and who, as resting both on academical distinction and
connection with the great world, did not know, and did
not represent, the sentiments of the Colleges. Accordingly, drifting with the current of London opinion themselves, which the necessities of the state and the
convenience of the Government, and Parliamentary
agitation, had for some time made more and more
favourable to Emancipation, those considerable persons
returned for answer, that the important act might be
passed any day, and that men would go to bed and
rise again, without being at all the wiser or more
anxious for what had taken place. The Minister seems
to have committed himself to this opinion ; and, in
consequence, confident of a successful issue of the
experiment, he took a bold, and as it turned out, an
unlucky step. Member for the University as he was,
and elected on the very ground of his opposition to the
Catholic claims, he resolved on resigning his seat, and
presenting himself for re-election, with an avowed
change of opinions. He did this, or at least his friends
for him, under the conviction that his triumphant
appeal to the votes of the academical constituency, on
which he reckoned, would be the best evidence to his
Master that the feeling of the country had undergone
that revolution which had already, openly or secretly,
taken place among statesmen. And hence the extraordinary vehemence of the contest which followed ; the
country party, which was represented by the Colleges,
being confident of swaying the determination of the king
and ejecting the Minister from office, if it managed to
eject him from the representation.

Political importance is of course the protection of those who possess it. They who can do so much for or against a Minister, can do as much for themselves ; and in consequence, the Colleges of Oxford and Cambridge are perhaps the best protected interests in the whole country. They have endured the most formidable attacks, without succumbing. It was against the wall of Magdalen College, as it has been expressed, that James the Second ran his head. That College received the brunt of the monarch's attack, and in the strength of the nation repelled it. Twenty years ago, when Reform was afloat, when boroughs were disfranchised, corporations created, sees united, dioceses rearranged, chapters remodelled, church property redistributed, and every parsonage perplexed with parliamentary papers of inquiry and tables of returns, the Colleges alone escaped. A determined attack was made upon them by the Ministry of the day, and great apprehensions were excited in the minds of their members. However, calm, perhaps selfish, calculators at Oxford said : " Nothing can touch us ; the Establishment will go, but not the Colleges : " and certainly after one or two sessions, after strong speeches in Parliament from Secretaries of State and experimentalists in Education, and after committees, gatherings, and manifestoes on the part of the members of Colleges, it was owned by friends of Government, that its attempt upon them was a mistake and a failure, and the sooner Government gave it up, the better for Government.

There is no political power in England like a College in the Universities ; it is not a mere local body, as a corporation or London company ; it has allies in every part of the country. When the mind is most impressible, when the affections are warmest, when associations are made for life, when the character is most ingenuous and the sentiment of reverence is most powerful, the future landowner, or statesman, or lawyer, or clergyman comes up to a College in the Universities. There he forms friendships, there he spends his happiest days ; and, whatever is his career there, brilliant or obscure, virtuous or vicious, in after years, when he looks back on the past, he finds himself bound by ties of gratitude and regret to the memories of his College life. He has received favours from the Fellows, he has dined with the Warden or Provost ; he has unconsciously imbibed to the full the beauty and the music of the place. The routine of duties and observances, the preachings and the examinations and the lectures, the dresses and the ceremonies, the officials whom he feared, the buildings or gardens that he admired, rest upon his mind and his heart, and the shade of the past becomes a sort of shrine to which he makes continual silent offerings of attachment and devotion. It is a second home, not so tender, but more noble and majestic and authoritative. Through his life he more or less keeps up a connection with it and its successive sojourners. He has a brother or intimate friend on the foundation, or he is training up his son to be a member of it. When then he hears that a blow is levelled at the Colleges, and that they are in commotion, —that his own College, Head and Fellows, have met together, and put forward a declaration calling on its members to come up and rally round it and defend it, a chord is struck within him, more thrilling than any other ; he burns with *esprit de corps* and generous indignation ; and he is driven up to the scene of his early education, under the keenness of his feelings, to vote, to sign, to protest, to do just what he is told to do, from confidence in the truth of the representations made to him, and from sympathy with the appeal. He appears on the scene of action ready for battle on the appointed day, and there he meets others like himself, brought up by the same summons ; he gazes on old faces, revives old friendships, awakens old reminiscences, and goes back to the country with the renewed freshness of youth upon him.   Thus, wherever you look, to the North or South of England, to the East or West, you find the interest of the Colleges dominant ; they extend their roots all over the country, and can scarcely be overturned, certainly not suddenly overturned, without a revolution.

The consequences on the Colleges themselves are not satisfactory.   They are withdrawn in an especial way from the action and the influence of public opinion, than which there is no greater stimulant to right action, as things are, nor a more effective security against dereliction of duty.   The Colleges, left to themselves, in the course of last century became shamefully indolent and inactive.   They were in no sense any longer places of education ; they were for the most part mere clubs, and sinecures, and almshouses, where the inmates did little but enjoy themselves.   They did next to nothing for the youth confided to them ; suffered them to follow their own ways and enjoy their own liberty, and often in their own persons set them a very bad example of using it. Visitor they practically had none ; and there was but one power which could have exerted authority over them, and most naturally and suitably too ; I mean the University ; but the University could do nothing.   The University had no means of acting upon the Colleges ; it was but a name or a privilege ; it was not a body or a power. This seems to me the critical evil in the present state of the English Universities, not that the Colleges are strong, but that the University has no practical or real jurisdiction over them.   Over the members of Colleges it has jurisdiction, but even then, not as such, but because they are its own members also; over the Head of the College, over the Fellows, over the corporate body, over its property, over its officers, over its acts and regulations within its own precincts, the University has no practical jurisdiction at all. The Tutor indeed is a University office by the Statutes, but the College has made it its own.

In matter of fact the only mode of affecting the Colleges has been by the gradual stress of persevering efforts, by incessant agitation, and by improving the tone and enlightening the minds of their members,—by indirect means altogether. At the beginning of this century, when matters were at the worst at Oxford, some zealous persons attempted to bring the University to bear upon the Colleges. The degrees were at that time given upon no *bonâ fide* examination. The youth, who had passed his three or four years at the place, and wished to graduate, chose his examiners, and invited them to dinner, which the ceremony of examination preceded. Now a degree is a University, not a College distinction ; and the admirable persons, to whom I have alluded, made an effort to restore to the University the power and the practice of ascertaining by a *bona fide* examination the proficiency of every one of its members, who was a candidate for it. Could there be a case in which the right of the University was more clear ? It gave a privilege, and, one might surely think, had a right to lay down the conditions of giving it. Yet it found itself unable to exact of all its members, what was so imperatively its duty, and so natural. The Colleges had first to be persuaded to concede, what the University was so reasonable in requiring. What took place in detail, has never perhaps been published to the world : so much, however, is notorious, that for thirty years one College, by virtue of ancient rights, was able to stand out against the University, and demanded and obtained degrees for its junior members without examination. A generation passed, before its Fellows, acted on by the example and sympathizing in the sentiments of the academical society around them, consented to do for themselves what the University had in vain attempted to do for them.

The University has thus gradually progressed ever since that time; not indeed towards the recovery of that power of jurisdiction, which properly belongs to it, but in separate and particular measures of improvement. One measure was attempted nearly thirty years ago, by an eminent person, still alive, and well known in Dublin, and was thwarted by parties who are long dead; so that it may be spoken of without pain to any one. There are at Oxford several Societies or Houses, which have practically the rank and rights of Colleges, though they have not the legal *status*, or the property. Some of these at that date supported themselves by taking as members those, who, either would not be received, or had actually been sent away, by the Colleges. The existence then of these Societies mainly depended on the sufferance within the University of incompetent, idle, or riotous young men. As they had no endowments, they asked high terms for admission, which of course they could not fail in obtaining from those, who needed to be in some Society or other, with a view to academical advantages, and who could not secure a place in any other body. Evidently, nothing would have been more fatal to such establishments than any successful effort to purify the University of unworthy members. Now, in the gradual advance of reforms, it was attempted by the able person I speak of to introduce an examination of all members on their matriculation. But the independence and the interests of both endowed and not endowed Houses, were at once touched by such a proposition; and a vigorous opposition was set on foot, in particular by the Head of one Society, which abounded in gownsmen of the unsatisfactory character I have been describing. Of course he might as well have shut up his Hall at once, and taken lodgings in High Street, as consent to a measure which would have simply cut off the supply from which it was filled. The private interest prevailed over the public; had the question fairly come before the members of the Colleges generally, it might perhaps have been carried in the affirmative; but it had to be decided first in the board of Heads of Houses, and they were typical specimens of those very Collegiate vices of which I have been speaking. An oligarchy indeed of twenty-four men, perpetual, sovereign, absolutely sheltered from public opinion, and purely irresponsible in their proceedings; standing aloof from the Academical body itself, and intensely scornful towards its judgments, too well entrenched to be susceptible of fear and too majestic to be swayed by flattery or ridicule, they were a prodigy in the England of the nineteenth century.

> Omnis enim per se Divûm natura necesse 'st
> Immortali ævo summâ cum pace fruatur,
> Semota ab nostris rebus, sejunctaque longe:
> Nam privata dolore omni, privata periclis,
> Ipsa suis pollens opibus, nil indiga nostri,
> Nec bene promeritis capitur, nec tangitur ir.

These authorities naturally were unwilling to handle a question, which concerned so nearly some of themselves; and to this day, though separate Colleges properly insist on the necessary qualifications, in the case of those who are to be admitted to their Lectures, the University itself is not allowed to exercise its reasonable right of examining its members before it matriculates them. It may here be added, that this time-honoured usurpation and abuse, the old Hebdomadal Board, which every thoughtful person felt could not much longer continue, has, amid the jubilations and thanksgivings of all parties, and with scarcely a sigh or murmur from any quarter whatever, expired ignominiously under the Act passed in the last Session of Parliament, 18 Vict.

As to that Act, however, its history is but a fresh illustration of the foregoing remarks. It did not dare to touch the real seat of existing evils, by restoring or giving jurisdiction to the University over the Colleges, much as it professed to effect in the way of radical reform. And in the passage of the Bill through the House of Commons, unless I am mistaken, Ministers found it impossible to get beyond that part of it which related to University alterations. As soon as it went on to legislate for the Colleges, the opposition was too strong for them, and the whole subject was postponed by Parliament, and made over for the consideration of a small Commission, with so many checks and limitations upon its proceedings, that there is reason for fearing that, whatever comes of them, the University will not be less enslaved by the Collegiate interest than it is at present.*

---

* Since this was written, there have been far larger changes in the polity and system of this University.

CHAPTER XX.

UNIVERSITIES AND SEMINARIES:
L'ECOLE DES HAUTES ETUDES.

NO two institutions are more distinct from each other in character, than Universities and Seminaries; and their very difference might seem a pledge that they would not come into collision with each other. Seminaries are for the education of the clergy; Universities for the education of laymen. They are for separate purposes, and they act in separate spheres; yet, such is human infirmity, perhaps they ever will be rivals in their actual working. So at least it has been in time past. Universities grew out of the Episcopal Schools; and then, as time went on, they returned evil for good, and gradually broke the strength, and drained away the life of the institution which had given them birth; an institution too, which was of far more importance to the Church than themselves. Universities are ornaments indeed and bulwarks to Religion; but Seminaries are essential to its purity and efficiency. It is plain then, if the action and interests of the two institutions have conflicted, which side the Church would take in the quarrel. She would side for the injured party, against the aggressor; for the party more important to her, against the party less so. Universities then for a long season have been sustaining the punishment of past ambition; and it seems hardly right to close this survey of them without saying a few words about them under this aspect.

As Seminaries are so necessary to the Church, they are one of her earliest appointments. Scarcely had the New Dispensation opened, when, following the example of the Schools of the Temple and of the Prophets under the Old, St. John is recorded, over and above the public assemblies of the faithful, to have had about him a number of students whom he familiarly instructed ; and, as time went, and power was given to the Church, this School for ecclesiastical learning was placed under the roof of the Bishop. In Rome especially, where we look for the pattern to which other churches are to be conformed, the clergy, not of the city only, but of the provinces, were brought under the immediate eye of the Pope. The Lateran Church, his first Cathedral, had a Seminary attached to it, which remained there till the pontificate of Leo the Tenth, when it was transferred into the heart of the city. The students entered within its walls from the earliest childhood ; but they were not raised from minor orders till the age of twenty, nor did they reach the priesthood till after the trial of many years. Strict as a monastic noviciate, it nevertheless included polite literature in its course ; and a library was attached to it for the use of the seminarists. Here was educated about the year 310, St. Eusebius, afterwards in Arian times the celebrated Bishop of Vercellæ ; and in the dark age which followed, it was the home from childhood of some of the greatest Popes, St. Gregory the Second, St. Paul the First, St. Leo the Third, St. Paschal, and St. Nicholas the First. This venerable Seminary, called anciently the School of the Pontifical Palace, has never failed. Even when the barbarians were wasting the face of Italy, and destroying its accumulations of literature, the great Council of Rome, under Pope Agatho, as I mentioned above, could testify, not indeed to the theological science of the school in that miserable age, but to its faithful preservation of the unbroken teaching of revealed truth and of the traditions of the Fathers. In the thirteenth century, we find it in a flourishing condition, and St. Thomas and Albertus Magnus lecturing in its halls.

Such a prerogative of perpetuity was not enjoyed elsewhere. Europe lay submerged under the waters of a deluge; and, when they receded, schools had to be refounded as well as churches. One of the principal results of Charlemagne's visit to Rome, was the reform or revival of education, both secular and ecclesiastical; and on his return to the north he addressed his well-known letter on the subject to the chapters and monastic bodies through his Empire. Henceforth the Pope made Seminaries obligatory in every Diocese: as to the laity, they attended the public Schools spoken of in a former Chapter.

Seminaries then were long in possession before Universities were imagined; and Universities rose out of them. And, when Universities were established, in order to preserve the *equilibrium* between clerical and lay education, it was decreed, by the authority of the Canons, that secular learning should be studied in the Seminaries, and that each Cathedral should maintain masters for its teaching. It was foreseen that, unless this was done, Universities would supply a higher and a wider education than the Episcopal Schools; and that the clergy would either become inferior to the monks and the laity, or would be drawn within the precincts and influence of Universities.

The latter of these inconveniences actually took place. The lectures in the Universities, after all, were necessarily superior to those which a Seminary could furnish. Accordingly, Colleges for ecclesiastical students were founded in their neighbourhood, and the Cathedral Schools fell in reputation, and were gradually deserted. The youths, who would have found their natural home there, sometimes entered the Colleges aforesaid, sometimes attended the schools of the Regulars, sometimes lived in lodgings as other students. It is sufficient to refer to the Lives of the Medieval Saints for instances of ordination taking place from or at the Universities without Seminary training; take, for example, St. Raymund, St. John of Matha, St. Thomas of Canterbury, St. Edmund, St. John Nepomucene, St. Caietan, St. Carlo, St. Ignatius and his companions, or St. Francis of Sales,—men, who lived in very various ages and countries, and some of whom had to repel the shameless assaults, to which their defenceless condition, in the midst of great cities, exposed them. And thus it was, that by the date of the Council of Trent, Seminaries had all but ceased to exist; and the candidates for the Priesthood, who had any learning and any religious training, either gained it for themselves, as they could, amid the mixed concourse of a University, or as members of Colleges, which had themselves suffered materially in their discipline from University contact.

There would be danger to their faith and religious temper, as well as to their morals. In Universities, subjects of every sort were disputed publicly; and boys, who ought to have been schooled at a Seminary in distrust of the intellect and modesty of speculation, were suffered to imbibe a critical, carping, curious spirit, most unbecoming in an ecclesiastic, on the interpretation of difficulties of Scripture, or on the deepest questions of theology. And the state of things became still more grave, when Protestantism arose, and its adherents found means of introducing themselves into the Professorial chairs.

It must be recollected, too, that none but the more able, or more wealthy, or more pushing, could succeed in paying their way at a University. But the majority of ecclesiastics would be poor, and without any great energy or enterprise. These, in the decay of Seminaries, were thrown for education upon the parish schools, which were obviously unequal to the task.

Such was the state of things, to which the Council of Trent put an end. Episcopal Seminaries were restored ; ecclesiastical Colleges in Universities suppressed ; the profounder studies were to be taught under the Bishop's eye : but, to make the observance of this rule easier, it was provided that poorer Dioceses might unite to establish a Provincial Seminary, where the students of each would be all educated together. Such, I suppose, in its ecclesiastical position is the College of Maynooth ; and it is able in consequence to present a staff of Professors, and it exhibits an amount and quality of learning and talent, which invest it almost with a University character.

A further step in the same direction has been taken by the present Pope. Without interfering with the constitution of the Seminaries of his States, he has founded at Rome, at considerable expense, the Seminario Pio, which is to be filled with young ecclesiastics, taken from all dioceses, selected from the whole number on the principle of merit. Their course lasts for nine years, and embraces philosophy, scholastic theology, Holy Scripture, the Fathers, canon law, rites, and ecclesiastical history. It has Professorial Chairs, and the power of granting degrees in Theology and Canon Law: it is in fact an ecclesiastical University.

It cannot be denied, that, while Seminaries have been

fostered and advanced during these last centuries, Universities have been out of favour. Two only were founded, as it would appear, in the sixteenth century, and these were expressly intended to counteract the spread of Protestantism. The last great Medieval University was the famous foundation, or foundations, at Alcala, due to the munificence of Cardinal Ximenes, in the year 1500. Since that date, it has been usual rather to bestow on Collegiate institutions the privileges of Universities, or in other words to erect a University in a College, than to adhere to the medieval type. Such appears to be the nature of the University, which, with the recognition of the British Government, has lately been founded at Quebec. To the same distinction another College seems tending, unless civil obstacles hinder it, which to us is of especial interest, for the sake of the prelate who founded it, from its progress hitherto, and because its Superior is an Irishman : I mean *L'Ecole des Hautes Etudes* at Paris. But, above all, it will have a definite place, if it proceeds, as it promises to do, in the history of Universities, and for that reason deserves some distinct mention here.

It was commenced by the immediate predecessor of the present Archbishop of Paris, a prelate of glorious memory ; whose blood, offered in behalf of his flock, seems already to have borne those fruits, which are the usual result of suffering in the cause of religion, and to have called down from Heaven upon his flock the blessings which he so ardently desired for them. As one of his scholars in the seat of learning which he has founded, expresses it,

> Audiit, et, miseratus oves per prælia promptus,
> Perque neces varias fertur, pia victima, pastor.
> Heu scelus infandum ! ruptæ dum fœdera pacis

Nectere, et insanos tentas cohibere furores,
Occidis, ac moriens extremâ voce " Beatos,
Si nostro," exclamas, " cessaret sanguine sanguis !"

Nor has the Archbishop's been the only blood by
which his Institution has been sanctified, nor is that Institution the only school of devotion and science, which
has occupied the spot on which it is placed.   That spot
was long ago, for centuries, the home of theologians,
and it has become in the generation before us the scene
and monument of Martyrs.   It is no other than the
famous Carmes, where, on the terrible outburst of the
Revolution, in 1792, so many Bishops and Priests of
France were massacred.

This of course is not the occasion for enumerating
the noble foundations which of old time were brought
under the shadow of the great University of Paris, the
first school of the Church.   I have touched upon the subject in a former Chapter.   Nations, provinces, monastic
bodies, had their several houses there, and royal personages and wealthy ecclesiastics rejoiced to leave endowments there for the benefit of religion and learning.
The southern and more healthy bank of the river was
allotted to it, and its manifold establishments gathered
round the hill of St. Genevieve.   The Carmelites were
originally at an inconvenient distance from the Saint,
till Philip the Fair, King of France, gave them ground
at the foot of her hill, sufficient for a Church and a
Monastery.   This was about the year 1300; and for the
last two centuries before the dreadful events, to which I
have referred, it is described, in particular, as having
been one of the most peaceable asylums of science and
faith.   When the Revolution came, and the clergy,
hindered, by their duty to the Church, from taking the
oaths which were presented for their acceptance, were

subjected to an imprisonment which was to end in death, the Carmelite Convent was one of the buildings selected for their confinement. Here, or rather in the small church attached to the Convent, in the month of August, 1792, were crowded, first 120, and at length as many as 175 or 200, according to various accounts, of all ranks and ages of the clergy.

The first prisoners seem to have been the secular clergy of the city ; to these were added a number of superannuated priests, who lived on pensions, and then a number of youthful seminarists. Besides these, were three Bishops, various Professors and Preachers, and the heads of certain religious congregations and collegiate bodies. The second of September was the day of their memorable conflict with the powers of evil, then for a brief season in the ascendant. On that day were imprisoned together in the house and garden of the Carmes (besides the Seculars), Benedictines, Capuchins, Cordeliers, Sulpicians, disbanded Jesuits, members of the Sorbonne, and of the College of Navarre. The revolutionary tribunal held its sitting in one of the rooms of the Convent, and pronounced them guilty of disloyalty to France ; and then the revolutionary soldiers impatiently burst in upon the prisoners to carry its sentence into execution. The massacre lasted for three hours ; eighty priests were slaughtered in the garden ; the walls of the orangery at its end, now a chapel, are still stained, or rather daubed over, with their blood. On about a hundred others the outward door of the Convent was opened for their passage into the street ; they were called forward one by one; the assassins stood in double file, and, as their victims ran the gauntlet between them, above sixty perished under their blows, thirty-six or thirty-eight escaping into the city. These noble soldiers of the Church waited for their turn, and went to death and died, with their office books in their hands, and its psalms and prayers upon their tongues.

To have lived in Paris then, and to have heard the report, and seen the tokens, of what was going on, was to have had some share in her agony, who of old time looked upon One uplifted on the Cross; yet, bitter as the sorrow must have been, surely it was lighter after all, than that which has oppressed the Catholic heart at other miserable seasons. It was surely lighter than that which overspread Christendom at the time when religion was overthrown in England, while, for a long course of years, for the greater part of a century, some fresh deed of sacrilege was perpetrated day by day, and a false-hearted clergy and a cowardly laity allowed the monarch and his nobles in their deeds of violence and avarice. For the death of traitors makes no sign, and whispers scarce a hope of a revival; but a martyrdom is a victory, and a Church which falls from an external blow, rises again by its inward vigour. This is fulfilled before our eyes in the instance of France, and of that memorable spot of which I have been speaking. Good reason why the late Archbishop should have placed his new institution in that sanctuary of martyrs, himself destined so soon afterwards to be gathered to their company.

Institutions, which are to thrive and last, generally have humble beginnings, sometimes a scope narrower than that which they eventually profess; as there has been enough to suggest, even in the sketches which have been set before the reader in these pages. So has it been, so is it still perhaps, in the case of the school now under consideration. Its first object, when it opened in 1845, was one indeed of high importance in itself, being no less than that of providing Professors for the *petits seminaires* of France. However, it is also described as " a noviciate of ecclesiastics intended for teachers of the young clergy," which is something of an advance in dignity and moment upon the object as originally conceived. When the title was given, by which the school is now designated, does not appear ; but an " Ecole des Hautes Etudes," also promises, or presages, more than the first profession of its founder. It speaks of high studies, and studies for their own sake, which hardly is equivalent to a school for schoolmasters. Perhaps it was discovered, as soon as attention was directed to the subject, that, in order to teach well, more must be learned by the teacher than he has formally to impart to the pupil ; that he must be above his work, and know, and know accurately and philosophically, what he does not actually profess. Accordingly, we find the students are instructed, not only in the languages, but in the literatures, of Greece, Rome, and France ; in general history ; and in philosophy, and in the bearings of religion upon it,—in which probably are included the study of the Evidences of Christianity, of the objections made to it and their refutation. Nor is the direct cultivation of their minds forgotten ; the perfection of our intellectual nature seems to be judgment ; and what judgment is in the conduct of life, such is taste in our social intercourse, in literature, and the fine arts. Now we are told that it is provided, with a largeness of view which does honour to the projectors of the Institution, that its students, though ecclesiastical, should be made acquainted with the ideas and sentiments, the tone of mind, and character of thought, and method of expression, which distinguish the great writers both of ancient and modern times ; in order that, while they exercise themselves in composition, they may have a really good standard to work by, and may learn even unconsciously to imitate what has become familiar to them by frequent perusal.

Nor is this the limit of their studies; the present Archbishop has added mathematics, physics, and geology. Little is evidently now wanting to complete a University course ; and accordingly we find they have been led for some time to present themselves for the formal examinations which are the condition of an academical degree. Two years ago they numbered as many as thirty-two licentiates in arts; and the doctorate, which is preceded by the study of the Fathers and ecclesiastical history, had then been attained by three. Meanwhile the Synod of Paris has made the Institution the metropolitan school of the province. Moreover, an association has been formed for founding burses in favour of poorer students, to which the ladies of the higher classes and the curés of Paris are liberally contributing.

The Institution would have no pretension to the historical name of " University," while it was confined to ecclesiastics ; and the present Archbishop, pursuing the process of development, which had been so rapid in its movements before him, has opened it to the laity. The two descriptions of students are kept distinct, except at lecture, examinations, and literary meetings. The lay youths are received, as it would appear, after the age of eighteen, and are educated for the Professions, while they gain of course the benefit of being imbued with sound principles of religion. Literature and mathematics form their principal studies ; they are practised, moreover, as well as the ecclesiastics, in exercises of a logical character, in elocution and composition. Many of these youths pass on to the *Ecole Polytechnique*, or other government schools ; or even belong to them, while they attend lectures at the Carmes.

The cause of truth, never dominant in this world, has its ebbs and flows. It is pleasant to live in a day, when the tide is coming in. Such is our own day ; and, without forgetting that there are many rocks on the shore to throw us back and break our advance for the moment, and to task our patience before we cover them,—that physical force is now on the world's side, and that the world will be provoked to more active enmity against the Church in proportion to her success,—still we may surely encourage ourselves by a thousand tokens all around us now, that this is our hour, whatever be its duration, the hour for great hopes, great schemes, great efforts, great beginnings. We may live indeed to see but little built, but we shall see much founded. A new era seems to be at hand, and a bolder policy is showing itself. In particular, the Church feels herself strong enough in the provisions and safeguards which a painful experience has suggested against prospective dangers, to recommence the age of Universities. Louvain revived twenty years ago ; a new University of Paris seems to be in prospect, or at least in hope ; the report is current that a University is soon to be erected in Austria ; and the University of Ireland is proving its possibility by entering on its work, and presaging its future success by its triumph over the difficulties of its commencement.

THE MISSION OF ST. BENEDICT.

(From the ATLANTIS *of January,* 1858.)

THE MISSION OF ST. BENEDICT.

I.

AS the physical universe is sustained and carried on in dependence on certain centres of power and laws of operation, so the course of the social and political world, and of that great religious organization called the Catholic Church, is found to proceed for the most part from the presence or action of definite persons, places, events, and institutions, as the visible cause of the whole. There has been but one Judæa, one Greece, one Rome; one Homer, one Cicero; one Cæsar, one Constantine, one Charlemagne. And so, as regards Revelation, there has been one St. John the Divine, one Doctor of the Nations. Dogma runs along the line of Athanasius, Augustine, Thomas. The conversion of the heathen is ascribed, after the Apostles, to champions of the truth so few, that we may almost count them, such as Martin, Patrick, Augustine, Boniface. Then there is St. Antony, the father of monachism; St. Jerome, the interpreter of Scripture; St. Chrysostom, the great preacher.

Education follows the same law: it has its history in Christianity, and its doctors or masters in that history. It has had three periods:—the ancient, the medieval, and the modern; and there are three Religious Orders in those periods respectively, which succeed, one the other, on its public stage, and represent the teaching given by the Catholic Church during the time of their ascendancy. The first period is that long series of centuries, during which society was breaking or had broken up, and then slowly attempted its own re-construction; the second may be called the period of re-construction; and the third dates from the Reformation, when that peculiar movement of mind commenced, the issue of which is still to come. Now, St. Benedict has had the training of the ancient intellect, St. Dominic of the medieval; and St. Ignatius of the modern. And in saying this, I am in no degree disrespectful to the Augustinians, Carmelites, Franciscans, and other great religious families, which might be named, or to the holy Patriarchs who founded them; for I am not reviewing the whole history of Christianity, but selecting a particular aspect of it.

Perhaps as much as this will be granted to me without great hesitation. Next, I proceed to contrast these three great masters of Christian teaching with each other. To St. Benedict, then, who may fairly be taken to represent the various families of monks before his time and those which sprang from him (for they are all pretty much of one school), to this great Saint let me assign, for his discriminating badge, the element of Poetry; to St. Dominic, the Scientific element; and to St. Ignatius, the Practical.

These characteristics, which belong respectively to the schools of the three great Teachers, grow out of the circumstances under which they respectively entered upon their work. Benedict, entrusted with his mission almost as a boy, infused into it the romance and simplicity of boyhood. Dominic, a man of forty-five, a graduate in theology, a priest and a canon, brought with him into religion that maturity and completeness of learning which he had acquired in the schools. Ignatius, a man of the world before his conversion, transmitted as a legacy to his disciples that knowledge of mankind which cannot be learned in cloisters. And thus the three several Orders were (so to say), the births of Poetry, of Science, and Practical Sense.

And here another coincidence suggests itself. I have been giving these three attributes to the three Patriarchs whom I have specified, severally, from a *bonâ-fide* regard to their history, and without at all having any theory of philosophy in my eye. But after having so described them, it certainly did strike me that I had un-intentionally been illustrating a somewhat popular notion of the day, the like of which is attributed to authors with whom I have as little sympathy as with any persons who can be named. According to these speculators, the life, whether of a race or of an individual of the great human family, is divided into three stages, each of which has its own ruling principle and characteristic. The youth makes his start in life, with " *hope* at the prow, and *fancy* at the helm ; " he has nothing else but these to impel or direct him ; he has not lived long enough to exercise his reason, or to gather in a store of facts ; and, because he cannot do otherwise, he dwells in a world which he has created. He begins with illusions. Next, when at length he looks about for some surer footing than imagination gives him, he may have recourse to reason, or he may have recourse to facts ; now facts are external to him, but his reason is his own : of the two, then, it is easier for him to exercise his reason than to ascertain facts. Accordingly, his first mental revolu-tion, when he discards the life of aspiration and affection which has disappointed him, and the dreams of which he has been the sport and victim, is to embrace a life of logic : this, then, is his second stage,—the metaphysical. He acts now on a plan, thinks by system, is cautious about his middle terms, and trusts nothing but what takes a scientific form. His third stage is when he has made full trial of life ; when he has found his theories break down under the weight of facts, and experience falsify his most promising calculations. Then the old man recognizes at length, that what he can taste, touch, and handle, is trustworthy, and nothing beyond it. Thus he runs through his three periods of Imagination, Reason, and Sense ; and then he comes to an end, and is not ;— a most impotent and melancholy conclusion.

Undoubtedly a Catholic has no sympathy in so heartless a view of life, and yet it seems to square with what I have been saying of the three great Patriarchs of Christian teaching. And certainly there is a truth in it, which gives it its plausibility. However, I am not concerned here to do more than to put my finger on the point at which I should diverge from it, both in what I have been saying and what I must say concerning them. It is true then, that history, as viewed in these three Saints, is, somewhat after the manner of the theory I have mentioned, a progress from poetry through science to practical sense or prudence ; but then this important *proviso* has to be borne in mind at the same time, that what the Catholic Church once has had, she never has lost. She has never wept over, or been angry with, time gone and over. Instead of passing from one stage of life to another, she has carried her youth and middle age along with her, on to her latest time. She has not changed possessions, but accumulated them, and has brought out of her treasure-house, according to the occasion, things new and old. She did not lose Benedict by finding Dominic ; and she has still both Benedict and Dominic at home, though she has become the mother of Ignatius. Imagination, Science, Prudence, all are good, and she has them all. Things incompatible in nature, coëxist in her ; her prose is poetical on the one hand, and philosophical on the other.

Coming now to the historical proof of the contrast I have been instituting, I am sanguine in thinking that one branch of it is already allowed by the consent of the world, and is undeniable. By common consent, the palm of religious Prudence, in the Aristotelic sense of that comprehensive word, belongs to the School of Religion of which St. Ignatius is the Founder. That great Society is the classical seat and fountain (that is, in religious thought and the conduct of life, for of ecclesiastical politics I speak not), the school and pattern of discretion, practical sense, and wise government. Sublimer conceptions or more profound speculations may have been created or elaborated elsewhere ; but, whether we consider the illustrious Body in its own constitution, or in its rules for instruction and direction, we see that it is its very genius to prefer this most excellent prudence to every other gift, and to think little both of poetry and of science, unless they happen to be useful. It is true that, in the long catalogue of its members, there are to be found the names of the most consummate theologians, and of scholars the most elegant and accomplished ; but we are speaking here, not of individuals, but of the body itself. It is plain that the body is not over-jealous about its theological traditions, or it certainly would not suffer Suarez to controvert with Molina, Viva with Vasquez, Passaglia with Petavius, and Faure with Suarez, de Lugo, and Valentia. In this intellectual freedom its members justly glory ; inasmuch as they have set their affections, not on the opinions of the Schools, but on the souls of men. And it is the same charitable motive which makes them give up the poetry of life, the poetry of ceremonies,—of the cowl, the cloister, and the choir,—content with the most prosaic architecture, if it be but convenient, and the most prosaic neighbourhood, if it be but populous. I need not then dwell longer on this wonderful Religion, but may confine the remarks which are to follow to the two Religions which historically preceded it—the Benedictine and the Dominican.*

One preliminary more, suggested by a purely fanciful analogy :—As there are three great Patriarchs on the high road and public thoroughfare of Christian Education, so there were three chief Patriarchs in the first age of the chosen people. Putting aside Noe and Melchisedec, and Joseph and his brethren, we recognize three venerable fathers,—Abraham, Isaac, and Jacob, and what are their characteristics ? Abraham, the father of many nations ; Isaac, the intellectual, living in solitary simplicity, and in loving contemplation ; and Jacob, the persecuted and helpless, visited by marvellous providences, driven from place to place, set down and taken up again, ill-treated by those who were his debtors, suspected because of his sagacity, and betrayed by his eager faith, yet carried on and triumphing amid all troubles by means of his most faithful and powerful guardian-archangel.

2.

St. Benedict, then, like the great Hebrew Patriarch, was the " Father of many nations." He has been styled "the Patriarch of the West," a title which there are many reasons for ascribing to him. Not only was he the first to establish a perpetual Order of Regulars in

---

* Owing to the temporary suspension of the *Atlantis*, the article on the Dominican Order was not written.

Western Christendom; not only, as coming first, has he had an ampler course of centuries for the multiplication of his children; but his Rule, as that of St. Basil in the East, is the normal rule of the first age of the Church, and was in time generally received even in communities which in no sense owed their origin to him. Moreover, out of his Order rose, in process of time, various new monastic families, which have established themselves as independent institutions, and are able in their turn to boast of the number of their houses, and the sanctity and historical celebrity of their members. He is the representative of Latin monachism for the long extent of six centuries, while monachism was one; and even when at length varieties arose, and distinct titles were given to them, the change grew out of him;—not the act of strangers who were his rivals, but of his own children, who did but make a new beginning in all devotion and loyalty to him. He died in the early half of the sixth century; at the beginning of the tenth rose from among his French monasteries the famous Congregation of Cluni, illustrated by St. Majolus, St. Odilo, Peter the Venerable, and other considerable personages, among whom is Hildebrand, afterwards Pope Gregory the Seventh. Then came, in long succession, the Orders or Congregations of Camaldoli under St. Romuald, of Vallombrosa, of Citeaux, to which St. Bernard has given his name, of Monte Vergine, of Fontvrault; those of England, Spain, and Flanders; the Silvestrines, the Celestines, the Olivetans, the Humiliati, besides a multitude of institutes for women, as the Gilbertines and the Oblates of St. Frances, and then at length, to mention no others, the Congregation of St. Maur in modern times, so well known for its biblical, patristical, and historical works, and for its learned members. Montfaucon, Mabillon, and their companions. The pane-gyrists of this illustrious Order are accustomed to claim for it in all its branches as many as 37,000 houses, and, besides, 30 Popes, 200 Cardinals, 4 Emperors, 46 Kings, 51 Queens, 1,406 Princes, 1,600 Archbishops, 600 Bishops, 2,400 Nobles, and 15,000 Abbots and learned men.*

Nor are the religious bodies which sprang from St. Benedict the full measure of what he has accomplished, —as has been already observed. His Rule gradually made its way into those various monasteries which were of an earlier or of an independent foundation. It first coalesced with, and then supplanted, the Irish Rule of St. Columban in France, and the still older institutes which had been brought from the East by St. Athanasius, St. Eusebius, and St. Martin. At the beginning of the ninth century it was formally adopted throughout the dominions of Charlemagne. Pure, or with some admixture, it was brought by St. Augustine to England; and that admixture, if it existed, was gradually eliminated by St. Wilfrid, St. Dunstan, and Lanfranc, till at length it was received, with the name and obedience of St. Benedict, in all the Cathedral monasteries† (to mention no others), excepting Carlisle. Nor did it cost such regular bodies any very great effort to make the change, even when historically most separate from St. Benedict; for the Saint had taken up for the most part what he found, and his Rule was but the expression of the genius of monachism in those first times of the Church, with a more exact adaptation to their needs than could elsewhere be met with.

---

* Helyot, Hist. Mon. Ziegelbauer, Litt. Hist. Soame's Mosheim, vol. ii., p. 26. Brockie, Præf. ad Regul. Buckingham's bible in the Middle Ages, p. 81, etc., etc.

† Butler, June 22.

So uniform indeed had been the monastic idea before his time, and so little stress had been laid by individual communities on their respective peculiarities, that religious men passed at pleasure from one body to another.* St. Benedict provides in his Rule for the case of strangers coming to one of his houses, and wishing to remain there. If such a one came from any monastery with which the monks had existing relations, then he was not to be received without letters from his Abbot ; but, in the instance of "a foreign monk from distant parts," who wished to dwell with them as a guest, and was content with their ways, and conformed himself to them, and was not troublesome, " should he in the event wish to stay for good," says St. Benedict, " let him not be refused ; for there has been room to make trial of him, during the time that hospitality has been shown to him : nay, let him even be invited to stay, that others may gain a lesson from his example ; for in every place we are servants of one Lord and soldiers of one King."†

3.

The unity of idea, which, as these words imply, is to be found in all monks in every part of Christendom, may be described as a unity of object, of state, and of occupation. Monachism was one and the same everywhere, because it was a reaction from that secular life, which has everywhere the same structure and the same characteristics. And, since that secular life contained in it many objects, many states, and many occupations, here was a special reason, as a matter of principle, why the reaction from it should bear the badge of unity, and

---

* Thomassin, Disc. Eccl., t. i., p. 705. Calmet, Reg. Ben., t. ii., p. 25. Mabillon, Acta Sæc. iv., p. 1, præf., p. xxx. Annal., t. i., præf., § 19.
   † Reg., c. 61,

should be in outward appearance one and the same everywhere. Moreover, since that same secular life was, when monachism arose, more than ordinarily marked by variety, perturbation and confusion, it seemed on that very account to justify emphatically a rising and revolt against itself, and a recurrence to some state which, unlike itself, was constant and unalterable. It was indeed an old, decayed, and moribund world, into which Christianity had been cast. The social fabric was overgrown with the corruptions of a thousand years, and was held together, not so much by any common principle, as by the strength of possession and the tenacity of custom. It was too large for public spirit, and too artificial for patriotism, and its many religions did but foster in the popular mind division and scepticism. Want of mutual confidence would lead to despondency, inactivity, and selfishness. Society was in the slow fever of consumption, which made it restless in proportion as it was feeble. It was powerful, however, to seduce and deprave ; nor was there any *locus standi* from which to combat its evils ; and the only way of getting on with it was to abandon principle and duty, to take things as they came, and to do as the world did. Worse than all, this encompassing, entangling system of things, was, at the time we speak of, the seat and instrument of a paganism, and then of heresies, not simply contrary, but bitterly hostile, to the Christian profession. Serious men not only had a call, but every inducement which love of life and freedom could supply, to escape from its presence and its sway.

Their one idea then, their one purpose, was to be quit of it ; too long had it enthralled them. It was not a question of this or that vocation, of the better deed, of the higher state, but of life and death. In later times a variety of holy objects might present themselves for devotion to choose from, such as the care of the poor, or of the sick, or of the young, the redemption of captives, or the conversion of the barbarians ; but early mona-chism was flight from the world, and nothing else. The troubled, jaded, weary heart, the stricken, laden con-science, sought a life free from corruption in its daily work, free from distraction in its daily worship ; and it sought employments as contrary as possible to the world's employments,—employments, the end of which would be in themselves, in which each day, each hour, would have its own completeness ;—no elaborate under-takings, no difficult aims, no anxious ventures, no uncertainties to make the heart beat, or the temples throb, no painful combination of efforts, no extended plan of operations, no multiplicity of details, no deep calculations, no sustained machinations, no suspense, no vicissitudes, no moments of crisis or catastrophe ;— nor again any subtle investigations, nor perplexities of proof, nor conflicts of rival intellects, to agitate, harass, depress, stimulate, weary, or intoxicate the soul.

Hitherto I have been using negatives to describe what the primitive monk was seeking ; in truth monachism was, as regards the secular life and all that it implies, emphatically a negation, or, to use another word, a *mortification ;* a mortification of sense, and a mortifica-tion of reason. Here a word of explanation is necessary. The monks were too good Catholics to deny that reason was a divine gift, and had too much common sense to think to do without it. What they denied themselves was the various and manifold exercises of the reason ; and on this account, because such exercises were excite-ments. When the reason is cultivated, it at once begins to combine, to centralize, to look forward, to look back, to view things as a whole, whether for speculation or for action ; it practises synthesis and analysis, it discovers, it invents. To these exercises of the intellect is opposed simplicity, which is the state of mind which does not combine, does not deal with premisses and conclusions, does not recognize means and their end, but lets each work, each place, each occurrence stand by itself,— which acts towards each as it comes before it, without a thought of anything else. This simplicity is the temper of children, and it is the temper of monks. This was their mortification of the intellect ; every man who lives, must live by reason, as every one must live by sense ; but, as it is possible to be content with the bare necessities of animal life, so is it possible to confine ourselves to the bare ordinary use of reason, without caring to improve it or make the most of it. These monks held both sense and reason to be the gifts of heaven, but they used each of them as little as they could help, reserving their full time and their whole selves for devotion ;—for, if reason is better than sense, so devotion they thought to be better than either ; and, as even a heathen might deny himself the innocent indulgences of sense in order to give his time to the cultivation of the reason, so did the monks give up reason, as well as sense, that they might consecrate themselves to divine meditation.

Now, then, we are able to understand how it was that the monks had a unity, and in what it consisted. It was a unity, I have said, of object, of state, and of occupation. Their object was rest and peace ; their state was retirement ; their occupation was some work that was simple, as opposed to intellectual, viz., prayer, fasting, meditation, study, transcription, manual labour, and other unexciting, soothing employments. Such was their institution all over the world ; they had eschewed the busy mart, the craft of gain, the money-changer's bench, and the merchant's cargo. They had turned their backs upon the wrangling forum, the political assembly, and the pantechnicon of trades. They had had their last dealings with architect and habit-maker, with butcher and cook; all they wanted, all they desired, was the sweet soothing presence of earth, sky, and sea, the hospitable cave, the bright running stream, the easy gifts which mother earth, "justissima tellus," yields on very little persuasion. "The monastic institute," says the biographer of St. Maurus, "demands *Summa Quies*, the most perfect quietness;"* and where was quietness to be found, if not in reverting to the original condition of man, as far as the changed circumstances of our race admitted; in having no wants, of which the supply was not close at hand; in the "nil admirari;" in having neither hope nor fear of anything below; in daily prayer, daily bread, and daily work, one day being just like another, except that it was one step nearer than the day just gone to that great Day, which would swallow up all days, the day of everlasting rest?

4

However, I have come into collision with a great authority, M. Guizot, and I must stop the course of my argument to make my ground good against him. M. Guizot, then, makes a distinction between monachism in its birth-place, in Egypt and Syria, and that Western institute, of which I have made St. Benedict the representative. He allows that the Orientals mortified the intellect, but he considers that Latin monachism was the seat of considerable mental activity. "The desire for retirement," he says, "for contemplation, for a marked

* Mabillon, Act Benedict., t. iv., p. 1, p. xxxvii.

rupture with civilized society, was the source and fundamental trait of the Eastern monks : in the West, *on the
contrary*, and especially in Southern Gaul, where, at the
commencement of the fifth century, the principal monasteries were founded, it was in order to live in common,
with a view to conversation as well as to religious edification, that the first monks met.   The monasteries of
Lerins, of St. Victor, and many others, were especially
great schools of theology, the focus of intellectual movement.   It was by no means with solitude or with
mortification, but with discussion and activity, that they
there concerned themselves."*   Great deference is due
to an author so learned, so philosophical, so honestly
desirous to set out Christianity to the best advantage ;
yet, I am at a loss to understand what has led him to
make such a distinction between the East and West, and
to assign to the Western monks an activity of intellect,
and to the Eastern a love of retirement.

It is quite true that instances are sometimes to be
found of monasteries in the West distinguished by much
intellectual activity, but more, and more striking, instances are to be found of a like phenomenon in the
East.   If, then, such particular instances are to be taken
as fair specimens of the state of Western monachism,
they are equally fair specimens of the state of Eastern
also ; and the Eastern monks will be proved more intellectual than the Western, by virtue of that greater
interest in doctrine and in controversy which given individuals or communities among them have exhibited.
A very cursory reference to ecclesiastical history will
be sufficient to show us that the fact is as I have stated
it.   The theological sensitiveness of the monks of Marseilles, Lerins, or Adrumetum, it seems, is to be a proof

* History of Civilization, vol. ii., p. 65, Bohn ; and so Ampère.

of the intellectualism generally of the West : then, why is not the greater sensitiveness of the Scythian monks at Constantinople, and of their opponents, the Acœmetæ, an evidence in favour of the East ? These two bodies of Religious actually came all the way from Constantinople to Rome to denounce one another, besieging, as it were, the Holy See, and the former of them actually attempting to raise the Roman populace against the Pope, in behalf of its own theological tenet. Does not this show activity of mind ? I venture to say that, for one intellectual monk in the West, a dozen might be produced in the East. The very reproach, thrown out by secular historians against Greeks in general, of over-subtlety of intellect, applies in particular, if to any men, to certain classes or certain communities of Eastern monks. These were sometimes orthodox, quite as often heretical, but inexhaustible in their argumentative resources, whether the one or the other. If Pelagius be a monk in the West, on the other hand, Nestorius and Eutyches, both heresiarchs, are both monks in the East ; and Eutyches, at the time of his heresy, was an old monk into the bargain, who had been thirty years abbot of a convent, and whom age, if not sanctity, might have saved from this abnormal use of his reason. His partizans were principally monks of Egypt ; and they, coming up in force to the pseudo-synod of Ephesus, in aid of a theological thesis, kicked to death the patriarch of Constantinople, and put to flight the Legate of the Pope, all in consequence of their intellectual susceptibilities. A century earlier, Arius, on starting, carried away into his heresy as many as seven hundred nuns ;* what have the Western convents to show, in the way of controversial activity, comparable with a fact like this ? I do

* Epiph. Hær., 69.

not insist on the zealous and influential orthodoxy of
the monks of Egypt, Syria, and Asia Minor in the
fourth century, because it was probably nothing else but
an honourable adhesion to the faith of the Church, without any serious exercise of mind ; but turn to the great
writers of Eastern Christendom, and consider how many
of them figure at first sight as monks ;—Chrysostom,
Basil, Gregory Nazianzen, Epiphanius, Ephrem, Amphi-
lochius, Isidore of Pelusium, Theodore, Theodoret, perhaps
Athanasius.   Among the Latin writers no great names
occur to me but those of Jerome and Pope Gregory ; I
may add Paulinus, Sulpicius, Vincent, and Cassian, but
Jerome is the only learned writer among them.   I have
a difficulty, then, even in comprehending, not to speak
of admitting, M. Guizot's assertion, a writer who does
not commonly speak without a meaning or a reason.

But, after all, however the balance of intellectualism
may lie between certain convents or individuals in the
East and the West, such particular instances of mental
activity are nothing to the purpose, when taken to
measure the state of the great body of the monks ; certainly not in the West, with which in this paper I am
exclusively concerned.   In taking an estimate of the
Benedictines, we need not trouble ourselves about the
state of monachism in Egypt, Syria, Asia Minor, and
Constantinople, as it existed after the fourth century,
when the true monastic tradition was passing from the
East to the West.   In the fourth century, the Eastern
Monks simply follow the defined and promulgated doctrine of the Church, and in following it are guilty of no
exercise of reason; their intellectualism proper, which is
foreign to the genius of their institute, begins with the
fifth.   Taking, then, the great tradition of St. Antony,
St. Pachomius, and St. Basil in the East, and then tracing

it into the West by the hands of St. Athanasius, St. Martin, and their contemporaries, we shall find no historical facts but what admit of a fair explanation, consistent with the views which we have laid down above about monastic simplicity, bearing in mind always, what holds in all matters of fact, that there never was a rule without its exceptions.

5.

Every rule has its exceptions; but, further than this, when exceptions occur, they are commonly likely to be great ones. This is no paradox; illustrations of it are to be found everywhere. For instance, we may conceive a climate very fatal to children, and yet those who survive growing up to be strong men; and for a plain reason, because those alone could have passed the ordeal who had robust constitutions. Thus the Romans, so jealous of their freedom, when they resolved on the appointment of a supreme ruler for an occasion, did not do the thing by halves, but made him a Dictator. In like manner, a mere trifling occurrence, or an ordinary inward impulse, would be powerless to snap the bond which keeps the monk fast to his cell, his oratory, and his garden. Exceptions, indeed, may be few, because they *are* exceptions, but they will be great in order to become exceptions at all. It must be a serious emergence, a particular inspiration, a sovereign command, which brings the monk into political life; and he will be sure to make a great figure in it, else why should he have been torn from his cloister at all? This will account for the career of St. Gregory the Seventh or of St. Dunstan, of St. Bernard or of Abbot Suger, as far as it was political: the work they had to do was such as none could have done but a monk with his superhuman single-minded-

ness and his pertinacity of purpose. Again, in the case
of St. Boniface, the Apostle of Germany, and in that of
others of the missionaries of his age, it seems to have
been a particular inspiration which carried them abroad ;
and it is observable after all how soon most of them
settled down into the mixed character of agriculturists
and pastors in their new country, and resumed the tranquil life to which they had originally devoted themselves
As to the early Greek Fathers, some of those whom we
have instanced above are only *primâ facie* exceptions,
as Chrysostom, who, though he lived with the monks
most austerely for as many as six years, can hardly be
said to have taken on himself the responsibilities of their
condition, or to have simply abandoned the world.
Others of them, as Basil, were scholars, philosophers,
men of the world, before they were monks, and could
not put off their cultivation of mind or their learning
with their secular dress ; and these would be the very
men, in an age when such talents were scarce, who would
be taken out of their retirement by superior authority,
and who therefore cannot fairly be quoted as ordinary
specimens of the monastic life.

Exceptio probat regulam : let us see what two Doctors
of the Church, one Greek, one Latin, both rulers, both
monks, say concerning the state, which they at one time
enjoyed, and afterwards lost. " You tell me," says St.
Basil, writing to a friend from his solitude, " that it was
little for me to describe the place of my retirement,
unless I mentioned also my habits and my mode of life ;
yet really I am ashamed to tell you how I pass night and
day in this lonely nook. I am like one who is angry
with the size of his vessel, as tossing overmuch, and
leaves it for the boat, and is seasick and miserable still.
However, what I propose to˙do is as follows, with the hope

of tracing His steps who has said, 'If any one will come after Me, let him deny himself.' We must strive after a quiet mind. As well might the eye ascertain an object which is before it, while it roves up and down without looking steadily at it, as a mind, distracted with a thousand worldly cares, be able clearly to apprehend the truth. One who is not yoked in matrimony is harassed by rebellious impulses and hopeless attachments; he who is married is involved in his own tumult of cares: is he without children? he covets them; has he children? he has anxieties about their education. Then there is solicitude about his wife, care of his house, oversight of his servants, misfortunes in trade, differences with his neighbours, lawsuits, the merchant's risks, the farmer's toil. Each day, as it comes, darkens the soul in its own way; and night after night takes up the day's anxieties, and cheats us with corresponding dreams. Now, the only way of escaping all this is separation from the whole world, so as to live without city, home, goods, society, possessions, means of life, business, engagements, secular learning, that the heart may be prepared as wax for the impress of divine teaching. Solitude is of the greatest use for this purpose, as it stills our passions, and enables reason to extirpate them. Let then a place be found such as mine, separate from intercourse with men, that the tenor of our exercises be not interrupted from without. Pious exercises nourish the soul with divine thoughts. Soothing hymns compose the mind to a cheerful and calm state. Quiet, then, as I have said, is the first step in our sanctification; the tongue purified from the gossip of the world, the eyes unexcited by fair colour or comely shape, the ear secured from the relaxation of voluptuous songs, and that especial mischief, light jesting. Thus, the mind, rescued from dissipation from without, and sensible allurements, falls back upon itself, and thence ascends to the contemplation of God."* It is quite clear that at least St. Basil took the same view of the monastic state as I have done.

So much for the East in the fourth century; now for the West in the seventh. "One day," says St. Gregory, after he had been constrained, against his own wish, to leave his cloister for the government of the Universal Church, "one day, when I was oppressed with the excessive trouble of secular affairs, I sought a retired place, friendly to grief, where whatever displeased me in my occupations might show itself, and all that was wont to inflict pain might be seen at one view." While he was in this retreat, his "most dear son, Peter," with whom, ever since the latter was a youth, he had been intimate, surprised him, and he opened his grief to him. "My sad mind," he said, "labouring under the soreness of its engagements, remembers how it went with me formerly in this monastery, how all perishable things were beneath it, how it rose above all that was transitory, and, though still in the flesh, went out in contemplation beyond that prison, so that it even loved death, which is commonly thought a punishment, as the gate of life and the reward of labour. But now, in consequence of the pastoral charge, it undergoes the busy work of secular men, and for that fair beauty of its quiet, is dishonoured with the dust of the earth. And often dissipating itself in outward things, to serve the many, even when it seeks what is inward, it comes home indeed, but is no longer what it used to be."† Here is the very same view of the monastic state at Rome which St. Basil had in Pontus, viz., retirement and repose. There have been great Religious Orders since, whose atmosphere has been con-

* Ep. 2. *Vid.* Supr. p. 63.　　† Dial., i. 1. *Vid.* Essays, vol. ii., p. 284.

flict, and who have thriven in smiting or in being smitten. It has been their high calling ; it has been their peculiar meritorious service ; but, as for the Benedictine, the very air he breathes is peace.

6.

I have now said enough both to explain and to vindicate the biographer of St. Maurus, when he says that the object, and life, and reward of the ancient monachism was "summa quies,"—the absence of all excitement, sensible and intellectual, and the vision of Eternity. And therefore have I called the monastic state the most poetical of religious disciplines. It was a return to that primitive age of the world, of which poets have so often sung, the simple life of Arcadia or the reign of Saturn, when fraud and violence were unknown. It was a bringing back of those real, not fabulous, scenes of innocence and miracle, when Adam delved, or Abel kept sheep, or Noe planted the vine, and Angels visited them. It was a fulfilment in the letter, of the glowing imagery of prophets, about the evangelical period. Nature for art, the wide earth and the majestic heavens for the crowded city, the subdued and docile beasts of the field for the wild passions and rivalries of social life, tranquillity for ambition and care, divine meditation for the exploits of the intellect, the Creator for the creature, such was the normal condition of the monk. He had tried the world, and found its hollowness ; or he had eluded its fellowship, before it had solicited him ;—and so St. Antony fled to the desert, and St. Hilarion sought the sea shore, and St. Basil ascended the mountain ravine, and St. Benedict took refuge in his cave, and St. Giles buried himself in the forest, and St. Martin chose the broad river, in order that the world might be shut out

6 *   **25**

of view, and the soul might be at rest. And such a rest of intellect and of passion as this is full of the elements of the poetical.

I have no intention of committing myself here to a definition of poetry ; I may be thought wrong in the use of the term ; but, if I explain what I mean by it, no harm is done, whatever be my inaccuracy, and each reader may substitute for it some word he likes better. Poetry, then, I conceive, whatever be its metaphysical essence, or however various may be its kinds, whether it more properly belongs to action or to suffering, nay, whether it is more at home with society or with nature, whether its spirit is seen to best advantage in Homer or in Virgil, at any rate, is always the antagonist to *science.* As science makes progress in any subject-matter, poetry recedes from it. The two cannot stand together ; they belong respectively to two modes of viewing things, which are contradictory of each other. Reason investigates, analyzes, numbers, weighs, measures, ascertains, locates, the objects of its contemplation, and thus gains a scientific knowledge of them. Science results in system, which is complex unity ; poetry delights in the indefinite and various as contrasted with unity, and in the simple as contrasted with system. The aim of science is to get a hold of things, to grasp them, to handle them, to comprehend them ; that is (to use the familiar term), to *master* them, or to be superior to them. Its success lies in being able to draw a line round them, and to tell where each of them is to be found within that circumference, and how each lies relatively to all the rest. Its mission is to destroy ignorance, doubt, surmise, suspense, illusions, fears, deceits, according to the " Felix qui potuit rerum cognoscere causas " of the Poet, whose whole passage, by the way, may be taken as drawing

out the contrast between the poetical and the scientific.*
But as to the poetical, very different is the frame of
mind which is necessary for its perception. It demands,
as its primary condition, that we should not put ourselves above the objects in which it resides, but at their
feet ; that we should feel them to be above and beyond
us, that we should look up to them, and that, instead of
fancying that we can comprehend them, we should take
for granted that we are surrounded and comprehended
by them ourselves. It implies that we understand them
to be vast, immeasurable, impenetrable, inscrutable,
mysterious ; so that at best we are only forming conjectures about them, not conclusions, for the phenomena
which they present admit of many explanations, and we
cannot know the true one. Poetry does not address the
reason, but the imagination and affections ; it leads to
admiration, enthusiasm, devotion, love. The vague, the
uncertain, the irregular, the sudden, are among its attributes or sources. Hence it is that a child's mind is so
full of poetry, because he knows so little ; and an old
man of the world so devoid of poetry, because his experience of facts is so wide. Hence it is that nature is
commonly more poetical than art, in spite of Lord
Byron, because it is less comprehensible and less patient
of definitions ; history more poetical than philosophy ;
the savage than the citizen ; the knight-errant than the
brigadier-general ; the winding bridle-path than the

---

* Me verò primùm dulces ante omnia Musæ . . .
   Accipiant, *cælique vias et sidera monstrent*, etc., etc.
   Sin, has ne possim naturæ accedere partes,
   Frigidus obstiterit circùm præcordia sanguis,
   Rura mihi et rigui placeant in vallibus amnes, etc.
And so again :
     Felix, qui potuit rerum cognoscere *causas*, etc.
     Fortunatus et ille, Deos qui novit agrestes, etc.

straight railroad ; the sailing vessel than the steamer ;
the ruin than the spruce suburban box ; the Turkish
robe or Spanish doublet than the French dress coat.
I have now said far more than enough to make it clear
what I mean by that element in the old monastic life,
to which I have given the name of the Poetical.

Now, in many ways the family of St. Benedict answers
to this description, as we shall see if we look into its
history. Its spirit indeed is ever one, but not its outward
circumstances. It is not an Order proceeding from one
mind at a particular date, and appearing all at once in
its full perfection, and in its extreme development, and
in form one and the same everywhere and from first to
last, as is the case with other great religious institutions ;
but it is an organization, diverse, complex, and irregular,
and variously ramified, rich rather than symmetrical,
with many origins and centres and new beginnings and
the action of local influences, like some great natural
growth ; with tokens, on the face of it, of its being a
divine work, not the mere creation of human genius.
Instead of progressing on plan and system and from the
will of a superior, it has shot forth and run out as if
spontaneously, and has shaped itself according to events,
from an irrepressible fulness of life within, and from the
energetic self-action of its parts, like those symbolical
creatures in the prophet's vision, which " went every one
of them straight forward, whither the impulse of the
spirit was to go." It has been poured out over the
earth, rather than been sent, with a silent mysterious
operation, while men slept, and through the romantic
adventures of individuals, which are well nigh without
record ; and thus it has come down to us, not risen up
among us, and is found rather than established. Its
separate and scattered monasteries occupy the land,

each in its place, with a majesty parallel, but superior, to that of old aristocratic houses. Their known antiquity, their unknown origin, their long eventful history, their connection with Saints and Doctors when on earth, the legends which hang about them, their rival ancestral honours, their extended sway perhaps over other religious houses, their hold upon the associations of the neighbourhood, their traditional friendships and compacts with other great landlords, the benefits they have conferred, the sanctity which they breathe,—these and the like attributes make them objects, at once of awe and of affection.

7.

Such is the great Abbey of Bobbio, in the Apennines, where St. Columban came to die, having issued with his twelve monks from his convent in Benchor, county Down, and having spent his life in preaching godliness and planting monasteries in half-heathen France and Burgundy. Such St. Gall's, on the lake of Constance, so called from another Irishman, one of St. Columban's companions, who remained in Switzerland, when his master went on into Italy. Such the Abbey of Fulda, where lies St. Boniface, who, burning with zeal for the conversion of the Germans, attempted them a first time and failed, and then a second time and succeeded, and at length crowned the missionary labours of forty-five years with martyrdom. Such Monte Cassino, the metropolis of the Benedictine name, where the Saint broke the idol, and cut down the grove, of Apollo. Ancient houses such as these subdue the mind by the mingled grandeur and sweetness of their presence. They stand in history with an accumulated interest upon them, which belongs to no other monuments of the past. Whatever there is of venerable authority in other foundations, in Bishops' sees, in Cathedrals, in Colleges, respectively, is found in combination in them. Each gate and cloister has had its own story, and time has engraven upon their walls the chronicle of its revolutions. And, even when at length rudely destroyed, or crumbled into dust, they live in history and antiquarian works, in the pictures and relics which remain of them, and in the traditions of their place.

In the early part of last century the Maurist Fathers, with a view of collecting materials for the celebrated works which they had then on hand, sent two of their number on a tour through France and the adjacent provinces. Among other districts the travellers passed through the forest of Ardennes, which has been made classical by the prose of Cæsar, and the poetry of Shakespeare. There they found the great Benedictine Convent of St. Hubert;* and, if I dwell awhile upon the illustration which it affords of what I have been saying, it is not as if twenty other religious houses which they visited would not serve my purpose quite as well, but because it has come first to my hand in turning over the pages of their volume. At that time the venerable abbey in question had upon it the weight of a thousand years, and was eminent above others in the country in wealth, in privileges, in name, and, not the least recommendation, in the sanctity of its members. The lands on which it was situated were its freehold, and their range included sixteen villages. The old chronicle informs us that, about the middle of the seventh century,

* Voyage Littéraire. *Vid.* also Calmet, Lorraine, t. i., p. 1043. Moreri, art. S. Hubert. Gallia Christ., t. iii. p. 966. Mabillon, Annal. Bened., t. ii., pp. 16, 441, 606. Bucherii, Gest. Tungr. etc., t. i., p. 153. Helyot, Ordres Mon., t. vi., p. 296.

St. Sigibert, the Merovingian, pitched upon Ardennes and its neighbourhood for the establishment of as many as twelve monasteries, with the hope of thereby obtaining from heaven an heir to his crown. Dying prematurely, he but partially fulfilled his pious intention, which was taken up by Pepin, sixty years afterwards, at the instance of his chaplain, St. Beregise; so far, at least, as to make a commencement of the abbey of which we are speaking. Beregise had been a monk of the Benedictine Abbey of St. Tron, and he chose for the site of the new foundation a spot in the midst of the forest, marked by the ruins of a temple dedicated to the pagan Diana, the goddess of the chase. The holy man exorcised the place with the sign of the Cross; and, becoming abbot of the new house, filled it either with monks, or, as seems less likely, with secular canons. From that time to the summer day, when the two Maurists visited it, the sacred establishment, with various fortunes, had been in possession of the land.

On entering its precincts, they found it at once full and empty: empty of the monks, who were in the fields gathering in the harvest; full of pilgrims, who were wont to come day after day, in never-failing succession, to visit the tomb of St. Hubert. What a series of events has to be recorded to make this simple account intelligible! and how poetical is the picture which it sets before us, as well as those events themselves, which it presupposes, when they come to be detailed! Were it not that I should be swelling a passing illustration into a history, I might go on to tell how strict the observance of the monks had been for the last hundred years before the travellers arrived there, since Abbot Nicholas de Fanson had effected a reform on the pattern of the French Congregation of St. Vanne. I might relate how, when a simple monk in the Abbey of St. Hubert, Nicholas had wished to change it for a stricter community, and how he got leave to go off to the Congregation just mentioned, and how then his old Abbot died suddenly, and how he himself to his surprise was elected in his place. And I might tell how, when his mitre was on his head, he set about reforming the house which he had been on the point of quitting, and how he introduced for that purpose two monks of St. Vanne ; and how the Bishop of Liege, in whose diocese he was, set himself against his holy design, and how some of the old monks attempted to poison him ; and how, though he carried it into effect, still he was not allowed to aggregate his Abbey to the Congregation whose reform he had adopted ; but how his good example encouraged the neighbouring abbeys to commence a reform in themselves, which issued in an ecclesiastical union of the Flemish Houses.

All this, however, would not have been more than one passage, of course, in the adventures which had befallen the abbey and its abbots in the course of its history. It had had many seasons of decay before the time of Nicholas de Fanson, and many restorations, and from different quarters. None of them was so famous or important as the reform effected in the year 817, about a century after its original foundation, when the secular canons, who anyhow had got in, were put out, and the monks put in their place, at the instance of the then Bishop of Liege, who had a better spirit than his successor in the time of Nicholas. The new inmates were joined by some persons of noble birth from the Cathedral, and by their suggestion and influence the bold measure was taken of attempting to gain from Liege the body of the great St. Hubert, the Apostle of Ardennes

Great, we may be sure, was the resistance of the city where he lay ; but Abbot Alreus, the friend and fellow-workman of St. Benedict of Anian, the first Reformer of the Benedictine Order before the date of Cluni, went to the Bishop, and he went to the Archbishop of Cologne ; and then both prelates went to the Emperor Louis le Debonnaire, the son of Charlemagne, whose favourite hunting ground the forest was ; and he referred the matter to the great Council of Aix-la-Chapelle, whence a decision came in favour of the monks of Ardennes. So with great solemnity the sacred body was conveyed by water to its new destination ; and there in the Treasury, in memorial of the happy event, the Maurist visitors saw the very chalice of gold, and the beautiful copy of the Gospels, ornamented with precious stones, given to the Abbey by Louis at the time. Doubtless it was the handiwork of the monks of some other Bene-dictine House, as must have been the famous Psalter, of which the visitors speak also, written in letters of gold, the gift of Louis's son, the Emperor Lothaire ; and there he sits in the first page, with his crown on his head, his sceptre in one hand, his sheathed sword in the other, and something very like a fleur-de-lys buckling on his ermine robe at the shoulder :—which precious gift, that is, the Psalter with all its pictures, two cen-turies after came most unaccountably into the possession of the Lady Helvidia of Aspurg, who gave it to her young son Bruno, afterwards Pope Leo the Ninth, to learn the Psalms by ; but, as the young Saint made no progress in his task, she came to the conclusion that she had no right to the book, and so she ended by making a pilgrimage to St. Hubert with Bruno, and, not only gave back the Psalter, but made the offering of a Sacra-mentary besides.

But to return to the relics of the Saint ; the sacred body was taken by water up the Maes. The coffin was of marble, and perhaps could have been taken no other way ; but another reason, besides its weight, lay in the indignation of the citizens of Liege, who might have interfered with a land journey, and in fact did make several attempts, in the following years, to regain the body. In consequence, the good monks of Ardennes hid it within the walls of their monastery, confiding the secret of its whereabouts to only two of their community at a time ; and they showed in the sacristy to the devout, instead, the Saint's ivory cross and his stole, the sole of his shoe and his comb, and Diana, Marchioness of Autrech, gave a golden box to hold the stole. This, however, was in after times ; for they were very loth at first to let strangers within their cloisters at all ; and in 838, when a long spell of rain was destroying the crops, and the people of the neighbourhood came in procession to the shrine to ask the intercession of the Saint, the cautious Abbot Sewold, availing himself of the Rule, would only admit priests, and them by threes and fours, with naked feet, and a few laymen with each of them. The supplicants were good men, however, and had no notion of playing any trick : they came in piety and devotion, and the rain ceased, and the country was the gainer by St. Hubert of Ardennes. And thenceforth others, besides the monks, became interested in his stay in the forest.

And now I have said something in explanation why the courtyard was full of pilgrims when the travellers came. St. Hubert had been an object of devotion for a particular benefit, perhaps ever since he came there, certainly as early as the eleventh century, for we then have historical notice of it. His preference of the forest to the city, which he had shown in his life-time before his conversion, was illustrated by the particular grace or miraculous service, for which, more than for any other, he used his glorious intercession on high. He is famous for curing those who had suffered from the bite of wild animals, especially dogs of the chase, and a hospital was attached to the Abbey for their reception. The sacristan of the Church officiated in the cure ; and with rites which never indeed failed, but which to some cautious persons seemed to savour of superstition. Certainly they were startling at first sight ; accordingly a formal charge on that score was at one time brought against them before the Bishop of Liege, and a process followed. The Bishop, the University of Louvain, and its Faculty of Medicine, conducted the inquiry, which was given in favour of the Abbey, on the ground that what looked like a charm might be of the nature of a medical regimen.

However, though the sacristan was the medium of the cure, the general care of the patients was left to externs. The hospital was served by secular priests, since the monks heard no confessions save those of their own people. This rule they observed, in order to reserve themselves for the proper duties of a Benedictine,—the choir, study, manual labour, and transcription of books ; and, while the Maurists were ocular witnesses of their agricultural toils, they saw the diligence of their penmanship in its results, for the MSS. of their Library were the choicest in the country. Among them, they tell us, were copies of St. Jerome's Bible, the Acts of the Councils, Bede's History, Gregory and Isidore, Origen and Augustine.

The Maurists report as favourably of the monastic buildings themselves as of the hospital and library. Those buildings were a chronicle of past times, and of the changes which had taken place in them. First there were the poor huts of St. Beregise upon the half-cleared and still marshy ground of the forest; then came the building of a sufficient house, when St. Hubert was brought there; and centuries after that, St. Thierry, the intimate friend of the great Pope Hildebrand, had renewed it magnificently, at the time that he was Abbot. He was sadly treated in his lifetime by his monks, as Nicholas after him; but, after his death, they found out that he was a Saint, which they might have discovered before it; and they placed him in the crypt, and there he and another holy Abbot after him lay in peace, till the Calvinists broke into it in the sixteenth century, and burned both of them to ashes. There were marks too of the same fanatics on the pillars of the nave of the Church; which had been built by Abbot John de Wahart in the twelfth century, and then again from its foundations by Abbots Nicholas de Malaise and Romaclus, the friend of Blosius, four centuries later; and it was ornamented by Abbot Cyprian, who was called the friend of the poor; and doubtless the travellers admired the marble of the choir and sanctuary, and the silver candelabra of the altar given by the reigning Lord Abbot; and perhaps they heard him sing solemn Mass on the Assumption, as was usual with him on that feast, with his four secular chaplains, one to carry his Cross, another his mitre, a third his gremial, and a fourth his candle, and accompanied by the pealing organ and the many musical bells, which had been the gift of Abbot Balla about a hundred years earlier. Can we imagine a more graceful union of human with divine, of the sweet with the austere, of business and of calm, of splendour and of simplicity, than is displayed in a great religious house after this pattern, when unrelaxed in its observance, and pursuing the ends for which it was endowed?

8.

The monks have been accused of choosing beautiful spots for their dwellings ; as if this were a luxury in ascetics, and not rather the necessary alleviation of their asceticism. Even when their critics are kindest, they consider such sites as chosen by a sort of sentimental, ornamental indolence. "Beaulieu river," says Mr. Warner in his topography of Hampshire, and, because he writes far less ill-naturedly than the run of authors, I quote him, " Beaulieu river is stocked with plenty of fish, and boasts in particular of good oysters and fine plaice, and is fringed quite to the edge of the water with the most beautiful hanging woods. In the area enclosed are distinct traces of various fishponds, formed for the use of the convent. Some of them continue perfect to the present day, and abound with fish. A curious instance occurs also of monkish luxury, even in the article of water ; to secure a fine spring those monastics have spared neither trouble nor expense. About half a mile to the south-east of the Abbey is a deep wood ; and at a spot almost inaccessible is a cave formed of smooth stones. It has a very contracted entrance, but spreads gradually into a little apartment, of seven feet wide, ten deep, and about five high. This covers a copious and transparent spring of water, which, issuing from the mouth of the cave, is lost in a deep dell, and is there received, as I have been informed, by a chain of small stone pipes, which formerly, when perfect, conveyed it quite to the Abbey. It must be confessed the monks in general displayed an elegant taste in the choice of their situations. Beaulieu Abbey is a striking proof of this. Perhaps few spots in the kingdom could have been pitched upon better calculated for monastic seclusion than this. The deep woods, with which it is almost environed, throw an air of gloom and solemnity over the scene, well suited to excite religious emotions ; while the stream that glides by its side afforded to the recluse a striking emblem of human life : and at the same time that it soothed his mind by a gentle murmuring, led it to serious thought by its continual and irrevocable lesson."*

The monks were not so soft as all this, after all ; and if Mr. Warner had seen them, we may be sure he would have been astonished at the stern, as well as sweet simplicity which characterized them. They were not dreamy sentimentalists, to fall in love with melancholy winds and purling rills, and waterfalls and nodding groves ; but their poetry was the poetry of hard work and hard fare, unselfish hearts and charitable hands. They could plough and reap, they could hedge and ditch, they could drain ; they could lop, they could carpenter ; they could thatch, they could make hurdles for their huts ; they could make a road, they could divert or secure the streamlet's bed, they could bridge a torrent. Mr. Warner mentions one of their luxuries,—clear, wholesome water ; it was an allowable one, especially as they obtained it by their own patient labour. If their grounds are picturesque, if their views are rich, they made them so, and had, we presume, a right to enjoy the work of their own hands. They found a swamp, a moor, a thicket, a rock, and they made an Eden in the wilderness. They destroyed snakes ; they extirpated wild cats, wolves, boars, bears ; they put to flight or they converted rovers, outlaws, robbers. The gloom of the forest departed, and the sun, for the first time since the Deluge

* Vol. i., p. 237, etc.

shone upon the moist ground. St. Benedict is the true man of Ross.

> Who hung with woods yon mountain's sultry brow?
> From the dry rock who made the waters flow?
> Whose causeway parts the vale with shady rows?
> Whose seats the weary traveller repose?
> He feeds yon almshouse, neat, but void of state,
> When Age and Want sit smiling at the gate;
> Him portioned maids, apprenticed orphans blessed,
> The young who labour, and the old who rest.

And candid writers, though not Catholics, allow it. Even English, and much more foreign historians and antiquarians, have arrived at a unanimous verdict here. "We owe the agricultural restoration of great part of Europe to the monks," says Mr. Hallam. "The monks were much the best husbandmen, and the only gardeners," says Forsyth. "None," says Wharton, "ever improved their lands and possessions more than the monks, by building, cultivating, and other methods." The cultivation of Church lands, as Sharon Turner infers from Doomsday Book, was superior to that held by other proprietors, for there was less wood upon them, less common pasture, and more abundant meadow. "Wherever they came," says Mr. Soame on Mosheim, "they converted the wilderness into a cultivated country; they pursued the breeding of cattle and agriculture, laboured with their own hands, drained morasses, and cleared away forests. By them Germany was rendered a fruitful country." M. Guizot speaks as strongly: "The Benedictine monks were the agriculturists of Europe; they cleared it on a large scale, associating agriculture with preaching." *

---

* Hallam, Middle Ages, vol. iii., p. 436. Forsyth, Antiqu., vol. i., pp. 37. 44, 179. Turner, Anglo-Sax., vol. ii., p. 167. Murdoch's Mosheim, vol. ii., p. 21, etc. Guizot, Hist. Civil., vol. ii., p. 75, Bohn.

St. Benedict's direct object indeed in setting his monks to manual labour was neither social usefulness nor poetry, but penance ; still his work was both the one and the other. The above-cited authors enlarge upon its use, and I in what I am writing may be allowed to dwell upon its poetry ; we may contemplate both its utility to man and its service to God in the aspect of its poetry. How romantic then, as well as useful, how lively as well as serious, is their history, with its episodes of personal adventure and prowess, its pictures of squatter, hunter, farmer, civil engineer, and evangelist united in the same individual, with its supernatural colouring of heroic virtue and miracle ! When St. Columban first came into Burgundy with his twelve young monks, he placed himself in a vast wilderness, and made them set about cultivating the soil. At first they all suffered from hunger, and were compelled to live on the barks of trees and wild herbs. On one occasion they were for five days in this condition. St. Gall, one of them, betook himself to a Swiss forest, fearful from the multitude of wild beasts ; and then, choosing the neighbourhood of a mountain stream, he made a cross of twigs, and hung some relics on it, and laid the foundation of his celebrated abbey. St. Ronan came from Ireland to Cornwall, and chose a wood, full of wild beasts, for his hermitage, near the Lizard. The monks of St. Dubritius, the founder of the Welsh Schools, also sought the woods, and there they worked hard at manufactures, agriculture, and road making. St. Sequanus placed himself where " the trees almost touched the clouds." He and his companions, when they first explored it, asked themselves how they could penetrate into it, when they saw a winding footpath, so narrow and full of briars that it was with difficulty that one foot followed another. With much labour and with torn clothes they succeeded in gaining its depths, and stooping their heads into the darkness at their feet, they perceived a cavern, shrouded by the thick interlacing branches of the trees, and blocked up with stones and underwood. "This," says the monastic account, "was the cavern of robbers, and the resort of evil spirits." Sequanus fell on his knees, prayed, made the sign of the Cross over the abyss, and built his cell there. Such was the first foundation of the celebrated abbey called after him in Burgundy.[*]

Sturm, the Bavarian convert of St. Boniface, was seized with a desire, as his master before him in his English monastery, of founding a religious house in the wilds of Pagan Germany; and setting out with two companions, he wandered for two days through the Buchonian forest, and saw nothing but earth, sky, and large trees. On the third day he stopped and chose a spot, which on trial did not answer. Then, mounting an ass, he set out by himself, cutting down branches of a night to secure himself from the wild beasts, till at length he came to the place (described by St. Boniface as "locum silvaticum in eremo, vastissimæ solitudinis"), in which afterwards arose the abbey and schools of Fulda. Wunibald was suspicious of the good wine of the Rhine where he was, and, determining to leave it, he bought the land where Heidensheim afterwards stood, then a wilderness of trees and underwood, covering a deep valley and the sides of lofty mountains. There he proceeded, axe in hand, to clear the ground for his religious house, while the savage natives looked on sullenly, jealous for their hunting-grounds and sacred trees. Willi-

---

* Neander, Memorials, pp. 436, 451, 473, Bohn. Rader, Bavaria Sacra. Calles, Ann. Germ., t. i., pp. 200, 276, 317, 318. Guizot, Civil., vol. ii., p 134. Whitaker's Cornwall, vol. ii., p. 196. Fosbroke, Antiq. p. 16.

bald, his brother, had pursued a similar work on system; he had penetrated his forest in every direction and scattered monasteries over it. The Irish Alto pitched himself in a wood, half way between Munich and Vienna. Pirminius chose an island, notorious for its snakes, and there he planted his hermitage and chapel, which at length became the rich and noble abbey and school of Augia Major or Richenau.*

The more celebrated School of Bec had a similar beginning at a later date, when Herluin, an old soldier, devoted his house and farm to an ecclesiastical purpose, and governed, as abbot, the monastery which he had founded. "You might see him," says the writer of his life, "when office was over in church, going out to his fields, at the head of his monks, with his bag of seed about his neck, and his rake or hoe in his hand. There he remained with them hard at work till the day was closing. Some were employed in clearing the land of brambles and weeds; others spread manure; others were weeding or sowing; no one ate his bread in idleness. Then when the hour came for saying office in church, they all assembled together punctually. Their ordinary food was rye bread and vegetables with salt and water; and the water muddy, for the well was two miles off."† Lanfranc, then a secular, was so edified by the simple Abbot, fresh from the field, setting about his baking with dirty hands, that he forthwith became one of the party;‡ and, being unfitted for labour, opened in the house a school of logic, thereby to make money for the community. Such was the cradle of the scholastic theology; the last years of the patristic, which were

---

* Meyrick's Willibald, p. 68.　Bavaria Sacra, p. 119.　Petri, Suevia Eccles., p. 96.　Calles Ann. Germ., t. i., p. 191.

† Butler's Lives, Aug. 20.　　　　‡ Apud. Mabillon Act. Bened.

nearly contemporaneous, exhibit a similar scene,—St. Bernard founding his abbey of Clairvaux in a place called the Valley of Wormwood, in the heart of a savage forest, the haunt of robbers, and his thirteen companions clearing a homestead, raising a few huts, and living on barley or cockle bread with boiled beech leaves for vegetables.*

How beautiful is Simeon of Durham's account of Easterwine, the first abbot after Bennet of St. Peter's at Wearmouth! He was a man of noble birth, who gave himself to religion, and died young. "Though he had been in the service of King Egfrid," says Simeon, "when he had once left secular affairs, and lain aside his arms, and taken on him the spiritual warfare instead, he was nothing but the humble monk, just like any of his brethren, winnowing with them with great joy, milking the ewes and cows, and in the bakehouse, the garden, the kitchen, and all house duties, cheerful and obedient. And, when he received the name of Abbot, still he was in spirit just what he was before to every one, gentle, affable, and kind; or, if any fault had been committed, correcting it indeed by the Rule, but still so winning the offender by his unaffected earnest manner, that he had no wish ever to repeat the offence, or to dim the brightness of that most clear countenance with the cloud of his transgression. And often going here and there on business of the monastery, when he found his brothers at work, he would at once take part in it, guiding the plough, or shaping the iron, or taking the winnowing fan, or the like. He was young and strong, with a sweet voice, a cheerful temper, a liberal heart and a handsome countenance. He partook of the same food as his brethren, and under the same roof. He slept in

* Thomass. Disc. Eccl. t. iii., p. 513.

the common dormitory, as before he was abbot, and he continued to do so for the first two days of his illness, when death had now seized him, as he knew full well. But for the last five days he betook himself to a more retired dwelling; and then, coming out into the open air and sitting down, and calling for all his brethren, after the manner of his tender nature, he gave his weeping monks the kiss of peace, and died at night while they were singing lauds."[*]

9.

This gentleness and tenderness of heart seems to have been as characteristic of the monks as their simplicity; and if there are some Saints among them, who on the public stage of history do not show it, it was because they were called out of their convents for some special purpose, and, as I have said above, exceptions to a rule are commonly great exceptions. Bede goes out of his way to observe of King Ethelbert, on St. Austin's converting him, that "he had learned from the teachers and authors of his salvation that men were to be drawn heavenwards, and not forced." Aldhelm, when a council had been held about the perverse opinions of the British Christians, seconding the principle which the Fathers of it laid down, that "schismatics were to be convinced, not compelled," wrote a book upon their error and converted many of them. Wolstan, when the civil power failed in its attempts to stop the slave trade of the Bristol people, succeeded by his persevering preaching. In the confessional he was so gentle, that penitents came to him from all parts of England.[†] This has been the spirit of the monks from the first; the student

---

[*] P. 93.   The passage seems taken from Bede.
[†] Bede, Hist. Eccles., i. 26.   William of Malmesb. Ponfic. Angl.

of ecclesiastical history may recollect a certain passage in St. Martin's history, when his desire to shield the Spanish heretics from capital punishment brought him into great difficulties* with the usurper Maximus.

Works of penance indeed and works of mercy have gone hand in hand in the history of the monks ; from the Solitaries in Egypt down to the Trappists of this day, it is one of the points in which the unity of the monastic idea shows itself. They have ever toiled for others, while they toiled for themselves ; nor for posterity only, but for their poor neighbours, and for travellers who came to them. St. Augustine tells us that the monks of Egypt and of the East made so much by manual labour as to be able to freight vessels with provisions for impoverished districts. Theodoret speaks of a certain five thousand of them, who by their labour supported, besides themselves, innumerable poor and strangers. Sozomen speaks of the monk Zeno, who, though a hundred years old, and the bishop of a rich Church, worked for the poor as well as for himself. Corbinian in a subsequent century surrounded his German Church with fruit trees and vines, and sustained the poor with the produce. The monks of St. Gall, already mentioned, gardened, planted, fished, and thus secured the means of relieving the poor and entertaining strangers. "Monasteries," says Neander, "were seats for the promotion of various trades, arts, and sciences. The gains accruing from their combined labour were employed for the relief of the distressed. In great famines, thousands were rescued from starvation."† In a scarcity at the beginning of the twelfth century, a monastery in the neighbourhood of Cologne distributed

---

* *Vid.* Supr. p. 198.
† Eccl. Hist., vol. vii., p. 331, Bohn.

in one day fifteen hundred alms, consisting of bread, meat, and vegetables. About the same time St. Bernard founded his monastery of Citeaux, which, though situated in the waste district described above, was able at length to sustain two thousand poor for months, besides extraordinary alms bestowed on others. The monks offered their simple hospitality, uninviting as it might be, to high as well as low ; and to those who scorned their fare, they at least could offer a refuge in misfortune or danger, or after casualties.

Duke William, ancestor of the Conqueror, was hunting in the woods about Jumieges, when he fell in with a rude hermitage.* Two monks had made their way through the forest, and with immense labour had rooted up some trees, levelled the ground, raised some crops, and put together their hut. William heard their story, not perhaps in the best humour, and flung aside in contempt the barley bread and water which they offered him. Presently he was brought back wounded and insensible : he had got the worst in an encounter with a boar. On coming to himself, he accepted the hospitality which he had refused at first, and built for them a monastery. Doubtless he had looked on them as trespassers or squatters on his domain, though with a religious character and object. The Norman princes were as good friends to the wild beasts as the monks were enemies: a charter still exists of the Conqueror, granted to the abbey of Caen,† in which he stipulates that its inmates should not turn the woods into tillage, and reserves the game for himself.

Contrast with this savage retreat and its rude hospitality the different, though equally Benedictine picture of

* Duchesne, Script. North., p. 236.
† Turner, Middle Ages, vol. v., p. 89.

the sacred grove of Subiaco, and the spiritual entertainment which it ministers to all comers, as given in the late pilgrimage of Bishop Ullathorne: "The trees," he says, "which form the venerable grove, are very old, but their old age is vigorous and healthy. Their great grey roots expose themselves to view with all manner of curling lines and wrinkles on them, and the rough stems bend and twine about with the vigour and ease of gigantic pythons. . . . Of how many holy solitaries have these trees witnessed the meditations! And then they have seen beneath their quiet boughs the irruption of mailed men, tormented by the thirst of plunder and the passion of blood, which even a sanctuary held so sacred could not stay. And then they have witnessed, for twelve centuries and more, the greatest of the Popes, the Gregories, the Leos, the Innocents, and the Piuses, coming one after another to refresh themselves from their labours in a solitude which is steeped with the inspirations and redolent with the holiness of St. Benedict."*

What congenial subjects for his verse would the sweetest of all poets have found in scenes and histories such as the foregoing, he who in his Georgics has shown such love of a country life and country occupations, and of the themes and trains of thought which rise out of the country! Would that Christianity had a Virgil to describe the old monks at their rural labours, as it has had a Sacchi or a Domenichino to paint them! How would he have been able to set forth the adventures and the hardships of the missionary husbandmen, who sang of the Scythian winter, and the murrain of the cattle, the stag of Sylvia, and the forest home of Evander! How could he have pourtrayed St. Paulinus or St. Serenus in his garden, who could draw so beautiful a picture of the old

* P. 37.

Corycian, raising amid the thicket his scanty pot-herbs upon the nook of land, which was "not good for tillage, nor for pasture, nor for vines!" How could he have brought out the poetry of those simple labourers, who has told us of that old man's flowers and fruits, and of the satisfaction, as a king's, which he felt in those innocent riches! He who had so ͵huge a dislike of cities, and great houses, and high society, and sumptuous banquets, and the canvass for office, and the hard law, and the noisy lawyer, and the statesman's harangue,—he who thought the country proprietor as even too blessed, did he but know his blessedness, and who loved the valley, winding stream, and wood, and the hidden life which they offer, and the deep lessons which they whisper,—· how could he have illustrated that wonderful union of prayer, penance, toil, and literary work, the true " otium cum dignitate," a fruitful leisure and a meek-hearted dignity, which is exemplified in the Benedictine! That ethereal fire which enabled the Prince of Latin poets to take up the Sibyl's strain, and to adumbrate the glories of a supernatural future,—that serene philosophy, which has strewn his poems with sentiments which come home to the heart,—that intimate sympathy with the sorrows of human kind and with the action and passion of human nature,—how well would they have served to illustrate the patriarchal history and office of the monks in the broad German countries, or the deeds, the words, and the visions of a St. Odilo or a St. Aelred !

What a poet deliberately chooses for the subject of his poems must be in its own nature poetical. A poet indeed is but a man after all, and in his proper person may prefer solid beef and pudding to all the creations of his own " fine frenzy," which, in his character of poet, are his meat and drink. But no poet will ever commit his poetical reputation to the treatment of subjects which do not admit of poetry. When, then, Virgil chooses the country and rejects the town, he shows us that a certain aspect of the town is uncongenial with poetry, and that a certain aspect of the country is congenial. Repose, intellectual and moral, is that quality of country life which he selects for his praises ; and effort, and bustle, and excitement is that quality of a town life which he abhors. Herein then, according to Virgil, lies the poetry of St. Benedict, in the " secura quies et nescia fallere vita," in the absence of anxiety and fretfulness, of schemes and scheming, of hopes and fears, of doubts and disappointments. Such a life,—living for the day without solicitude for the morrow, without plans or objects, even holy ones, here below ; working, not (so to say) by the piece, but as hired by the hour ; sowing the ground with the certainty, according to the promise, of reaping ; reading or writing this present week without the consequent necessity of reading or writing during the next ; dwelling among one's own people without distant ties ; taking each new day as a whole in itself, an addition, not a complement, to the past ; and doing works which cannot be cut short, for they are complete in every portion of them,—such a life may be called emphatically Virgilian. They, on the contrary, whose duty lies in what may be called *undertakings*, in science and system, in sustained efforts of the intellect or elaborate processes of action,— apologists, controversialists, disputants in the schools, professors in the chair, teachers in the pulpit, rulers in the Church,—have a noble and meritorious mission, but not so poetical a one. When the bodily frame receives an injury, or is seized with some sudden malady, nature may be expected to set right the evil, if left to itself, but she requires time ; science comes in to shorten the pro-

cess, and is violent that it may be certain.   This may be
taken to illustrate St. Benedict's mode of counteracting
the miseries of life.   He found the world, physical and
social, in ruins, and his mission was to restore it in
the way, not of science, but of nature, not as if setting
about to do it, not professing to do it by any set time or
by any rare specific or by any series of strokes, but so
quietly, patiently, gradually, that often, till the work was
done, it was not known to be doing.   It was a restoration, rather than a visitation, correction, or conversion,
The new world which he helped to create was a growth
rather than a structure.   Silent men were observed
about the country, or discovered in the forest, digging,
clearing, and building ; and other silent men, not seen,
were sitting in the cold cloister, tiring their eyes, and
keeping their attention on the stretch, while they pain-
fully deciphered and copied and re-copied the manuscripts
which they had saved.   There was no one that " con-
tended, or cried out," or drew attention to what was
going on ; but by degrees the woody swamp became a
hermitage, a religious house, a farm, an abbey, a village,
a seminary, a school of learning, and a city.   Roads and
bridges connected it with other abbeys and cities, which
had similarly grown up ; and what the haughty Alaric
or fierce Attila had broken to pieces, these patient me-
ditative men had brought together and made to live
again.

And then, when they had in the course of many years
gained their peaceful victories, perhaps some new invader
came, and with fire and sword undid their slow and persevering toil in an hour.   The Hun succeeded to the
Goth, the Lombard to the Hun, the Tartar to the Lombard ; the Saxon was reclaimed only that the Dane
might take his place.   Down in the dust lay the labour

and civilization of centuries,—Churches, Colleges, Cloisters, Libraries,—and nothing was left to them but to begin all over again; but this they did without grudging, so promptly, cheerfully, and tranquilly, as if it were by some law of nature that the restoration came, and they were like the flowers and shrubs and fruit trees which they reared, and which, when ill-treated, do not take vengeance, or remember evil, but give forth fresh branches, leaves, or blossoms, perhaps in greater profusion, and with richer quality, for the very reason that the old were rudely broken off. If one holy place was desecrated, the monks pitched upon another, and by this time there were rich or powerful men who remembered and loved the past enough to wish to have it restored in the future. Thus was it in the case of the monastery of Ramsey after the ravages of the Danes. A wealthy Earl, whose heart was touched, consulted his Bishop how he could best promote the divine glory: the Bishop answered that they only were free, serene, and unsolicitous, who renounced the world, and that their renunciation brought a blessing on their country. "By their merit," he said, "the anger of the Supreme Judge is abated; a healthier atmosphere is granted; corn springs up more abundantly; famine and pestilence withdraw; the state is better governed; prisons are opened; the fetters unbound; the shipwrecked relieved." He proceeded to advise him, as the best of courses, to give ground for a monastery, and to build and endow it. Earl Alwin observed in reply, that he had inherited some waste land in the midst of marshes, with a forest in the neighbourhood, some open spots of good turf, and others of meadow; and he took the Bishop to see it. It was in fact an island in the fens, and as lonely as religious men could desire. The gift was accepted, workmen were collected, the pious peasants round about gave their labour. Twelve monks were found from another cloister; cells and a chapel were soon raised. Materials were collected for a handsome church; stones and cement were given; a firm foundation was secured; scaffolding and machinery were lent; and in course of time a sacred edifice and two towers rose over the desolate waste, and renewed the past;—a learned divine from France was invited to preside over the monastic schools.*

10.

Here then I am led, lastly, to speak of the literary labours of the Benedictines, but I have not room to do more than direct attention to the peculiar character of their work, and must leave the subject of their schools for some future opportunity. Here, as in other respects above noticed, the unity of monachism shows itself. What the Benedictines, even in their latest literary developments, have been, in St. Maur in the seventeenth century, and at Solesme now, such were the monks in their first years. One of the chief occupations of the disciples of St. Pachomius in Egypt was the transcription of books. It was the sole labour of the monks of St. Martin in Gaul. The Syrian solitaries, according to St. Chrysostom, employed themselves in making copies of the Holy Scriptures. It was the occupation of the monks of St. Equitius and of Cassiodorus, and of the nunnery of St. Cæsarius. We read of one holy man preparing the skins for writing, of another selling his manuscripts in order to gain alms for the poor, and of an abbess writing St. Peter's Epistles in letters of gold. St. David had shown the same reverence to St. John's Gospel. Abbot Plato filled his own and other monas-

* *Vid.* Turner, Anglo-Saxons, vol. iii., p. 468.

teries with his beautifully written volumes.* During the short rule of Abbot Desiderius at Monte Cassino, his monks wrote out St. Austin's fifty Homilies, his Letters, his Comment upon the Sermon on the Mount, upon St. Paul and upon Genesis ; parts of St. Jerome and St. Ambrose, part of St. Bede, St. Leo's Sermons, the Orations of St. Gregory Nazianzen ; the Acts of the Apostles, the Epistles and the Apocalypse ; various histories, including that of St. Gregory of Tours, and of Josephus on the Jewish War, Justinian's Institutes, and many ascetic and other works ; of the Classics, Cicero de Naturâ Deorum, Terence, Ovid's Fasti, Horace, and Virgil. Maurus Lapi, a Camaldolese, in the fifteenth century, copied a thousand volumes in less than fifty years. Jerome, a monk in an Austrian monastery, wrote so great a number of books that, it is said, a wagon with six horses would scarcely suffice to draw them. Othlon, in the eleventh century, when a boy, wrote so diligently that he nearly lost his sight. That was in France ; he then went to Ratisbon, where he wrote nineteen missals, three books of the Gospel, two books of Epistle and Gospel, and many others. Many he gave to his friends, but the list is too long to finish. The Abbot Odo of Tournay " used to exult," according to his successor, " in the number of writers which the Lord had given him. Had you gone into his cloister, you might have seen a dozen young men sitting in perfect silence, writing at tables constructed for the purpose. All Jerome's Commentaries on the Prophets, all the works of St. Gregory, all that he could find of Austin, Ambrose, Isidore, Bede, and the Lord Anselm, Abbot

---

* Pallad, c. 39. Cassian, Inst., iv., 12. Calmet, Reg., t. ii., p. 150. Thomassin, Disc. Eccl., t. iii., p. 505. Ziegelbaum, Hist. Litt. Bened, t. ii., p. 510.

of Bec, and afterwards Archbishop of Canterbury, he caused to be diligently transcribed." *

These tranquil labourers found a further field in the illumination and binding of the transcribed volumes, as they had previously been occupied in the practice necessary for the then important art of calligraphy. It was not running hand that the monks had to learn; for it was no ephemeral expression of their own thoughts which their writing was to convey, but the formal transcript, for the benefit of posterity, of the words of inspired teachers and Doctors of the Church. They were performing what has been since the printer's work; and it is said that from the English monks is derived the small letter of the modern Roman type. In France the abbeys of Fontenelle, Rheims, and Corbie were especially famed for beauty of penmanship in the age of Charlemagne,† when literature was in its most depressed state. Books intended for presents, such as that which the mother of Leo the Ninth presented to St. Hubert, and, much more, if intended for sacred uses, were enriched with gold and silver plates and precious stones. Here was a commencement of the cultivation of the fine arts in those turbulent times,—a quiet, unexciting occupation, which went on inside the monasteries, whatever rivalries or heresies agitated Christendom outside of them, and which, though involving, of course, an improvement in the workmanship as time went on, yet in the case of every successive specimen, whatever exact degree of skill or taste each exhibited, had its end in itself, as though there had been no other specimen before or after.

* Annal. Camald., t. vii., p. 300 : *vid.* other instances in Maitland's Dark Ages, and Buckingham's Bible in the Middle Ages, who, however, is deficient in references.

† Guizot's Hist. Civil., vol. ii., p. 236, Bohn.

Brower, in his work on the Antiquities of Fulda, gives us a lively picture of the various tranquil occupations which were going on at one time within the monastic walls. "As industrious bees," he says, "their work never flagging, did these monks follow out their calling. Some of them were engaged in describing, here and there upon the parchment, the special letters and characters which were to be filled in; others were wrapping or binding the manuscripts in handsome covers; others were marking out in red the remarkable sentences or the heads of the chapters. Some were writing fairly what had been thrown together at random, or had been left out in the dictation, and were putting every part in fair order. And not a few of them excelled in painting in all manner of colours, and in drawing figures."* He goes on to refer to an old manuscript there, which speaks of the monks as decorating their church, and of their carpenters' work, sculpture, engraving, and brass work.

I have mentioned St. Dunstan in an earlier page, as called to political duties, which were out of keeping with the traditionary spirit of his Order; here, however, he shows himself in the simple character of a Benedictine. He had a taste for the arts generally, especially music. He painted and embroidered; his skill in smith's work is recorded in the well-known legend of his combat with the evil one. And, as the monks of Hilarion joined gardening with psalmody, and Bernard and his Cistercians joined field work with meditation, so did St. Dunstan use music and painting as directly expressive or suggestive of devotion. "He excelled in writing, painting, moulding in wax, carving in wood and bone, and in work in gold, silver, iron, and brass," says the

* P. 45.

writer of his life in Surius. " And he used his skill in musical instruments to charm away from himself and others their secular annoyances, and to rouse them to the thought of heavenly harmony, both by the sweet words with which he accompanied his airs, and by the concord of those airs themselves."* And then he goes on to mention how on one occasion, when he had hung his harp against the wall, and the wind brought out from its strings a wild melody, he recognized in it one of the antiphons in the Commune Martyrum, " Gaudete in Cœlis," etc., and used it for his own humiliation.

As might be expected, the monasteries of the South of Europe would not be behind the North in accomplishments of this kind. Those of St. Gall, Monte Cassino, and Solignac, are especially spoken of as skilled in the fine arts. Monte Cassino excelled in illumination and in mosaic, the Camaldolese in painting, and the Olivetans in wood-inlaying.†

II.

While manual labour, applied to these artistic purposes, ministered to devotion, on the other hand, when applied to the transcription and multiplication of books, it was a method of instruction, and that peculiarly Benedictine, as being of a literary, not a scientific nature. Systematic theology had but a limited place in ecclesiastical study prior to the eleventh and twelfth centuries ; Scripture and the Fathers were the received means of education, and these constituted the very text on which the pens of the monks were employed. And thus they would be becoming familiar with that kind of knowledge which was proper to their vocation, at the same time

* *Vid.* also Whitaker's Cornwall, vol. i., p. 167, and the whole chapter.
† Meehan's Marchese, p. xxiv.

that they were engaged in what was unequivocally a manual labour; and, in providing for the religious necessities of posterity, they were directly serving their own edification. And this again had been the practice of the monks from the first, and is included in the *unity* of their profession. St. Chrysostom tells us that their ordinary occupation in his time was "to sing and pray, to read Scripture, and to transcribe the sacred text."[*] As the works of the early Fathers gradually became the literary property of the Church, these, too, became the subject-matter of the reading and the writing of the monks. " For him who is going on to perfection," says St. Benedict in his Rule, "there are the lessons of the Holy Fathers, which lead to its very summit. For what page, what passage of the Old or New Testament, coming as it does with divine authority, is not the very exactest rule of life? What book of the Holy Catholic Fathers does not resound with this one theme, how we may take the shortest course to our Creator?" But I need not here insist on this characteristic of monastic study, which, especially as regards the study of Scripture, has been treated so fully and so well by Mr. Maitland in his " Essays on the Dark Ages."

The sacred literature of the monks went a step further. They would be naturally led by their continual perusal of the Scriptures and the Fathers to attempt to compare and adjust these two chief sources of theological truth with each other. Hence resulted the peculiar character of the religious works of what may be especially called the Benedictine period, the five centuries between St. Gregory and St. Anselm. The age of the Fathers was well nigh over; the age of the Schoolmen was yet to come; the ecclesiastical writers

* Hist. Litter. de St. Maur. 1770, p. 21.

of the intervening centuries employed themselves for the most part in arranging and digesting the patristical literature which had come down to them ; they either strung together choice passages of the Fathers in *catenæ*, as a running illustration of the inspired text, or they formed them into a comment upon it. The *Summæ Sententiarum* of the same centuries were works of a similar character, while they also opened the way to the intellectual exercises of the scholastic period ; for they were lessons or instructions arranged according to a scheme or system of doctrine, though they were still extracted from the works of the Fathers, and though the matter of those works suggested the divisions or details of the system. Moreover, such labours, as much as transcription itself, were Benedictine in their spirit, as well as in their subject-matter ; for where there was nothing of original research, nothing of brilliant or imposing result, there would be nothing to dissipate, elate, or absorb the mind, or to violate the simplicity and tranquillity proper to the monastic state.

The same remark applies to a further literary employment in which the Benedictines allowed themselves, and which is the last I shall here mention, and that is the compilation of chronicles and annals, whether ecclesiastical, secular, or monastic. So prominent a place does this take in their literature, that the author of the *Asceticon*, in the fourth volume of Dom Francois's Bibliothèque des Ecrivains Bénédictins, does not hesitate to point to the historical writings of his Order as constituting one of its chief claims, after its Biblical works, on the gratitude of posterity. " This," he says, " is the praise especially due to the monks, that they have illustrated Holy Scripture, rescued history, sacred and profane, from the barbarism of the times, and have handed down to posterity so many lives both of Saints and of Bishops."* Here again is a fresh illustration of the Benedictine character ; for first, those histories are of the most simple structure and most artless composition, and next, from the circumstance of their being commonly narratives of contemporary events, or compilations from a few definite sources of information which were at hand, they involved nothing of that laborious research and excitement of mind which is demanded of the writer who has to record a complex course of history, extending over many centuries and countries, and who aims at the discovery of truth, in the midst of deficient, redundant, or conflicting testimony. "The men who wrote history," says Mr. Dowling, speaking of the times in question, "did not write by rule ; they only put down what they had seen, what they had heard, what they knew. Very many of them did what they did as a matter of moral duty. The result was something *sui generis ;* it was not even what *we* call history at all. It was, if I may so speak, something more, an actual admeasurement rather than a picture ; or, if a picture, it was painted in a style which had all the minute accuracy and homely reality of the most domestic of the Flemish masters, not the lofty hyperbole of the Roman school, nor the obtrusive splendour, not less unnatural, of the Venetian. In a word, history, as a subject of criticism, is an art, a noble and beautiful *art ;* the historical writings of the middle ages is *nature.*"†

Mention is made in this passage of the peculiarity in monastic historiography, that it proceeded from the motive of religious duty. This must always have been

---

* P. 379. Printing, another tranquil work, was introduced into Italy by the Benedictines of Subiaco. *Vid.* Dr. Ullathorne's Pilgrimage.

† Introd. Eccles. Hist., p. 56.

the case in consequence of the monastic profession; however, we have here, in addition to the presumption, actual evidence, and not on one occasion only, of the importance which the Benedictine Order attached to these notices and memorials of past times. In the year 1082, for instance, the Abbot Marquand of New Corbie, in Saxony, seems to have sent an order to all churches and monasteries subject to his rule to send to him severally the chronicles of their own places. Abbot Wichbold repeated the order sixty years later, and Abbot Thierry in 1337 addressed to the provosts and rectors subject to him a like injunction.* Again, in 1481 the Abbot of Erfurdt addressed a letter to the Fathers of the Reform of Bursfeld, with the view of persuading them to take part in a similar work. "If you were to agree among yourselves," he says, "and make a statute to the effect that every Prelate is under an obligation to compose annals and histories of his monastery, what could be better, what more useful, what more interesting, whether for knowing or for reading?"†

It is easier to conjecture what those literary works would be, in which a Benedictine would find himself at liberty to engage, than to pretend to point out those from which his vocation would debar him; yet Mabillon, equally with de Rancé, implied that all subjects do not come alike to him. Here we are recalled to the well-known controversy between these two celebrated men. The Abbot of La Trappe, the Cistercian de Rancé, writing to his own people, put forth some statements on the subject of the studies proper to a monk, which

---

* Ziegelbaur, t. ii., p. 401.

† *Ibid.*, t. i., p. 424. For lists of monastic histories, *vid.* Mr. Dowling, Introd. E. H., p. 260; the Asceticon as above, § 26. Ziegelbaur, t. ii., p. 398. Balmez., Prot. and Cath., p. 195.

seemed to reflect upon the learned Maurists. Mabillon, one of them, replied, in a learned vindication of himself and his brethren. The Abbot had maintained that study of whatever kind should be kept in strict subordination to manual labour, and should not extend to any books except the Scriptures and the ascetic treatises of the Fathers. Mabillon, on the other hand, without denying the necessity of manual labour, to which the Maurists themselves devoted an hour a day, seemed to allow to the Benedictine the free cultivation of the intellect, and an unlimited range of studies. When they explained themselves, each combatant would appear to have asserted more than he could successfully maintain ; yet after all there was a considerable difference of view between them, which could not be removed. The critical question was whether certain historical instances, which Mabillon urged in his favour, were to be considered exceptions or not to the rule of St. Benedict. I have certainly maintained in an earlier page of this Essay that such instances as Alcuin, Paschasius, or Lanfranc are no fair specimens of the Benedictine profession, and must not be taken to represent the monks generally. Lest, however, in saying this, I may be thought to be evading the testimony of history, as adduced by a writer, authoritative at once by his learning and as spokesman of the great Congregation of St. Maur, I think it well to extract in my behalf some of his own admissions, which seem to me fully to bear out what I have been laying down above about the spirit and mission of his Order.

For instance, he frankly concedes, or rather maintains, that the scholastic method of teaching theology and philosophy is foreign to the profession of a Benedictine, as such. "Why," he asks, "need we cultivate these

sciences in the way of disputation ? Why not as positive sciences, explaining questions and resolving doubts
as they occur ? Why is it not more than enough for
religious pupils to be instructed in the more necessary
principles of the science, and thereby to make progress
in the study of the Scriptures and the Fathers ? What
need of this perpetual syllogizing in form, and sharp
answers to innumerable objections, as is the custom in
the schools ?" Elsewhere he contrasts the mode of
teaching a subject, as adopted by the early Fathers, with
that which the Schoolmen introduced. "The reasonings
of the Fathers," he says, "are so full, so elegantly set
forth, as to be everywhere redolent of the sweetness and
vigour of Christian eloquence, whereas scholastic theology is absolutely dry and sterile." Elsewhere he says
that " in the study of Holy Scripture consists the entire
science of monks." Again, he says of Moral Theology,
" As monks are rarely destined to the cure of souls, it
does not seem necessary that they should give much
time to the science of Morals." And though of course
he does not forbid them the study of history, which we
have seen to be so congenial to their calling, yet he
observes of this study, when pursued to its full extent,
" It seems to cause much dissipation of mind, which is
prejudicial to that inward compunction of heart, which
is so especially fitting to the holy life of a monk." Again,
observing that the examination of ancient MSS. was the
special occupation of the Maurists in his time, he says,
" They who give themselves to this study have the more
merit with God, in that they have so little praise with
men. Moreover, it obliges them to devote the more
time to solitude, which ought to be their chief delight.
I confess it is a most irksome and unpleasant labour ;
however, it gives much less trouble than transcription,

which was the most useful work of our early monks."
Elsewhere, speaking of the celebrated Maurist editions
of the Fathers, he observes, " Labour, such as this, which
is undergone in silence and in quietness, is especially
compatible with true tranquillity of mind and the mastery of the passions, provided we labour as a duty, and
not for glory.*

I trust the reader will be so good as to keep in mind
that I am all along speaking of the Benedictine life
historically, and as I might speak of any other historical
fact; not venturing at all on what would be the extreme
presumption of any quasi-doctrinal or magisterial exposition of it, which belongs to those only who have
actually imbibed its tradition. This being clearly understood, I think I may interpret Mabillon to mean that
(be the range of studies lawful to a monk what it may)
still, whatever literary work requires such continuous portions of time as not to admit of being suspended at a
moment's notice, whatever is so interesting that other
duties seem dull and heavy after it, whatever so exhausts
the power of attention as to incapacitate for attention
to other subjects, whatever makes the mind gravitate
towards the creature, is inconsistent with monastic simplicity. Accordingly, I should expect to find that
controversy was uncongenial to the Benedictine, because
it excited the mind, and metaphysical investigations,
because they fatigued it; and, when I met such instances as St. Paschasius or St. Anselm, I should deal
with them as they came and as I could. Moreover,
I should not look to a Benedictine for any elaborate and
systematic work on the history of doctrine, or of heresy, or
for any course of patristical theology, or any extended

* Stud. Monast., ed. 1732; t. i., pp. 52, 135; t. ii., p. 2; t. i., pp. 145,
147, 191, 64.

ecclesiastical history, or any philosophical disquisitions upon history, as implying a grasp of innumerable details, and the labour of using a mass of phenomena to the elucidation of a theory, or of bringing a range of multifarious reading to bear upon one point ; and that, because such efforts of mind require either an energetic memory devoted to matters of time and place, or, instead of the tranquil and plodding study of one book after another, the presence of a large library, and the distraction of a vast number of books handled all at once, not for perusal, but for reference.   Perhaps I am open to the charge of refining, in attempting to illustrate the principle which I seem to myself to detect in the Benedictine tradition ; but the principle itself which I have before me is clear enough, and is expressed in the advice which is given to us by a sacred writer : " The words of the wise are as goads, and nails deeply fastened in ; *more than these, my son, require not :* of making many books there is no end, and much study is an affliction of the flesh."

To test the truth of this view of the Benedictine mission, I cannot do better than appeal as a palmary instance to the Congregation of St. Maur, an intellectual school of Benedictines assuredly.   Now what, in matter of fact, is the character of its works ?   It has no Malebranche, no Thomassin, no Morinus ; it has no Bellarmine, no Suarez, no Petavius ; it has no Tillemont or Fleury,— all of whom were more or less its contemporaries ; but it has a Montfaucon, it has a Mabillon, it has a Sainte Marthe, a Coustant, a Sabbatier, a Martene,—men of immense learning and literary experience ; it has collators and publishers of MSS. and of inscriptions, editors of the text and of the versions of Holy Scripture, editors and biographers of the Fathers, antiquarians, annalists, paleographists,—with scholarship indeed, and criticism, and theological knowledge, admirable as often as elicited by the particular subject on which they are directly employed, but conspicuously subordinate to it.

If we turn to other contemporary Congregations of St. Benedict we are met by the same phenomenon. Their labours have been of the same modest, patient, tranquil kind. The first name which occurs to me is that of Augustine Calmet, of the Congregation of St. Vanne. His works are biblical and antiquarian ;—a literal Comment on Scripture with Dissertations, a dictionary of the Bible, a Comment on the Benedictine Rule, a history of Lorraine. I cast my eyes round the Library, in which I happen at the moment to be writing ; what Benedictine authors meet them ? There is Ceillier, also of the Congregation of St. Vanne ; Bertholet, of the same Congregation ; Cardinal Aguirre of Salamanca ; Cressy of Douai ; Pez of Mölk on the Danube ; Lumper of St. George in the Hercynian Forest ; Brockie of the Scotch College at Ratisbon ; Reiner of the English Congregation. Their Works are of the same complexion,—historical, antiquarian, biographical, patristical,—calling to mind the line of study traditionally pursued by a modern ecclesiastical congregation, the Italian Oratory. I do not speak of Ziegelbauer, Francois, and other Benedictines, who might be added, because they have confined themselves to Benedictine Antiquities, and every Order will write about itself.

And so of the Benedictine Literature from first to last. Ziegelbauer, who has just been mentioned, has written four folio volumes on the subject. Now one of them is devoted to a catalogue and an account of Benedictine authors ;—of these, those on Scripture and Positive Theology occupy 110 pages ; those on history, 300 ; those on scholastic theology, 12 ; those on polemics, 12 ;

those on moral theology, 6. This surprising contrast may be an exaggeration of the fact, because there is much of repetition and digression in his survey, and his biographical notices vary in length ; but, after all allowances for such accidental unfairness in the list, the result must surely be considered as strikingly confirmatory of the account which I have been giving.

12.

But I must cut short an investigation which, though imperfect for the illustration of its subject, is already long for the patience of the reader. All human works are exposed to vicissitude and decay; and that the great Order of which I have been writing should in the lapse of thirteen centuries have furnished no instances of that general law is the less to be expected, in proportion to the extent of its territory, the independence of its separate houses, and the local varieties of its constitution. To say that peace may engender selfishness, and humility become a cloak for indolence, and a country life may be an epicurean luxury, is only to enunciate the over-true maxim, that every virtue has a vice for its first cousin. *Usum non tollit abusus ;* and the circumstance that Benedictine life admits of being corrupted into a mode of living which is not Benedictine, but its very contradictory, cannot surely be made an argument against its meritorious innocence, its resolute cheerfulness, and its strenuous tranquillity. We are told to be like little children ; and where shall we find a more striking instance than is here afforded us of that union of simplicity and reverence, that clear perception of the unseen, yet recognition of the mysterious, which is the characteristic of the first years of human existence ? To the monk heaven was next door ; he formed no plans, he had no cares ;

the ravens of his father Benedict were ever at his side. He "went forth" in his youth "to his work and to his labour" until the evening of life ; if he lived a day longer, he did a day's work more ; whether he lived many days or few, he laboured on to the end of them. He had no wish to see further in advance of his journey than where he was to make his next stage. He ploughed and sowed, he prayed, he meditated, he studied, he wrote, he taught, and then he died and went to heaven. He made his way into the labyrinthine forest, and he cleared just so much of space as his dwelling required, suffering the high solemn trees and the deep pathless thicket to close him in. And when he began to build, his architecture was suggested by the scene,—not the scientific and masterly conception of a great whole with many parts, as the Gothic style in a later age, but plain and inartificial, the adaptation of received fashions to his own purpose, and an addition of chapel to chapel and a wayward growth of cloister, according to the occasion, with half-concealed shrines and unexpected recesses, with paintings on the wall as by a second thought, with an absence of display and a wild, irregular beauty, like that of the woods by which he was at first surrounded. And when he would employ his mind, he turned to Scripture, the book of books, and there he found a special response to the peculiarities of his vocation ; for there supernatural truths stand forth as the trees and flowers of Eden, in a divine disorder, as some awful intricate garden or paradise, which he enjoyed the more because he could not catalogue its wonders. Next he read the Holy Fathers, and there again he recognized a like ungrudging profusion and careless wealth of precept and of consolation. And when he began to compose, still he did so after that mode which nature and revelation had taught him, avoiding curious knowledge, content with incidental ignorance, passing from subject to subject with little regard to system, or care to penetrate beyond his own homestead of thought,—and writing, not with the sharp logic of disputants, or the subtle analysis of philosophers, but with the one aim of reflecting in his pages, as in a faithful mirror, the words and works of the Almighty, as they confronted him, whether in Scripture and the Fathers, or in that "mighty maze" of deeds and events, which men call the world's history, but which to him was a Providential Dispensation.

Here the beautiful character in life and death of St. Bede naturally occurs to the mind, who is, in his person and his writings, as truly the pattern of a Benedictine as is St. Thomas of a Dominican ; and with an extract from the letter of Cuthbert to Cuthwin concerning his last hours, which, familiarly as it is known, is always pleasant to read, I break off my subject for the present.

"He was exceedingly oppressed," says Cuthbert of St. Bede, "with shortness of breathing, though without pain, before Easter Day, for about a fortnight ; but he rallied, and was full of joy and gladness, and gave thanks to Almighty God day and night and every hour, up to Ascension Day ; and he gave us, his scholars, daily lectures, and passed the rest of the day in singing the Psalms, and the night too in joy and thanksgiving, except the scanty time which he gave to sleep. And as soon as he woke, he was busy in his customary way, and he never ceased with uplifted hands giving thanks to God. I solemnly protest, never have I seen or heard of any one who was so diligent in thanksgiving.

"He sang that sentence of the blessed Apostle Paul, 'It is a dreadful thing to fall into the hands of the Living God,' and many other passages of Scripture, in which he warned us to shake off the slumber of the soul, by anticipating our last hour. And he sang some verses of his own in English also, to the effect that no one could be too well prepared for his end, viz., in calling to mind, before he departs hence, what good or evil he has done, and how his judgment will lie. And he sang too the antiphons, of which one is, 'O King of Glory, Lord of Angels, who this day hast ascended in triumph above all the heavens, leave us not orphans, but send the promise of the Father upon us, the Spirit of Truth, alleluia.' And when he came to the words, 'leave us not orphans,' he burst into tears, and wept much. He said, too, 'God scourgeth every son whom He receiveth,' and, with St. Ambrose, 'I have not so lived as to be ashamed to have been among you, nor do I fear to die, for we have a good Lord.'

"In those days, besides our lectures and the Psalmody, he was engaged in two works; he was translating into English the Gospel of St. John, as far as the words, 'But what are these among so many,' and some extracts from the *Notæ* * of Isidore. On the Tuesday before Ascension Day he began to suffer still more in his breathing, and his feet were slightly swollen. However, he went through the day, dictating cheerfully, and he kept saying from time to time, 'Take down what I say quickly, for I know not how long I am to last, or whether my Maker will not take me soon.' He seemed to us to be quite aware of the time of his going, and he passed that night in giving of thanks, without sleeping. As soon as morning broke, that is on the Wednesday, he urged us

---

* The Bollandists have not been able to determine which of St. Isidore's works is here intended. "Notæ" means "Musical Notes," according to Du Cange. According to Lebœuf in Ampère, Hist. Litter. t. iii., p. 253, the word means "penmanship."

to make haste with the writing which we had begun. We did so till nine o'clock, when we walked in procession with the Relics of the Saints, according to the usage of that day. But one of our party said to him, 'Dearest Master, one chapter is still wanting; can you bear our asking you about it?' He answered, 'I can bear it; take your pen and be ready, and write quickly.' At three o'clock he said to me, 'Run fast, and call our priests, that I may divide among them some little gifts which I have in my box.' When I had done this in much agitation, he spoke to each, urging and entreating them all to make a point of saying Masses and prayers for him. Thus he passed the day in joy until the evening, when the above-named youth said to him, 'Dear Master, there is yet one sentence not written;' he answered, 'Write quickly.' Presently the youth said, 'Now it is written;' he replied, 'Good, thou hast said the truth; *consummatum est;* take my head into thy hands, for it is very pleasant to me to sit facing my old praying place, and thus to call upon my Father.' And so, on the floor of his cell, he sang, 'Glory be to Father, Son, and Holy Ghost,' and, just as he had said 'Holy Ghost,' he breathed his last, and went to the realms above."

It is remarkable that this flower of the Benedictine school died on the same day as St. Philip Neri,—May 26; Bede on Ascension Day, and Philip on the early morning after the feast of Corpus Christi. It was fitting that two saints should go to heaven together, whose mode of going thither was the same; both of them singing, praying, working, and guiding others, in joy and exultation, till their very last hour.

V.

THE BENEDICTINE SCHOOLS.

(From the ATLANTIS *of* January, 1859.)

V.

THE BENEDICTINE SCHOOLS.

I.

WE read in history of great commanders, who, when an overwhelming force was directed against them on the plain, and success was for the time impossible, submitted to necessity, and, with plans afterwards to be developed, retired up the mountain passes in their rear, where nature had provided a safe halting-place for brave men who could not advance, and would not turn in flight. There, behind the lofty crag, the treacherous morass, and the thick wood, they nursed their confidence of victory, and waited patiently for an issue, which was not less certain because it was delayed. On came the haughty foe, with cries of defiance ; and when at length he thought he had them at his mercy, he found that first he must do battle with the adamantine rocks, which sternly rose up in defence of fugitives who had invoked their aid. Then he stood for a while irresolute, till the difficulties of his position ended his deliberation, and forced upon him a retreat in his turn, while the lately besieged hosts were once more in motion, and pressed upon the baffled foe, who had neither plan of campaign nor base of operations to fall back upon.

Such is the history of Christian civilization. It gave

6*

way before the barbarians of the north and the fanatics of the south; it fled into the wilderness with its own books and those of the old social system which it was succeeding. It obeyed the direction given it in the beginning,—when persecuted in one place, to flee away to another; and then at length the hour of retribution came, and it advanced into the territories from which it had retired. St. Benedict is the historical emblem of its retreat, and St. Dominic of its return.

I do not say that its retreat in the first centuries was made with the intent of its return in the medieval. There was no oracular voice which proclaimed what would be the course and fortune of the war; no secret tradition which whispered to the initiated the tactic that ought to be pursued. It is a sufficient explanation of the double movement, that they who feel their weakness are used to give way, and they who feel their strength are used to push forward. The corruptions of Roman society caused Christians to despair of ever mending it, and to look out for that better world which was destined to supersede it. The evil which they experienced, the good for which they sighed, the promise in which they confided, wrought in them the persuasion that the end of all things was at hand; and this persuasion made them patient under inconveniences which they felt to be only temporary. "Behold, my brethren," says Pope Gregory about the year 600, "we already see with our eyes what we are used to hear in prophecy. Day by day is the world assaulted by fresh and thickening blows. Out of that innumerable Roman *plebs* what a mere remnant are ye at this day! yet incessant scourges are still in action; sudden adversities thwart you; new and unforeseen slaughters wear you away. For, as in youth, the body is in vigour, the chest is strong, the neck muscular, and the arms plump, but in old age the stature is bent, the neck is withered and stooping, the chest pants, the energies are feeble, and breath is wanting for the words ; so the world too once was vigorous, robust for the increase of its kind, green in its health, and opulent in its resources, but now on the contrary it is laden with the weight of years, and is fast sinking into the grave by its ever-multiplying maladies. Beware, then, of giving your heart to that which, as even your senses tell you, cannot last for ever." * Commonly the presentiment wore a more definitely supernatural expression than is found in this extract. Not sense merely, but the prophecies were directly invoked, which spoke of that great enemy of the Church, who was to be the herald of the Second Advent ; and the rudiments of a new order of things were descried in the manifest tokens of an expiring world.

In all times, indeed, the multitude, whether from religious feeling or from superstition, is prone to portend some impending catastrophe from the occurrence of any startling phenomenon of nature. An eclipse, a comet, a volcanic eruption, is to them the omen of coming evil. But in the early centuries of the Church the expectation extended to the learned and the saintly. It was the posture of mind of confessors and doctors. As St. Gregory looked out for Antichrist in the sixth century, so had the Martyrs of Lyons in the second, St. Cyprian in the third, St. Hilary and St. Chrysostom in the fourth, and St. Jerome in the fifth. It was the sober judgment of the wisest and the most charitable, that the world was too bad to mend, and that destruction was close upon it.

What would be the practical result of such a belief ?

* Hom. i. 1.

That which I have partly described in my remarks on the mission of St. Benedict; evidently, to leave the world to itself. Evils which threaten to continue we try to remedy; but what was the use of spending one's strength in reforming a state of things which would go to pieces, if let alone, and, if ever so much meddled with, would go to pieces too, nay, the sooner, perhaps, for the meddling? Hence it was the prevalent disposition, as I have said, of Christians of the first centuries, and no irrational disposition, either to leave the world or to put up with it, not to set about influencing it. "Let us go hence," said the Angels in the doomed sanctuary of the chosen people. "Come ye out of her, my people," was the present bidding of inspiration. Those who would be perfect obeyed it, and became monks. Monachism therefore was a sort of recognized emigration from the old world. St. Antony had found out a new coast, the true *eldorado* or gold country; and on the news of it thousands took their departure year after year for the diggings in the desert. The monks of Egypt alone soon became an innumerable host. As times got worse, Basil in the East, and Benedict in the West, put themselves at the head of fresh colonies, bound for the land of perpetual peace. There they sat them down, over against Babylon, and waited for the coming judgment and the end of all things. Those who remained in the world, waited too. To undergo patiently what was,—to make the best of it, to use it, as far as it could be used, for religious purposes,—was their wisdom and their resolve. If they took another course, they would be wasting strength and hope upon a shadow, and losing the present for a future which would never come. They had no large designs or profound policy. It was their aim that things should just last their time. They patched them up as best they might, they made shift, and lived from hand to mouth; and they followed events, rather than created them. Nor, when they undertook great labours and began works pregnant with consequences, did they perceive whither they were going.

How different in this respect is the spirit of the first Gregory, already cited, from that of Hildebrand, the seventh! Gregory the First did not understand his own act, when he converted the Anglo-Saxons; nor Ambrose, when he put Theodosius to penance. The great Christian Fathers laid anew the foundations of the world, while they thought that its walls were tottering to the fall, and that they already saw the fires of judgment through the chinks. They refuted Arianism, which they named the forerunner of the last woe, with reasonings which were to live for ages; and they denounced the preachers of a carnal millennium, without anticipating that wonderful temporal reign of the saints which was to be manifested in medieval times. They propounded broad principles, but did not carry them out into their inevitable consequences. How slow were they to define doctrine, when disputes arose about its meaning or its bearing! How patient they seem to us of imperial encroachments on ecclesiastical rights, when we view them by the side of the great Popes who came after them! How tamely do they conduct themselves when the civil magistrate interferes with their jurisdiction, or takes the initiative in points of discipline or order, in questions of property, and matrimonial causes! How contented or resigned are they to avail themselves of such education as the state provided for their use; sending their children to the pagan schools, before they have teachers of their own, and, even when at length they have them, adopting the *curriculum* of studies which those pagan schools had devised !

In fact, in the minds of those high saints, "the wish was father to the thought." Religious men will always desire, will always be prone to believe, the approach of that happier order of things, which sooner or later is to be. This hope was the form in which the deep devotion of those primitive times showed itself; and if it did not continue in its full expression beyond them, this was because experience had thrown a new light upon the course of Divine Providence in the world. With the multitude, indeed, as I have said, who know little of history, and in whom religious fear is a chief element, the anticipation of the Last Day revived, and revives, from time to time. At the end of the tenth century, when a thousand years had passed over the Church, the sense of impending destruction was so vivid as even to affect the transfer and disposal of property, and the repair of sacred buildings. However, when we seek in theologians for the apprehension, we shall find that it is a characteristic of the old Empire far more than of the barbarian kingdoms which succeeded to it. The barbarian world was young, as the Roman world was effete. Youth is the season of hope; and, according as things looked more cheerful, so did they look more lasting, and to-day's sunshine became the sufficient promise of a long summer. A fervent preacher here or there, St. Norbert or St. Vincent Ferrer, may have had forebodings of the end of all things; or an astrologer or a schismatizing teacher may have traded on the belief; but the men of gravity and learning after the time of Gregory the First, for the most part, set their faces against speculations about the future.

Bede, after speaking of the six ages of the world, says,

that " as no one of the former ages has consisted exactly of a thousand years, it follows that the sixth too, under which we live, is of uncertain length, known to Him alone who has bidden His servants watch. For," he continues, " whereas all saints naturally love the hour of His advent, and desire it to be near, still, we run into danger if we presume to conclude or to proclaim, either that the hour is near or that it is far off."* Raban and Adson, who witnessed or heard of the splendours of Charlemagne, go so far as to indulge the vision of a great king of the Franks, who, in time to come, is to reign religiously, ere the fulfilment of the bad times of the end.† Theodulf indeed predicts that they were coming ; but, even when the popular excitement was at its height, in the last years of the tenth century, Richard and Abbo of Fleury, and the Adson above mentioned, set themselves against it. Hardly was the dreaded crisis over, when men took heart, and began to restore and deco-rate the Churches ; hardly had the new century run its course, when Pope Paschal the Second held a Council at Florence against Raynerius, the archbishop of that city, who had preached of the coming end.‡ Such was the change of sentiment which followed after the Pontificate of St. Gregory, the last and saddest of a line of Fathers, who thought the world was on the verge of dissolution.

The names which I have been introducing show that, among these converts to a more hopeful view of things, were Benedictine monks, members of those very associations which had given up the world as lost, and

---

* De Rat. Temp. 66, 67. Elsewhere, he speaks of *futura* tempora sub Antichristo, in Sam. iv., 2, p. 300.

† Raban, de Antichr. opp. t. vi., p. 178. Adson, ap. Alcuin, t. ii., p. 529.

‡ So Malvenda, t. i. p. 118, calling the prelate "Fluentinus ; " *vid.* Ughelli, t. iii., p. 77.

had quitted it accordingly. And the position which they occupy in their own body is sufficient evidence that what they held, their brethren held also; and that the actual changes which had taken place in the framework of society had been followed by a change of sentiment in these religious bodies. When we look into history, to see where these preachers of new hopes were, as well as who, we find the fact plain beyond all denial; for it is the monk Alcuin who was Charlemagne's instructor, and head of the school of the palace; the monk Theodulf who was a political *employé* of the same Emperor, and bishop of Orleans; and the monk Raban who was archbishop of Mayence. How could the cloister-loving monk have come to such places of station, unless he had experienced some singular change in his sentiments? And these instances, it must be allowed, are only samples of a phenomenon which is not uncommon in these centuries. Here then we have something to explain. Why should Benedictines leave those sweet country-homes which St. Benedict bequeathed to them for the haunts of men, the seats of learning, archiepiscopal sees, and king's courts? St. Jerome had said, when Monachism was young: "If the priest's office be your choice, if a bishop's work or dignity be your attraction, live a town life, and save your soul in saving others. But, if you wish to be a monk, that is a solitary, in fact as well as in name, what have you to do with towns?" "A monk's office," he says elsewhere, "is not a teacher's but a mourner's, who bewails either himself or the world."* This, doubtless, was the primary aim and badge of the religious institute; and if, among uncongenial offices, there were one more uncongenial to it than another, it was that of a ruler or a master of the faithful. The monk did not lecture, teach,

* Ad Paulin. Ep. 58; adv. Vigil. fin.

controvert, lay down the law, or give the word of command; and for this simple reason, because he did not speak at all, because he was bound to silence. He who had given up the use of his tongue, could neither be preacher nor disputant. It follows, we repeat, that a singular change must have taken place by the ninth century in the ecclesiastical position of a monk, when we find instances of his acting so differently from St. Jerome's teaching and example in the fifth.

I touched, in the Essay to which I have already referred, upon this seeming anomaly in the history of the Benedictines, while I was describing them in outline; if I did not then dwell upon it and investigate its limits, this was because I thought it advisable first to trace out the general idea of the monastic state, with as little interruption as was possible, without risking the confusion which would arise in my delineation from a premature introduction of the historical modifications to which that idea has actually been subjected. Now, however, the time has come for taking up what in that former sketch I passed over; and I propose accordingly here, after a brief reference to the circumstances under which these modifications appeared, and to the extent to which they spread, to direct attention to the principal instance of them, viz., the literary employments of the monks, and to show how singularly, after all, these employments, as carried out, were in keeping with the main idea of the monastic rule, even though they seem at first sight scarcely contained in its letter. I stated, on that former occasion, that the substance of the monastic life was "summa quies;" that its object was rest, its state retirement, and its occupations such as were unexciting and had their end in themselves. That the literature in question was consistent with these conditions will be clearly seen, when I come to describe it; first, however, let me consider the circumstances which called for it, and the hold which it had upon the general body.

2.

It is rare, indeed, to find the profession and the history of any institution running exactly in one and the same groove. The political revolutions which issued in the rule of Charlemagne, changing, as they did, the currents of the world, and the pilotage of St. Peter's bark, became a severe trial of the consistency of an Order, like the Benedictine, of which the maxims and the aims are grave, definite, and fixed. Demands of action and work would be made on it, by the exigencies of the times, at variance with its genius, and it would find itself in the dilemma of failing in efficiency on the one hand, or in faithfulness to its engagements on the other. It would be incurring either the impatience of Society, which it disappointed, or the remonstrances of its own subjects, whom it might be considered to betray.

And indeed a greater shock can hardly be fancied than that which would overtake the peaceful inhabitant of the cloister, on his finding that, after all, he so intimately depended still upon this moribund world, which he had renounced for ever, that the changes which were taking place in its condition were affecting his own. Such men, whether senators like Paulinus, or courtiers like Arsenius, or legionaries like Martin, had one and all, in their respective places and times, left the responsibilities of earth for the anticipations of heaven.* They had sought, in the lonely wood or the silent mountain top, the fair uncorrupted form of nature, which spoke

---

* "Omnibus idem propositus scopus erat, idemque finis, nempe secessus à sæculi tumultu et corruptelis." Mabillon, Annal. t. i., p. 215.

only of the Creator. They had retired into deserts, where they could have no enemies but such as fast and prayer could subdue. They had gone where the face of man was not, except as seen in pale, ascetic apparitions like themselves. They had secured some refuge, whence they might look round at the sick world in the distance, and see it die. But, when that last hour came, it did but frustrate all their hopes, for, instead of an old world at a distance, they found they had a young world close to them. The old order of things died, sure enough; but then a new order took its place, and they themselves, by no will or expectation of their own, were in no small measure its very life. The lonely Benedictine rose from his knees and found himself a city. This was the case, not merely here or there, but everywhere; Europe was new mapped, and the monks were the principle of mapping. They had grown into large communities, into abbeys, into corporations with civil privileges, into land-holders with tenants, serfs, and baronial neighbours; they had become centres of population, the schools of the most cherished truths, the shrines of the most sacred confidences. They found themselves priests, rulers, legislators, feudal lords, royal counsellors, missionary preachers, controversialists; and they comprehended that unless they fled anew from the face of man, as St. Antony in the beginning, they must bid farewell to the hope of leading St. Antony's life.

In this choice of difficulties, when there was a duty to stay and a duty to take flight, the monastic bodies were not unwilling to come to a compromise with the age, and, reserving their fidelity to St. Benedict, to undertake those functions to which both the world and the Church called them. Such, that is, for the most part, was the resolve of those who found themselves in this perplexity ; but it could not be supposed that there were no Antonies on earth still, and that these would be satisfied to adopt it.   On the contrary, there were holy men who were but impelled into a re-action of the most rigid asceticism by this semblance of a reconciliation between their brethren and the world.   Such was St. Romuald in the tenth century, the founder of the Camaldolese, who, through a long life of incredible austerities, was ever forming new monastic stations, and leaving them when formed, from love of solitude.   Such St. Bruno, the founder of the Carthusians, whose conversion, as described in the well-known legend, points to the union in his day of intellectual gifts and dissoluteness of life. " Come, dear friend," he is represented as saying to some companions, concerning the awful death which he had witnessed, " what is to become of us ?   If a man of this doctor's rank and repute, of such literary, such scientific attainments, of such seeming-virtuous life, of so wide a reputation, is thus indubitably damned,what is to become of poor creatures of no estimation, such as we are? "*   Such, again, was St. Stephen of Grandimont, who, when two Cardinals came to see and wonder at him in his French desert, excused himself by saying, " How could we serve churches and undertake cures who are dead to the world, and have every member of our body cut off from this life, with neither feet to walk, nor tongues to speak withal ? "†   These, and others such, sought out for themselves a seclusion and silence, most congenial to the original idea of monachism, but incompatible with those active duties,—missions, the pastoral office, teaching in the schools, and disputations with heresy,—which at the time there were none but monks to fulfil.

Would that nothing worse than the demand of such

* Marten. Ampl. Coll. t. vi., p. 153.   † *Ibid.*, p. 1063.

sacred duties brought the monasteries into the world, and drove these reformers into the desert! The law of God was often broken by the monks, as well as the rule of St. Benedict. Grave moral disorders arose within their walls; and that partly indeed from the seductions of ease, wealth, and the homage of mankind, but in a great measure also from the political troubles of the times, which exposed them to the tyranny of the military chief or the violence of the marauder. Relaxation will easily take place in a religious community, when, from whatever circumstance, it cannot observe its rule; and what orderly observance could there be when the country round about was the seat of war and rapine? Nay, a simpler process of monastic degeneracy followed from the high hand of military power. Kings seized the temporalities of the abbeys for their favourites, and made licentious soldiers bishops and abbots; and these, by their terrors and their bribes, fostered a lax irreligious party in the heart of these communities up and down the country. This part of the history, however, does not concern us in these pages, which are devoted to the consideration of the real work of the Benedictine, not to the injuries or interruptions which it has sustained, or to corruptions which are not its own.

On the other hand, not kings alone interfered with St. Benedict. A not less forcible overruling of his tradition took place from another quarter, where there was authority for the act, and where nothing would be done except on religious principles and with religious purposes. It was a more serious interference, for the very reason that it was a legal one, proceeding from the Church herself. According to the maxim, " sacramenta propter homines," she has never hesitated to consider, in this sense of the maxim, that "the end justifies the means;" and since Regulars of whatever sort are her own creation, she can of course alter, or adapt, or change, or bring to nought, according as her needs require, the institutions which she has created. Necessity has no law, and charity has no reserves; and she has acted accordingly. She brought the Benedictine from his cloister into the political world; but, as far as she did so, let it be observed, it was her act and not his. If then, on account of the necessities of the day, she has over-ruled his resolve, and made him do what neither his tradition nor his wishes suggested, such instances cannot fairly be taken, either as specimens of Benedictine work, or as modifications of the Benedictine idea.

And such cases abound. St. Benedict himself had with difficulty contemplated a priest as being in the ranks of his children; laying it down in his Rule, " If a priest asks to be received in any monastery, his request must not quickly be granted; but if he persists, the whole discipline of the rule is binding on him without any relaxation."—*C.* 60. But Pope Gregory, who had himself been torn violently from the cloister to fill the Pontifical throne, spared his religious brethren as little as he had been spared himself. He made a number of them bishops. From his own convent on the Cælian he sent Augustine and his companions to be apostolic missionaries to the Anglo-Saxons, and he designed to put the entire episcopate and priesthood of the newly-converted race, and thereby their secular concerns, into the hands of the monks.* As to the Archbishops of Canterbury, they actually were monks down to the twelfth century.† This is but a specimen of what was

* Thomassin. Disc. Eccl. t. i., p. 674.

† " Uno excepto, qui ob hanc præsumptionem et alia depositus per Romanum Pontificem fuit." Eadmer ap. Nat. Alex. t. vi., p. 599. St. Thomas in consequence made himself a monk, when he came to the see.

largely carried out by the Holy See on the continent in the centuries which followed Gregory ; but, I repeat, the Pope's action is external to the Benedictines, who are as little compromised by his consecrating hand as by the iron glove of the feudal tyrant.

To whatever extent, however, these innovations went, whether they were simple profanations, or were made and ratified by the wise policy of those who had a right to make them, and whatever show they make in history from the circumstance of their necessary connection with public events, with principal cities, and with prominent men, we cannot speak of them as constituting any great exception to the monastic discipline, or as exerting any considerable influence on the monastic spirit, till we have surveyed the religious institutions of Christendom as a whole, and measured them by the side of the general view thus obtained. I had occasion in my former Essay to speak of the condition of the early monks, their various families, the rise of the Benedictines, and the process of assimilation and absorption, by which at length St. Benedict gathered under his own rule the disciples of St. Martin, St. Cæsarius, and St. Columban. And even when the whole monastic body was Benedictine, it was not on that account moulded upon one type, or dependent upon one centre. As it had not spread out from one origin, so neither was it homogeneous in its construction nor simple and concordant in its action. It propagated itself variously, and had much of local character in its secondary dispositions. We cannot be certain what it was in one place by knowing what it was in another. One house attained more nearly to what may be called its normal idea than another, and therefore we have no right to argue that such quasi-secularizations as I have noticed extended much further than those particular cases which history has handed down to us.

And then, on the other hand, we must bear in mind how vast was the whole multitude of persons who professed the monastic life, and, compared with it, how small was the number of those who were called away to active political duties or who gave themselves to literature or science. They might all be subtracted from the sum total of religious, and, as far as number goes, they would not have been missed. I have already referred to the exuberance of Egyptian monachism. Antony left to Pachomius the rule of 50,000. Posthumus of Memphis presided over 5,000 ; Ammon over 3,000. In the one city of Oxyrinchus there were 10,000. Hilarion in Syria had from 2,000 to 3,000. Martin of Gaul was followed to the grave by 2,000 of his disciples. At that date the sees of the whole of Christendom, according to Bingham, did not go much beyond 1,700.* If every bishop then had been a monk, the general character of monastic life would not have been much affected. In a later age, the monastery of Bangor contained 2,000; that of Banchor, county Down, according to St. Bernard, "many thousand monks," one of whom founded as many as 100 monasteries in various places.† Again, the Episcopal Sees of France are given in the *Gallia Christiana* as 160, including the provinces of Utrecht, Cologne, and Treves ; and precisely that number of monastic houses is said to have been founded in that country by St. Maur alone, in the very first years of the Benedictines. Trithemius, at the end of the fifteenth century, numbers the Benedictine convents as 15,000 ;‡ and, though we are

---

* Thomassin. Disc. Eccles. t. i., p. 702. Gibbon, ch. 37. Bingh. Antiqu. b. 9.

† Camden, Hist. vol. iii., p. 618.

‡ Milman, Latin Christ. vol. i., p. 398.

not to suppose that each of them had the 2,000 subjects which we find at Bangor, the lowest average will swell the sum total of monks to a vast multitude. In the beginning of the previous century, a census of the Benedictines was taken by John the Twenty-second, to which Helyot refers, according to which the Order, from its commencement up to that time, had had 22,000 archbishops and bishops, and of saints alone, 40,000. Vague calculations or statements are sufficient to represent general truths; it is difficult to determine what is the per-centage of heroic virtue in a population of regulars; if we say at random, as many saints as one in the hundred, even at this rate the number of Benedictines would reach 4,000,000, and the Episcopal portion would be only the one hundred and eightieth part of the whole Order.

More data, then, than we need, will be left to us in history, to determine the monastic vocation, even though we strike out from the list of its disciples every monk who took any secular office, as of prelate, lecturer, or disputant; nay, though we formed all those who undertook such duties into evidence of an opposite mode of life. But in fact, these very men, who in one way or another were engaged in work, which St. Benedict has not recognized by name, are themselves specimens of fidelity to their founder, and impress the Benedictine type of sanctity upon their literary or political undertakings. The proverb, " naturam expellas furcâ," etc., holds true of religion. Whatever has life has in it a conservative principle, and a power of assimilation. Where the religious spirit was strong, it would overcome obstacles in its exercise, and revive after overthrows, and would make for itself preternatural channels for its operations, when its legitimate course was denied to it. Neither the functions of an Apostle, nor of a schoolmaster, are much akin to those of a monk ; nevertheless, in a given individual, they may be reconciled, or the one merged in the other. The Benedictine missionary soon relapsed into the laborious husbandman ; the champion of the faith flung his adversary, and went back to his plough or his pen ; the bishop, like Peter Damian, effected, or like Boniface, contemplated, a return in his old age to the cloister which he had left. As to the schools of learning, it will be my business now to show how undisputatious was the master, and how unexciting the studies.

3.

The rise and extension of these Schools seems to me as great an event in the history of the Order as the introduction of the sacerdotal office into the number of its functions. If Pope Gregory took a memorable step in turning the monks of his convent into missionary bishops, charged with the conversion of England, much more remarkable was the act of Pope Vitalian, in sending the old Greek monk Theodore to the same island, to fill the vacant see of Canterbury. I call it more remarkable, because it introduced an actual tradition into the Benedictine houses, and consecrated a system by authority. It is true that from an early date in the history of monachism, extensive learning had been combined with the profession of a monk. St. Jerome was only too fond of the Cicero and Horace, whom he put aside ; and, if out of the whole catalogue of ecclesiastics I had to select a literary Father, the monk Jerome, *par excellence*, would be he. In the next century Claudian Mamercus, of Vienne, employed the leisure which his monastic profession gave him to gain an extensive knowledge of Greek and Latin literature. He collected a library of Greek,

Roman, and Christian books, " quam totam, monachus," says Sidonius of him, " virente in ævo, secretâ bibit institutione." * And in the century after, Cassiodorus, the contemporary of St. Benedict, is well known for combining sacred and classical studies in his monastery. The tradition, however, of the cloister was up to that time against profane literature, añd Theodore reversed it.

Theodore made his appearance at the end of the century which the missionary Augustine opened, and just about the time when the whole extent of England had been converted to the Christian faith. He brought with him Greek as well as Latin Classics, and set up schools for both the learned languages in various parts of the country. Henceforth the curriculum of the Seven Sciences is found in the Benedictine Schools. From Theodore † proceeded Egbert and the school of York ; from Egbert came Bede and the school of Jarrow ; from Bede, Alcuin and the schools of Charlemagne at Paris, Tours, and Lyons. From these came Raban and the school of Fulda ; from Raban, Walafrid and the school of Richenau, Lupus and the school of Ferrières. From Lupus, Heiric, Remi, and the school of Rheims ; from Remi, Odo of Cluni ; from the dependencies of Cluni, the celebrated Gerbert, afterwards Pope Sylvester the Second, and Abbo of Fleury, whom I have already introduced to the reader's notice, though not by name, in the former part of this sketch, as repaying a portion of the debt which the Franks owed to the Anglo-Saxons, by opening the schools of Ramsey Abbey, after the inroad of the Danes.

In addressing myself, then, at length, to the ques-

---

* Mabillon Annal. Bened. t. i., p. 32.

† *Vid.* Daniel, Etudes Classiques, p. 100, etc. ; Launoy, de Scholis, Opp t. iv., 1.

tion, how such studies can be considered in keeping with the original idea of the monastic state, I think it right to repeat an explanation which I made at an earlier stage of the discussion, to the effect that I am proposing nothing more than a survey of the venerable order of St. Benedict from without; and I claim leave to do as much as this by the same right by which the humblest among us may freely and without offence gaze on sun, moon, and stars, and form his own private opinion, true or false, of their materials and their motions. And with this proviso, I remind the reader, if I have not sufficiently done so already, that the one object, immediate as well as ultimate, of Benedictine life, as history presents it to us, was to live in purity and to die in peace. The monk proposed to himself no great or systematic work, beyond that of saving his soul. What he did more than this was the accident of the hour, spontaneous acts of piety, the sparks of mercy or beneficence, struck off in the heat, as it were, of his solemn religious toil, and done and over almost as soon as they began to be. If to-day he cut down a tree, or relieved the famishing, or visited the sick, or taught the ignorant, or transcribed a page of Scripture, this was a good in itself, though nothing was added to it to-morrow. He cared little for knowledge, even theological, or for success, even though it was religious. It is the character of such a man to be contented, resigned, patient, and incurious; to create or originate nothing; to live by tradition. He does not analyze, he marvels; his intellect attempts no comprehension of this multiform world, but on the contrary, it is hemmed in, and shut up within it. It recognizes but one cause in nature and in human affairs, and that is the First and Supreme; and why things happen day by day in this way, and not in that, it refers immediately to His will.* It loves the country, because it is His work; but "man made the town," and he and his works are evil. This is what may be called the Benedictine idea, viewed in the abstract; and, as being such, I gave it, in my former Essay, the title of "poetical," when contrasted with that of other religious orders; and I did so, because I considered I saw in it a congeniality, *mutatis mutandis*, with the spirit of a great Roman Poet, who has perhaps a better title to that high name than any one else, at least in this respect, as having received a wider homage than others, and that among nations in time, place, and character, further removed from each other.†

Now, supposing the historical portrait of the Benedictine to be such as this, and that we were further told, that he was concerned with study and with teaching, and then were asked, keeping in mind the notion of his

---

* Quoties videtur contra naturam aliquid evenire, quodammodo non contra naturam est, quia rerum natura hoc habet eximium, ut à quo est, semper ejus obtemperet jussis. Paschas. p. 155, Opp. ed. 1618.

† This analogy between the monastic institute and Virgil is recognized by Cassiodorus, who, after impressing on his monks, in the first place, the study of Holy Scripture and the Fathers, continues, "However, the most holy Fathers have passed no decree, binding us to repudiate secular literature; for in fact such reading prepares the mind in no slight measure for understanding the sacred writings." Presently, "In some cases indeed, Frigidus obstiterit circum præcordia sanguis," so as to hinder a man's perfect mastery whether of human or divine letters; but even with but a poor measure of knowledge, *he may be able to choose the life which follows in the next verse*, "Rura mihi et rigui placeant in vallibus amnes;" for "*it is even congenial to monks to have the care of a garden, to till the land, and to take interest in a good crop of apples.*"—De Inst. div. litt. 28. Here, by the bye, is in fact the same contrast between the "Felix qui" and the "Fortunatus et ille," which I have suggested to the reader in my former article (*Supr.* p. 387, note). Mr. Keble, in a passage of his beautiful Prelections, p. 648, considers Virgil to allude to Lucretius in the "Felix," and to ascribe to himself the "Fortunatus."

poetry of character, to guess what books he studied and what sort of pupils he taught, we should without much difficulty conclude that Scripture would be his literature, and that children would be the members of his school.*
And, if we were further asked what was likely to be, after Scripture, the subject-matter of the schooling imparted to these boys, probably we should not be able to make any guess at all ; but we surely should not be very much surprised to be told that the same spirit which led him to prefer the old basilicas for worship instead of any new architecture of his own inventing, and to honour his emperor or king with spontaneous loyalty more than by theological definitions, had also induced him, in the matter of education, to take up with the old books and subjects which he found ready to his hand in the pagan schools, as far as he could religiously do so, rather than to venture on any experiments or system of his own.† This, as I have already intimated, was the case. He adopted the Roman curriculum, professed the Seven Sciences, beginning with Grammar, that is, the Latin classics, and, if he sometimes finished with them, it was because his boys left him ere he had time to teach them more. The subjects he chose were his fit recompense for choosing them. He adopted the Latin writers from his love of prescription, because he found them in possession. But there were in fact no writings, after Scripture, more congenial, from their fresh and natural beauty and their freedom from intellectualism, to the monastic temperament. Such were his schoolbooks ;

---

* "Mos in Benedictino ordine usatissimus scholas instituere, et pueros cùm pietate tum litteris imbuere." Dachery in Lanfranc. Opp. p. 28. Brower. Antiqu. Fuld., pp. 35-38.

† On the monastic schools taking up the imperial, *vid*. Guizot, Civil, vol. ii., p. 100, etc. *Vid*. also Ampère, Hist. Lit., t. ii., p. 277.

and as " the boy is father of the man," the little monks, who had heard them read or pored over them, when they grew up filled the atmosphere of the monastery with the tasks and studies with which they had thus been imbued in their childhood.

For so it was, strange as it seems to our ideas, these boys were monks*—monks as truly as those of riper years. About St. Benedict's time the Latin Church innovated upon the discipline of former centuries, and allowed parents not only to dedicate their infants to a religious life, but to do so without any power on the part of those infants, when they came to years of reason, to annul the dedication. This discipline continued for five or six centuries, beginning with the stern Spaniards, nor ending till shortly before the pontificate of Innocent the Third. Divines argued in behalf of it from the case of infant baptism, in which the sleeping soul without being asked, is committed to the most solemn of engagements ; from that of Isaac on the Mount, and of Samuel, and from the sanction of the Mosaic Law ; and they would be confirmed in their course by the instances of compulsion, not uncommon in the early centuries, when high magistrates or wealthy heads of families were suddenly seized on by the populace or by synods, and, against their remonstrances, tonsured, ordained, and consecrated, before they could well take breath and realize to themselves their change of station. Nor must we forget the old Roman law, the spirit of which they had inherited, and which gave to the father the power even of life and death over his refractory offspring.

However, childhood is not the age at which the severity of the law would be felt, which bound a man by his parent's act to the service of the cloister. While these

* Thomass. Disc. Eccles, t. i., 821.

oblates were but children, they were pretty much like other children; they threw a grace over the stern features of monastic asceticism, and peopled the silent haunts of penance with a crowd of bright innocent faces. "Silence was pleased," to use the poet's language, when it was broken by the cheerful, and sometimes, it must be confessed, unruly voices of a set of school-boys. These would sometimes, certainly, be inconveniently loud, especially as St. Benedict did not exclude from his care lay-boys, destined for the world. It was more than the devotion of some good monks could bear; and they preferred some strict Reform, which, among its new provisions, prohibited the presence of these uncongenial associates. But, after all, it was no great evil to place before the eyes of austere manhood and unlovely age a sight so calculated to soften and to cheer. It was not adolescence, with its curiosity, its pride of knowledge and its sensitiveness, with its disputes and emulations, with its exciting prizes and its impetuous breathless efforts, which St. Benedict undertook to teach; he was no professor in a University. His convent was an infant school, a grammar school, and a seminary; it was not an academy. Indeed, the higher education in that day scarcely can be said to exist. It was a day of bloodshed and of revolution; before the time of life came when the University succeeds the School, the student had to choose his profession. He became a clerk or a monk, or else he became a soldier.

The fierce northern warriors, who had won for themselves the lands of Christendom with their red hands, rejoiced to commit their innocent offspring to the custody of religion and of peace. Nay, sometimes with the despotic will, of which I have just now spoken, they, dedicated them, from or before their birth, to the service of Heaven. They determined that some at least of their lawless race should be rescued from the contamination of blood and licence, and should be set apart in sacred places to pray for their kindred. The little beings,* of three or four or five years old, were brought in the arms of those who gave them life to accept at their bidding the course in which that life was to run. They were brought into the sanctuary, spoke by the mouth of their parents, as at the font, put out their tiny hand for the sacred corporal to be wrapped round it, received the cowl, and took their place as monks in the monastic community. In the first ages of the Benedictine Order, these children were placed on a level with their oldest brethren. They took precedence according to their date of admission, and the grey head gave way to them in choir and refectory, if junior to them in monastic standing. They even voted in the election of abbot, being considered to speak by divine instinct, as the child who cried out, "Ambrose is Bishop." † If they showed waywardness in community meetings, inattention at choir, ill behaviour at table, which certainly was not an impossible occurrence, they were corrected by the nods, the words, or the blows of the grave brother who happened to be next them : it was not till an after time that they had a prefect of their own, except in school hours.

That harm came from this remarkable discipline is only the suggestion of our modern habits and ideas ; that it was not expedient for all times, follows from the

* Calmet, Reg. Bened., t. ii., pp. 2, 4, 116, 278, 325-6, 380, 385. *Vid.* also Thomassin. Disc. Eccl., t. i., p. 821, and Magagnotti's Dissert. in Fleury's Disc. Pop. Dei.

† Calmet, t. ii., p. 324. This early dedication of the monk might tend to suggest or defend the abuse of boy priests. *Vid.* St. Bernard, de Off. Ep. 7.

fact that at a certain date it ceased to be permitted. However, that, in those centuries in which it was in force, its result was good, is seen in the history of the heroic men whom it nurtured, and might have been anticipated from the principle which it embodied. The monastery was intended to be the paternal home, not the mere refuge of the monk : it was an orphanage, not a reformatory ; father and mother had abandoned him, and he grew up from infancy in the new family which had adopted him. He was a child of the house ; there were stored up all the associations of his wondering boyhood, and there would lie the hopes and interests of his maturer years. He was to seek for sympathy in his brethren, and to give them his own sympathy in return. He lived and died in their presence. They prayed for his soul, cherished his memory, were proud of his name, and treasured his works. A pleasing illustration of this brotherly affection meets us in the life of Walafrid Strabo, Abbot of Richenau, whose poems, written by him when a boy of fifteen and eighteen, were preserved by his faithful friends, and thus remain to us at this day. Walafrid is but one out of many, whose names are known in history, dedicated from the earliest years to the cloister. St. Boniface, Apostle of Germany, was a monk at the age of five ; St. Bede came to Wiremouth at the age of seven ; St. Paul of Verdun is said by an old writer to have left his cradle for the cloister ; St. Robert entered it as soon as he was weaned ; Pope Paschal the Second was taken to Cluni, Ernof to Bec, the Abbot Suger to St. Denis, from their " most tender infancy."

4.

Infants can but gaze about at what surrounds them.

and their learning comes to them through their eyes. In the instances I have been considering, their minds would receive the passive impressions which were made on them by the monastic scene, and would be moulded by the composed countenances and solemn services which surrounded them. Such was the education of these little ones, till perhaps the age of seven ; when, under the title of " pueri," [*] they commenced their formal school-time, and committed to memory their first lesson. That lesson was the Psalter—that wonderful manual of prayer and praise, which, from the time when its various portions were first composed down to the last few centuries, has been the most precious *viaticum* of the Christian mind in its journey through the wilderness. In early times St. Basil speaks of it as the popular devotion in Egypt, Africa, and Syria ; and St. Jerome had urged its use upon the Roman ladies whom he directed. All monks were enjoined to know it by heart ; the young ecclesiastics learned it by heart ; no bishop could be ordained without knowing it by heart ; and in the parish schools it was learned by heart. The Psalter, with the Lord's Prayer and Creed, constituted the *sine quâ non* condition of discipleship. At home pious mothers, as the Lady Helvidia, the mother of St. Leo the Ninth, taught their children the Psalter. It was only, then, in observance of a universal law [†] that the Benedictine children were taught it ;—they mastered it, and then they passed into the secular schoolroom, and were introduced to the study of grammar.[‡]

---

[*] Calmet, t. i., p. 495.

[†] Thomass. Disc., t. ii., p. 280, etc.

[‡] The following sketch is drawn up from the works of the Benedictines, in Bibl. Max. Patr., tomm. 14, 15, 17, 18, 21 ; Mabillon's Acta SS. Bened. ; Ceillier's Auteurs, tomm. 18-20 ; Neander's Hist., vol vi., (Bohn); Guizot,

By Grammar, it is hardly necessary to say, was not meant, as now, the mere analysis or rules of language, as denoted by the words etymology, syntax, prosody; but rather it stood for scholarship, that is, such an acquaintance with the literature of a language as is implied in the power of original composition and the *vivâ voce* use of it. Thus Cassiodorus defines it to be " skill in speaking elegantly, gained from the best poets and orators;" St. Isidore, " the science of speaking well;" and Raban, " the science of interpreting poets and historians, and the rule of speaking and writing well." In the monastic school, the language of course was Latin; and in Latin literature first came Virgil; next Lucan and Statius; Terence, Sallust, Cicero; Horace, Persius, Juvenal; and of Christian poets, Prudentius, Sedulius, Juvencus, Aratus. Thus we find that the monks of St. Alban's, near Mayence, had standing lectures in Cicero, Virgil, and other authors. In the school of Paderborne there were lectures in Horace, Virgil, Statius, and Sallust. Theodulf speaks of his juvenile studies in the Christian authors, Sedulius and Paulinus, Aratus, Fortunatus, Juvencus, and Prudentius, and in the classical Virgil and Ovid. Gerbert, afterwards Sylvester the Second, after lecturing his class in logic, brought it back again to Virgil, Statius, Terence, Juvenal, Persius, Horace, and Lucan. A work is extant of St. Hildebert's, supposed to be a school exercise; it is scarcely more than a cento of Cicero, Seneca, Horace, Juvenal, Persius, Terence, and other writers. Horace he must have almost known by heart.

Hist. Civil., vol. ii., (Bohn); Ampère, Hist. Lit. t. iii., and two recent works, Mgr. Landriot's Ecoles Littéraires, and P. Daniel's Etudes Classiques, to which I am much indebted for many points of detail. *Vid.* also M. l'Abbé Lalanne's Influence des Pères, and P. Cahour's Etudes Classiques.

Considering the number of authors which have to be studied in order to possessing a thorough knowledge of the Latin tongue, and the length to which those in particular run which are set down in the above lists, we may reasonably infer, that with the science of Grammar the Benedictine teaching began and ended, excepting of course such religious instruction as is rather the condition of Christian life than the acquisition of knowledge. At fourteen, when the term of boyhood was completed,[*] the school-time commonly ended too, the lay youths left for their secular career, and the monks commenced the studies appropriate to their sacred calling. The more promising youths, however, of the latter class were suffered or directed first to proceed to further secular studies ; and, in order to accompany them, we must take some more detailed view of the curriculum, of which Grammar was the introductory study.

This curriculum,[†] derived from the earlier ages of heathen philosophy, was transferred to the use of the Church on the authority of St. Augustine, who in his *de Ordine* considers it to be the fitting and sufficient preparation for theological learning. It is hardly necessary to refer to the history of its formation ; we are told how Pythagoras prescribed the study of arithmetic, music, and geometry ; how Plato and Aristotle insisted on grammar and music, which, with gymnastics, were the substance of Greek education ; how Seneca speaks, though not as approving, of grammar, music, geometry, and astronomy, as the matter of education in his own day ; and how Philo, in addition to these, has named logic and rhetoric. Augustine, in his enumeration of them, begins with arithmetic and grammar, including

[*] Calmet, Reg., t. i., p. 495.
[†] Brucker, Phil. t. iii., p. 594, etc. Appul. Florid. iv. 20.

under the latter history; then he speaks of logic and rhetoric; then of music, under which comes poetry, as equally addressing the ear; lastly, of geometry and astronomy, which address the eye. The Alexandrians, whom he followed, arranged them differently; viz., grammar, rhetoric, and logic or philosophy,* which branched off into the four mathematical sciences of arithmetic, music, geometry, and astronomy. And this order was adopted in Christian education, the first three sciences being called the Trivium, the last four the Quadrivium.

Grammar was taught in all these schools; but for those who wished to proceed further than the studies of their boyhood, seats of higher education had been founded by Charlemagne in the principal cities of his Empire, under the name of public schools,† which may be considered the shadow, and even the nucleus of the Universities which arose in a subsequent age. Such were the schools of Paris, Tours, Rheims, and Lyons in France; Fulda in Germany; Bologna in Italy. Nor did they confine themselves to the Seven Sciences above mentioned, though it is scarcely to be supposed that, in any science whatever, except Grammar, they professed to impart more than the elements. Thus we read of St. Bruno of Segni (A.D. 1080), after being grounded in the " litteræ humaniores," as a boy, by the monks of St. Perpetuus near Aste, seeking the rising school of Bologna for the " altiores scientiæ."‡ St. Abbo of Fleury (A.D. 990), after mastering, in the monastery of that place,

---

* The Quadrivium was called "philosophy." Ampère, t. iii., p. 267.

† Charlemagne's schools taught Grammar, Rhetoric, Leges, Canones, Theology biblical and patristical. *Vid.* Thomass. Disc. t. iii., pp. 271-294; Ampère Hist., t. iii., p. 267.

‡ Vit. ap. Brun. Opp. ed. 1759.

grammar, arithmetic, logic, and music, went to Paris and Rheims for philosophy and astronomy ; and afterwards taught himself rhetoric and geometry. Raban (A.D. 822) left the school of Fulda for a while for Alcuin's lectures, and learned Greek of a native of Ephesus. Walafrid (A.D. 840) passed from Richenau to Fulda. St. William (A.D. 908), dedicated by his parents to St. Benedict at St. Michael's near Vercellæ, proceeded to study at Pavia. Gerbert (A.D. 990), one of the few cultivators of physics, after Fleury and Orleans, went to Spain.* St. Wolfgang (A.D. 994), after private instruction, went to Richenau. Lupus (A. D. 840), after Ferrières, was sent for a time to Fulda. Fulbert too of Chartres (A. D. 1000), though not a monk, may be mentioned as sending his pupils in like manner to finish their studies at schools of more celebrity than his own.†

History furnishes us with specimens of the subjects taught in this higher education. We read of Gerbert lecturing in Aristotle's Categories and the Isagogæ of Porphyry; St. Theodore taught the Anglo-Saxon youths Greek and mathematics ; Alcuin, all seven sciences at York ; and at some German monasteries there were lectures in Greek,‡ Hebrew, and Arabic. The monks of St. Benignus at Dijon gave lectures in medicine; the abbey of St. Gall had a school of painting and engra-

---

* Brucker, t. iii., p. 646.

† Thomass. Disc. t. ii., pp. 296-8.

‡ Fredegodus of Canterbury (A.D. 960) wrote in Greek. *Vid.* Cave's Hist. Litt. in nom. In the Life of St. Odo of Canterbury we read that his patron Athelm "Græcâ et Latinâ linguâ magistris edocendum eum tradidit, quarum linguarum *plerisque* tunc temporis in gente Anglorum usus erat, à discipulis beatæ memoriæ Theodori archiepiscopi profectus. Factusque est in utrâque linguâ valdè gnarus, ita ut posset poemata fingere, continuare prosam, et omnia, quicquid ei animo sederet, luculentissimo sermone proferre." Mabillon, Act. Sæc. v., p. 289

ving ; the blessed Tubilo of that abbey was mathematician, painter, and musician.* We read of another monk
of the same monastery, who was ever at his carpentry
when he was not at the altar ; and of another, who
worked in stone. Hence Vitruvius was in repute with
them. Another accomplishment was that of copying
manuscripts, which they did with a perfection unknown
to the scholastic age which followed them.†

These manual arts, far more than the severer sciences,
were the true complement of the Benedictine ideal of
education, which, intellectually considered, was, after all,
little more than a fair or a sufficient acquaintance with
Latin literature. Such is the testimony of the ablest
men of the time. " To pass from Grammar to Rhetoric,
and then in course to the other liberal sciences," says
Lupus, speaking of France, is "fabula tantum."‡ " It has
ever been the custom in Italy," says Glaber Radulphus,
writing of the year 1000, " to neglect all arts but Grammar." § Grammar, moreover, in the sense in which we
have defined it, is no superficial study, nor insignificant
instrument of mental cultivation, and the school-task of
the boy became the life-long recreation of the man.
Amid the serious duties of their sacred vocation the
monks did not forget the books which had arrested and
refined their young imagination. Let us turn to the
familiar correspondence of some of these more famous
Benedictines, and we shall see what were the pursuits of
their leisure, and the indulgences of their relaxation.

---

* I quoted in my former article a passage from Brower on the arts
cultivated at Fulda. For a parallel in the East, *vid.* the account of the
monks of Theodore Studita, Vit. p. 29, Sismond.

† Guizot, Civil., t. ii., p. 236 ; Hallam, Lit. i., 1, 87.

‡ Ep. 1.

§ Muratori, Dissert. xliii., p. 831.

Alcuin, in his letters to his friends, quotes Virgil again and again; he also quotes Horace, Terence, Pliny, besides frequent allusions to the heathen philosophers Lupus quotes Horace, Cicero, Suetonius, Virgil, and Martial. Gerbert quotes Virgil, Cicero, Horace, Terence, and Sallust. Petrus Cellensis quotes Horace, Seneca, and Terence. Hildebert quotes Virgil and Cicero, and refers to Diogenes, Epictetus, Crœsus, Themistocles, and other personages of ancient history. Hincmar of Rheims quotes Horace. Paschasius Radbert's favourite authors were Cicero and Terence. Abbo of Fleury was especially familiar with Terence, Sallust, Virgil, and Horace; Peter the Venerable, with Virgil and Horace; Hepidann of St. Gall took Sallust as a model of style.*

Nor is their anxiety less to enlarge the range of their classical reading. Lupus asks Abbot Hatto through a friend for leave to copy Suetonius's Lives of the Cæsars, which is in the monastery of St. Boniface in two small *codices.* He sends to another friend to bring with him the Catilinarian and Jugurthan Wars of Sallust, the *Verrines* of Cicero, and any other volumes which his friend happens to know either that he has not, or possesses only in faulty copies, bidding him withal beware of the robbers on his journey. Of another friend he asks the loan of Cicero's *de Rhetoricâ*, his own copy of which is incomplete, and of Aulus Gellius. In another letter he asks the Pope for Cicero's *de Oratore*, the Institutions of Quintilian, and the commentary of Donatus upon Terence. In like manner Gerbert tells Abbot Gisilbert that he has the beginning of the *Ophthalmicus* of the philosopher Demosthenes, and the end of Cicero's *Pro rege Deiotaro ;* and he wants to

---

* The School of Ouen produced 500 writers in 50 years. Landriot, p. 138. *Vid.* the curious Letter of Gunzo, Marten., Ampl. Coll. t. i., col. 294.

know if he can assist in completing them for him. He asks a friend at Rome to send him by Count Guido the copies of Suetonius and Aurelius, which belong to his archbishop and himself; he requests Constantine, the lecturer (scholasticus) at Fleury, to bring him Cicero's *Verrines* and *de Republicâ*, and he thanks Remigius, a monk of Treves, for having begun to transcribe for him the Achilleid of Statius, though he had been unable to proceed with it for want of a copy. To other friends he speaks of Pliny, Cæsar, and Victorinus. Alcuin's Library contained Pliny, Aristotle, Cicero, Virgil, Statius, and Lucan ; and he transcribed Terence with his own hand.

Not only the memory of their own youth, but the necessity of transmitting to the next generation what during it they had learned themselves, kept them loyal to their classical acquirements. They were, in this aspect of their history, not unlike the fellows in our modern English universities, who first learn and then teach. It is impossible, indeed, to overlook their resemblance generally to the elegant scholar of a day which is now waning, especially at Oxford, such as Lowth or Elmsley, Copleston or Keble, Howley or Parr, who thought little of science or philosophy by the side of the authors of Greece and Rome. Nor is it too much to say that the Colleges in the English Universities may be considered in matter of fact to be the lineal descendants or heirs of the Benedictine schools of Charlemagne.* The modern of course has vastly the advantage in the comparison ; for he is familiar with Greek, has an exacter criticism and purer taste, and a more refined cultivation of mind. He writes, verse at least, far better than the Benedictine, who had commonly little idea of it ; and

* *Vid.* infr. vol. iii., pp. 225, 6.

he has the accumulated aids of centuries in the shape of dictionaries and commentaries. I am not writing a panegyric on the classical learning of the dark age, but describing what it was ; and, with this object before me, I observe that, whatever the monks had not, a familiar knowledge and a real love they had of the great Latin writers, and I assert, moreover, that that knowledge and love were but in keeping with the genius and character of their institute. For they instinctively recognized in the graceful simplicity of Virgil or of Horace, in his dislike of the great world, of political contests and of ostentatious splendour, in his unambitious temper and his love of the country, an analogous gift to that religious repose, that distaste for controversy, and that innocent cheerfulness which were the special legacy of St. Benedict to his children. This attachment to the classics is well expressed by a monk of Paderborn,[*] who, when he would describe the studies of the place, suffers his prose almost to dissolve into verse, as he names his beloved authors.

Viguit Horatius,   magnus et Virgilius,
Crispus et Sallustius,   et urbanus Statius.

Ludusque fuit omnibus,   *insudare versibus,*
Et dictaminibus   *juɔundisque cantibus.*

The latter of these stanzas, as they may be called, illustrates what we have wished to express, in speaking of the classical temperament of the Benedictines. As far as they allowed themselves in any recreation, which was not of a sacred nature, they found it in these beautiful authors, who might be considered as the prophets of the human race in its natural condition.

---

[*] *Vid.* Daniel. p. 115. Landriot, p. 139.

How strongly they contrast in this respect with the scholastic age which swallowed them up! Amid the religious or ecclesiastical matters which were the subject of their correspondence, questions of grammar and criticism are mooted, and a loving curiosity about the nicety of languages is temperately indulged. Whether *rubus* is masculine or feminine is argued from analogy and by induction; Ambrose makes it feminine, and the names of trees, which have no plurals, are feminine, as *populus, fraxinus;* on the other hand Virgil makes it masculine, and Priscian allows it to be an exception to the rule. Again, is it *dispexeris* or *despexeris?* Priscian says *despicio,* and makes *de* answer to the Greek κατὰ, *down;* but the Greek in the Psalm is, not κατίδης, but ὑπερίδης, *above.* Again, is the penultima of *voluerimus* long or short? long, says Servius on Virgil.* They carry their fidelity to the Classics into their own poetical compositions; far from resigning themselves to that merely rhythmical versification, which is ever grateful to the popular ear, which had been in use from the Augustan age, and which afterwards developed into *rhyme,*† they rather affect the archaisms and the licences of the classical times. "Contraria rerum," "genus omne animantum," "retundier," "formarier," "benedicier," "scribier," "indupediret," "indunt," savour of Ennius or Lucretius rather than of Virgil. They keep to the Augustan metres, and they are never unwilling to use them. Their theological treatises begin, their epistles to kings end, with hexameters and pentameters. They moralize, they protest, they soothe their sorrows, they ask favours, they compile chronicles, they record their journeys in heroics, elegiacs, and epigrams. They are

---

* Alcuin, Ep. 23; Lupus, Ep pp. 5, 8, 20, 34.

† *Vid.* Muratori Dissert. 40.

versifiers, one and all, or at least those whose names or works are best known in history, or in our libraries. The habit was formed at school, and it endured through life. Some indeed, as Lupus or Gerbert, had too many occupations to indulge in it ; but others, as Theodulf, bishop of Orleans, return to it in the evening of life, after the manner of Gregory Nazianzen in patristic times, or Lord Wellesley in our own. Bede, Alcuin, Aldhelm, Raban, Theodulf, Hildebert, Notgar, Adelhard, Walafrid, Agobard, Florus, Modoin, Heiric, Gerbert, Angilbert, Herman, Abbo, Odo, Hucbald, Lupus, Fridouard, Paschasius, with many others, all wrote verse. I am not insinuating that they wrote it so happily as the Patriarch of Constantinople or the Governor-General of India ; on the contrary, it was not their *forte ;* but Florus, for instance, is eloquent, and Walafrid Virgilian.[*] Their subjects, when most sacred, are such as the great phenomena of nature, the country, woods, mountains, flocks, and herds, plants, flowers, and others which I have called Benedictine. I have no space for extracts ; but here is one, as a specimen of what I mean, when I speak of the alliance of St. Benedict and Virgil. It is the conclusion of the Hortulus of Walafrid, and presents us with a very pretty picture of an old monk amid children and fruit trees :—

> Hæc tibi servitii munuscula vilia parvi
> Strabo tuus, Grimalde pater ! . . . . . .
> Ut, cùm conseptu viridis consederis horti,
> Inter apricatas frondenti germine malos,
> Persicus imparibus crines ubi dividit umbris,
> Dum tibi cana legunt tenerâ lanugine poma

---

* Du Pin, however, says, "Theodulf's poems are very fine." **Cent. viii.**, p. 126, ed. 1699. "Tolerable poetry," says Dr. Murdock, on Mosheim, vol. ii., p. 151.

Ludentes pueri, schola lætabunda tuorum,
Atque volis ingentia mala capacibus indunt,
Grandia conantes includere corpora palmis,
Quo moneare habeas nostri, pater alme, laboris,
Dum relegis quæ dedo volens, interque legendum
Et vitiosa secas bonus, et meliora reformas.

I have taken a liberty with the last line, which any
how is somewhat feeble.

Their prose is superior to their verse ; it has little
claim indeed to the purity of taste and of vocabulary,
which we call classical ; but it is good Latin both in
structure and in idiom. At any rate the change is
wonderful, when we pass from the Benedictine centuries
to the Dominican which followed.

In so speaking I have no disrespectful meaning as regards those great authors whose Latinity happens not
to be equal to their sanctity or their intellectual power.
Their merit, in respect to language, is of a different
kind ; it consists in their success in making the majestic
and beautiful Latin tongue minister to scientific uses,
for which it was never intended. But, because they
have this merit of their own, that is no reason why we
should deny to the writers who preceded them the praise
of being familiar with the ancient language itself, a
praise which is justly theirs, though seldom allowed to
them. The writers of the Benedictine centuries are supposed to have the barbarism, without the science, of the
Dominican period ; and modern critics, who wish to be
fair, seem to consider it a great concession, if they grant
that an age must at least have some smattering in classical literature, which, as the foregoing pages show, is
ever quoting it and referring to it. Thus Mr. Hallam, in
the opening chapter of his Literature of Europe, can but
say, " Alcuin's own poems *could at least not* have been

written by one *unacquainted* with Virgil." Again: "From
this time, though *quotations* from the Latin poets, especially Ovid and Virgil, and *sometimes* from Cicero, are *not
very* frequent, they occur sufficiently to show that manuscripts had been brought to *this* side of the Alps.—*p. 7.*
Some pages lower he says, quoting some of St. Adelhard's
verses, "the quotation from Virgil in the ninth century
perhaps deserves remark, though in one of Charlemagne's
monasteries it is not by any means *astonishing ;* " as if
Virgil were not the text-book in the northern schools, as
my foregoing quotations make clear, and ignorance, in
that day, when it was to be found, had not its special
seat in the southern side of the Alps, rather than in France
and Germany. Passages such as these in men of wide
research are simply perplexing. I ask myself whether
I have rightly understood their words, or whether I
read wrongly the historical facts which they profess to
be generalizing. Perhaps it is that I assume without
warrant that the quotations of Alcuin and the rest are
bonâ fide such, and not derived, as some have said, from
catenas of passages, commonplace books, or traditionary
use ; * but such an account of them is absolutely inconsistent, first, with the testimonies which I have above
cited, as to the actual studies of the young, and next,
with the literary habits which those studies actually
formed in the persons who were exercised in them. Can
it be that critics of the nineteenth century, possessing

* "Bede . . had some familiarity with Virgil, Ovid, Lucan, Statius,
and even Lucretius . . . It may be questioned, however, whether many
of the citations from ancient authors, often adduced from medieval writers,
as indicating their knowledge of such authors, are more than traditionary,
almost proverbial, insulated passages, brilliant fragments, broken off from
antiquity, and reset again and again by writers borrowing them from each
other, but who had never read another word of the lost poet, orator, or
philosopher."—Milman, Latin Christ. vol. ii., p. 39.

the fine appreciation of classical poetry, imparted in the public schools of England, glance their eye over the rude versification of Theodulf or Alcuin, and consider it the measure of the secular learning which gave it birth? M. Guizot, Protestant as he is, is a fairer and kinder judge of the cloister literature than Mr. Hallam or Dean Milman.

5.

And now, to prevent misapprehension of my meaning in this review of the Benedictine Schools, I have two remarks to make before I bring it to an end, one on each side of the description to which that review has led me.

On the one hand, the classical studies and tastes which I have been illustrating, even though foreign to the monastic masses, as they may be called,—even though historically traceable to the mission of St. Theodore from the Holy See to England,—must still be regarded a true offspring of the Benedictine discipline, and in no sense the result of seasons or places, of relaxation and degeneracy. At first sight, indeed, there is some plausibility in saying that with the change of times a real change came over a portion of the great family of monks, and that however usefully employed, Cassiodorus or Theodore, Alcuin or Walafrid, did certainly fall from their proper vocation, and did really leave it to Romuald and others like him, to be, not only the most faithful imitators, but the only true children of the ancient monachism. And, in confirmation of this view, it might be added that the same circumstances which led the monks to literary pursuits, led them to political entanglements also, and that in the same persons, as Theodulf, Lupus, and Gerbert, learning and secular engagements were combined ; and that, as no one would say that the cares of office were proper to a monk's vocation, as little could be fairly included in it classical attainments. Whatever be the best mode of treating this difficulty, which of course demands a candid and equitable consideration, here, in addition to what I have said by the way, I shall make one answer of a different kind, which seems to me conclusive, and there leave the question. When, then, I am asked whether these studies are but the accidents and the signs of a time of religious declension, I reply that they are found in those very persons, on the contrary, who were pre-eminent in devotional and ascetic habits, and who were so intimately partakers in the spirit of mortification, whether of St. Benedict or St. Romuald, that they have come down to us with the reputation of saints,—nay, have actually received canonization or beatification. Theodore himself is a saint; Alcuin and Raban are styled "beati;" Hildebert is "venerable;" Bede and Aldhelm are saints; and we can say the same of St. Angilbert, St. Abbo, St. Bertharius, St. Adalhard, St. Odo, and St. Paschasius Radbert. At least Catholics must feel the full force of this argument; for they cannot permit themselves to attribute any dereliction of vocation to those, whom the Church holds up as choice specimens of divine power, and, as being such, sealed by miracle for eternal bliss.

This is my remark on one side the question; on the other, it must not of course be supposed,—indeed my last remark negatives the idea,—that critical scholarship or classical erudition was the business of life, even in the case of this minority of the monastic family, who took so prominent a part in the education of their time. I have distinctly said that, after their school years, the monks were as little taken up with the classics, *exceptis excipiendis*, as members of parliament or country gentlemen at the present day. They had their serious engagements, as statesmen have now, though of a different kind, and to these they gave themselves. Theology was their one study; to theology secular literature ministered, first as an aid and an ornament, then as a relaxation, amid the mental exertion which it involved. Nor was this literature cultivated without some holy jealousy on the part of the cultivators; "nuces pueris;"—there was a time of life when it ought to be put aside; there was even a danger of its seductiveness. Alcuin himself, if we may trust the account, reproved on one occasion the study, at least of the poets; and in one of his extant letters he complains of a former pupil, then raised to the episcopate, for preferring Virgil to his old master Flaccus, that is, to himself, and prays that "the four Gospels, not the twelve Æneids, may fill his breast."—*Ep.* 129. St. Paschasius, too, in spite of his love for Terence and Cicero, expresses a judgment, in one passage of his comment upon Ezekiel (*Bibl. Max. P.* t. xiv., p. 788), against the elder monks being occupied with the heathen poets and philosophers. Lanfranc, when an Irish Bishop asked him some literary question, made answer, "Episcopale propositum non decet operam dare hujusmodi studiis; we passed in these our time of youth, but, when we took on ourselves the pastoral care, we bade them farewell." —*Ep.* 33. The instance of Pope Gregory is well known: when the Bishop of Vienne had been led to lecture in the classics, he wrote, "A fact has come to our ears, which we cannot name without a blush, that you, my brother, lecture on literature" (grammatica).—*Ep.* xi. 54. Such occupations, indeed, were in those centuries generally and reasonably held to be inconsistent with the calling of a Bishop.* St. Jerome speaks as strongly in an earlier age.

* *Vid.* Thomass. Disc. Eccl., t. ii., pp. 268-286.

What was true of the Bishop was on the whole true of
the monk also ; he might perhaps have special duties as
the *scholasticus* of his monastery, but ordinarily, while
his manual labour was either in the field or in the *scrip-
torium*, so his intellectual exercises were for the most
part combined with his devotional, and consisted in the
study of the sacred volume. This was mainly what at
that time was meant by theology. " Theologia, hoc est,
Scripturarum meditatio," says Thomassin.—*Disc. Eccl.* t.
ii., p. 288. Their theology was a loving study and exposition of Holy Scripture, according to the teaching
of the Fathers, who had studied and expounded it before
them. It was a loyal adherence to the teaching of the
past, a faithful inculcation of it, an anxious transmission
of it to the next generation. In this respect it differed
from the theology of the times before and after them.
Patristic and scholastic theology each involved a creative
action of the intellect ; that this is the case as regards
the Schoolmen need not be proved here ; nor is it less
true, though in a different way, of the theology of the
Fathers. Origen, Tertullian, Athanasius, Chrysostom,
Augustine, Jerome, Leo, are authors of powerful, original
minds, and engaged in the production of original works.
There is no greater mistake, surely, than to suppose that
a revealed truth precludes originality in the treatment of
it. The contrary is acknowledged in the case of secular
subjects, in which it is the very triumph of originality,
not to invent or discover what is not already known,
but to make old things read as if they were new, from
the novelty of aspect in which they are placed. This
faculty of investing with associations, of applying to
particular purposes, of deducing consequences, of impressing upon the imagination, is creative ; and though
false associations, applications, deductions, and impres-

sions are often made, and were made by some theologians of the early Church, such as Origen and Tertullian, this does but prove that originality is not co-extensive with truth. And so in like manner as to Scripture; to enter into the mind of the sacred author, to follow his train of thought, to bring together to one focus the lights which various parts of Scripture throw upon his text, and to give adequate expression to the thoughts thus evolved, in other words, the breadth of view, the depth, or the richness, which we recognize in certain early expositions, is a creation. Nor is it an inferior faculty to discriminate, rescue, and adjust the truth, which a fierce controversy threatens to tear in pieces, at a time when the ecclesiastical atmosphere is thick with the dust of the conflict, when all parties are more or less in the wrong, and the public mind has become so bewildered as not to be able to say what it does or what it does not hold, or even what it held before the strife of ideas began. In such circumstances, to speak the word evoking order and peace, and to restore the multitude of men to themselves and to each other, by a reassertion of what is old with a luminousness of explanation which is new, is a gift inferior only to that of revelation itself.

This gift is not the characteristic of the history, nor is it akin to the spirit or the object, as I have described them, of the Benedictine Order. At the time of which I am writing, the Christian athlete, after running one length of the stadium, was taking breath before commencing a second course : the Christian combatant was securing his conquests in the wide field of thought by a careful review and catalogue of them, before going forth to make new ones. He was fitly represented, therefore, at such a season, by the Benedictine, faithful, conscientious, affectionate, and obedient, like the good steward who keeps an eye on all his master's goods, and preserves them from waste or decay. First, then, he compared, emendated, and transcribed the text of Scripture ; next he transcribed the Fathers who directly or indirectly commented on it ; then he attached to its successive portions such passages from the Fathers as illustrated them; then he fused those catenated passages into one homogeneous comment of his own : and there he stopped. He seldom added anything original. In such a task the skill would lie in the happy management and condensation of materials brought together from very various quarters, and here he would find the advantage of the literary habits gained in his early education. A taste for criticism would be another result of it, which we see in Bede, and which would result in so much of leaning to the literal interpretation of Scripture as was consistent with the profession of editing and republishing, as it may be called, the comments of the Fathers. We see this tendency in Alcuin, Paschasius, and especially in Druthmar. Indeed, Alcuin's greatest work was the revision of the Scripture text.[*] Other commentators were Ansbert, Smaragdus, Haymo, Remi, and the Irish Sedulius, if he was a Benedictine. The most widely celebrated, however, of these works was the *Glossa Ordinaria* of Walafrid, which was in great measure an abridgement of Raban's Catena, and became a standard authority in the centuries which followed.

6.

But times were approaching when such peaceful labours were not sufficient for the Church's need, and when theo-

[*] "Codex, Alcuini labor, in Vallicellensi Bibliothecâ asservatur." Baron. an. 778.

logy required to be something more than the rehearsal of
what her champions had achieved and her sages had
established in ages passed away. As the new Christian
society, which Charlemagne inaugurated, grew, its intellect grew with it, and at last began to ask questions and
propose difficulties, which *catenæ* and commentaries could
not solve. Hard-headed objectors were not to be subdued by the reverence for antiquity and the amenities of
polite literature ; and, when controversies arose, the
Benedictines found themselves, from the necessity of the
times, called to duties which were as uncongenial to the
spirit of their founder as the political engagements of St.
Dunstan or St. Bernard. Nor must it be supposed that
the other parts of Christendom did not furnish matters
demanding keen theological acumen, even though none
had arisen in the Frankish Churches themselves. And
here, I conceive, we have this remarkable confirmation
of the identity of the Benedictine character, that, in proportion as these matters were in substance already
decided by the Fathers, they acquitted themselves well
in the controversy, and in proportion as these matters
demanded some original explanations, the monastic disputants were less successful. And in speaking of them,
I speak of course of their age itself, of which they were
the leading teachers, and which they represent. And I
speak, not of individual monks, who would have the
natural talents, the intellectual acuteness and subtlety
of other men, but of the action of the monasteries, considered as bodies and historically, which is the true measure of the mental discipline to which their Rule subjected
them. I speak of those whose direct duty lay, by virtue of
their vocation, not in confronting doubts but in suppress-
ing them, and who were not likely on the whole to succeed
in exercises of reason in which they had no practice.

One of the countries to which I allude, as being at the era of Charlemagne the seat of theological error, was Spain, then under the power of the Saracens. The victorious infidels, in spite of their general toleration of Catholicism, of course could not avoid inflicting on it the most serious injuries. One of these was the decay or destruction of its schools,* and the want of education in its priesthood, which was the consequence. Another injury lay in the circumstance that Mahometanism, being a misbelief or heresy, more than a direct denial of the faith, might think it had a right to interfere with it, and had a tendency to corrupt it by the insinuation of its own opinions and traditions about Christian facts and doctrines. Mahomet is said to have been indebted to the teaching of a Nestorian monk, and the demolition of images was one of the watchwords of his armies. Now, from Spain at this time proceeded the heresy of the Adoptionists, which is of a Nestorian character ; and it was in Spain that Claudius of Turin matured those uncatholic opinions, especially on the subject of images, which have given him a place in ecclesiastical history.

The conflict with Nestorianism had been completed long before the time of Charlemagne ; accordingly the theologians of the age, in refuting it, had but to repeat the arguments which they found ready for them in the pages of the Fathers. Alcuin was one of those who undertook the controversy, and proved himself abundantly prepared for the work. "Paulinus and Alcuin," says Professor Döllinger, "proved their point with a degree of theological acumen, and with a knowledge of the Fathers, which in that age may surprise us."†

* "The Spanish Latin of that period was unquestionably extremely corrupt." Neander Hist., vol. vi., p. 118.

† Cox's Translation, vol. iii., p. 60.

Such was their success, when the doctrine in question had already been defined ; but, on the other hand, the question with which Claudius's name is connected, the honour due to images, was still *sub judice*, and when the ecumenical decision came from Nicæa, from whatever cause, the Franks misunderstood and disputed it. The same great council of Frankfort, which condemned the Adoptionists, acted as a protection to the Iconoclasts of Constantinople. I am far indeed from insinuating that the Fathers of the Frankish churches really differed from the definition which came to them from the East ; but even for a century afterwards those churches regarded it, to say the least, with dissatisfaction.

Meanwhile the spirit of inquiry was alive and operative even within the hearts of these peaceful monastic communities themselves. We find it, as it would seem, in one of the immediate friends and pupils of Alcuin. Fredegis, of the school of York, to whom he addressed various of his letters and works, and whom he made his successor at Tours, has left behind him an argumentative fragment of so strange a nature that it has been thought a mere exercise in disputation and not a portion of a serious work.* He starts, moreover, with a proposition in favour of the supremacy of reason as contrasted with authority, which, though admitting of a Catholic explanation, is capable also of being made the basis of a philosophy to which I shall immediately have occasion to allude.† Soon after, Gotteschalc, a monk of Orbais, taught that the decree of divine predestination has direct reference to the lost as well as the saved ; and about the same time Ratramn of the monastery of Corbie, opposed the Catholic doctrine of the

Vid. Ittig. Biblioth., p. 313.
† *Vid.* Neander, vol. vi., p. 161 ; Baluz. Miscell., t. ii., p. 56

Holy Eucharist. But these intellectual movements within the Benedictine territory were eclipsed by a manifestation of the sceptical spirit which came from a country, where from its prevalent religious temperament such a phenomenon was little to have been expected.

There was a portion of the Western Church which had never been included in the Roman Empire, and but partially, if at all, included within the range of the Benedictine discipline. While that discipline made its way northward, became the instrument of Anglo-Saxon conversion, and even supplanted the rule of Columban in the French monasteries, the countrymen of Columban remained faithful to their old monachism, descended southwards a second time, and retaliated on the convents of the continent by a fresh introduction of themselves and their traditions. At this period, whatever may have been their literary attainments, they were most remarkable for a bold independence of mind, a curiosity, activity, and vigour of thought, which contrasted strongly with the genius of Bede and Raban. Their strength lay in those exercises of pure reason which go by the name of "philosophy," or of "wisdom." Thus in an ancient writer the Irish Scots are spoken of as "*sophiâ* clari."[*] By Heric of Auxerre, in the passage so often quoted, they are described as "*philosophorum greges*," venturing across the stormy sea to the wide continent of Europe. And so in the legendary account, by a monk of St. Gall, of the Irish scholars who accosted the Frankish Emperor, they are represented as crying out, "Who wants *wisdom?* who will buy *wisdom?*" Dunstan, again, is said to have learned "*philosophy*" in Ireland ; and Benedict of Aniane, the second founder of the Benedictines, is expressly described as looking with suspicion on their

* Brucker Philos., t. iii., p. 574.

6 *   31

syllogistic method, which was so hostile to the habits of mind which his own Order cultivated. These Irish scholars, indeed, were too sincere Catholics, viewing them in the mass, to warrant this jealousy; but it was not without foundation, as we shall see, as regards individuals, and at least would be amply justified in the judgments of those who differed so much from them in mental characteristics as did the Benedictines. On the other hand, there was much in the Anglo-Saxon temper intimately congenial with the latter: then, as now, the occupants of the British soil seem to have been practical rather than speculative, fond of hard work rather than of hard thought, tenacious of what they had received, jealous of novelty, the champions of law and order. Thus the English and Irish may be said so far to represent respectively the two great Orders which came in succession on the stage of ecclesiastical history; and, as they were not without their collisions at home, so we detect some instances, and may conjecture others, of their rivalry as missionaries and teachers in central Europe. We read, for instance, in the history of St. Boniface, that one of his antagonists, in his organization of the Churches which he had founded in Germany, was an Irish priest of the name of Clement. Boniface relates, if his account is to be received to the letter, that this priest neither allowed the authority of Jerome, Augustine, or Gregory, nor of the sacred canons; that he maintained the marriage of bishops; argued from Scripture in defence of marriage with a sister-in-law, and taught a sort of universalism. Also he had to report to Pope Zacharias the false teaching of another Scottish or Irish priest, named Samson, in relation to the Sacraments.* Another Irishman, with whom Boniface had a quarrel, was Virgil,

* Boniface, Epp. 82, p. 237.

afterwards Bishop of Salzburgh, who has been acknowledged, as well as Boniface, for a saint. He offended Boniface by maintaining what seems like a doctrine of the existence of *antipodes*.

The antagonism between the two schools extended into the next century. Of course John Scotus Erigena, whom Charles the Bald placed in the chair of Alcuin in the School of the Palace, is the palmary specimen of the philosophical party among the Irish monks. This remarkable man, while acknowledging the authority of Revelation, propounded it as a first principle of his speculations, as Fridegis had done before him, that reason must come first, and authority second. Such a proposition indeed was faulty only in its application ; for St. Austin himself had laid it down in his treatise *de Ordine.* It is self-evident, that we should not know what was revelation and what was not, unless we used our reason to decide the point. Whatever we are obliged in the event to learn from external sources, our process of inquiry must begin from within. The ancient Father to whom I have referred propounds both the principle and the sense in which it is true. "We learn things necessarily in two ways," he says, "by authority and by reason. Tempore auctoritas, re autem ratio prior est ;" but Erigena, as is generally agreed, accounted reason, not only as the ultimate basis of religious truth, but the direct and proper warrant for it ; and, armed with this principle, he proceeded to take part in the two controversies which I have already had occasion to mention, the Predestinarian and the Eucharistic. "The writings have come to us," says the church of Lyons, speaking of his tendencies, like Clement's, to universalism, "the writings have come to us, vaniloqui et garruli hominis, who, disputing on divine prescience and predestination with human, or, as he boasts, philosophical reasonings, without any deference to Scripture, or regard to the authority of the Holy Fathers, has dared to define by his own independent assertion what is to be held and followed." Thus Erigena adopted Clement's argumentative basis as well as his doctrine. His views upon reason and authority are distinctly avowed in the first book of his work, *De divisione naturæ.* "You are not ignorant," he argues, "that what is prius naturâ ranks higher than what is prius tempore. We have been taught," referring apparently to St. Austin, "that reason is prior in nature, authority in time ; now, whereas nature was created together with time, authority did not begin with the beginning of time and nature ; on the other hand, reason had its origin with nature and time in the first beginning of things." The Scholar replies to him, " Reason itself teaches this ; for authority has proceeded from right reason, reason by no means from authority. For all authority which is not approved by right reason is weak ; whereas right reason, when it is fortified in its own strength, settled and immovable, need not be corroborated by the concurrence of any authority."—*Lib.* 1. *n.* 71. In like manner, in the commencement of his work on Predestination, while appealing to St. Austin, he makes philosophy and religion convertible terms.*

Erigena was succeeded in the Schola Palatii by Mannon, who inherited his master's doctrine. He himself had called Plato the greatest of philosophers, and Aristotle the most subtle of investigators ; and, according to the testimony of Friar Bacon, he was a successful interpreter of the latter writer ; and Mannon, in like manner, has left commentaries on Plato's *de Legibus* and *de Republicâ*

* Guizot Civil.. t. ii., p. 375.

and on Aristotle's Ethics. About the same time flourished in France another Irishman, named Macarius; and he too showed the same leaning towards pantheism which has been imputed to Erigena.* From him this error was introduced into the monastery of Corbie. At a latter date we hear of one Patrick, who from his name may be considered as an Irishman, holding the same heterodox opinion about the Eucharist which Ratramn and Erigena advanced.†

As to the two controversies, which have been mentioned more than once, while they exemplify to us the *scholasticismus ante scholasticos* then in action, they afford fresh illustrations also of the insufficiency of such instruments as the Church at that time had in her service to meet this formidable antagonist of her religious supremacy. No mind equal to Erigena appeared on the side of traditionary teaching ; and the vigour with which the Adoptionists were condemned and the *Filioque* inserted in the Creed did not manifest itself in the dealing of the Frankish Synods with the bold doctrine of Gotteschalc and Ratramn. Gotteschalc, as I have said, was a monk of Orbais. We suddenly find him asserting categorically that the reprobate have been predestined to damnation from eternity. Raban and the Synod of Mentz condemned this doctrine. Hincmar and the Synod of Quiercy condemn it also ; and Pardulus, bishop of Laon, writes against it. Then Lupus writes, if not in defence of Gotteschalc, at least not in accordance with Hincmar, who, in distress for a champion, has recourse to no other than Erigena, and Erigena, as might be expected from what has been said above, proceeds to commit himself to an extreme doctrine of universalism,

* Lanigan Hist., vol. iii., p. 320.
† *Vid.* Rather. Ep. apud Dach. Spic., t. i., p. 375.

as Gotteschalc had to an extreme predestinarianism.
Upon this, Florus and Prudentius write against Erigena;
and Remigius, explaining or espousing the thesis of
Gotteschalc, writes against the three Epistles of Raban,
Hincmar, and Pardulus.   Hincmar replies in a second
Synod of Quiercy ; and the Bishops of Lorraine rejoin
in the Synod of Valence.   The controversy ceases rather
than terminates at the Synod of Savonnières, in which
all parties were represented, and in which four important
articles were received, bearing indirectly on the subject
of dispute, but leaving without distinct notice the original
position of Gotteschalc.

In the Eucharistic controversy, which lasted through
several centuries, the Benedictine Paschasius, supported
by Haimo, Hincmar, and Ratherius, expounded the traditionary doctrine afterwards defined : but his statements
were met by the dissent, or the hesitation, as it would
appear, of men of his own schools, Raban, Ratramn,
Amalarius, Heribald, Heriger, Druthmar, and Florus.
At the end of two centuries indeed appeared the great
Benedictines Lanfranc and Anselm, who dealt successfully with this as well as other controversies.   But it
must be recollected that, though their school of Bec is
confessedly the historical fountain-head of the new theology which was making its way into Christendom, it is
as far from a specimen of the Benedictine character in
matters of teaching, as imperial minds such as their
brother-monk and contemporary, Hildebrand, can be
considered in ecclesiastical politics

7.

And thus the period, properly Benedictine, ended ;
this honour being shown by Providence to the great
Order from which it is named, in reward for its long and

patient services to religion, that, though its monks were not to be immediately employed by the Church in the special sense in which they had been her ministers for some hundreds of years, still they should be the first to point out, and that they should hansel, those new weapons, which Orders of a different genius were destined to wield against a new description of opponents.

Nor is it without significancy that the Anglo-Saxon Church, itself the creation of the Benedictines, and the seat from which their influence went out for the education or conversion of Europe, from the Baltic to the Bay of Biscay, should have its share in this honour; and that, as Theodore was brought all the way from Tarsus to Canterbury, so Lanfranc from Lombardy and Anselm from Piedmont should successively fill the archiepiscopal throne of Theodore.

THE ABERDEEN UNIVERSITY PRESS LIMITED.

EDITOR'S NOTES

Rise and Progress of Universities

p. 13. *Paris ... University*: The medieval University of Paris, along with twenty-one other French universities, was swept away by the Revolution of 1789 and replaced by a group of *écoles spéciales* in Paris and by professional *facultés* in the provinces. The University of London, founded in 1836, was at this time an examination board only.

p. 15. *St. Irenaeus*: St. Irenaeus (*c.* 130–200), Bishop of Lyons, first great Christian theologian, author of *Adversus Omnes Haereses*.

p. 15. *St. Anthony*: St. Anthony (Antony) of Egypt (d. 356), desert hermit and founder of a company of hermits.

p. 15. *St. Didymus*: St. Didymus the Blind (*c.* 313–398), Alexandrian theologian and prolific apologist.

p. 18. *Pisistratus*: Pisistratus (560–527 BC), Cimon (512–449 BC), and Pericles (496–429 BC), Athenian statesmen.

p. 19. *Plutarch*: Plutarch (AD 46–120), biographer of antiquity, author of *Parallel Lives*.

p. 19. *Phidias*: Phidias (*c.* 490–415 BC), Athenian sculptor.

p. 19. *Anaxagoras*: Anaxagoras (*c.* 500–428 BC), pre-Socratic philosopher.

p. 20. *Mithridates*: Mithridates VI (d. 73 BC), king in Asia Minor (Ionia or modern western Turkey), conquered by the Romans.

p. 25. *Alcuin*: Alcuin (*c.* 735–804), English monk who, as adviser to Charlemagne, inspired the so-called Carolingian Renaissance.

p. 25. *St. Germain-des-Prés*: St. Germain-des-Prés, monastery founded in the eighth century, long a centre of learning, now within the confines of Paris.

p. 26. *Lipsius*: Justus Lipsius (1547–1608), Flemish historian and Latinist.

p. 27. *Salvete*: Drinking song celebrating the new 'Athenians', students from all nations at a medieval university.

p. 27. *Wood*: Anthony Wood (1632–1695), antiquarian and historian of Oxford.

p. 28. *St. Edmund, St. Richard, St. Thomas Cantilupe*: St. Edmund (*c.* 1180–1240), St. Richard (1197–1253), St. Thomas Cantilupe (*c.* 1218–1282), English bishops associated with Oxford as students or instructors or both.

p. 28. *Scotus, Hales, Occam, Bacon, Bradwardine, Middleton*: John Duns Scotus (*c.* 1264–1308), Alexander of Hales (*c.* 1170–1245), William of Occam (*c.* 1300–1349), Roger Bacon (*c.* 1214–1292), Thomas Bradwardine (*c.* 1290–1349), Richard Middleton (*c.* 1240–1300), all leading medieval thinkers and all associated at one time or another with Oxford and Paris.

p. 29. *Gregory*: St. Gregory I, 'the Great' (*c.* 540–604), pope from 590. The reference here is to Gregory's dispatch of St. Augustine to Canterbury to convert the English, 'angeli, non Angli.'

p. 29. *Huber*: V. A. Huber, author of *Die Englischen Universitäten* (1839).

p. 30. *Claude Lorraine or Poussin*: Claude Lorraine (1600–1682), Nicolas Poussin (1594–1664), French neo-classical painters.

p. 31. *Augustine and Paulinus*: St. Augustine of Canterbury (d. 605), St. Paulinus of York (d. 644), both foreign churchmen sent to England by Gregory I.

p. 31. *Pole*: Reginald Pole (1500–1558), last Catholic Archbishop of Canterbury.

p. 32. *Fisher*: St. John Fisher (1469–1535), Bishop of Rochester, executed by Henry VIII.

p. 34. *Cleanthes*: Cleanthes (*c.* 330–230 BC), stoic philosopher, best known for his *Hymn to Zeus*.

p. 34. *Zeno*: Zeno of Citium (*c.* 336–264 BC). Founder of Stoicism.

p. 34. *Marcus*: Marcus Aurelius (AD 121–180), a stoic and Roman Emperor (161–180).

p. 35. *Cicero*: Marcus Tullius Cicero (106–43 BC), Roman orator and statesman, often called 'Tully' by educated Englishmen in the nineteenth century.

p. 35. *Gregory*: St. Gregory Nazianzus (329–389), theologian, one of the three 'Cappodocian Fathers' of the Church whom Newman particularly revered. Gregory had been a student in Athens.

p. 35. *Horace*: Horace (65–8 BC), great lyric poet of the Augustan age, often quoted by Newman. He too had been a student in Athens.

p. 36. *Eunapius*: Eunapius (*c.* 325–390), stoic philosopher.

p. 38. *Basil*: St. Basil 'the Great' (*c.* 330–379), theologian and monastic founder, also from Cappodocia, a fellow student of Gregory Nazianzus in Athens. Basil's brother, St. Gregory of Nyssa (*c.* 330–395), was the third of the 'Cappodocian Fathers'.

p. 38. *Mr. Russell*: William Howard Russell (d. 1907), a product of Trinity College, Dublin, joined the staff of *The Times* of London in 1843. As a foreign correspondent, he covered the Crimean War (in which Newman took keen interest) and the American Civil War.

p. 40. *Plato*: Plato (427–347 BC), pupil of Socrates, teacher of Aristotle, one of the giants of the western philosophical tradition.

p. 40. *Thucydides*: Thucydides (460–400 BC), historian of the Peloponnesian Wars, still a model of historical research and presentation.

p. 40. *Augustus*: Gaius Octavianus Augustus (63BC–AD14), grand-nephew of Julius Caesar and first Roman Emperor.

p. 40. *Attalus*: Attalus, a king in Asia Minor, third century BC.

p. 40. *Ptolemies*: The Ptolemies, 331–30 BC, were a dynasty that emerged in Egypt with the break up of the empire of Alexander the Great. The last Ptolemy ruler was the fabled Cleopatra.

p. 40. *Hadrian*: Hadrian, Roman Emperor (117–138).

p. 42. *Epicurus*: Epicurus (341–270 BC), a Greek Philosopher who taught that the avoidance of pain and the cultivation of pleasure were the highest human goods.

p. 43. *Theophrastus ... Hadrian the Syrian*: all these thinkers and writers displayed their doctrines in Athens from the fifth through the third centuries BC.

p. 46. *Sophronius*: Sophronius (560–638), Patriarch of Jerusalem, controversialist, who witnessed the fall of Jerusalem to the Saracens. It is unclear as to the 'Eusebius' Newman refers to as 'the bosom friend of Sophronius', who – Sophronius, that is – was much involved in the Christological controversies of the seventh century.

p. 46. *Celsus*: Celsus (*c.* 135–190) was a pagan controversialist whose attack on Christianity is known through Origen's response to it.

p. 46. *Emperor Julian*: Flavius Claudius Julianus, 'Julian the Apostate' (332–363), was the last pagan Roman Emperor.

p. 54. *Protagoras*: Protagoras (fifth century BC), considered founder of the Sophist school of philosophy: 'Man is the measure of all things'.

p. 54. *Hippias or Prodicus*: Hippias (*c.* 481–411 BC) and Prodicus (*c.* 470–404 BC), sophist disciples of Protagoras.

p. 54. *Hippocrates*: Hippocrates (*c.* 460–377 BC), Greek scientist and 'Father of Medicine'.

p. 55. *Orpheus*: In Greek mythology, Orpheus's music had the power to arouse even inanimate objects and almost delivered his wife Eurydice from the confines of Hades.

p. 56. *Mr. Grote*: George Grote (1794–1871) wrote a ten-volume *History of Greece* (1846–1856). Numa, a legendary king of Rome, eighth century BC.

p. 57. *Diogenes ... sent to Rome*: The sojourn in Rome by the three Athenian philosophers occurred about 155 BC.

p. 57. *Cato*: Marcus Porcius Cato 'the Elder' (234–149 BC) was renowned for his personal and public austerity.

p. 59. '*Fortes fortuna adjuvat*': Fortune favours the brave.

p. 61. *'fallentis semita vitae'*: pathway of a retiring life.

p. 62. *'hoc erat in votis'*: 'This is what I wished for. Persian luxury, my boy, I hated.' Horace.

p. 63. *'otium cum dignitate'*: repose with dignity. 'otium': godlike repose.

p. 63. *Virgil to Juvenal*: Virgil the epic poet (70–19 BC), Juvenal the satirist (*c.* AD 60–140).

p. 63. *Cincinnatus to Pliny*: Cincinnatus (*c.* 490–420 BC), Roman soldier and dictator. Pliny 'the Younger' (61–114), littérateur and Roman imperial administrator.

p. 64. *George the Second*: George II (1683–1760), King of Great Britain and Ireland, 1727–1760.

p. 66. *'Ne sutor ultra crepidam'*: 'Let the cobbler stick to his last.' Pliny.

p. 67. *Peter ... John*: Peter and John were Irish-born thirteenth-century Aristotelians who taught in Naples and Paris.

p. 67. *Moore*: Thomas Moore (1779–1852), Irish poet, historian, and biographer.

p. 70. *Hildebrands ... Guizot's*: Hildebrand, St. Gregory VII (*c.* 1021–1085), pope from 1073; Ghislieri, St. Pius V (1504–1572), pope from 1566; Winfrid (his Anglo Saxon name), St. Boniface (680–754), apostle of Germany; St. Francis Xavier (1506–1552), missionary to India and Japan.

p. 70. *'Quantula ... mundus!'*: With how little wisdom the world is ruled.

p. 70. *Guizot*: François Guizot (1787–1874), French statesman and historian, an admirer of British political institutions.

p. 71. *Malebranche*: Nicolas Malebranche (1638–1715), French philosopher and, like Newman, an Oratorian.

p. 73. *Abelard*: Peter Abelard (1079–1142), monk, noted logician, controversial philosopher, lover of Héloise.

p. 73. *Arius*: Arius (*c.* 250–336), heresiarch who challenged the doctrine of the divinity of Christ.

p. 76. '*portaque emittit eburna*': literally, 'he sends him through the gates of ivory.' Virgil. The reference is to Aeneas coming out of the underworld where he had been given a foretaste of the future glories of Rome.

p. 77. *Orpheus . . . Solon*: Orpheus, as the mythical first of the poets, set standards for society until replaced by the more formal and systematic civil directors, like Lycurgus, legendary law-giver, Solon (*c.* 638–559), Athenian law-giver, and Deioces, King of Media, whom Herodotus (*Histories*) described as an ideal ruler.

p. 81. *Vir bonus . . . servat*: 'Who is a good man? He who is respectful of tradition and obeys the law.' Horace.

p. 82. *Theophrastus and Demetrius*: Theophrastus (d. 287 BC), Athenian philosopher, successor of Aristotle as head of the Lyceum. Demetrius (*c.* 350–280 BC), Macedonian administrator, credited with the foundation of the great library in Alexandria.

p. 86. *St. Philip*: St. Philip Neri (1515–1595), founder of the Oratory, called by Newman (p. 88) the 'Amabile Santo'.

p. 88. '*potuit . . . non fecit*': 'he who could transgress and does not, could do evil and does not.'

p. 91. *Callisthenes*: Callisthenes (*c.* 360–327 BC), historian, nephew of Aristotle and follower of Alexander the Great.

p. 92. *Dryden's celebrated Ode*: '*Alexander's Feast*', by John Dryden (1631–1700).

p. 92. *Eumenes*: Eumenes (*c.* 361–316 BC), secretary to Philip of Macedon and his son, Alexander.

p. 95. *John the Twenty-second*: John XXII (1249–1334), pope (at Avignon) from 1316.

p. 96. *Ammianus . . . Philostratus*: Ammianus Marcelinus (*c.* 330–400), pagan historian who wrote fairly about Christianity. Philostratus (*c.* 180–250), author of the *Vita* of Apollonius of Tyana, legendary seer and magician.

p. 96. *Emperor Claudius*: (10 BC–AD 54), Roman emperor from 41.

p. 97. *Clement*: St. Clement of Alexandria (*c.* 150–215).

p. 97. *Cave*: William Cave (1637–1713), prolific antiquarian, author of *Antiquitates Apostolicae* (1676).

p. 97. *Origen*: (c. 185–254), prolific Alexandrian theologian, author of *De Principiis*.

p. 97. *St. Anatolius*: (d. 283), Aristotelian scholar and Bishop of Alexandria.

p. 97. *St. Athanasius*: (c. 296–373), theologian and Bishop of Alexandria, great opponent of Arianism, a Church Father to whom Newman was particularly devoted.

p. 97. *St. Gregory Thaumaturgus*: St. Gregory the Wonder Worker (Thaumaturgus) (c. 213–170), theologian and Bishop of Pontus, a disciple of Origen.

p. 98. *Alexandrian Neo-Platonists*: Of the Alexandrian neo-Platonists Newman mentions here, the most distinguished was Plotinus (c. 205–171), author of the *Enneads*.

p. 99. *Alexandrian School*: Of the scholars of Alexandria Newman mentions here, the most notable are Galen (131–201) for his researches in medicine and pharmacology and Ptolemy (c. 100–178), mathematician and geographer, who formulated a geocentric explanation of the universe.

p. 100. Augustus assumed imperial power in 27 BC and Justinian died in 565. Emperor Theodosius II (401–450) codified Roman law enacted during the preceding century (438). The code outlawed paganism.

p. 102. *Agricola*: Gnaeus Julius Agricola (40–93) was a Roman general who conquered a large part of Britain. His biographer was Tacitus (55–120).

p. 103. *Writers of reputation*: Among the Roman writers mentioned here, the most notable was Lucan (39–65), poet and statesman, and his uncle, Seneca 'the Younger,' playwright and philosopher, tutor to the mad Emperor Nero, who ultimately forced him (and Lucan as well) to commit suicide.

p. 103. *Rusticus*: St. Rusticus (d. 461), monk and bishop in France, missionary to Britain, a strong opponent of the Arians.

p. 103. *St. Jerome*: (c. 342–420), ascetic, hermit, prodigious scholar, translator of the Bible into Latin (the *Vulgate*).

p. 103. *St. Germanus*: (c. 650–733), Patriarch of Constantinople, defender of icons and promoter of devotion to the Virgin Mary.

p. 108. *Tertullian*: (c. 160–220), theologian and apologist. His rigorist views led him to join the heretical Montanist sect.

p. 113. *Agatho*: (c. 600–681), pope from 678.

p. 115. *Vitalian . . . or Leo*: Vitalian: (d. 672), pope from 657.

p. 115. *Leo*: St. Leo III (d. 816), pope from 795. In 800 he crowned Charlemagne, King of the Franks (742–814), as the first Holy Roman Emperor.

p. 117. *Alaric . . . Theodoric*: Of the barbarian chieftains mentioned here, the most notable were Alaric (c. 370–410), King of the Visigoths, who sacked Rome in 410, and Theodoric (454–526), King of the Ostrogoths, who conquered most of Italy at the beginning of the sixth century. Theodoric's rule was considered benign and highly successful.

p. 118. *The Antonines*: the 'five good emperors' (Nerva, Trajan, Hadrian, Antoninus Pius, and Marcus Aurelius) who ruled in succession from 96 till 180. This was a period of general peace and prosperity, the so-called 'Silver Age' of Roman history.

p. 124. *St. Celestine I*: (d. 432), pope from 422. He is said to have sent St. Patrick to Ireland.

p. 125. *Döllinger*: Johann von Döllinger (1799–1890), immensely productive Church historian, who seceded from the Catholic Church in the wake of the definition of papal infallibility at the First Vatican Council (1870).

p. 125. *St. Finian*: St. Finian (usually spelled Finnian) of Clonnard (d. 549), monk and abbot.

p. 126. *St. Columba . . . St. Fridolin*: St. Columba (c. 521–597), Irish-born monk and missionary.

p. 126. St. Fridolin (d. 510), Irish-born monk and missionary to the Rhineland.

p. 128. *Erigena . . . St. Virgil*: John Scotus Erigena (c. 810–877), Irish-born neo-Platonist philosopher, head of the cathedral school in Paris in the generation after Charlemagne.

p. 128. *St. Virgil*: (*c.* 700–784), Irish-born monk, mathematician, and missionary, called 'the Apostle of Carinthia,' died as Bishop of Salzburg.

p. 129. *St. Bede ... St. Thomas*: St. Bede 'the Venerable' (*c.* 673–735), monk and biblical scholar, called the 'Father of English History' by reason of his *Historia Ecclesisastica Gentis Anglorum* (731).

p. 129. *St. Thomas*: St. Thomas à Becket (*c.* 1118–1170), Lord Chancellor of England and later Archbishop of Canterbury, murdered in his cathedral.

p. 132. *Hence at this very moment*: Newman refers here to the hostile reaction to what was popularly called in England 'the Papal Aggression,' occasioned by Pius IX's decree (September 29 1850) restoring a conventional Catholic hierarchy to England and Wales.

p. 141. *a great warrior now no more*: Arthur Wellesley, Duke of Wellington, victor at Waterloo and Prime Minister at the time of the passage of Catholic Emancipation (1829), died in 1852.

p. 141. *Julius ... Martin*: Newman cites St. Julius I (d. 352), pope from 337, St. Silverius (d. 538), pope from 536, and St. Martin I (d. 655), pope from 649, as pontiffs who resisted the secular power at great personal cost.

p. 141. *Gaeta*: In the wake of the revolutions of 1848, Pius IX was forced into an eighteen-month exile in Gaeta, a town south of Rome and within the border of what was then the Kingdom of Naples.

p. 142. *Josephine statutes*: Joseph II, Holy Roman Emperor in title and Emperor of Austria in fact (1765–1790), enacted a series of laws removing Catholicism from its privileged position and placing it more directly under the power of the State. The legislation became a dead letter with the emperor's death.

p. 146. *Pius the Sixth*: Pius VI (1717–1799), pope from 1775, died in France as a prisoner of Napoleon.

p. 146. *Pius the Seventh*: Pius VII (1740–1823), pope from 1800, was also a prisoner of Napoleon and was freed only after the emperor's defeat.

p. 147. *an old system shattered some sixty years ago*: that is, by the cataclysm of the French Revolution of 1789.

p. 152. *Theodore*: St. Theodore of Tarsus (*c.* 602–690), Greek-born papal diplomat and missionary, died as Archbishop of Canterbury.

p. 152. *Egbert*: St. Egbert (d. 729), English-born monk who migrated to Ireland and later was a missionary in Germany.

p. 152. *Benedict Biscop*: St. Benedict Biscop (*c.* 628–690), English nobleman who became a monk in France and then in England; accompanied by John the archcantor of St. Peter's Basilica, he strongly promoted the Roman liturgy; his life was written by St. Bede.

p. 154. *Bulaeus*: César du Boulay who published (1673) a multi-volume and largely mythical 'history' of the University of Paris from the time of Charlemagne.

p. 158. *the recent Act of Parliament*: reform legislation, passed in 1854, which gravely altered the constitution of the Oxford Newman had known and loved.

p. 159. *Hebdomadal Board*: the traditional governing board of the University of Oxford, composed of the heads of the individual colleges, the Provost of Oriel, the Master of Balliol, and so forth.

p. 161. *Mr. Prescott*: William Prescott (1796–1859), American historian, author of *A History of Ferdinand and Isabella* (1838).

p. 161. *Cardinal Ximénes*: Francisco Ximénes de Cisneros (1436–1517), Archbishop of Toledo, confessor to Queen Isabella and afterward regent during the minority of her grandson, the Emperor Charles V.

p. 166. *Alfred*: Alfred 'the Great' (840–899), King of Wessex, greatest of the pre-conquest Anglo-Saxon rulers, reputed to have been a patron of learning.

p. 166. *Henry the First of England*: Henry I (1068–1135), King of England from 1100, youngest son of William the Conqueror.

p. 166. *Mr. Hallam*: Henry Hallam (1777–1859), English littérateur, author of *View of Europe in the Middle Ages* (1818); his son, Arthur Henry, was an intimate of Tennyson, who wrote '*In Memoriam*' to mark young Hallam's premature death.

p. 168. *Fleury*: Claude Fleury (1640–1725), French priest and prolific ecclesiastical historian, author of *Histoire ecclésiastique* (20 vols., 1691–1720).

p. 168. *Lanfranc*: (*c.* 1005–1089), Italian-born monk; controversial both doctrinally and politically, he died as Archbishop of Canterbury. His successor was St. Anselm.

p. 168. *William of Malmesbury*: (*c.* 1080–1143), English monk and historian, who wrote both ecclestiastical and secular history, *Gesta Regum Anglorum* and *Gesta Pontificum Anglorum*.

p. 168. *William of Jumièges*: (d. 1076), monk-chronicler of the Dukes of Normandy.

p. 169. *Vacarius*: (d. 1175), celebrated Italian lawyer and legal scholar who taught at Oxford and later in the cathedral school in York. Inerius, a generation younger, taught law at Bologna.

p. 169. *Muratori*: Ludovico Antonio Muratori (1672–1750), librarian and archivist at Modena and Milan; he discovered the oldest extant list of New Testament writings (eighth century), which is appropriately called the Muratorian Canon.

p. 170. *Selden*: John Selden (1584–1654), historian and legal scholar, a moderate supporter of Parliament during the English Civil War.

p. 170. "*Dat . . . pedes*": "Galen gives riches, and Justinian bestows honours; but genus and species must go on foot." The meaning seems to be that while the study of science brings wealth and the study of the law – the Emperor Justinian (d. 565) was a great law-giver – political and social advancement, the logician's art will not even earn the price of a good horse.

p. 171. *Robert Pullus or Pulleyne*: (d. 1146), native of Exeter, one of the first theology masters at Oxford, who, after a stint in Paris, went to Rome, where he was made a cardinal and where he was a severe critic of Abelard. Oseney was a monastery near Oxford.

p. 171. *Leland*: John Leland (1506–1552), chaplain to Henry VIII and antiquarian, who argued that the Anglican Church represented a return to Arthurian times.

p. 171. *St. Bernard*: St. Bernard of Clairvaux (1090–1153), monk and monastic reformer, founder of the Cistercian branch of Benedictine monasticism; mystic, spiritual director to the great and the lowly, defender of orthodoxy, one of the giants of the Middle Ages.

p. 171. "*turbantibus aequora ventis*": "more than equal to the conflicting winds."

p. 172. *Quintillian*: (35–96), Roman rhetorician, whose central doctrine was that effective oratory amounted to a good man saying good things.

p. 173. *William of Champeaux*: (*c.* 1070–1121), scholastic philosopher, was abbot of the monastery of St. Victor in Paris, where he proved a strong opponent of Abelard, died as Bishop of Chalons.

p. 173. *Peter Lombard*: (*c.* 1100–1160), the 'Master of Sentences', the title he earned with the publication (1148–1150) of *Sententiarum Libri Quatuor*, a vast compilation of quotations from the Church Fathers, *sententia* meaning opinion or statement.

p. 173. *Abbot Rupert*: Rupert of Deutz (*c.* 1070–1129), German monk, mystic, and scholastic theologian.

p. 173. *Hugh of St. Victor*: (*c.* 1096–1141), German-born theologian and mystic, joined William of Champeaux at St. Victor in Paris, where his careful scholarship paved the way for the great schoolmen of the next century.

p. 173. *Albertus Magnus*: Albert the Great (Albertus Magnus) (*c.* 1200–1280), Dominican theologian and teacher of St. Thomas Aquinas, much imbued in his thought by Aristotelian and Arabic models; he foreshadowed Aquinas's synthesis of philosophy and theology.

p. 173. *The Angelic Doctor*: St. Thomas Aquinas (*c.* 1225–1274), '*Doctor Communis*' and '*Doctor Angelicus*', the pinnacle of medieval thought and still a measure of the Catholic intellect.

p. 174. *Emperor Frederick the Second*: Frederick II (1194–1250), Holy Roman Emperor, warrior and statesman, one of the most spectacular celebrities of the Middle Ages, whom his contemporaries nicknamed '*Stupor Mundi*', founder of the University of Naples (1240), where Aquinas learned his first lessons from Peter of Ireland.

p. 175. *John of Salisbury*: (*c.* 1115–1180), philosopher, Latinist, and papal diplomat, student of Abelard at Paris, the first of medieval thinkers to be acquainted with the logical works of Aristotle.

p. 175. *Sharon Turner*: (1768–1847), London-born author of *The History of England from the Earliest Times to the Norman Conquest* (1799–1805).

p. 176. *St. Edmund*: St. Edmund of Abingdon (*c.* 1180–1240), Archbishop of Canterbury, had in his younger years taught Aristotelian logic at Oxford, where he is still commemorated in the foundation of St. Edmund's Hall, said to have been built on the site of his residence.

p. 176. *Nicholas Breakspeare:* (*c.* 1100–1159), monk and papal diplomat, afterward, from 1154, Pope Hadrian IV, the only Englishman ever to ascend the throne of Peter.

p. 176. "*Et procul ... Oxoniaeque.*": "Both far and near Frenchman and Englishman have recognised on an equal footing what is done at Paris and at Oxford."

p. 176. *the Lollards:* the followers of the heterodox Oxford theologian, John Wycliffe (1329–1384).

p. 177. *French wars:* The happy union of the universities at Paris and Oxford was ruptured by what historians call the Hundred Years War (1337–1453), initiated by the dynastic ambitions of England's Edward III (d. 1377) in France.

p. 178. *Gerson:* Jean de Gerson (1363–1429), French churchman, spiritual writer, and influential controversialist, author of *De Consolatione Theologiae*, modelled on Boethius's *De Consolatione Philosophiae.*

p. 179. *Kehama:* "Curses are like young chickens, they always come home to roost". '*The Curse of Kehama*' (1810), by Robert Southey (1774–1843).

p. 179. *Morier:* James Justinian Morier (1780–1849), British ambassador to Persia, published (1824) a romantic novel called *The Adventures of Haji Baba Ispahan.*

p. 180. *Charicles:* Wilhelm Bekker (1796–1846), whose German novel (1830) tells the romantic story of the goddess-like Charicleia, daughter of a priest of Apollo, and her lover, Knemon – a typical fiction during an era in which the classical education still prevailed.

p. 181. *the Edinburgh Review:* founded in 1802. It was an organ of the Whig party and from the beginning espoused various liberal causes. Prominent among its writers were Hazlitt and Macaulay. Walter Scott wrote for its early issues but then withdrew, complaining about its political orientation. It offered consistently negative criticism of the likes of Wordsworth and Coleridge. In 1836 Thomas Arnold of Rugby published in the *Review* a harsh critique of Newman and his tractarian colleagues in an article called 'The Oxford Malignants'.

p. 187. *Professor Vaughan:* Henry Vaughan (1811–1885), Fellow of Oriel (with Newman) 1835–1842, Regius Professor of Modern History at Oxford 1848–1858, a keen supporter of university reform, later practised law.

p. 187. *Fr. Dalgairns*: John Dalgairns (1818–1876), an Oxford disciple of Newman, was received into the Catholic Church by Father Dominic Barberi shortly before his mentor. He joined the Oratory in Birmingham in 1846, but in later years, when he was located at the Oratory in London, he and Newman grew estranged.

p. 189. *"desursum . . . pacifica"*: see p. 199 where Newman provides a translation.

p. 189. *"altera Trojae Pergama"*: The Pergamum was the citadel in Troy; the later city of Pergama was designated by Virgil as a kind of simulated Troy. Therefore Pergama was "another Troy". Newman uses this classical allusion to suggest a rather modest proverb: a university should be a home away from home.

p. 193. *Sabellius*: (early third century), probably a Roman, preached an heretical unitarianism.

p. 193. *The Gnostics*: Gnosticism in its many manifestations emphasised the special *gnosis* or knowledge which enabled man to give proper vent to his spirituality. Some gnostic sects assumed a philosophical form, many others lapsed into magic and mythology. Common to most of them was a sharp dichotomy between the good spirit and the evil flesh. As a consequence most Christian Gnostics considered Christ's human body to be a phantasm.

p. 193. *Apollinaris*: or Apollinarius (*c.* 310–390), theologian and bishop, much involved in the Christological controversies of his time, whose minimalist views about the humanity of Christ led to his condemnation and to his secession from the Church.

p. 193. *St. Cyril*: (*c.* 315–386), Bishop of Jerusalem, author of the *Catecheses* (347), a set of doctrinal instructions for catechumens.

p. 193. *Ephesine Council*: The Council of Ephesus (431) which condemned Nestorianism, the belief that in Christ were present two persons, one human and the other divine. A consequence was the proclamation of Mary as the *Theotokos*, the God-bearer – that is, of her divine motherhood.

p. 196. *Mount St. Geneviève*: Mont Sainte-Geneviève in Paris rises up from the left bank of the Seine, not far from the Sorbonne, the medieval university. The Pantheon is located there today.

p. 197. *Peter of Blois*: (1070–1117), Parisian philosopher, one of the few intellectual luminaries in the period between the fading of the school of St. Victor and the rise of the schoolmen.

p. 200. *Arnold of Brescia*: (d. 1155), Italian-born reformer, reputed to have been a pupil of Abelard in Paris. He incurred the wrath of ecclesiastical and secular authorities by his denial of the sacrament of penance and his assertion that sinful priests could not validly administer the sacraments, as well as by his call for political reform. Reconciled to the Church at the end, he was nevertheless executed.

p. 200. *St. Ivo*: (*c.* 1040–1116), Bishop of Chartres, the most learned canonist of his time and a prolific commentator on all aspects of church law.

p. 200. *Desire of wine ... vanquished*: The poetry quoted is from Milton's *Samson Agonistes* (1671).

p. 202. *fiery eloquence of a Saint*: The reference is to St. Bernard, who was the implacable foe of Abelard (and of Arnold of Brescia).

p. 202. "*Heu, vitam perdidi ... agendo*": "Woe is me, I have lost my life by painstakingly accomplishing nothing." Seneca.

p. 204. *the Dominicans*: The Order of Preachers, founded by St. Dominic Guzman (1170–1221), was one of several new religious congregations which sprang up during the early thirteenth century, reflective of the revival of urban and commercial life in western Europe. The Dominicans, as well as their contemporaries, the Franciscan friars, played a crucial role in the evolution of genuine universities out of the previous monastic and cathedral schools.

p. 205. *St. Kevin*: (d. 618), Irish monk and abbot.

p. 207. *John Lech or Leach*: John de Lecke (d. 1313), Archbishop of Dublin from 1311.

p. 207. *Clement the Fifth*: Clement V (1264–1314), pope from 1305, transferred the papacy from Rome to Avignon.

p. 208. *Alexander de Bicknor*: (d. 1349), English-born administrator in Ireland, Archbishop of Dublin in 1317, defrocked and excommunicated for embezzlement in 1325.

p. 211. *Sixtus the Fourth*: (1414–1484), pope from 1471, a too typical renaissance prelate in his extravagance and his obsession with Italian politics; he founded the Sistine Choir, built the Sistine Chapel and greatly expanded the Vatican Library.

p. 214. *convitto*: a living together.

p. 216. *the Premonstrants*: The Premonstratensian Canons were founded by St. Norbert (*c.* 1080–1134) at Prémontré, near Laon. The Norbertines, as they were popularly known, modelled their style of life on the Cistercians of St. Bernard. They were especially prominent in medieval England and Hungary. ('Canons' in this context means religious who lived under a semi-monastic rule – more like monks, that is, than friars.)

p. 216. *The Carmelites*: The Order of Our Lady of Mount Carmel was founded in Palestine *c.* 1150, though it claimed a connection to the hermits of Mount Carmel of very early Christian times and even to the Old Testament prophet, Elijah. After the crusades the Carmelites migrated to Europe where they assumed the form of a conventional order of friars.

p. 217. *Henry the Third*: Henry III (1207–1272), King of England and Ireland from 1216. His reign was marked by civil disturbances and his own political and military ineptitude.

p. 217. *Theobald*: (d. 1161), French-born (Normandy) monk and, from 1138, Archbishop of Canterbury.

p. 218. *Parva domus . . . ignota casis*: The first three lines are untranslatable with the material omitted ("&c., &c."). The last four lines: Poverty is our total abode, where the household gods bring no fruitfulness. Nor does abundance ever visit this sickly Parnassus. Some higher status to lift us to our lecture halls is unknown in these huts.

p. 219. *St. Louis*: St. Louis IX (1214–1270), King of France from 1226, austere and idealistic, died while on crusade.

p. 219. *Philip Augustus*: Philip II Augustus (1165–1223), King of France from 1180, grandfather of Louis IX and also a crusader.

p. 220. *Constantinople*: During the Fourth Crusade (1202–1204), the crusaders captured and sacked Constantinople. They then established a Latin kingdom in Byzantium which lasted till 1261 and of which Baldwin, the Flemish nobleman to whom Newman refers here, was the first king.

p. 222. *Henry of Monmouth*: (1387–1422), youthful friend of Falstaff and, from 1413, King Henry V.

p. 223. *Wars of the Roses*: Between 1455 and 1485 two factions within the royal family competed militarily for the throne: the House of Lancaster symbolised by the red rose on its coat of arms, and the House of York with its white rose; hence the Wars of the Roses.

p. 224. *civil war*: The Civil War between King Charles I and the Parliament, 1642–1646.

p. 224. "*Chronica … Angligenenses.*": "If you take account of history, when the men of Oxford go to battle, a few months later the wrath spreads throughout the land."

pp. 231–232. *Sir Robert Peel*: (1788–1850), Conservative politician and Member of Parliament for the University of Oxford, steered the Catholic Emancipation Bill through the House of Commons (1829). This departure from his previous policy led to his defeat at the by-election that followed, a defeat in which Newman, then a young Fellow of Oriel, rejoiced heartily.

p. 233. *Magdalen College*: In 1687, James II (1633–1701), King of England and Ireland 1685–1688, a convert to Catholicism, attempted to appoint a Catholic President of the Magdalen College, Oxford. The resistance of the fellows of the college was symptomatic of the overall antipathy toward James and his religion, which culminated in the 'Glorious Revolution' of 1688.

p. 233. *Twenty years ago*: Beginning with the reform of the franchise in 1832, the British Parliament launched a whole set of sweeping administrative and ecclesiastical reforms; these latter were largely responsible for prompting Newman and his friends to launch the Oxford Movement.

p. 236. *At the beginning of this century*: The reference is to the passage in 1800 of the Examination Statute at Oxford, which initiated the recovery from the decadence that had marked the university through the eighteenth century.

p. 238. *Omnis … nec tangitur ir.* Nature of itself is divine, and so necessarily it enjoys immortality with the greatest serenity. It is remote from all our affairs, and separated a long way off. Detached from all sorrow, all danger, Nature flourishes by its own riches, and shares nothing of our destitution. Neither does it depend upon merit, nor is it affected by anger.

p. 239. *18 Vict.*: Traditionally Acts of Parliament were recorded consistent with each year of the current monarch's reign. Hence '18 Vict.' meant the Act was passed in the eighteenth year of the reign of Queen Victoria, 1854. This was the Act reforming the structure of the University of Oxford.

p. 242. *Seminaries were then long in possession*: True enough in an extended sense of the word, but 'seminary' only came into ordinary Catholic parlance with the institutions set up after the Council of Trent in the sixteenth century.

p. 243. *St. Raymund*: St. Raymund of Pennafort (*c.* 1190–1275), Spanish canonist who studied law at Bologna.

p. 243. *St. Carlo*: St. Charles Borromeo (San Carlo) (1538–1584), nephew of Pope Pius IV, architect of the Council of Trent, reforming Archbishop of Milan.

p. 243. *St. Ignatius*: St. Ignatius Loyola (*c.* 1493–1556), Spanish ex-soldier and founder of the Society of Jesus; among his original six companions, all students in the University of Paris, was St. Francis Xavier.

p. 243. *St. Francis of Sales*: (1567–1622), French bishop and spiritual director, author of two landmark books: *Introduction to the Devout Life* (1608) and *Treatise on the Love of God* (1616).

p. 244. *College of Maynooth*: St. Patrick's College, Maynooth, fifteen·miles northwest of Dublin, the first seminary in Ireland, opened in 1795 with the partial relaxation of the anti-Catholic penal laws.

p. 245. *University ... at Quebec*: The Catholic Laval University was founded in Quebec in 1852. *L'Ecole des hautes études* of which Newman speaks evolved into what was called later the *Institut Catholique* (and was also called the *Ecole des Carmes*, since its first locale was the Carmelite church on the Rue de Vaugirard). The more famous *Ecole pratique des hautes études* is the research centre in the (secular) University of Paris, established as an *école spéciale* in 1869.

p. 245. *A prelate of glorious memory*: Newman refers here to Archbishop Affre, shot on the Parisian barricades during the revolution of June 1848.

pp. 245–6. *Audiit ... sanguis!*: The pastor, the godly victim, hears the call, and, having compassion for his sheep, he is seen making his way through the battle and the sundry scenes of death. Then, alas, the unspeakable crime! While you try to restore the ruptured peace treaties, and try to contain the insane furies, you fall, and dying you cry out in a loud voice, "Blessed we are if bloodshed should cease by the shedding of our blood."

p. 246. *the famous Carmes*: The reference is to the martyrs of September 1792, when upward of 1400 Catholics (including 225 priests) were massacred by the radical revolutionaries in Paris alone, many of them at the same Carmelite church were attempts were being made, sixty years later, to establish a Catholic university.

Mission of St. Benedict

p. 366. *St. Benedict*: of Nursia (*c.* 480–550), Roman educated, retired first as a hermit to a cave near Subiaco and while there founded several monasteries peopled by like-minded ascetics; *c.* 525 he settled on Monte Cassino, where he remained till his death.

p. 369. *Suarez to controvert with*: All nine of the theologians listed here were Jesuits of the sixteenth and seventeenth centuries.

p. 371. *Congregation of Cluni*: The monastery of Cluny, in Burgundy, was founded in 910. Under a series of reforming abbots – notably St. Odo (d. 959) and St. Odilo (994–1048) – Cluny came to represent a reassertion of primitive Benedictine ideals, with special emphasis upon a cultivation of the individual monk's spiritual life as well as upon a solemn and splendid liturgy. On its administrative side, Cluny, along with the houses it founded or those that imitated it, stressed sound financial organisation, free from any lay interference. Eventually the Cluniac system included hundreds of foundations across France, Italy, and England. Its influence declined sharply toward the end of the Middle Ages, but Cluny itself survived until 1790.

p. 371. *Congregations of Camaldoli*: The Camaldolese, an order of hermits founded by St. Romuald (*c.* 950–1027), at Camaldoli, near Arezzo, in central Italy, whose emphasis was on the cultivation of individual asceticism.

p. 371. *The Congregation of Saint-Maur*: founded in France in 1621, as part of a general reform movement within Benedictinism. Named for St. Maurus (sixth century), a companion of St. Benedict, the congregation quickly established a reputation for high scholarship, especially in patristic studies. The Maurists were suppressed by the Revolutionary regime in 1790.

p. 372. St. Dunstan (*c.* 909–988), monk and Abbot of Glastonbury, which he made a centre of learning; he died as Archbishop of Canterbury.

p. 372. *Carlisle*: The Diocese of Carlisle was founded in 1133; the governing board of its cathedral – the chapter – was composed of Augustinian canons rather than Benedictine monks, as was common elsewhere.

p. 372. *Helyot et al.*: (footnote) For those interested in pursuing the sources Newman used in these essays – incomplete and sometimes confusing as his citations are – consult Oliver L. Kapsner (ed.), *A Benedictine Bibliography*, 3 vols. (Collegeville MN: The Liturgical Press, 1962–1982), a work of truly monumental scholarship.

p. 373. *Reg., c. 61* (footnote): The *Regula* or Rule, divided into chapters, was drawn up by St. Benedict and has remained the overall guide of the western monastic vocation ever since. It called for a patriarchal form of government, each monastery, independent of every other, ruled by an abbot who is chosen by vote. The major requirement of the monk, according to the Rule, is to perform the *Opus Dei*, the Divine Office of communal prayer and liturgy, from which work, study, and private prayer take their inspiration. All property is held in common. The monk, besides the usual religious vows, swears to observe 'stability', that is, to remain permanently in the house in which he has been professed.

p. 377. *"justissima tellus"*: "the most bountiful soil".

p. 378. *Lérins*: the name of two islands off the coast of the French Riviera, upon one of which an abbey was founded by St. Honoratus (*c.* 350–429). It became a famed centre of learning and boasted association at one time or another with the likes of St. Patrick, St. Hilary of Arles (403–440), and St. Vincent of Lérins (d. 450), who framed the famous threefold test of Catholicity ('what has been believed everywhere, always, and by all'), which had such a profound affect upon Newman.

p. 379. *Pelagius*: (d. *c.* 425), a British or Irish hermit, who proposed a doctrine denying the full deleterious force of original sin, hence the optimistic heresy called Pelagianism, opposed most strenuously by St. Augustine of Hippo.

p. 379. *Nestorius*: (d. *c.* 451), Syrian-born monk, taught the double personality of Christ, a view condemned by the Council of Ephesus (431); nonetheless a remnant of Nestorians survived into the fourteenth century.

p. 379. *Eutyches*: (*c.* 378–454), a monk in Constantinople, carried his abhorrence of Nestorianism to the opposite extreme by positing a single divine nature in Christ; this view, Monophysitism, was condemned at the Council of Chalcedon (451).

p. 379. *pseudo-synod*: In 449 a council was held at Ephesus under Monophysite domination, which was repudiated by the Church, east and west, and earned the derisive name 'The Robber Council' from the dismissal of it by Pope St. Leo I, 'the Great' (d. 461), as 'non judicium sed latrocinium.'

p. 381. *Abbot Suger*: (*c.* 1081–1151), Statesman and historian, Abbot of Saint-Denis, near Paris, remembered mostly for his political activities.

p. 387. *Lord Byron*: George Gordon, Lord Byron (1788–1824), romantic poet, author of *Childe Harold* (1818) and *Don Juan* (1824).

p. 387. *Me vero . . . agrestes*:

> May the sweet Muses receive me truly before all else
> > and show me the stars and the pathways of the heavens . . .
> But if I should be unable to approach these natural phenomena,
> > the chill blood shall congeal within my breast.
> Then let me take pleasure in country places and valley-streams . . .
> Happy the man who understands the causes of things . . .
> Fortunate is he who knows the country gods.
> > > > Virgil, *Eclogues*, Bk. IX, L. 190ff.

p. 389. *Bobbio*: a village forty miles northeast of Genoa, where St. Coumbanus (*c.* 550–615), Irish-born monk and missionary (not to be confused with his contemporary, St. Columba), founded an abbey in 612.

p. 389. *St. Gall's*: The foundation of the abbey of St. Gallen in Switzerland dates from a century after its patron, St. Gall (*c.* 550–645), Irish-born monk and disciple of St. Columbanus.

p. 389. *Abbey of Fulda*: The Benedictine abbey of Fulda in Hesse was founded by a disciple of St. Boniface, who was buried there; it was a centre of missionary work among the Saxons.

p. 390. *St. Hubert*: (d. 727), the so-called 'Apostle of the Ardennes', Bishop of Liège, patron of huntsmen and of those who suffer from hydrophobia.

p. 391. *secular canons*: members of cathedral chapters who were not monks or 'regular' canons, like the Augustinians. It is not clear what meaning Newman attaches to the term here.

p. 393. *Leo the Ninth*: (1002–1054), pope from 1048, controversial reformer during whose pontificate occurred the final break between the Catholic and the Eastern Orthodox churches.

p. 400. *St. Dubritius*: (sixth century), Bishop of Llandaff in Wales, who, legend says, crowned King Arthur of the Round Table.

p. 401. "*locum . . . solitudinis*": "a deserted wooded place, a vast solitude."

p. 402. *School of Bec*: The Norman monastery of Bec, located between Rouen and Lisieux, and founded in 1041, arguably ranks with Fulda and Cluny among the most influential of medieval Benedictine establishments. Founded in 1041, it counted among its monks Lanfranc and St. Anselm. Fallen into decay in the seventeenth century, it was reconstructed by the Maurists. It was suppressed in 1790.

p. 403. *Simeon of Durham*: (*c.* 1060–1130), monk and chronicler, author of histories of the diocese of Durham and of the kings of England.

p. 403. *St. Peter's at Wearmouth*: The abbey of St. Peter of Wearmouth, on the banks of the Tyne, was founded in 674 by St. Benedict Biscop.

p. 404. *Aldhelm*: St. Aldhelm (d. 709), monk and abbot, esteemed in his time as a writer and poet in Latin, first Bishop of Sherborne, a diocese merged in the eleventh century into Salisbury.

p. 407. *Subiaco*: a town forty miles east of Rome where St. Benedict first retired from the world; he founded twelve monasteries in the vicinity.

p. 407. *Bishop Ullathorne*: William Bernard Ullathorne (1806–1889), three years a cabin boy, then a monk at Downside Abbey, then, after ordination, a missionary in Australia, then (before the restoration of the hierarchy) Vicar Apostolic of the West and Central Districts in England, and finally, in 1850, the strong-minded Bishop of Birmingham till a year before his death. Ullathorne was always a firm friend of Newman and played an important role in the latter's promotion to the cardinalate (1879).

p. 412. *St. Pachomius*: of Egypt (*c.* 290–346) stands in the history of Eastern Christian monasticism as the intermediary between the hermit-ideal of St. Anthony and the developed communitarianism of St. Basil.

p. 412. *St. Chrysostom*: St. John Chrysostom (*c.* 347–407), Bishop of Constantinople, biblical scholar, liturgist, preacher extraordinaire, one of the Greek Fathers of the Church to whom Newman was so deeply devoted.

p. 412. *Cassiodorus*: (*c.* 490–580), Roman nobleman, senator, and legal scholar turned monk, strong advocate of the union of sacred and profane studies in Christian education.

p. 414. *Fontenelle, Rheims, and Corbie*: Benedictine monasteries founded in France during the Merovingian era, that is, before the ascendancy of Charlemagne.

p. 415. *Christopher Brower*: (or Brouwer), Jesuit antiquarian, author of *Vita S. Sturmi, primi abbatis Fuldensis* (1616).

p. 417. *Mr. Maitland*: Samuel Roffey Maitland (1792–1866), *The Dark Ages* (1853).

p. 418. *catenae*: literally chains or links, a term used to designate collections of commentaries on biblical passages linked together verse by verse; the most celebrated example, Thomas Aquinas's *Catena Aurea* on the Gospels.

p. 419. *Mr Dowling*: John Goulter Dowling (1805–1841), *An Introduction to the Critical Study of Ecclesiastical History* (1838).

p. 421. *The Abbot*: Armand de Rancé (1626–1700), Abbot of La Trappe, Cistercian monastery in Normandy founded in 1122, who inaugurated a programme of strict observance of the primitive Benedictine Rule, with its emphasis upon prayer, austere asceticism, and manual labour, and its suspicion of scholarly endeavour: hence the term 'Trappists' to designate monks who have adopted this form of monasticism.

p. 421. *Mabillon*: Jean Mabillon (1632–1707) most celebrated of the Maurist scholars, who, in his *Traité des études monastiques* (1591), challenged de Rancé's interpretation of the Rule.

p. 424. "*The words ... the flesh*": Ecclesiastes 12: 11.

p. 424. *Tillemont*: Louis de Tillemont (1637–1698), French priest and historian, trained at Jansenist Port-Royal, who wrote a sixteen-volume ecclesiastical history.

p. 424. *Bellarmine*: St. Robert Bellarmine (1524–1621), Jesuit theologian and controversialist, afterward cardinal, the single greatest Catholic thinker of the Counter Reformation era.

p. 425. For the Benedictine chroniclers Newman lists here, see Kapsner (ed.), *Bibliography*.

p. 426. *Usum . . . abusus*: Abuse does not take away utility.

The Benedictine Schools
p. 437. *Ambrose*: St. Ambrose (*c.* 339–397), Bishop of Milan, ranked with Jerome, Gregory the Great and Augustine of Hippo as one of the ancient Doctors of the Latin Church. He excommunicated the Emperor Theodosius I for having connived at a massacre of some of his political enemies (390); only after the Emperor had done public penance did Ambrose reconcile him to the Church.

p. 438. *St. Vincent Ferrer*: (*c.* 1350–1419), Dominican preacher, missionary, and penitent.

p. 442. "*Omnibus . . . et corruptelis.*" (footnote): "To all, the same objective was given, and the same end, namely, withdrawal from the tumult and corruption of the world."

p. 446. "*Uno excepto . . . Pontificem fuit.*" (footnote): "With one exception, a man who, because of this arrangement and other matters, was deposed by the pope."

p. 448. *Bingh.* (footnote): Joseph Bingham (1668–1723), *Origines Ecclesiasticae*, 2 vols. (1850).

p. 449. "*naturam expella furca*": "You can drive out nature with a pitch fork, but it will always come back." Horace, *Odes*, Bk. IV, L. 24.

p. 451. For the authorities Newman cites here, see Kapsner (ed.), *Bibliography*.

p. 453. *Quoties videtur . . . obtemperet jussis.* (footnote): As often as something seems to occur contrary to nature in a certain way, it really does not, because the nature of things has this requirement, that what a thing genuinely is, always conforms to nature's commands.

p. 454. "*Mos in Benedictino . . . imbuere.*" (footnote): The common practice among the Benedictines is to set up schools and to instruct pupils in piety and letters.

p. 460. *St. Isidore*: (*c.* 560–636), Archbishop of Seville, renowned preacher and prolific author, whose works were widely utilised during the Middle Ages.

p. 467. *Viguit ... cantibus*: Horace flourishes and so do great Virgil, Sallustius Crispus and the suave Statius. It was a game for all the pupils to sweat over verses and precepts and sweet songs.

pp. 469–70. *Haec tibi ... lanugine poma ... meliora reformas*:

Good Father Grimaldus, I envy you these small gifts and the humble service you offer ... When you contemplate the greenery of your walled garden and sun yourself among the sprouting buds and under the apple trees, the peach tree gives you some shade, and the playful children, enrolled in this joyous school, gather fruit for you in honour of your grey and thinning hairs. You want to enclose your great apple trees and to confide all these living things to capable hands, and so you bring to our consciousness, dear Father, our own work. While you gather up what I cheerfully cede to you, you also benignly root up what is worthless and prune that which needs improvement.

p. 471. *Milman* (footnote): Henry Hart Milman (1791–1868), Professor of Poetry at Oxford and later Dean of St. Paul's, author of *History of Latin Christianity* (1855).